Wicked Men and Fools

Wicked Men and Fools

A SCOTTISH CRIME ANTHOLOGY

Edited by

BRIAN D. OSBORNE

and

RONALD ARMSTRONG

Published in 2000 by
Birlinn Limited
8 Canongate Venture
5 New Street
Edinburgh
EH8 8BH

ISBN 1 84158 100 3

British Library Cataloguing-in-Publication Data
A catalogue record for this book is available from the British Library

Typeset by Textype, Cambridge
Printed and bound by
Omnia Books Limited, Glasgow

Contents

†

NOTE: The titles given in quotation marks have been supplied by the
editors and do not appear in the original texts

1

FOREWORD

✝

> Coffins stood round, like open presses,
> That shaw'd the dead in their last dresses;
> And by some devilish cantraip sleight,
> Each in its cauld hand held a light:
> By which heroic Tam was able
> To note upon the haly table,
> A murderer's banes, in gibbet-airns;
> Twa span-lang, wee, unchristen'd bairns;
> A thief new-cutted frae a rape –
> Wi' his last gasp his gab did gape:
> Five tomahawks wi' bluid red-rusted:
> Five scimitars wi' murder crusted:
> A garter which a babe had strangled;
> A knife a father's throat had mangled –
> Whom his ain son o' life bereft –
> The grey hairs yet stack to the heft;
> Wi' mair o' horrible and awfu'
> Which even to name wad be unlawfu'.

Tam o' Shanter's vision of the horrors set out on the Communion Table of 'Alloway's auld, haunted kirk' forms a fitting start for our consideration of crime in Scotland as represented in literary form past and present.

Robert Burns, of course, drew an appropriate moral from Tam's adventures, and suggested that:

> Whene'er to drink you are inclin'd,
> Or cutty sarks run in your mind,
> Think! ye may buy the joys o'er dear

An odd conclusion for a man who did not, himself, ever very conspicuously refrain from drink or thinking of cutty sarks.

Sex and drink have certainly been among the most frequently occurring causes of criminal behaviour in Scotland, but there are other keynotes in the history of crime in Scotland and we have attempted to look at some of them in this anthology. We have taken a very broad view of crime, and include, for example, an early specimen of road rage. We have taken an equally broad view of the word 'Scottish' and have not hesitated to include such a quintessentially English writer as Dorothy L. Sayers when she happens to write, vividly and amusingly, of a Scottish crime.

We have tried to remember that murder is not the only crime and that the classic detective story is not the only form of writing about crime. With this is mind we have drawn our material from a wide range of sources, non-fiction as well as fiction, poetry as well as prose.

Crime is such an all-pervading subject that we have thought it best to break the wealth of material into six broad categories. In the first of these – 'The Criminal Mind' – we look at the individual criminal, his motives and his actions. From there we move on to what must be considered a Scottish speciality, political crime, in the shape of a chapter entitled 'Treason, Feud and Foray'. 'The Bloody Deed' brings together our selection of writing on crimes against the person – murder, assault, body snatching and the like. 'Catch the Thief!' collects a wide variety of writing about theft in all its varied manifestations. Whether all the forms of theft discussed in this chapter are always and everywhere equally seriously considered as theft is a nice problem in comparative ethics. Poaching, as we shall explain, was traditionally held in the words of an old Gaelic proverb to be, if not exactly a non-criminal act, then at least a criminal act nobody should worry too much about committing:

> Slat a coille, breac a linne, fiadh a frithinn – trì mearlaidh de nach do gabh na Ghaidheil riamh nàire
> A branch from the wood, a trout from the pool, a deer from the deer forest – three thefts of which Highlanders are never ashamed

After the crime comes the investigation, the work of policemen and detectives, private and official, which forms the subject of our chapter 'Detection'. The volume is logically, and inexorably, rounded off by a consideration of the part that lawyers and judges play in 'Judgement'.

Crime in all its varied forms has attracted many of Scotland's greatest writers and has often shown them at their best and most gripping. Nor is this entirely surprising – after all crime does tend to find both victims and perpetrators at moments of tension and conflict and of such moments is great literature made. Indeed crime has had such a powerful influence on the Scottish imagination that this anthology could have been filled up with one category of writing, such as the great traditional ballads, which so often record dark deeds and their consequences – poems like *The Twa Corbies* with the crows' conversation over the body of 'a new slain knight' or the tale of *Lord Randal* poisoned by his true-love.

It is not accidental that our anthology starts and finishes with the works of Robert Louis Stevenson. Stevenson, of all the great Scottish writers, perhaps responded most strongly to the dark side of life, to the criminal and to the person who has stepped outside the law. Many of the most striking Stevenson characters are the ones who have taken the fateful step outside the law and convention – from the eponymous Dr Jekyll of our first extract to the rebellious Archie Weir of our last extract, through a remarkable cast of characters in between.

Surely everyone's abiding memory of *Treasure Island* isn't of the young hero, Jim Hawkins or of the frankly dull Squire Trelawney or Dr Livesey, but of the piratical, one-legged sea-cook, Long John Silver. In *Kidnapped* the Jacobite agent Alan Breck Stewart is a much livelier and more interesting character than the dull, but decent, Lowland Whig David Balfour. In his shorter fiction, too, Stevenson's interest in matters criminal comes out clearly – stories such as *Markheim* and *The Body-Snatcher* testify to this.

Stevenson, from his earliest years, was in rebellion against his ancestry and his parentally-selected career path and threw himself with enthusiasm into the bohemian life of an Edinburgh student, then set out to live by literature and to live as he wished to live rather than as convention dictated he should. These influences perhaps predisposed him to an interest in, or even a sympathy for, those who had rebelled against society.

There will be texts in this anthology, like *Weir of Hermiston*, which will be familiar to many readers – there will be others, like Lord Ruthven's account of *The Murder of Rizzio* which will, to most readers, be quite unknown. In all cases we have chosen self-contained pieces or extracts long enough to provide a worthwhile experience, and have provided explanatory material to introduce the authors whose works we have used and to place the extract its historical and literary context.

As always in an anthology the selection has been the consequence of editorial tastes (or perhaps editorial prejudices) and we have selected what interested us, what engaged us and what informed us. Fortunately, with a rich and remarkably varied author list ranging from Anon. to Robert Burns, from John Buchan to Robert Louis Stevenson, from Kenneth Grahame to Josephine Tey, we feel that our readers will stand a very fair chance of being equally interested, engaged and informed.

The title of this anthology – *Wicked Men and Fools* – is another example of our indebtedness to Robert Louis Stevenson. As David Balfour eventually gets off the Isle of Earraid in *Kidnapped* he reflects:

I have seen wicked men and fools, a great many of both; and I believe they both get paid in the end; but the fools first.

Brian D. Osborne
Ronald Armstrong
May 2000

2
THE CRIMINAL MIND
Introduction

†

Perhaps the definitive portrait of the criminal mind is one of a Scot drawn by an Englishman. In Act One, Scene IV of the Scottish Play, Macbeth has just learned that part one of the witches' prophecy has been fulfilled and he is now Thane of Cawdor. He now begins to consider the horrible possibility of murdering Duncan:

> . . . I am Thane of Cawdor.
> If good, why do I yield to that suggestion
> Whose horrid image doth unfix my hair
> And make my seated heart knock at my ribs
> Against the use of nature? Present fears
> Are less than horrible imaginings.
> My thought, whose murder yet is but fantastical,
> Shakes so my single state of man
> That function is smother'd in surmise,
> And nothing is but what is not.

Later the Englishman Shakespeare seems to show a strange awareness of the ideal of Highland hospitality, which Macbeth would abuse, were he to carry out the assassination:

> . . . as his host,
> Who should against his murderer shut the door,
> Not bear the knife myself.

Scots writers themselves were slower to seize upon the literary potential of the criminal mind but when they did they reaped a rich harvest. The exploits of pirates and freebooters might hardly have existed in readers' imaginations had it not been for Ballantyne and Barrie, and the notion of the divided self had to have a Hogg and a Stevenson in order to fully explore its possibilities. Hogg's 'Calvinist Gothic' novel from 1824, *The Private Memoirs and Confessions of a Justified Sinner*, is a psychological study unmatched at that time or possibly since. Here is the description by another character of Robert Wringhim, the evil half of the dual personality:

I never in my life saw any human being, whom I thought so like a fiend. If a demon could inherit flesh and blood, that youth is precisely such a being as I could conceive that demon to be.

Something of the same insight is brought to a blood-curdling pitch in Stevenson's *Strange Case of Dr Jekyll and Mr Hyde*, and our first extract is taken from this work. This sensationally successful 'shilling shocker' has entered the world-wide canon of crime and horror and has been the subject of numerous adaptations for stage and screen. It is a superior take on the Victorian obsession with violent crime and the stream of sensational literature of the 'penny dreadful' type. It borrows from them something of the seductive power and intoxication of crime. On a different level altogether, the peculiarly Scottish notion of the 'divided self' that is found in Hogg and in *Jekyll and Hyde* can be traced on the one hand to beliefs about possession and witchcraft; and on the other hand, to emerging ideas about psychology and personality that at times seem to prefigure Freud.

There was another more obvious source for *Jekyll and Hyde*. As an Edinburgh man himself, and a lawyer, Stevenson knew all about the actual case of the notorious Deacon Brodie with his 'double life', who had featured in the capital's criminal lore in the eighties of the previous century. Stevenson, together with W.E. Henley, wrote a play, *Deacon Brodie*, and although it achieved no great commercial success, it did contain some graphic phrases reminiscent of the later work. Here, for example, is Brodie's soliloquy as he dons a disguise prior to sallying forth from his locked room on one of his criminal excursions:

BRODIE: Now for one of the Deacon's headaches! Rogues all, rogues all! (*Goes to clothes-press and proceeds to change his coat.*) On with the new coat and into the new life! Down with the Deacon and up with the robber! Eh God! How still the house is! There's something in hypocrisy after all. If we were as good as we seem, what would the world be? The city has its vizard on, and we – at night we are our naked selves. Trysts are keeping, bottles cracking, knives are stripping; and here is Deacon Brodie flaming forth the man of men he is! How still it is! . . . My father and Mary [his sister]. Well! The day for them, the night for me; the grimy cynical night that makes all cats grey, and all honesties of one complexion. Shall a man not have <u>half</u> a life of his own? Not eight hours out of twenty-four? (*Takes out money.*) Where's the blunt? I must be cool tonight, or . . . steady, Deacon, you must win; damn you, you must! You must win back the dowry that you've stolen, and marry [off] your sister, and pay your debts, and gull the world a little longer! (*As he blows out the lights*) The Deacon's going to bed – the poor sick Deacon! Allons! (*Throws up the window and looks out).* Only the stars to see me! (*Addressing the bed*) Lie there, Deacon! Sleep and be well tomorrow. As for me, I'm a man once more till morning.

There is something of Mr Hyde in that last remark. Indeed there is also something similar to the spirited defiance of the ultimate outlaw that is Macpherson of the old song *Macpherson's Farewell*, which we include in Burns's version. This is sandwiched between *Jekyll and Hyde* and another Stevenson piece, from *Treasure Island*, included, because in Long John Silver we have one of the great villains of world literature. Silver is, though, quite different from the kind of 'wicked men' we have been discussing. If Stevenson appears to have a metaphysical interest in evil, it is subtler by far than that of most exponents of the horror genre, for example, his Long John Silver has many appealing, if not absolutely redeeming, features, including humour and intelligence. Curiously, too, Stevenson allows him to escape the horrible fate of most of his kind, such as a real Scottish pirate, Captain Kidd, hanged at Execution Dock, or the pirate chief in our next extract, taken from J. M. Barrie's *Peter and Wendy*, a little-read book version of the play *Peter Pan*.

The pirate in this case is of course another immortal, Captain Jas. Hook, Old Etonian, and his fate is to go to the Crocodile. Here the psychological model is different again. Not so much the 'divided self' – although it has always been the practice to have Hook and Mr Darling, father of Wendy and the boys, played by the same actor – as an immensely complex study of evil, racked by memories, fear, and in some sense guilt.

It may seem odd that we are treating figures from children's literature as serious representations of evil and crime, but the modern notion of writing for children has changed so as to presume an adult readership – consider the *Harry Potter* phenomenon of our day – largely because of the scope of achievement of a few greats, like Barrie and Stevenson. And of the third member of the great triumvirate, with perhaps the most Scottish name of them all, Kenneth Grahame. His loveable rogue, Toad of Toad Hall, is not a deep-dyed villain like Hook or Silver, but he is a rogue all right – and because of him *The Wind in the Willows* can lay claim to be the first book to describe dangerous driving of a motor-car.

So, three Scots in the Pantheon of children's literature – Stevenson, Barrie, Grahame – created magnificent rascals and lawbreakers. All of them now have had the dubious honour of being adapted by Disney for the cinema. What next? Can they all look forward to featuring in theme parks?

The next extract could not be more different in its cool account of what must be at best doubtful as a crime – sedition. This was at a time when to go on strike or take part in a demonstration for parliamentary reform was seen as a direct attack on the State, and when three martyrs were made in a skirmish at Bonnybridge. The excerpt is taken from the diaries of Henry, Lord Cockburn, *Memorials of His Time*, and gives a very personal view of the 'Radical War' of 1820, when the government forces of law and order became extremely timorous about rebellion and civil war. Cockburn, as a Whig and supporter of the Opposition party, doesn't see it that way.

Finally, we include a short story from another writer who could be termed a 'one-off'. Saki's stories have distinctive edgy flavours and none more than this one, *Sredni Vashtar*, a shocking little tale of family hatred. Saki (H.H. Munro) may have made use of experience he gained while serving for a brief period as a policeman – he must be unusual in this respect, although, coincidentally, George Orwell was also a policeman for a while, and in the same place, Burma. To complete the coincidence, Orwell also used a pseudonym – his real name was the very Scottish sounding Eric Blair.

Incident of the Letter

from Strange Case of Dr Jekyll and Mr Hyde

ROBERT LOUIS STEVENSON (1850–1894)

'*Conceived, written, rewritten, re-rewritten, and printed inside ten weeks*' *– this, the darkest of Stevenson's short fiction pieces, was produced early in 1885 (published the following year), while Stevenson was living at 'Skerryvore' in Bournemouth with his American wife Fanny Osbourne. At first he had simply written the tale (which was probably inspired by a bad dream) as a 'shocker' in which Dr Jekyll used the persona of Hyde as a disguise for his nefarious crimes. The major revision he undertook produced the world-famous story of a dual personality, much-filmed and otherwise adapted, and a key text in what we now call the Gothic genre, if not out-and-out horror. The dual nature of the central character has become a fixture in our imaginative landscape and 'Jekyll and Hyde' has certainly entered the language. The story also in a way seems to anticipate Freudian imagery. Stevenson himself described it as 'a body, a vehicle for that strong sense of man's double being, which must at times come in upon and overwhelm the mind of every thinking creature'.*

The Scottish writer who had previously mined these psychological possibilities to greatest effect had been James Hogg, in The True Confessions of A Justified Sinner. *Stevenson's intent was probably less serious – his description of it as a 'fine bogey tale' was very much in the Scots tradition of the macabre.*

It has often been remarked that the setting of the Strange Case *in London actually more closely resembles the Edinburgh of Stevenson's youthful wild excesses. In the same vein, his first version of the story bears considerable similarity to the true story of Deacon Brodie, the outwardly respectable citizen of that city who had led a horrific double life of crime in the previous century. The tale was retold for the stage (with much success) by Stevenson and W.E. Henley in* Deacon Brodie OR The Double Life – a Melodrama in Five Acts and Eight Tableaux *(1880). William Brodie came from a respectable family and was Deacon of the City Carpenters (or wrights) who embarked on a series of violent robberies at night, when he was supposedly at home inside a locked room. Henley and Stevenson's play ends with Brodie being run through by a Bow Street Runner – in reality he was hanged on a gallows which he had himself designed not long before. (There is a short extract from the play in the introduction to this section.)*

Jekyll and Hyde *is of course much more complex but has been no less appealing to the reading public then and now. It sold more than 40,000 copies in six months and soon became regarded as the kind of moral tale which attracts the notice of such as ministers of the Kirk. The book can also be regarded as a kind of prototype science fiction – there are, for example, numerous references to chemistry which was indeed the topical science of the time.*

In the chosen extract Mr Utterson, a lawyer friend of Dr Jekyll, visits him in the aftermath of the dreadful murder of an MP, Sir Danvers Carew. Jekyll hands him a letter which appears to be a confession by the sinister Mr Hyde. 'Appears to be' – because all is not quite as it seems, and, in an unusual little passage, Stevenson shows Utterson's head clerk virtually playing the role of detective and handwriting expert. The dialogue at this point becomes rather like that of a Sherlock Holmes story, two years before the first of these appeared from the pen of Arthur Conan Doyle.

It was late in the afternoon, when Mr Utterson found his way to Dr Jekyll's door, where he was at once admitted by Poole, and carried down by the kitchen offices and across a yard which had once been a garden, to the building which was indifferently known as the laboratory or the dissecting rooms. The doctor had bought the house from the heirs of a celebrated surgeon; and his own tastes being rather chemical than anatomical, had changed the destination of the block at the bottom of the garden. It was the first time that the lawyer had been received in that part of his friend's quarters; and he eyed the dingy windowless structure with curiosity, and gazed round with a distasteful sense of strangeness as he crossed the theatre, once crowded with eager students now lying gaunt and silent, the tables laden with chemical apparatus, the floor strewn with crates and littered with packing straw, and the light falling dimly through the foggy cupola. At the further end, a flight of stairs mounted to a door covered with red baize; and through this Mr Utterson was at last received into the doctor's cabinet. It was a large room, fitted round with glass presses, furnished, among other things, with a cheval-glass and a business table, and looking out upon the court by three dusty windows barred with iron. The fire burned in the grate; a lamp was set lighted on the chimney shelf, for even in the houses the fog began to lie thickly; and there, close up to the warmth, sat Dr Jekyll, looking deadly sick. He did not rise to meet his visitor, but held out a cold hand and bade him welcome in a changed voice.

'And now,' said Mr Utterson, as soon as Poole had left them, 'you have heard the news?'

The doctor shuddered. 'They were crying it in the square,' he said. 'I heard them in my dining room.'

'One word,' said the lawyer. 'Carew was my client, but so are you, and I want to know what I am doing. You have not been mad enough to hide this fellow?'

'Utterson, I swear to God,' cried the doctor. 'I swear to God I will never set eyes on him again. I bind my honour to you that I am done with him in this world. It is all at an end. And indeed he does not want my help; you do not know him as I do; he is safe, he is quite safe; mark my words, he will never more be heard of.'

The lawyer listened gloomily; he did not like his friend's feverish manner. 'You seem pretty sure of him,' said he; 'and for your sake, I hope you may be right. If it came to a trial, your name might appear.'

'I am quite sure of him,' replied Jekyll; 'I have grounds for certainty that I cannot share with anyone. But there is one thing on which you may advise me. I have – I have received a letter; and I am at a loss whether I should show it to the police. I should like to leave it in your hands, Utterson; you would judge wisely I am sure; I have so great a trust in you.'

'You fear, I suppose, that it might lead to his detection?' asked the lawyer.

'No,' said the other. 'I cannot say that I care what becomes of Hyde; I am quite done with him. I was thinking of my own character, which this hateful business has rather exposed.'

Utterson ruminated awhile; he was surprised at his friend's selfishness, and yet relieved by it. 'Well,' said he, at last, 'let me see the letter.'

The letter was written in an odd, upright hand and signed 'Edward Hyde': and it signified, briefly enough, that the writer's benefactor, Dr Jekyll, whom he had long so unworthily repaid for a thousand generosities, need labour under no alarm for his safety as he had means of escape on which he placed a sure dependence. The lawyer liked this letter well enough; it put a better colour on the intimacy than he had looked for; and he blamed himself for some of his past suspicions.

'Have you the envelope?' he asked.

'I burned it,' replied Jekyll, 'before I thought what I was about. But it bore no postmark. The note was handed in.'

'Shall I keep this and sleep upon it?' asked Utterson.

'I wish you to judge for me entirely,' was the reply. 'I have lost confidence in myself.'

'Well, I shall consider,' returned the lawyer. 'And now one word more: it was Hyde who dictated the terms in your will about that disappearance?'

The doctor seemed seized with a qualm of faintness; he shut his mouth tight and nodded.

'I knew it,' said Utterson. 'He meant to murder you. You have had a fine escape.'

'I have had what is far more to the purpose,' returned the doctor solemnly: 'I have had a lesson – O God, Utterson, what a lesson I have had!' And he covered his face for a moment with his hands.

On his way out, the lawyer stopped and had a word or two with Poole. 'By the by,' said he, 'there was a letter handed in today: what was the messenger like?' But Poole was positive nothing had come except by post; 'and only circulars by that,' he added.

This news sent off the visitor with his fears renewed. Plainly the letter had come by the laboratory door; possibly, indeed, it had been written in the cabinet; and if that were so, it must be differently judged, and handled with the more caution. The newsboys, as he went, were crying themselves hoarse along the footways: 'Special edition. Shocking murder of an MP'. That was the funeral oration of one friend and client; and he could not help a certain apprehension lest the good name of another should be sucked down in the eddy of the scandal. It was, at least, a ticklish decision that he had to make; and self-reliant as he was by habit, he began to cherish a longing for advice. It was not to be had directly; but perhaps, he thought, it might be fished for.

Presently after, he sat on one side of his own hearth, with Mr Guest, his head clerk, upon the other, and midway between, at a nicely calculated distance from the fire, a bottle of a particular old wine that had long dwelt unsunned in the foundations of his house. The fog still slept on the wing above the drowned city, where the lamps glimmered like carbuncles; and through the muffle and smother of these fallen clouds, the procession of the town's life was still rolling in through the great arteries with a sound as of a mighty wind. But the room was gay with firelight. In the bottle the acids were long ago resolved; the imperial dye had softened with time, as the colour grows richer in stained windows; and the glow of hot autumn afternoons on hillside vineyards, was ready to be set free and to disperse the fogs of London. Insensibly the lawyer melted. There was no man from whom he kept fewer secrets than Mr Guest; and he was not always sure that he kept as many as he meant. Guest had often been on business to the doctor's; he knew Poole; he could scarce have failed to hear of Mr Hyde's familiarity about the house; he might draw conclusions: was it not as well, then, that he should see a letter which put that mystery to rights? And above all since Guest, being a great student and critic of handwriting, would consider the step natural and obliging? The clerk, besides, was a man of counsel; he would scarce read so strange a document without dropping a remark; and by that remark Mr Utterson might shape his future course.

'This is a sad business about Sir Danvers,' he said.

'Yes, sir, indeed. It has elicited a great deal of public feeling,' returned Guest. 'The man, of course, was mad.'

'I should like to hear your views on that,' replied Utterson. 'I have a document here in his handwriting; it is between ourselves, for I scarce know what to do about it; it is an ugly business at the best. But there it is; quite in your way: a murderer's autograph.'

Guest's eyes brightened, and he sat down at once and studied it with passion. 'No, sir,' he said; 'not mad; but it is an odd hand.'

'And by all accounts a very odd writer,' added the lawyer.

Just then the servant entered with a note.

'Is that from Doctor Jekyll, sir?' inquired the clerk. 'I thought I knew the writing. Anything private, Mr Utterson?'

'Only an invitation to dinner. Why? Do you want to see it?'

'One moment. I thank you, sir,' and the clerk laid the two sheets of paper alongside and sedulously compared their contents. 'Thank you, sir,' he said at last, returning both; 'it's a very interesting autograph.'

There was a pause, during which Mr Utterson struggled with himself. 'Why did you compare them, Guest?' he inquired suddenly.

'Well, sir,' returned the clerk, 'there's a rather singular resemblance; the two hands are in many points identical: only differently sloped.'

'Rather quaint,' said Utterson.

'It is, as you say, rather quaint,' returned Guest.

'I wouldn't speak of this note, you know,' said the master.

'No, sir,' said the clerk. 'I understand.'

But no sooner was Mr Utterson alone that night, than he locked the note into his safe where it reposed from that time forward. 'What!' he thought. 'Henry Jekyll forge for a murderer!' And his blood ran cold in his veins.

McPherson's Farewell

ROBERT BURNS (1759–1796)

James McPherson was a freebooter of considerable notoriety who brought fear and destruction to the counties of Aberdeen, Banff and Moray in the last years of the seventeenth century. Captured and sentenced to hang in the market place at Banff in November 1700, he is supposed to have composed a defiant song on the eve of execution and then played it on the fiddle, of which he was a recognised master.

Burns composed this lyric in September 1787, shortly after his tour of the Highlands, which took him close to Banff. There was an earlier form of the ballad in old song collections, but, typically, Burns transmuted this (relatively) base metal into gold with lyrical verses that perfectly capture the spirited air of defiance of the story. The dramatic tone is surely unsurpassed in Scots song – what William Scott Douglas described as 'the wild stanzas that Burns puts into the mouth of the daring desperado' – and unsurprisingly legend relates that McPherson concluded his defiance by breaking his fiddle at the very foot of the gallows.

The song was included in the second volume of James Johnson's Scots Musical Museum *which appeared in February 1788, in the period of heady success following the publication of the Kilmarnock Edition of* Poems Chiefly in the Scottish Dialect *in 1786. Burns had arrived in triumph in Edinburgh and was invited by Johnson, an unlettered music-seller, to contribute to the collection of Scots songs that eventually ran to six volumes. In a short time Burns virtually became the editor of the collection and through it poured 'the lyric flood' which in our day has arguably elevated Burns the songwriter to a position as high as Burns the poet.*

Farewell, ye dungeon's dark and strong,
The wretch's destinie!
McPherson's time will not be long,
On yonder gallows-tree.

chorus:

Sae rantingly, sae wantonly,
Sae dauntonly gae'd he:
He play'd a spring, and danc'd it round,
Below the gallows-tree.

O what is death but parting breath?
On many a bloody plain
I've dar'd his face, and in this place
I scorn him yet again!
Sae rantingly, etc.

Untie these bands from off my hands.
And bring to me my sword;
And there's no a man in all Scotland,
But I'll brave him at a word.
Sae rantingly, etc.

I've liv'd a life of sturt and strife;
I die by treacherie:
It burns my heart I must depart,
And not avenged be.
Sae rantingly, etc.

Now farewell light, thou sunshine bright,
And all beneath the sky!
May coward shame distain his name,
The wretch that dares not die!
Sae rantingly, etc.

'The Sea-Cook'

from Treasure Island

ROBERT LOUIS STEVENSON (1850–1894)

As well as co-writing Deacon Brodie, *W.E. Henley collaborated with Stevenson on three even more comprehensively forgotten plays but remained a close friend and, with his flamboyant nature, was affectionately described by the Scot as 'boisterous and piratic'. The latter epithet is interesting since Stevenson declared that Henley was his inspiration for the character of Long John Silver in* Treasure Island. *Again it might be noted that the two men first met when Henley was a patient in the Edinburgh Royal Infirmary – and that Henley limped because he had had one foot amputated in his youth.*

Treasure Island *first appeared in serialised form and then was published as Stevenson's first work of longer fiction. It did not attract much attention until after the critical success of* Kidnapped. *Ever since then it has been regarded as a classic of children's fiction and has been adapted on many occasions for stage and screen. Silver has become one of the two greatest fictional pirates, together with a fellow 'Scot', Captain Hook, Silver is a very modern and ambiguous sort of character – no less because Stevenson frees him from the sort of melodramatic justice which was the lot of most pirates, real or fictional. The relationship with Jim Hawkins in a way prefigures that of Alan Breck and David Balfour in* Kidnapped.

The notion of a yarn centred on an island has of course other links with Scotland and Scottish literature. Robinson Crusoe's 'original' was Alexander Selkirk from Largo in Fife and a more direct inspiration for Stevenson might be R.M. Ballantyne's The Coral Island, *published in 1858. The heading for this extract,* The Sea-Cook, *was his original title for the story.*

'No, not I,' said Silver. 'Flint was cap'n; I was quartermaster, along of my timber leg. The same broadside I lost my leg, old Pew lost his deadlights. It was a master surgeon, him that ampytated me – out of college and all –.Latin by the bucket, and what not; but he was hanged like a dog, and sun-dried like the rest, at Corso Castle. That was Roberts's men, that was, and comed of changing names to their ships – *Royal Fortune* and so on. Now, what a ship was christened, so let her stay, I says. So it was with the

Cassandra, as brought us all safe home from Malabar, after England took the *Viceroy of the Indies*; so it was with the old *Walrus*, Flint's old ship, as I've seen a-muck with the red blood and fit to sink with gold.'

'Ah!' cried another voice, that of the youngest hand on board, and evidently full of admiration, 'he was the flower of the flock, was Flint!'

'Davis was a man, too, by all accounts,' said Silver. 'I never sailed along of him; first with England, then with Flint, that's my story; and now here on my own account, in a manner of speaking. I laid my nine hundred safe, from England, and two thousand after Flint. That ain't bad for a man before the mast – all safe in bank. 'Tain't earning now, it's saving does it, you may lay to that. Where's all England's men now? I dunno. Where's Flint's? Why, most on 'em aboard here, and glad to get the duff – been begging before that, some on 'em. Old Pew, as had lost his sight, and might have thought shame, spends twelve hundred pound in a year, like a lord in Parliament. Where is he now? Well, he's dead now and under hatches; but for two year before that, shiver my timbers! the man was starving. He begged, and he stole, and he cut throats, and starved at that, by the powers!'

'Well, it ain't much use, after all,' said the young seaman.

' 'Tain't much use for fools, you may lay to it – that, nor nothing,' cried Silver. 'But now, you look here: you're young, you are, but you're as smart as paint. I see that when I set my eyes on you, and I'll talk to you like a man.'

You may imagine how I felt when I heard this abominable old rogue addressing another in the very same words of flattery as he had used to myself. I think, if I had been able, that I would have killed him through the barrel. Meantime, he ran on, little supposing he was overheard.

'Here it is about gentlemen of fortune. They lives rough, and they risk swinging, but they eat and drink like fighting-cocks, and when a cruise is done why it's hundreds of pounds instead of hundreds of farthings in their pockets. Now, the most goes for rum and a good fling, and to sea again in their shirts. But that's not the course I lay. I puts it all away, some here, some there, and none too much anywheres, by reason of suspicion. I'm fifty, mark you; once back from this cruise, I set up gentleman in earnest. Time enough, too, says you. Ah, but I've lived easy in the meantime; never denied myself o' nothing heart desires, and slep' soft and ate dainty all my days, but when at sea. And how did I begin? Before the mast, like you!'

'Well,' said the other, 'but all the other money's gone now, ain't it? You daren't show face in Bristol after this.'

'Why, where might you suppose it was?' asked Silver, derisively.

'At Bristol, in banks and places,' answered his companion.

'It were,' said the cook; 'it were when we weighed anchor. But my old missus has it all by now. And the "Spy-glass" is sold, lease and goodwill and rigging; and the old girl's off to meet me. I would tell you where, for I trust you; but it 'ud make jealousy among the mates.'

'And can you trust your missus?' asked the other.

'Gentlemen of fortune,' returned the cook, 'usually trust little among themselves, and right they are, you may lay to it. But I have a way with me, I have. When a mate brings a slip on his cable – one as knows me, I mean – it won't be in the same world with old John. There was some that was feared of Pew, and some that was feared of Flint; and Flint his own self was feared of me. Feared he was, and proud. They was the roughest crew afloat, was Flint's; the devil himself would have been feared to go to sea with them. Well, now, I tell you, I'm not a boasting man, and you seen yourself how easy I keep company; but when I was quartermaster, *lambs* wasn't the word for Flint's old buccaneers. Ah, you may be sure of yourself in old John's ship.'

'Well, I tell you now,' replied the lad, 'I didn't half a quarter like the job till I had this talk with you, John, but there's my hand on it now.'

'And a brave lad you were, and smart, too,' answered Silver, shaking hands so heartily that all the barrel shook, 'and a finer figurehead for a gentleman of fortune I never clapped my eyes on.'

By this time I had begun to understand the meaning of their terms. By a 'gentleman of fortune' they plainly meant neither more nor less than a common pirate, and the little scene that I had overheard was the last act in the corruption of one of the honest hands – perhaps of the last one left aboard. But on this point I was soon to be relieved, for Silver giving a little whistle, a third man strolled up and sat down by the party.

'Dick's square,' said Silver.

'Oh, I know'd Dick was square,' returned the voice of the coxswain, Israel Hands. 'He's no fool, is Dick.' And he turned his quid and spat. 'But look here,' he went on, 'here's what I want to know, Barbecue: how long are we a-going to stand off and on like a blessed bum-boat? I've had a'most enough o' Cap'n Smollett; he's hazed me long enough, by thunder! I want to go into that cabin, I do. I want their pickles and wines, and that.'

'Israel,' said Silver, 'your head ain't much account, nor ever was. But you're able to hear, I reckon; leastways, your ears is big enough. Now, here's what I say: you'll berth forward, and you'll live hard, and you'll speak soft, and you'll keep sober, till I give the word; and you may lay to that, my son.'

'Well, I don't say no, do I?' growled the coxswain. 'What I say is, when? That's what I say.'

'When! by the powers!' cried Silver. 'Well, now, if you want to know, I'll tell you when. The last moment I can manage; and that's when. Here's a first-rate seaman, Cap'n Smollett, sails the blessed ship for us. Here's this squire and doctor with a map and such – I don't know where it is, do I? No more do you, says you. Well, then, I mean this squire and doctor shall find the stuff, and help us to get it aboard, by the powers. Then we'll see. If I was sure of you all, sons of double Dutchmen, I'd have Cap'n Smollett navigate us half-way back again before I struck.'

'Why, we're all seamen aboard here, I should think,' said the lad Dick.

'We're all foc's'le hands, you mean,' snapped Silver. 'We can steer a course, but who's to set one? That's what all you gentlemen split on, first and last. If I had my way, I'd have Cap'n Smollett work us back into the trades at least; then we'd have no blessed miscalculations and a spoonful of water a day. But I know the sort you are. I'll finish with 'em at the island, as soon's the blunt's on board, and a pity it is. But you're never happy till you're drunk. Split my sides, I've a sick heart to sail with the likes of you!'

'Easy all, Long John,' cried Israel. 'Who's acrossin' of you?'

'Why, how many tall ships, think ye, now, have I seen laid aboard? and how many brisk lads drying in the sun at Execution Dock?' cried Silver, 'And all for this same hurry and hurry and hurry. You hear me? I seen a thing or two at sea, I have. If you would on'y lay your course, and a p'int to windward, you would ride in carriages, you would. But not you! I know you. You'll have your mouthful of rum tomorrow, and go hang.'

'Everybody know'd you was a kind of a chapling, John, but there's others as could hand and steer as well as you,' said Israel. 'They liked a bit o' fun, they did. They wasn't so high and dry, nohow, but took their fling, like jolly companions every one.'

'So?' says Silver. 'Well, and where are they now? Pew was that sort, and he died a beggar-man. Flint was, and he died of rum at Savannah. Ah, they was a sweet crew, they was!, on'y, where are they?'

'But,' asked Dick, 'when we do lay 'em athwart, what are we to do with 'em, anyhow?'

'There's the man for me!' cried the cook, admiringly. 'That's what I call business. Well, what would you think? Put 'em ashore like maroons? That would have been England's way. Or cut 'em down like that much pork? That would have been Flint's or Billy Bones's.'

'Billy was the man for that,' said Israel. ' "Dead men don't bite," says he. Well, he's dead now hisself; he knows the long and short on it now; and if ever a rough hand come to port, it was Billy.'

'Right you are,' said Silver, 'rough and ready. But mark you here: I'm an easy man – I'm quite the gentleman, says you, but this time it's serious. Dooty is dooty, mates. I give my vote – death. When I'm in Parlyment, and riding in my coach, I don't want none of these sea-lawyers in the cabin a-coming home, unlooked for, like the devil at prayers. Wait is what I say; but when the time comes, why let her rip!'

'John,' cries the coxswain, 'you're a man!'

'You'll say so, Israel, when you see,' said Silver. 'Only one thing I claim – I claim Trelawney. I'll wring his calf's head off his body with these hands. Dick!' he added, breaking off, 'you just jump up, like a sweet lad, and get me an apple, to wet my pipe like.'

You may fancy the terror I was in! I should have leaped out and run for it, if I had found the strength; but my limbs and heart alike misgave me. I heard Dick begin to rise, and then someone seemingly stopped him, and the voice of Hands exclaimed:

'Oh, stow that! Don't you get sucking of that bilge, John. Let's have a go of the rum.'

'Dick,' said Silver, 'I trust you. I've a gauge on the keg, mind. There's the key: you fill a pannikin and bring it up.'

Terrified as I was, I could not help thinking to myself that this must have been how Mr Arrow got the strong waters that destroyed him.

Dick was gone but a little while, and during his absence Israel spoke straight on in the cook's ear. It was but a word or two that I could catch, and yet I gathered some important news; for, besides other scraps that tended to the same purpose, this whole clause was audible: 'Not another man of them'll jine.' Hence there were still faithful men on board.

When Dick returned, one after another of the trio took the pannikin and drank – one 'To luck'; another with a 'Here's to old Flint'; and Silver himself saying, in a kind of song: 'Here's to ourselves, and hold your luff, plenty of prizes and plenty of duff.'

Just then a sort of brightness fell upon me in the barrel, and, looking up, I found the moon had risen, and was silvering the mizzen-top and shining white on the luff of the foresail; and almost at the same time the voice of the look-out shouted: 'Land ho!'

Hook or Me This Time

from Peter and Wendy

J. M. BARRIE (1860–1937)

This extract comes from the prose version of Peter Pan, *published in 1911, seven years after the Duke of York's Theatre in London had staged what must be the most famous first night of any play by a Scot at any time or place. It describes how Captain James Hook is defeated by Peter and the Lost Boy and how he finally meets his nemesis the Crocodile, which already has bitten off the hand that now is but a hook.*

James Barrie was born in Kirriemuir in Angus, the third son and seventh surviving child of David Barrie and Margaret Ogilvie. The first incident seized upon by many literary commentators on the life, career and psychology of Barrie was the death of his brother David in a skating accident at the age of fourteen. Some have argued that this was the germ of the idea about the boy who never grew up. Modern taste has perhaps turned a little against Barrie's whimsical but unique identification with children in his writing, although Hollywood continues to be fascinated by Peter, Hook and the others. Two filmed adaptations have been made in recent years and it has been remarked that ET – the Extra-terrestrial *also bears a close resemblance to* Peter Pan, *with flying and the secret world of children both being central ideas in that film. Despite fluctuations in taste there is no doubt that Barrie 'is indeed one of the immortals', (Peter Hollindale) because of his amazing story-telling facility.*

Hook is, of course, a pirate and makes up, along with Long John Silver, the most famous pair of pirates in all of Scottish, indeed world, literature. The fascination of Scots with the crime of piracy is perhaps founded on distant memories of Vikings and other fearsome raiders from the sea, as well as the careers of individuals like Captain Kidd, who came from Greenock (or possibly Dundee) and is probably the most (in)famous of historical pirates. Kidd sailed under a number of flags and had a vast number of exploits, but was finally taken at Boston and sent to London where, in 1701, he was hanged at the second attempt at Execution Dock. In Barrie's story, Hook's ship, the Jolly Roger *is lying in Kidd's Creek. There is something of the pirate in Peter too. He often sounds a buccaneering note of defiance, as in the title –* Hook or Me this Time.

What is often forgotten about Barrie's work is his humorous touch – humour was part of the appeal of successful plays like The Admirable Crichton *and* What Every Woman Knows. *In* Peter and Wendy, *too, humour is often apparent, as in the play itself. One running joke is interesting though probably incomprehensible to most young readers – the frequent references to James Hook having been at 'a famous public school' (Eton). In our extract, when facing certain defeat, Hook's mind is 'slouching in the playing fields of long ago' or 'watching the wall-game from a famous wall'. Barrie intended this quip for the amusement of the Llewelyn-Davies brothers (important in any consideration of Barrie), who were at Eton and would appreciate the joke.*

Appropriately enough, James Hook's last words here are 'Bad form' – in the play Peter Pan, *they were 'Floreat Etona'.*

Odd things happen to all of us on our way through life without our noticing for a time that they have happened. Thus, to take an instance, we suddenly discover that we have been deaf in one ear for we don't know how long, but, say, half an hour. Now such an experience had come that night to Peter. When last we saw him he was stealing across the island with one finger to his lips and his dagger at the ready. He had seen the crocodile pass by without noticing anything peculiar about it, but by and by he remembered that it had not been ticking. At first he thought this eerie, but soon he concluded rightly that the clock had run down.

Without giving a thought to what might be the feelings of a fellow-creature thus abruptly deprived of its closest companion, Peter at once considered how he could turn the catastrophe to his own use; and he decided to tick, so that wild beasts should believe he was the crocodile and let him pass unmolested. He ticked superbly, but with one unforeseen result. The crocodile was among those who heard the sound, and it followed him, though whether with the purpose of regaining what it had lost, or merely as a friend under the belief that it was again ticking itself, will never be certainly known, for, like all slaves to a fixed idea, it was a stupid beast.

Peter reached the shore without mishap, and went straight on; his legs encountering the water as if quite unaware that they had entered a new element. Thus many animals pass from land to water, but no other human of whom I know. As he swam he had but one thought: 'Hook or me this time.' He had ticked so long that he now went on ticking without knowing that he was doing it. Had he known he would have stopped, for to board the brig by the help of the tick, though an ingenious idea, had not occurred to him.

On the contrary, he thought he had scaled her side as noiseless as a mouse; and he was amazed to see the pirates cowering from him, with

Hook in their midst as abject as if he had heard the crocodile.

The crocodile! No sooner did Peter remember it than he heard the ticking. At first he thought the sound did come from the crocodile, and he looked behind him swiftly. Then he realized that he was doing it himself, and in a flash he understood the situation. 'How clever of me,' he thought at once, and signed to the boys not to burst into applause.

It was at this moment that Ed Teynte the quartermaster emerged from the forecastle and came along the deck. Now, reader, time what happened by your watch. Peter struck true and deep. John clapped his hands on the ill-fated pirate's mouth to stifle the dying groan. He fell forward. Four boys caught him to prevent the thud. Peter gave the signal, and the carrion was cast overboard. There was a splash, and then silence. How long has it taken?

'One!' (Slightly had begun to count.)

None too soon, Peter, every inch of him on tiptoe, vanished into the cabin; for more than one pirate was screwing up his courage to look round. They could hear each other's distressed breathing now, which showed them that the more terrible sound had passed.

'It's gone, captain,' Smee said, wiping his spectacles. 'All's still again.'

Slowly Hook let his head emerge from his ruff, and listened so intently that he could have caught the echo of the tick. There was not a sound, and he drew himself up firmly to his full height.

'Then here's to Johnny Plank,' he cried brazenly, hating the boys more than ever because they had seen him unbend. He broke into the villainous ditty:

> 'Yo ho, yo ho, the frisky plank,
> You walks along it so,
> Till it goes down and you goes down
> To Davy Jones below!'

To terrorize the prisoners the more, though with a certain loss of dignity, he danced along an imaginary plank, grimacing at them as he sang; and when he finished he cried, 'Do you want a touch of the cat before you walk the plank?'

At that they fell on their knees. 'No, no,' they cried so piteously that every pirate smiled.

'Fetch the cat, Jukes,' said Hook. 'It's in the cabin.'

The cabin! Peter was in the cabin! The children gazed at each other.

'Aye, aye,' said Jukes blithely, and he strode into the cabin. They followed him with their eyes; they scarce knew that Hook had resumed his song, his dogs joining in with him:

> 'Yo ho, yo ho, the scratching cat,
> Its tails are nine, you know,
> And when they're writ upon your back –'

What was the last line will never be known, for of a sudden the song was stayed by a dreadful screech from the cabin. It wailed through the ship, and died away. Then was heard a crowing sound which was well understood by the boys, but to the pirates was almost more eerie than the screech.

'What was that?' cried Hook.

'Two,' said Slightly solemnly

The Italian Cecco hesitated for a moment and then swung into the cabin. He tottered out, haggard.

What's the matter with Bill Jukes, you dog?' hissed Hook, towering over him.

'The matter wi' him is he's dead, stabbed,' replied Cecco in a hollow voice.

'Bill Jukes dead!' cried the startled pirates.

'The cabin's as black as a pit,' Cecco said, almost gibbering, 'but there is something terrible in there: the thing you heard crowing.'

The exultation of the boys, the lowering looks of the pirates, both were seen by Hook.

'Cecco,' he said in his most steely voice, 'go back and fetch me out that doodle-doo.'

Cecco, bravest of the brave, cowered before his captain, crying, 'No, no!' but Hook was purring to his claw.

'Did you say you would go, Cecco?' he said musingly.

Cecco went, first flinging up his arms despairingly. There was no more singing, all listened now; and again came a death-screech and again a crow.

No one spoke except Slightly. 'Three,' he said.

Hook rallied his dogs with a gesture. ''Sdeath and odds fish,' he thundered, 'who is to bring me that doodle-doo?'

'Wait till Cecco comes out,' growled Starkey, and the others took up the cry.

'I think I heard you volunteer, Starkey,' said Hook, purring again.

'No, by thunder!' Starkey cried.

'My hook thinks you did,' said Hook, crossing to him. 'I wonder if it would not be advisable, Starkey, to humour the hook?'

'I'll swing before I go in there,' replied Starkey doggedly, and again he had the support of the crew.

'Is it mutiny?' asked Hook more pleasantly than ever. 'Starkey's ring-leader.'

'Captain, mercy,' Starkey whimpered, all of a tremble now.

'Shake hands, Starkey,' said Hook, proffering his claw.

Starkey looked round for help, but all deserted him. As he backed Hook advanced, and now the red spark was in his eye. With a despairing scream the pirate leapt upon Long Tom and precipitated himself into the sea.

'Four,' said Slightly.

'And now,' Hook asked courteously, 'did any other gentleman say mutiny?' Seizing a lantern and raising his claw with a menacing gesture, 'I'll bring out that doodle-doo myself,' he said, and sped into the cabin.

'Five.' How Slightly longed to say it. He wetted his lips to be ready, but Hook came staggering out, without his lantern.

'Something blew out the light,' he said a little unsteadily.

'Something!' echoed Mullins.

'What of Cecco?' demanded Noodler.

'He's as dead as Jukes,' said Hook shortly.

His reluctance to return to the cabin impressed them all unfavourably, and the mutinous sounds again broke forth. All pirates are superstitious; and Cookson cried, 'They do say the surest sign a ship's accurst is when there's one on board more than can be accounted for.'

'I've heard,' muttered Mullins, 'he always boards the pirate craft at last. Had he a tail, captain?'

'They say,' said another, looking viciously at Hook, 'that when he comes it's in the likeness of the wickedest man aboard.'

'Had he a hook, captain?' asked Cookson insolently, and one after another took up the cry, 'The ship's doomed.' At this the children could not resist raising a cheer. Hook had wellnigh forgotten his prisoners, but as he swung round on them now his face lit up again.

'Lads,' he cried to his crew, 'here's a notion. Open the cabin door and drive them in. Let them fight the doodle-doo for their lives. If they kill him we're so much the better; if he kills them we're none the worse.'

For the last time his dogs admired Hook, and devotedly they did his bidding. The boys, pretending to struggle, were pushed into the cabin and the door was closed on them.

'Now, listen,' cried Hook, and all listened. But not one dared to face the door. Yes, one, Wendy, who all this time had been bound to the mast. It was for neither a scream nor a crow that she was watching; it was for the reappearance of Peter.

She had not long to wait. In the cabin he had found the thing for which he had gone in search – the key that would free the children of their manacles – and now they all stole forth, armed with such weapons as they could find. First signing to them to hide, Peter cut Wendy's bonds, and then nothing could have been easier than for them all to fly off together; but one thing barred the way, an oath, 'Hook or me this time.' So when he had freed Wendy, he whispered to her to conceal herself with the others, and himself took her place by the mast, her cloak around him so that he should pass for her. Then he took a great breath and crowed.

To the pirates it was a voice crying that all the boys lay slain in the cabin, and they were panic-stricken. Hook tried to hearten them, but like the dogs he had made them they showed him their fangs, and he knew that if he took his eyes off them now they would leap at him.

'Lads,' he said, ready to cajole or strike as need be, but never quailing for an instant, 'I've thought it out. There's a Jonah aboard.'

'Aye,' they snarled, 'a man wi' a hook.'

'No, lads, no, it's the girl. Never was luck on a pirate ship wi' a woman on board. We'll right the ship when she's gone.'

Some of them remembered that this had been a saying of Flint's. 'It's worth trying,' they said doubtfully.

'Fling the girl overboard,' cried Hook; and they made a rush at the figure in the cloak.

'There's none can save you now, missy,' Mullins hissed jeeringly.

'There's one,' replied the figure.

'Who's that?'

'Peter Pan the avenger!' came the terrible answer; and as he spoke Peter flung off his cloak. Then they all knew who 'twas that had been undoing them in the cabin, and twice Hook essayed to speak and twice he failed. In that frightful moment I think his fierce heart broke.

At last he cried, 'Cleave him to the brisket,' but without conviction.

'Down, boys, and at them,' Peter's voice rang out; and in another moment the clash of arms was resounding through the ship. Had the pirates kept together it is certain that they would have won, but the onset came when they were all unstrung, and they ran hither and thither, striking wildly, each thinking himself the last survivor of the crew. Man to man they were the stronger but they fought on the defensive only, which enabled the boys to hunt in pairs and choose their quarry. Some of the miscreants leapt into the sea, others hid in dark recesses, where they were found by Slightly, who did not fight, but ran about with a lantern which he flashed in their faces, so that they were half blinded and fell an easy prey to the reeking swords of the other boys. There was little sound to be heard but the clang of weapons, an occasional screech or splash, and Slightly monotonously counting—five—six—seven—eight—nine—ten—eleven.

I think all were gone when a group of savage boys surrounded Hook, who seemed to have a charmed life, as he kept them at bay in that circle of fire. They had done for his dogs, but this man alone seemed to be a match for them all. Again and again they closed upon him, and again and again he hewed a clear space. He had lifted up one boy with his hook, and was using him as a buckler, when another, who had just passed his sword through Mullins, sprang into the fray.

'Put up your swords, boys!' cried the newcomer. 'This man is mine.'

Thus suddenly Hook found himself face to face with Peter. The others drew back and formed a ring round them.

For long the two enemies looked at one another; Hook shuddering slightly, and Peter with the strange smile upon his face.

'So, Pan,' said Hook at last, 'this is all your doing.'

'Aye, James Hook,' came the stern answer, 'it is all my doing.'

'Proud and insolent youth,' said Hook, 'prepare to meet thy doom.'

'Dark and sinister man,' Peter answered.' Have at thee.'

Without more words they fell to, and for a space there was no advantage to either blade. Peter was a superb swordsman, and parried with dazzling rapidity; ever and anon he followed up a feint with a lunge that got past his foe's defence, but his shorter reach stood him in ill stead, and he could not drive the steel home. Hook, scarcely his inferior in brilliancy, but not quite so nimble in wrist play, forced him back by the weight of his onset, hoping suddenly to end all with a favourite thrust, taught him long ago by Barbecue at Rio; but to his astonishment he found this thrust turned aside again and again. Then he sought to close and give the quietus with his iron hook, which all this time had been pawing the air; but Peter doubled under it and, lunging fiercely, pierced him in the ribs. At sight of his own blood, whose peculiar colour, you remember, was offensive to him, the sword fell from Hook's hand, and he was at Peter's mercy.

'Now!' cried all the boys, but with a magnificent gesture Peter invited his opponent to pick up his sword. Hook did so instantly, but with a tragic feeling that Peter was showing good form.

Hitherto he had thought it was some fiend fighting him, but darker suspicions assailed him now.

'Pan, who and what art thou?' he cried huskily.

'I'm youth, I'm joy,' Peter answered at a venture, 'I'm a little bird that has broken out of the egg.'

This, of course, was nonsense, but it was proof to the unhappy Hook that Peter did not know in the least who or what he was, which is the very pinnacle of good form.

'To't again,' he cried despairingly.

He fought now like a human flail, and every sweep of that terrible sword would have severed in twain any man or boy who obstructed it; but Peter fluttered round him as if the very wind it made blew him out of the danger zone. And again and again he darted in and pricked.

Hook was fighting now without hope. That passionate breast no longer asked for life, but for one boon it craved; to see Peter bad form before it was cold for ever.

Abandoning the fight he rushed into the powder magazine and fired it.

'In two minutes,' he cried, 'the ship will be blown to pieces.'

Now, now, he thought, true form will show.

But Peter issued from the powder magazine with the shell in his hands, and calmly flung it overboard.

What sort of form was Hook himself showing? Misguided man though he was, we may be glad, without sympathizing with him, that in the end he was true to the traditions of his race. The other boys were flying around him now, flouting, scornful, and as he staggered about the deck striking up at them impotently, his mind was no longer with them; it was slouching in the playing fields of long ago, or being sent up for good, or watching the wall-game from a famous wall. And his shoes were right, and his waistcoat was right, and his tie was right, and his socks were right.

James Hook, thou not wholly unheroic figure, farewell.

For we have come to his last moment.

Seeing Peter slowly advancing upon him through the air with dagger poised, he sprang upon the bulwarks to cast himself into the sea. He did not know that the crocodile was waiting for him, for we purposely stopped the clock that this knowledge might be spared him: a little mark of respect from us at the end.

He had one last triumph, which I think we need not grudge him. As he stood on the bulwark looking over his shoulder at Peter gliding through the air, he invited him with a gesture to use his foot. It made Peter kick instead of stab.

At last Hook had got the boon for which he craved.

'Bad form,' he cried jeeringly, and went content to the crocodile.

Thus perished James Hook.

'Seventeen,' Slightly sang out, but he was not quite correct in his figures. Fifteen paid the penalty for their crimes that night, but two reached the shore: Starkey to be captured by the redskins, who made him nurse for all their papooses, a melancholy come-down for a pirate; and Smee, who henceforth wandered about the world in his spectacles, making a precarious living by saying he was the only man that Jas. Hook had feared.

Wendy, of course, had stood by taking no part in the fight, though watching Peter with glistening eyes, but now that all was over she became prominent again. She praised them equally, and shuddered delightfully when Michael showed her the place where he had killed one, and then she took them into Hook's cabin and pointed to his watch which was hanging on a nail. It said, 'half past one'!

The lateness of the hour was almost the biggest thing of all. She got them to bed in the pirates' bunks pretty quickly, you may be sure; all but Peter, who strutted up and down on deck, until at last he fell asleep by the side of Long Tom. He had one of his dreams that night, and cried in his sleep for a long time, and Wendy held him tight.

Mr Toad

from The Wind in the Willows

KENNETH GRAHAME (1859–1932)

This chapter from the classic children's story The Wind in the Willows, *(selling 80,000 copies a year or more for most of the century from its publication in 1908), presents to us the incorrigible Mr Toad in all his glory as 'traffic-queller' and 'road-hog'. The Scottish-born Kenneth Grahame seized upon the noise and intoxicating excitement of 'motor-cars' as suitable material for stories he told to his son Alastair, only a few years after their arrival on British roads. The temptation which these early motor-cars held is shown, and the invitation they gave to Grahame's amazingly anarchic Toad, to break the law and defy justice. In an earlier chapter Grahame gave this superb description of a speeding motor-car which seems almost to anticipate cinema animation:*

> *. . . far behind them they heard a faint warning hum, like the drone of a distant bee. Glancing back, they saw a small cloud of dust, with a dark centre of energy, advancing on them at incredible speed, while from out of the dust a faint 'Poop-poop!' wailed like an uneasy animal in pain. Hardly regarding it, they turned to resume their conversation, when in an instant (as it seemed) the peaceful scene was changed, and with a blast of wind and a whirl of sound that made them jump for the nearest ditch, it was on them! The 'Poop-poop' rang with a brazen shout in their ears, they had a moment's glimpse of an interior of glittering plate-glass and rich morocco, and the magnificent motor-car, immense, breath-snatching, passionate, with its pilot tense and hugging his wheel, possessed all earth and air for the fraction of a second, flung an enveloping cloud of dust that blinded and enwrapped them utterly, and then dwindled to a speck in the far distance, changing back into a droning bee once more.*

While the others are enraged or frightened, Toad is totally seduced by his first sight of the motor-car and, as the wise Rat predicted, he becomes possessed by a new craze and 'the poetry of motion'. He succumbs both to what we would call 'road rage ' and the temptation to steal a car.

Kenneth Grahame was a banker. He was born in Edinburgh in 1859 and lived there and in the small Argyllshire town of Inveraray, where his father was Sheriff Substitute, until the age of five, when his mother died. Thereafter he lived in England, in rural Berkshire. Grahame wrote comparatively little, although an earlier book for children, The Golden Age, *was much admired by, among others, Kaiser Wilhelm II. The* Wind in the Willows *has never lost its position as one of the great works of children's fiction and there are perhaps echoes of a Loch Fyne childhood in the love of nature which spills out of its pages.*

It was a bright morning in the early part of summer; the river had resumed its wonted banks and its accustomed pace, and a hot sun seemed to be pulling everything green and bushy and spiky up out of the earth towards him, as if by strings. The Mole and the Water Rat had been up since dawn very busy on matters connected with boats and the opening of the boating season; painting and varnishing, mending paddles, repairing cushions, hunting for missing boat-hooks, and so on; and were finishing breakfast in their little parlour and eagerly discussing their plans for the day, when a heavy knock sounded at the door.

'Bother!' said the Rat, all over egg. 'See who it is, Mole, like a good chap, since you've finished.'

The Mole went to attend the summons, and the Rat heard him utter a cry of surprise. Then he flung the parlour door open, and announced with much importance, 'Mr Badger!'

This was a wonderful thing, indeed, that the Badger should pay a formal call on them, or indeed on anybody. He generally had to be caught, if you wanted him badly, as he slipped quietly along a hedgerow of an early morning or a late evening, or else hunted up in his own house in the middle of the wood, which was a serious undertaking.

The Badger strode heavily into the room, and stood looking at the two animals with an expression full of seriousness. The Rat let his egg-spoon fall on the table-cloth, and sat open-mouthed.

'The hour has come!' said the Badger at last with great solemnity.

'What hour?' asked the Rat uneasily, glancing at the clock on the mantelpiece.

'*Whose* hour, you should rather say,' replied the Badger. 'Why, Toad's hour! The hour of Toad! I said I would take him in hand as soon as the winter was well over, and I'm going to take him in hand today!'

'Toad's hour, of course!' cried the Mole delightedly. 'Hooray! I remember now! *We'll* teach him to be a sensible Toad!'

'This very morning,' continued the Badger, taking an arm-chair, 'as I learnt last night from a trustworthy source, another new and exceptionally powerful motor-car will arrive at Toad Hall on approval or return. At this very moment, perhaps, Toad is busy arraying himself in those singularly hideous habiliments so dear to him, which transform him from a (comparatively) good-looking Toad into an Object which throws any decent-minded animal that comes across it into a violent fit. We must be up and doing, ere it is too late. You two animals will accompany me instantly to Toad Hall, and the work of rescue shall be accomplished.'

'Right you are!' cried the Rat, starting up. 'We'll rescue the poor unhappy animal! We'll convert him! He'll be the most converted Toad that ever was before we've done with him!'

They set off up the road on their mission of mercy, Badger leading the way. Animals when in company walk in a proper and sensible manner, in single file, instead of sprawling all across the road and being of no use or support to each other in case of sudden trouble or danger.

They reached the carriage-drive of Toad Hall to find, as the Badger had anticipated, a shiny new motor-car, of great size, painted a bright red (Toad's favourite colour), standing in front of the house. As they neared the door it was flung open, and Mr Toad, arrayed in goggles, cap, gaiters, and enormous overcoat, came swaggering down the steps, drawing on his gauntleted gloves.

'Hullo! come on, you fellows!' he cried cheerfully on catching sight of them. 'You're just in time to come with me for a jolly – to come for a jolly – for a – er – jolly –'

His hearty accents faltered and fell away as he noticed the stern unbending look on the countenances of his silent friends, and his invitation remained unfinished.

The Badger strode up the steps. 'Take him inside,' he said sternly to his companions. Then, as Toad was hustled through the door, struggling and protesting, he turned to the chauffeur in charge of the new motor-car.

'I'm afraid you won't be wanted today,' he said. 'Mr Toad has changed his mind. He will not require the car. Please understand that this is final. You needn't wait.' Then he followed the others inside and shut the door.

'Now, then!' he said to the Toad, when the four of them stood together in the hall. 'First of all, take those ridiculous things off!'

'Shan't!' replied Toad, with great spirit. 'What is the meaning of this gross outrage? I demand an instant explanation.'

Take them off him, then, you two,' ordered the Badger briefly.

They had to lay Toad out on the floor, kicking and calling all sorts of names, before they could get to work properly. Then the Rat sat on him, and the Mole got his motor-clothes off him bit by bit, and they stood him up on his legs again. A good deal of his blustering spirit seemed to have evaporated with the removal of his fine panoply. Now that he was merely Toad, and no longer the Terror of the Highway, he giggled feebly and looked from one to the other appealingly, seeming quite to understand the situation.

'You knew it must come to this, sooner or later, Toad,' the Badger explained severely. 'You've disregarded all the warnings we've given you, you've gone on squandering the money your father left you, and you're getting us animals a bad name in the district by your furious driving and your smashes and your rows with the police. Independence is all very well, but we animals never allow our friends to make fools of themselves beyond a certain limit, and that limit you've reached. Now, you're a good fellow in many respects, and I don't want to be too hard on you. I'll make one more effort to bring you to reason. You will come with me into the smoking-room, and there you will hear some facts about yourself, and we'll see whether you come out of that room the same Toad that you went in.'

He took Toad firmly by the arm, led him into the smoking-room, and closed the door behind them.

'*That's* no good!' said the Rat contemptuously. '*Talking* to Toad'll never cure him. He'll *say* anything.'

They made themselves comfortable in arm-chairs and waited patiently. Through the closed door they could just hear the long continuous drone of the Badger's voice, rising and falling in waves of oratory; and presently they noticed that the sermon began to be punctuated at intervals by long-drawn sobs, evidently proceeding from the bosom of Toad, who was a soft-hearted and affectionate fellow, very easily converted – for the time being – to any point of view.

After some three-quarters of an hour the door opened, and the Badger reappeared, solemnly leading by the paw a very limp and dejected Toad. His skin hung baggily about him, his legs wobbled, and his cheeks were furrowed by the tears so plentifully called forth by the Badger's moving discourse.

'Sit down there, Toad,' said the Badger kindly, pointing to a chair. 'My friends,' he went on, 'I am pleased to inform you that Toad has at last seen the error of his ways. He is truly sorry for his misguided conduct in the past, and he has undertaken to give up motor-cars entirely and for ever. I have his solemn promise to that effect.'

That is very good news,' said the Mole gravely.

'Very good news indeed,' observed the Rat dubiously, 'if only – *if* only –'

He was looking very hard at Toad as he said this, and could not help thinking he perceived something vaguely resembling a twinkle in that animal's still sorrowful eye.

'There's only one thing more to be done,' continued the gratified

Badger. 'Toad, I want you solemnly to repeat, before your friends here, what you fully admitted to me in the smoking-room just now. First, you are sorry for what you've done, and you see the folly of it all?'

There was a long, long pause. Toad looked desperately this way and that, while the other animals waited in grave silence. At last he spoke.

'No!' he said a little sullenly, but stoutly, 'I'm *not* sorry. And it wasn't folly at all! It was simply glorious!'

'What?' cried the Badger, greatly scandalized. 'You backsliding animal, didn't you tell me just now, in there –'

'O, yes, yes, in *there*,' said Toad impatiently. 'I'd have said anything in *there*. You're so eloquent, dear Badger, and so moving, and so convincing, and put all your points so frightfully well – you can do what you like with me in *there*, and you know it. But I've been searching my mind since, and going over things in it, and I find that I'm not a bit sorry or repentant really, so it's no earthly good saying I am, now, is it?'

'Then you don't promise,' said the Badger, 'never to touch a motor-car again?'

'Certainly not!' replied Toad emphatically. 'On the contrary, I faithfully promise that the very first motor-car I see, poop-poop! off I go in it!'

'Told you so, didn't I?' observed the Rat to the Mole.

'Very well, then,' said the Badger firmly, rising to his feet. 'Since you won't yield to persuasion, we'll try what force can do. I feared it would come to this all along. You've often asked us three to come and stay with you, Toad, in this handsome house of yours; well, now we're going to. When we've converted you to a proper point of view we may quit, but not before. Take him upstairs you two, and lock him up in his bedroom, while we arrange matters between ourselves.'

'It's for your own good, Toady, you know,' said the Rat kindly, as Toad, kicking and struggling, was hauled up the stairs by his two faithful friends. 'Think what fun we shall all have together, just as we used to, when you've quite got over this – this painful attack of yours!'

'We'll take great care of everything for you till you're well, Toad,' said the Mole, 'and we'll see your money isn't wasted, as it has been.'

'No more of those regrettable incidents with the police, Toad,' said the Rat, as they thrust him into his bedroom.

'And no more weeks in hospital, being ordered about by female nurses, Toad,' added the Mole, turning the key on him.

They descended the stair, Toad shouting abuse at them through the keyhole, and the three friends then met in conference on the situation.

'It's going to be a tedious business,' said the Badger, sighing. 'I've never seen Toad so determined. However, we will see it out. He must never be left an instant unguarded. We shall have to take it in turns to be with him, till the poison has worked itself out of his system.'

They arranged watches accordingly. Each animal took it in turns to sleep in Toad's room at night, and they divided the day up between them. At first Toad was undoubtedly very trying to his careful guardians. When his violent paroxysms possessed him he would arrange bedroom chairs in rude resemblance of a motor-car and would crouch on the foremost of them, bent forward and staring fixedly ahead, making uncouth and ghastly noises, till the climax was reached, when, turning a complete somersault, he would lie prostrate amidst the ruins of the chairs, apparently completely satisfied for the moment. As time passed, however, these painful seizures grew gradually less frequent, and his friends strove to divert his mind into fresh channels. But his interest in other matters did not seem to revive, and he grew apparently languid and depressed.

One fine morning the Rat, whose turn it was to go on duty, went upstairs to relieve Badger, whom he found fidgeting to be off and stretch his legs in a long ramble round his wood and down his earths and burrows. 'Toad's still in bed,' he told the Rat, outside the door. 'Can't get much out of him, except, "O, leave him alone, he wants nothing, perhaps he'll be better presently, it may pass off in time, don't be unduly anxious," and so on. Now, you look out, Rat! When Toad's quiet and submissive, and playing at being the hero of a Sunday-school prize, then he's at his artfullest. There's sure to be something up. I know him. Well, now I must be off.'

'How are you today, old chap?' inquired the Rat cheerfully, as he approached Toad's bedside.

He had to wait some minutes for an answer. At last a feeble voice replied, 'Thank you so much, dear Ratty! So good of you to inquire! But first tell me how you are yourself, and the excellent Mole?'

'O, we're all right,' replied the Rat. 'Mole,' he added incautiously, 'is going out for a run round with Badger. They'll be out till luncheon-time, so you and I will spend a pleasant morning together, and I'll do my best to amuse you. Now jump up, there's a good fellow, and don't lie moping there on a fine morning like this!'

'Dear, kind Rat,' murmured Toad, 'how little you realize my condition, and how very far I am from "jumping up" now – if ever! But do not trouble about me. I hate being a burden to my friends, and I do not expect to be one much longer. Indeed, I almost hope not.'

'Well I hope not, too,' said the Rat heartily. 'You've been a fine bother to us all this time, and I'm glad to hear it's going to stop. And in weather like this, and the boating season just beginning! It's too bad of you, Toad! It isn't the trouble we mind, but you're making us miss such an awful lot.'

'I'm afraid it *is* the trouble you mind, though,' replied the Toad languidly. 'I can quite understand it. It's natural enough. You're tired of bothering about me. I mustn't ask you to do anything further. I'm a nuisance, I know.'

'You are, indeed,' said the Rat. 'But I tell you, I'd take any trouble on earth for you, if only you'd be a sensible animal.'

If I thought that, Ratty,' murmured Toad, more feebly than ever, 'then I would beg you – for the last time, probably – to step round to the village as quickly as possible – even now it may be too late even now it may be too late – and fetch the doctor. But don't you bother. It's only a trouble, and perhaps we may as well let things take their course.'

'Why, what do you want a doctor for?' inquired the Rat, coming closer and examining him. He certainly lay very still and flat, and his voice was weaker and his manner much changed.

'Surely you have noticed of late –' murmured Toad. 'But no – why should you? Noticing things is only a trouble. Tomorrow, indeed, you may be saying to yourself, "O if only I had noticed sooner! If only I had done something!" But no; it's a trouble. Never mind – forget that I asked.'

'Look here, old man,' said the Rat, beginning to get rather alarmed, 'of course I'll fetch a doctor to you, if you really think you want him. But you can hardly be bad enough for that yet. Let's talk about something else.'

'I fear, dear friend,' said Toad, with a sad smile, 'that "talk" can do little in a case like this – or doctors either, for that matter; still, one must grasp at the slightest straw. And, by the way – while you are about it – I *hate* to give you additional trouble, but I happen to remember that you will pass the door – would you mind at the same time asking the lawyer to step up? It would be a convenience to me, and there are moments – perhaps I should say there is *a* moment – when one must face disagreeable tasks, at whatever cost to exhausted nature!'

'A lawyer! O, he must be really bad!' the affrighted Rat said to himself, as he hurried from the room, not forgetting, however, to lock the door carefully behind him.

Outside, he stopped to consider. The other two were far away, and he had no one to consult.

It's best to be on the safe side,' he said, on reflection. 'I've known Toad fancy himself frightfully bad before, without the slightest reason; but I've never heard him ask for a lawyer! If there's nothing really the matter, the doctor will tell him he's an old ass, and cheer him up; and that will be something gained. I'd better humour him and go; it won't take very long.' So he ran off to the village on his errand of mercy.

The Toad, who had hopped lightly out of bed as soon as he heard the key turned in the lock, watched him eagerly from the window till he disappeared down the carriage-drive. Then, laughing heartily, he dressed as quickly as possible in the smartest suit he could lay hands on at the moment, filled his pockets with cash which he took from a small drawer in the dressing-table, and next, knotting the sheets from his bed together and tying one end of the improvised rope round the central mullion of the handsome Tudor window which formed such a feature of his bedroom, he scrambled out, slid lightly to the ground, and, taking the opposite direction to the Rat, marched off light-heartedly, whistling a merry tune.

It was a gloomy luncheon for Rat when the Badger and the Mole at length returned, and he had to face them at table with his pitiful and unconvincing story. The Badger's caustic, not to say brutal, remarks may be imagined, and therefore passed over, but it was painful to the Rat that even the Mole, though he took his friend's side as far as possible, could not help saying, 'You've been a bit of a duffer this time, Ratty! Toad, too, of all animals!'

'He did it awfully well,' said the crestfallen Rat.

'He did *you* awfully well!' rejoined the Badger hotly. 'However, talking won't mend matters. He's got clear away for the time, that's certain, and the worst of it is, he'll be so conceited with what he'll think is his cleverness that he may commit any folly. One comfort is, we're free now, and needn't waste any more of our precious time doing sentry-go. But we'd better continue to sleep at Toad Hall for a while longer. Toad may be brought back at any moment – on a stretcher, or between two policemen.'

So spoke the Badger, not knowing what the future held in store, or how much water, and of how turbid a character, was to run under bridges before Toad should sit at ease again in his ancestral Hall.

Meanwhile, Toad, gay and irresponsible, was walking briskly along the high road, some miles from home. At first he had taken bypaths, and crossed many fields, and changed his course several times, in case of pursuit; but now, feeling by this time safe from recapture, and the sun smiling brightly on him, and all Nature joining in a chorus of approval to the song of self-praise that his own heart was singing to him, he almost danced along the road in his satisfaction and conceit.

'Smart piece of work that!' he remarked to himself, chuckling. 'Brain against brute force – and brain came out on the top – as it's bound to do.

Poor old Ratty! My! Won't he catch it when the Badger gets back! A worthy fellow, Ratty, with many good qualities, but very little intelligence and absolutely no education. I must take him in hand some day, and see if I can make something of him.'

Filled full of conceited thoughts such as these he strode along, his head in the air, till he reached a little town, where the sign of 'The Red Lion', swinging across the road half-way down the main street, reminded him that he had not breakfasted that day, and that he was exceedingly hungry after his long walk. He marched into the inn, ordered the best luncheon that could be provided at so short a notice, and sat down to eat it in the coffee-room.

He was about half-way through his meal when an only too familiar sound, approaching down the street, made him start and fall a-trembling all over. The poop-poop! drew nearer and nearer, the car could be heard to turn into the inn-yard and come to a stop, and Toad had to hold on to the leg of the table to conceal his overmastering emotion. Presently the party entered the coffee-room, hungry, talkative, and gay, voluble on their experiences of the morning and the merits of the chariot that had brought them along so well. Toad listened eagerly, all ears, for a time; at last he could stand it no longer. He slipped out of the room quietly, paid his bill at the bar, and as soon as he got outside sauntered round quietly to the inn-yard. 'There cannot be any harm,' he said to himself, 'in my only just *looking* at it!'

The car stood in the middle of the yard, quite unattended, the stable-helps and other hangers-on being all at their dinner. Toad walked slowly round it, inspecting, criticizing, musing deeply.

'I wonder,' he said to himself presently, 'I wonder if this sort of car *starts* easily?'

Next moment, hardly knowing how it came about, he found he had hold of the handle and was turning it. As the familiar sound broke forth, the old passion seized on Toad and completely mastered him, body and soul. As if in a dream he found himself, somehow, seated in the driver's seat; as if in a dream, he pulled the lever and swung the car round the yard and out through the archway; and, as if in a dream, all sense of right and wrong, all fear of obvious consequences, seemed temporarily suspended. He increased his pace, and as the car devoured the street and leapt forth on the high road through the open country, he was only conscious that he was Toad once more, Toad at his best and highest, Toad the terror, the traffic-queller, the Lord of the lone trail, before whom all must give way or be smitten into nothingness and everlasting night. He chanted as he flew, and the car responded with sonorous drone; the miles were eaten up under him as he sped he knew not whither, fulfilling his instincts, living his hour, reckless of what might come to him.

'To my mind,' observed the Chairman of the Bench of Magistrates cheerfully, 'the *only* difficulty that presents itself in this otherwise very clear case is, how we can possibly make it sufficiently hot for the incorrigible rogue and hardened ruffian whom we see cowering in the dock before us. Let me see: he has been found guilty on the clearest evidence, first, of stealing a valuable motor-car; secondly, of driving to the public danger; and, thirdly, of gross impertinence to the rural police. Mr Clerk, will you tell us, please, what is the very stiffest penalty we can impose for each of these offences? Without, of course, giving the prisoner the benefit of any doubt, because there isn't any.'

The Clerk scratched his nose, with his pen. 'Some people would consider,' he observed, 'that stealing the motor-car was the worst offence, and so it is. But cheeking the police undoubtedly carries the severest penalty, and so it ought. Supposing you were to say twelve months for the theft, which is mild, and three years for the furious driving, which is lenient, and fifteen years for the cheek, which was pretty bad sort of cheek, judging by what we've heard from the witness-box, even if you only believe one-tenth part of what you heard, and I never believe more myself – those figures, if added together correctly, tot up to nineteen years –'

'First-rate!' said the Chairman.

'– So you had better make it a round twenty years and be on the safe side,' concluded the Clerk.

'An excellent suggestion!' said the Chairman approvingly. 'Prisoner! Pull yourself together and try and stand up straight. It's going to be twenty years for you this time. And mind, if you appear before us again, upon any charge whatever, we shall have to deal with you very seriously!'

Then the brutal minions of the law fell upon the hapless Toad, loaded him with chains, and dragged him from the Court House, shrieking, praying, protesting; across the market-place, where the playful populace, always as severe upon detected crime as they are sympathetic and helpful when one is merely 'wanted', assailed him with jeers, carrots, and popular catch-words; past hooting schoolchildren, their innocent faces lit up with the pleasure they ever derive from the sight of a gentleman in difficulties; across the hollow-sounding drawbridge, below the spiky portcullis, under the frowning archway of the grim old castle, whose ancient towers soared high overhead; past guardrooms full of grinning soldiery off duty, past sentries who coughed in a horrid sarcastic way, because that is as much as a sentry on his post dare do to show his contempt and abhorrence of crime; up time-worn winding stairs, past men-at-arms in casquet and corselet of steel, darting threatening looks through their vizards; across courtyards, where mastiffs strained at their leash and pawed the air to get at him; past ancient warders, their halberds leant against the wall, dozing over a pasty and a flagon of brown ale; on and on, past the rack-chamber and the thumbscrew-room, past the turning that led to the private scaffold, till they reached the door of the grimmest dungeon that lay in the heart of the innermost keep. There at last they paused, where an ancient gaoler sat fingering a bunch of mighty keys.

'Oddsbodikins!' said the sergeant of police, taking off his helmet and wiping his forehead. 'Rouse thee, old loon, and take over from us this vile Toad, a criminal of deepest guilt and matchless artfulness and resource. Watch and ward him with all thy skill; and mark thee well, greybeard, should aught untoward befall, thy old head shall answer for this – and a murrain on both of them!'

The gaoler nodded grimly, laying his withered hand on the shoulder of the miserable Toad. The rusty key creaked in the lock, the great door clanged behind them, and Toad was a helpless prisoner in the remotest dungeon of the best-guarded keep of the stoutest castle in all the length and breadth of Merry England.

'A Civil War?'

from Memorials of his Time

HENRY COCKBURN (1779–1854)

In the aftermath of the Napoleonic Wars, widespread economic depression led to agitation for political reform and the right to organise. Lord Liverpool's Tory Government and many of their supporters became the victims of a paranoia – employing spies and 'agents provocateurs' – obsessed by the existence of sedition, real or imaginary, and the imminence of a working class rising The nearest this came to reality was the Peterloo Massacre of 1819 in Manchester. In Scotland the equivalent was the much less threatening but grandly named 'Radical War' of 1820.

Henry Cockburn gave this personal account, very much from the point of view of the Opposition Whigs, in his Memorials, *published in 1856. He makes it clear that a great deal of hysteria had gripped the bourgeoisie and panic measures were resorted to although, he believed, there was an absence of any real threat to public order. Walter Scott, as a Tory of the deepest dye, was meantime lined up on the side of hysteria and reaction; according to his biographer, Lockhart, he was 'ardent for actual and instant war', against the thousands of rebels he believed had taken up arms against the Government.*

Cockburn's version was much closer to the truth It was true that placards had called for strikes and that 60,000 had answered that call, largely in the West of Scotland. However, the accompanying call for rebellion and for a provisional government to be set up, brought a response which was snuffed out with ease. Around forty radicals marched to the Carron Ironworks near Falkirk in an attempt to seize guns. They were joined by a few others but at the so-called 'Battle of Bonnymuir' they were easily overcome by a force of troops. The Government reprisals were savage and out of all proportion: three leaders, Hardie, Baird and Wilson were executed for treason and nineteen others were transported. These men became radical martyrs in the tradition of Thomas Muir in 1793. A nationalistic tinge might be deduced from the wording of a banner carried at the time: 'Scotland Free or a Desart'.

✝

The year 1819 closed, and the new one opened, amidst the popular disturbances called, gravely by some, and jocularly by others, 'The Radical War'. The whole island was suffering under great agricultural and manufacturing distress. This was taken the usual advantage of by demagogues; and consequently there was considerable political excitement. Quite enough to require caution, and even to justify alarm. Its amount in Scotland was contemptible. But it was first exaggerated, and then exhibited as evidence of a revolutionary spirit, which nothing but Toryism and Castlereagh could check. It was determined therefore that the folly and violence of our western weavers should be considered as a civil war, and be dealt with accordingly. Edinburgh was as quiet as the grave, or even as Peebles, yet matters were so managed, that we were obliged to pass about a month as if an enemy had been drawing his lines round our very walls. The only curiosity in the affair now is the facility of spreading panic.

The Midlothian Yeomanry Cavalry was marched, in the middle of a winter night, to Glasgow; remained in that district a few days, did nothing, having nothing to do; and returned, as proud and as praised, as if fresh from Waterloo. The survivors of the old Edinburgh Gentlemen Volunteers were called together again, and disengaged a few soldiers by taking charge of the Castle, under their former and still unquenched Lieutenant-Colonel, Charles Hope, Lord President of the Court of Session. New offers of voluntary service were made, and accepted; and as the Whigs could not keep back, without seeming to encourage the enemy, once more did I prepare to gird on my sword as captain in a thing called 'The Armed Association', which was meant to be something more military than constables, and less military than soldiers. But this gallant battalion never assembled. In about a fortnight every sane eye saw that the whole affair was nonsense; and our Tory Colonel, Sir James Fergusson of Kilkerran, was too much ashamed of it to call us together even to be disbanded.

Some people however were clear that a blow would be struck by the Radical army – an army much talked of but never seen, on the last night of the year. The perfect facility with which a party of forty or fifty thousand weavers could march from Glasgow, and seize upon the Banks and the Castle of Edinburgh, without ever being heard of till they appeared in our streets, was demonstrated. Our magistrates therefore invited all loyal citizens to congregate, with such arms as they had, at various assigned posts. I repaired to the Assembly Rooms in George Street, with a stick, about eight in the evening. The streets were as quiet as on an ordinary Sunday; but their silence was only held by the excited to forebode the coming storm. There seemed to be nobody abroad except those who, like myself, were repairing to their forlorn hopes. On entering the large room, I found at least 400 or 500 grown gentlemen, pacing about, dressed coarsely, as if for work, and armed, according to taste or convenience, with bludgeons, fowling pieces, dirks, cane-swords, or other implements. A zealous banker laboured under two small swivels set on stocks, one under each arm. Frivolity, though much provoked, and a good deal indulged in in corners, was reproved as unbecoming the crisis. At last, about 10 p.m., the horn of the coach from Glasgow was heard, and the Lord Provost sent us word from the council chamber that we might retire for the night. We never met again.

Next summer a Commission of Oyer and Terminer was sent down for the trial of the rebels, with an English serjeant as prosecutor to keep us all right on the law of treason. The commissioners visited Stirling, Glasgow, Paisley, Ayr, and Dumbarton; and the result was, that several persons were convicted, and that three or four were executed. They were all guilty of high treason, no doubt, as any old woman is who chooses to charge a regiment of cavalry. But to make such a parade about such treason did no good either to the law or to the people. The whole affair was composed of three nearly equal parts – popular discontent, Government exaggeration, and public craze.

Sredni Vashtar

from the Short Stories of Saki

HECTOR HUGH MUNRO (1870–1916)

As will be evident from his name, Munro (or 'Saki' as he was generally known) had a policeman father who was of Scots extraction (as was his mother). Saki was born in Burma but was sent to England at the age of two, to be brought up by two aunts when his mother died suddenly. He went back out to Burma to a post with the military police in 1893, but finally illness forced him to return to England, where he made a career as a writer. In 1914 he enlisted as a soldier and was sent to France, where he was shot through the head while resting in a shell crater. The title of this short story shows some evidence of his familiarity with Far Eastern philosophy – the macabre quality is entirely Saki's own.

Saki's writing has always attracted a devoted following for its quality of dry detachment and a species of macabre humour, quite different from that of his namesake Neil Munro, creator of the gentle Para Handy. The sense of horror with which this story is infused comes from the child Conradin's hatred for his grown-up cousin – one does wonder if there is any connection with Saki's feelings for his female relatives. Kipling comes to mind as another Anglo–Indian writer who had hang-ups about his experience as a child of the East returned to England. Interestingly, Munro wrote a series of sketches called Not So Stories, *an obvious reference to Kipling's* Just So Stories *published in the same year, 1902.*

Conradin was ten years old, and the doctor had pronounced his professional opinion that the boy would not live another five years. The doctor was silky and effete, and counted for little, but his opinion was endorsed by Mrs De Ropp, who counted for nearly everything. Mrs De Ropp was Conradin's cousin and guardian, and in his eyes she represented those three-fifths of the world that are necessary and disagreeable and real; the other two-fifths, in perpetual antagonism to the foregoing, were summed up in himself and his imagination. One of these days Conradin supposed he would succumb to the mastering pressure of wearisome necessary things – such as illnesses and coddling restrictions and drawn-out dulness. Without his imagination, which was rampant under the spur of loneliness, he would have succumbed long ago.

Mrs De Ropp would never, in her honestest moments, have confessed to herself that she disliked Conradin, though she might have been dimly aware that thwarting him 'for his good' was a duty which she did not find particularly irksome. Conradin hated her with a desperate sincerity which he was perfectly able to mask. Such few pleasures as he could contrive for himself gained an added relish from the likelihood that they would be displeasing to his guardian, and from the realm of his imagination she was locked out – an unclean thing, which should find no entrance.

In the dull, cheerless garden, overlooked by so many windows that were ready to open with a message not to do this or that, or a reminder that medicines were due, he found little attraction. The few fruit-trees that it contained were set jealously apart from his plucking, as though they were rare specimens of their kind blooming in an arid waste; it would probably have been difficult to find a market-gardener who would have offered ten shillings for their entire yearly produce. In a forgotten corner, however, almost hidden behind a dismal shrubbery, was a disused tool-shed of respectable proportions, and within its walls Conradin found a haven, something that took on the varying aspects of a playroom and a cathedral. He had peopled it with a legion of familiar phantoms, evoked partly from fragments of history and partly from his own brain, but it also boasted two inmates of flesh and blood. In one corner lived a ragged-plumaged Houdan hen, on which the boy lavished an affection that had scarcely another outlet. Further back in the gloom stood a large hutch, divided into two compartments, one of which was fronted with close iron bars. This was the abode of a large polecat-ferret, which a friendly butcher-boy had once smuggled, cage and all, into its present quarters, in exchange for a long-secreted hoard of small silver. Conradin was dreadfully afraid of the lithe, sharp-fanged beast, but it was his most treasured possession. Its very presence in the tool-shed was a secret and fearful joy, to be kept scrupulously from the knowledge of the Woman, as he privately dubbed his cousin. And one day, out of Heaven knows what material, he spun the beast a wonderful name, and from that moment it grew into a god and a religion. The Woman indulged in religion once a week at a church near by, and took Conradin with her, but to him the church service was an alien rite in the House of Rimmon. Every Thursday, in the dim and musty silence of the tool-shed, he worshipped with mystic and elaborate ceremonial before the wooden hutch where dwelt Sredni Vashtar, the great ferret. Red flowers in their season and scarlet berries in the winter-time were offered at his shrine, for he was a god who laid some special stress on the fierce impatient side of things, as opposed to the Woman's religion, which, as far as Conradin could observe, went to great lengths in the contrary direction. And on great festivals powdered nutmeg was strewn in front of his hutch, an important feature of the offering being that the nutmeg had to be stolen. These festivals were of irregular occurrence, and were chiefly appointed to celebrate some passing event. On one occasion, when Mrs De Ropp suffered from acute toothache for three days, Conradin kept up the festival during the entire three days, and almost succeeded in persuading himself that Sredni Vashtar was personally responsible for the toothache. If the malady had lasted for another day the supply of nutmeg would have given out.

The Houdan hen was never drawn into the cult of Sredni Vashtar. Conradin had long ago settled that she was an Anabaptist. He did not pretend to have the remotest knowledge as to what an Anabaptist was, but he privately hoped that it was dashing and not very respectable. Mrs De Ropp was the ground plan on which he based and detested all respectability.

After a while Conradin's absorption in the tool-shed began to attract the notice of his guardian. 'It is not good for him to be pottering down there in all weathers,' she promptly decided, and at breakfast one morning she announced that the Houdan hen had been sold and taken away overnight. With her short-sighted eyes she peered at Conradin, waiting for an outbreak of rage and sorrow, which she was ready to rebuke with a flow of excellent precepts and reasoning. But Conradin said nothing: there was nothing to be said. Something perhaps in his white set face gave her a momentary qualm, for at tea that afternoon there was toast on the table, a delicacy which she usually banned on the ground that it was bad for him; also because the making of it 'gave trouble', a deadly offence in the middle-class feminine eye.

'I thought you liked toast,' she exclaimed, with an injured air, observing that he did not touch it.

'Sometimes,' said Conradin.

In the shed that evening there was an innovation in the worship of the hutch-god. Conradin had been wont to chant his praises, tonight he asked a boon.

'Do one thing for me, Sredni Vashtar.'

The thing was not specified. As Sredni Vashtar was a god he must be supposed to know. And choking back a sob as he looked at that other empty corner, Conradin went back to the void he so hated.

And every night, in the welcome darkness of his bedroom, and every evening in the dusk of the toolshed, Conradin's bitter litany went up: 'Do one thing for me, Sredni Vashtar.'

Mrs De Ropp noticed that the visits to the shed did not cease, and one day she made a further journey of inspection.

'What are you keeping in that locked hutch?' she asked. 'I believe it's guinea-pigs. I'll have them all cleared away.'

Conradin shut his lips tight, but the Woman ransacked his bedroom till she found the carefully hidden key, and forthwith marched down to the shed to complete her discovery. It was a cold afternoon, and Conradin had been bidden to keep to the house. From the furthest window of the dining-room the door of the shed could just be seen beyond the corner of the shrubbery, and there Conradin stationed himself. He saw the Woman enter, and then he imagined her opening the door of the sacred hutch and peering down with her short-sighted eyes into the thick straw bed where his god lay hidden. Perhaps, she would prod at the straw in her clumsy impatience. And Conradin fervently breathed his prayer for the last time. But he knew as he prayed that he did not believe. He knew that the Woman would come out presently with that pursed smile he loathed so well on her face, and that in an hour or two the gardener would carry away his wonderful god, a god no longer, but a simple brown ferret in a hutch. And he knew that the Woman would triumph always as she triumphed now, and that he would grow ever more sickly under her pestering and domineering and superior wisdom, till one day nothing would matter much more with him, and the doctor would be proved right. And in the sting and misery of his defeat, he began to chant loudly and defiantly the hymn of his threatened idol:

Sredni Vashtar went forth,
His thoughts were red thoughts and his teeth were white.
His enemies called for peace, but he brought them death.
Sredni Vashtar the Beautiful.

And then of a sudden he stopped his chanting and drew closer to the window-pane. The door of the shed still stood ajar as it had been left, and the minutes were slipping by. They were long minutes, but they slipped by nevertheless. He watched the starlings running and flying in little parties across the lawn; he counted them over and over again, with one eye always on that swinging door. A sour-faced maid came in to lay the table for tea, and still Conradin stood and waited and watched. Hope had crept by inches into his heart, and now a look of triumph began to blaze in his eyes that had only known the wistful patience of defeat. Under his breath, with a furtive exultation, he began once more again the pæan of victory and devastation. And presently his eyes were rewarded: out through that doorway came a long, low, yellow-and-brown beast, with eyes a-blink at the waning daylight, and dark wet stains around the fur of jaws and throat. Conradin dropped on his knees. The great polecat-ferret made its way down to a small brook at the foot of the garden, drank for a moment, then crossed a little plank bridge and was lost to sight in the bushes. Such was the passing of Sredni Vashtar.

'Tea is ready,' said the sour-faced maid; 'where is the mistress?'

'She went down to the shed some time ago,' said Conradin.

And while the maid went to summon her mistress to tea, Conradin fished a toasting-fork out of the sideboard drawer and proceeded to toast himself a piece of bread. And during the toasting of it and the buttering of it with much butter and the slow enjoyment of eating it, Conradin listened to the noises and silences which fell in quick spasms beyond the dining-room door. The loud foolish screaming of the maid, the answering chorus of wondering ejaculations from the kitchen region, the scuttering footsteps and hurried embassies for outside help, and then, after a lull, the scared sobbings and the shuffling tread of those who bore a heavy burden into the house.

'Whoever will break it to the poor child? I couldn't for the life of me!' exclaimed a shrill voice. And while they debated the matter among themselves, Conradin made himself another piece of toast.

3

TREASON, FEUD AND FORAY
Introduction

✝

This section could have furnished enough material for an entire anthology. Scotland's history is filled with incidents of political crimes, internal strife, feuding neighbours, unruly subjects, evil deeds done in the name of the state, in the cause of a family's advancement, in search of profit, in the name of a political belief and in the name of God.

From the murder of St Magnus in Orkney to Bruce's slaying of the Red Comyn in Dumfries the landscape of Scotland is blood-soaked and haunted by the memory of foul crimes and savage reprisals. We have, in the interests of facing up to our national shortcomings, tried to avoid the crimes caused by foreign war – with the exception of our final, fictional, extract, our selection of treason, feud and foray all arise from purely Scottish circumstances.

The description of Scotland's woes, given by Macduff in *Macbeth*:

> . . . Each new morn
> New widows howl, new orphans cry; new sorrows
> Strike heaven on the face, that it resounds
> As if it felt with Scotland . . .

could, all too easily have been said at many other times. The Macbeth story is itself, even after every allowance has been made for Shakespeare's political motivation in rewriting history from the winner's side, a fine example of the uncertainty of life as a Scottish ruler. As Shakespeare said elsewhere: 'uneasy lies the head that wears the crown'. A glance at the list of Scottish rulers will suggest that while job satisfaction may have been high the chances of a lengthy career and a quiet end were not always great.

Not that those lesser folk, who did not wear the crown, necessarily rested any easier. The common man was quite likely to get caught up in the machinations of his superiors and end up bearing arms in a cause of which he often knew little and cared less.

Scotland seem at times to be entirely filled with caves where one clan burned the members of another clan, with churches set on fire with the congregation inside, with castles whose garrisons surrendered on assurance of honourable terms and then were massacred. Few of these sanguinary episodes have quite the formality and the almost classical horror of the clan fight on the North Inch at Perth. The account of it given by Thomas Pennant in his *Tour in Scotland and Voyage to the Hebrides 1772* is brief, but telling.

> On this plain, in 1396, a private war between the clan Chattan, and the clan Kay was decided in a manner parallel to the combat between the Horatii and Curiatii. A cruel feud raged between these warlike tribes, which the king, Robert III, in vain endeavoured to reconcile: at length the Earls of Crawford and Dunbar proposed that the difference should be determined by the sword, by thirty champions on each side. The warriors were chosen, the day of combat fixed, the field appointed, the king and his nobility assembled as spectators. On reviewing the combatants, one of the clan Chattan (seized with a panic) was missing; when it was proposed, in order to form a parity of numbers, that one of the clan Kay should withdraw; but such was the spirit of that brave people, that not one could be prevailed on to resign the honour and danger of the day. At length one Henry Wind, a saddler, who happened accidentally to be present, offered to supply the place of the lost Macintosh, for the small sum of a French crown of gold. He was accepted; the combat began, and Henry fairly earned his pay, for by his prowess, victory declared itself in favour of his party. Of that of clan Chattan only ten and the volunteer were left alive, and every one of them dangerously wounded. Of the clan Kay only one survived, who declining so unequal a combat, flung himself into the Tay, and swam over unwounded to the opposite shore.

Reading this account one notes the enthusiasm of all the participants for the conflict and especially the willingness of Henry Wind to take part in another's quarrel. The King and his court also seem to have looked on the event as a form of aristocratic entertainment, the Scottish 14th century equivalent of a Roman gladiatorial contest. Perhaps, in truth the Scots are particularly given to feuding and fighting; certainly the 14th-century chronicler Froissart reported that the Scots reacted in a very hostile way to their French allies who had come to assist Robert II in his war with the English. The Scots, he tells us, said:

> Let them be told to return again, for we are sufficiently numerous in Scotland to fight our own quarrels, and do not want their company.

Our first extract comes from Walter Scott's *Tales of a Grandfather* and recounts the story of the Black Dinner – an incident from the early years of the reign of James II. The young James only came to the throne, of course, because of the murder of his father, James I, in the Blackfriars Monastery of Perth by a group of disaffected nobles

The Stuart dynasty did not enjoy a peaceful reign – James I had been captured by pirates and handed over to the English and remained a guest of the state, honoured but not free, for eighteen years. James II was killed by an exploding cannon, James III was killed fighting a rebellion – a rebellion in which his son, the future James IV was implicated. James IV died in action against foreign enemies at Flodden, to be succeeded by his infant son James V.

When James V came into manhood and his personal reign one of his actions was to attempt to stamp out the turbulent habits of the Borderers and curtail their age-old habits of reiving and stealing, cross-border theft and troublesome pretensions to independence. The story of how the King dealt with one of the most notable of these unruly subjects is told in the ballad of *Johnie Armstrang*.

The daughter of James V, Mary, had not her troubles to seek in her reign. Inheriting the Crown when she was six days old she was sent off to France as a little girl and married to the Dauphin at the age of fourteen. She was widowed when still a teenager and returned to Scotland to find her land in the throes of the Reformation. She married her cousin, Henry Stuart, Lord Darnley, but quickly found him to be an erratic and untrustworthy man. Darnley was involved in the murder of the Queen's Secretary, David Rizzio, and we include a long, detailed, first-hand analysis of this murder by one of the principal conspirators, Patrick Ruthven, who wrote his account of *The Murder of Rizzio* for Queen Elizabeth of England more or less on his death-bed.

Darnley's own end came less than a year after Rizzio's and Robert Chambers' account comes from his *Traditions of Edinburgh*. Mary was forced to abdicate a few weeks after Darnley's murder and spent her last twenty years of life a prisoner in England, busily plotting her restoration and Elizabeth of England's downfall before eventually being executed in 1587.

Although her son, James VI & I, boasted to his English Parliament that:

> Here I sit and govern with my Pen, I write and it is done, and by a Clearke of the Councill I govern Scotland now, which others could not doe by the sword

the taste for feud and foray had hardly died out in his ancient Kingdom. In 1640, during the Bishops' Wars, Campbell of Argyll, a supporter of the Covenanting side, was authorised to harry the lands of the Royalist Ogilvie Earl of Airlie. Politics, religious politics, was the immediate occasion but underlying this was a long tradition of clan conflict and rivalry between the Campbells and the Ogilvies. The story is told vividly in the anonymous ballad *The Bonnie House o'Airlie*.

Few crimes in Scottish history can have attracted more opprobrium to their instigators than the 'murder under trust' – The Massacre of Glencoe in 1692. Glencoe evoked horror and condemnation, not so much for the scale of the killing, which was hardly remarkable, but for the involvement of the highest in the land, the premeditation and the betrayal of trust. Too often painted as a Highland feud, as a Campbell versus Macdonald conflict, it is more precisely seen as a piece of state crime which was executed by a Campbell-led unit. The chilling words of the Scottish Secretary, the Master of Stair, to the Earl of Breadalbane (a Campbell) reveal the degree of planning, the ruthlessness of approach. Ethnic cleansing was not invented in the twentieth-century:

> The winter time is the only season in which we are sure the Highlanders cannot escape and carry their wives, bairns and cattle to the hills . . . This is the proper time to maul them in the long dark nights.

One of the great nineteenth-century historians, Thomas Babington Macaulay, wrote a vivid description of the Massacre in his *History of England* – he concluded:

> It is said, and may be but too easily believed, that the sufferings of the fugitives were terrible. How many old men, how many women with babes in their arms, sank down and slept their last sleep in the snow; how many having crawled, spent with toil and hunger, into nooks among the precipices, died in those dark holes, and were picked to the bone by the mountain ravens, can never be known. But it is probable that those who perished by cold, weariness, and want were not less numerous than those who were slain by the assassins. When the troops had retired, the Macdonalds crept out of the caverns of Glencoe, ventured back to the spot where the huts had formerly stood, collected the scorched corpses from among the smoking ruins, and performed some rude rites of sepulture. The tradition runs that the hereditary bard of the tribe took his seat on a rock which overhung the place of slaughter, and poured forth a long lament over his murdered brethren and his desolate home.

Even ahead of Glencoe in the catalogue of Scottish crimes, at least judged by their literary consequences, was Culloden and the repression of the Highlands which followed on the defeat of Jacobitism. One of the most vivid, and most immediate, responses to the slaughter at Drumossie Moor was that of the young Tobias Smollett, making his way as a doctor in London but shocked into the, possibly dangerous and certainly unwise, publication by the news from the North of *The Tears of Scotland*.

It is with something approaching relief that we turn to our last extract – still involving treason but mixed with some foreign espionage – and which besides is set in the world of fiction where 'they do but jest, poison in jest, no offence i' the world'. John Buchan's *The Thirty-Nine Steps* introduced Richard Hannay to the world in a classic tale of a man fighting against a group of spies and traitors in a pre-First World War setting. Our extract has Hannay on the run in Galloway.

'The Black Dinner'

from Tales of a Grandfather

SIR WALTER SCOTT (1771–1832)

Scott's Tales of a Grandfather *were conceived of in 1827, just as he was finishing work on his* Life of Napoleon. *Scott, working constantly to win free of bankruptcy, uneasy with the idea of rest and inactivity, wrote in his diary:*

> I have my proof-sheets, to be sure, but what are these to a whole day? A good thought came into my head to write Stories for little Johnnie Lockhart, from the History of Scotland . . . I will make, if possible, a book that a child shall understand, yet a man will feel some temptation to peruse should he chance to take it up.

The father of 'little Johnnie Lockhart' – John Gibson Lockhart – wrote of this work in his Life of Sir Walter Scott:

> [It] has, I have little doubt, extended the knowledge of Scottish history in quarters where little or no interest had ever before been awakened as to any other parts of that subject, except those immediately connected with Mary Stuart and the Chevalier.

Scott's approach to history in these tales may be too narrative and, indeed, too judgemental for modern academic fashion but Lockhart's verdict remains accurate. Scott was a splendid storyteller, not for nothing nicknamed 'The Wizard of the North' and he brings to life in Tales of a Grandfather *a host of stories from Scottish history – our extract is the story of the murder in 1440 of the young Douglas brothers in Edinburgh Castle by Sir William Crichton and Sir Alexander Livingstone.*

The ten-year-old James II, in front of whom the murder took place, was the victim of a power struggle between rival contesting factions of his nobility – his guardians Crichton and Livingstone contesting for position with the powerful House of Douglas.

The Douglas killing is also commemorated in the old ballad:

> Edinburgh Castle, towne and tower,
> God grant ye sink for sin!
> And that for the black denner
> Yerl Douglas gat therein.

✝

When James I was murdered, his son and heir, James II, was only six years old; so that Scotland was once more plunged into all the discord and confusions of a regency, which were sure to reach their height in a country where even the undisputed sway of a sovereign of mature age was not held in due respect, and was often disturbed by treason and rebellion.

The affairs of the kingdom, during the minority of James II, were chiefly managed by two statesmen, who seem to have been men of considerable personal talent, but very little principle or integrity. Sir Alexander Livingstone was guardian of the King's person; Sir William Crichton was Chancellor of the kingdom. They debated betwixt themselves the degree of authority attached to their respective offices, and at once engaged in quarrels with each other, and with one who was more powerful than either of them – the great Earl of Douglas.

That mighty house was now at the highest pitch of its greatness. The Earl possessed Galloway, Annandale, and other extensive properties in the south of Scotland, where almost all the inferior nobility and gentry acknowledged him as their patron and lord. Thus the Douglasses had at their disposal that part of Scotland, which from its constant wars with England, was most disciplined and accustomed to arms. They possessed the duchy of Touraine and lordship of Longueville in France, and they were connected by intermarriage with the Scottish royal family.

The Douglasses were not only powerful from the extent of lands and territories, but also from the possession of great military talents, which seemed to pass from father to son, and occasioned a proverb, still remembered in Scotland –

> So many, so good, as of the Douglasses have been,
> Of one sirname in Scotland never yet were seen.

Unfortunately, their power, courage, and military skill were attended with arrogance and ambition, and the Douglasses seemed to have claimed to themselves the rank and authority of sovereign princes, independent of the laws of the country, and of the allegiance due to the monarch. It was a common thing for them to ride with a retinue of a thousand horse, and as Archibald, the Earl of Douglas of the time, rendered but an imperfect allegiance even to the severe rule of James I it might be imagined that his power could not be easily restrained by such men as Crichton and Livingston – great indeed, through the high offices which they held, but otherwise of a degree far inferior to that of Douglas.

But when this powerful nobleman died, in 1439, and was succeeded by his son William, a youth of only sixteen years old, the wily Crichton began to spy an occasion to crush the Douglasses, as he hoped, for ever, by the destruction of the youthful earl and his brother, and for abating, by this cruel and unmerited punishment, the power and pride of this great family. Crichton proposed to Livingston to join him in this meditated treachery; and, though enemies to each other, the guardian of the King and the chancellor of the kingdom united in the vile project of cutting off two boys, whose age alone showed their innocence of the guilt charged upon them. For this purpose flattery and fair words were used to induce the young Earl, and his brother David, with some of their nearest friends, to come to court, where it was pretended that they would be suitable companions and intimates for the young King. An old adherent of the family greatly dissuaded the Earl from accepting this invitation, and exhorted him, if he went to Edinburgh in person, to leave at least his brother David behind him. But the unhappy youth, thinking that no treachery was intended, could not be diverted from the fatal journey.

The Chancellor Crichton received the Earl of Douglas and his brother on their journey, at his own castle of Crichton, and with the utmost appearance of hospitality and kindness. After remaining a day or two at this place, the two brothers were inveigled to Edinburgh castle, and introduced to the young King, who, not knowing the further purpose of his guardians, received them with affability, and seemed delighted with the prospect of enjoying their society.

On a sudden the scene began to change. At an entertainment which was served up to the Earl and his brother, the head of a black bull was placed on the table. The Douglasses knew this, according to a custom which prevailed in Scotland, to be the sign of death, and leaped from the table in great dismay. But they were seized by armed men who entered the apartment. They underwent a mock trial, in which all the insolencies of their ancestors were charged against them, and were condemned to immediate execution. The young King wept, and implored Livingston and Crichton to show mercy to the young noblemen, but in vain. These cruel men only reproved him for weeping at the death of those whom they called his enemies. The brethren were led out to the court of the castle, and beheaded without delay. Malcolm Fleming of Cumbernauld, a faithful adherent of their house, shared the same fate with the two brothers.

This barbarous proceeding was as unwise as it was unjust. It did not reduce the power of the Douglasses, but only raised general detestation against those who managed the affairs of James II.

Johnie Armstrang

from Walter Scott: Minstrelsy of the Scottish Border

ANONYMOUS

The tale of Johnie Armstrang or Armstrong of Gilnockie, told in this, one of the classic Border ballads, collected and edited by Walter Scott and published in 1801, is a story of lawlessness, feud, treachery, reiving and over-mighty subjects.

The Armstrongs, like the Eliots and many other Border families, had for generations been both a blessing and a curse to Scottish kings. A blessing, because their warlike habits and constant readiness made them both a significant part of any Scottish army and a valuable guard on the frontier with England. A curse, because they were a lawless and troublesome race, as likely to prey on Scots as on English (despite Johnie Armstrang's protestations of the exclusively English focus for his depredations – verses 20/21); many of the families spread across the Border with branches on both sides of the debatable land and dealt with the two governments on terms of some equality.

So troublesome a tribe were the Armstrongs that there are in fact two candidates for the tale of the King and John Armstrong: the first, Johnnie of Gilnockie executed in 1529 and the second, John, brother of Thomas Armstrong of Mangerston, executed in 1530. The poem will be seen to contain elements which identify it with both individuals – verse 1 speaks of the Laird of Gilnockie while verse 29 seems to relate to the brother of Armstrong of Mangerton. While it may be in some respects confusing and not totally reliable history (it is after all a ballad and probably of authorship linked to the Armstrong family), it remains a vivid description of rough life and rough death among the reiving clans of the Border.

The King of the story was the young James V, only 18 in 1530 and fairly recently entered on his personal reign. A near-contemporary chronicler, Robert Lindsay of Pitscottie, gives an account of the execution of Johnnie Armstrong and his retinue which echoes the envious words attributed to the King in verse 26, an envy which arose from the wealth and braggadocio of Armstrong:

> *What wants that knave that a King suld have,*
> *But the sword of honour and the crown!*

The ballad writer elsewhere (verse 6) indicates the King's recognition of Armstrong's state as a king in Liddesdale:

The King he movit his bonnet to him:
He ween'd he was a King as weel as he

which was very much the root of the problem: the quasi-independent state
of the Border clans, a matter which James was not prepared to tolerate.
Having come to the throne as an infant he had much personal experience
of over-mighty subjects; indeed the Earl of Angus, head of one of the
branches of the Douglas clan, had held him a prisoner between 1525 and
1528. Such formative experiences made him hostile to the pretensions of
the nobility and on his 1529 expedition into the Borders he had imprisoned
some of the great Border lords. The freebooter Johnnie Armstrong was
however a lesser figure against whom the King could act more freely and
use as an object lesson to demonstrate his power more safely.

Carlenrig, the site of the meeting between the King and Armstrong and
the site of Gilnockie's execution, lies between Hawick and Langholm in
the upper reaches of Teviotdale.

I

Sum speikis of lords, sum speikis of lairds,
And sic lyke men of hie degrie;
Of a gentleman I sing a sang,
Sum tyme call'd Laird of Gilnockie.

II

The King he wrytes a luving letter,
With his ain hand sae tenderly,
And he hath sent it to Johnie Armstrang,
To cum and speik with him speedily.

III

The Eliots and Armstrangs did convene;
They were a gallant cumpanie –
'We'll ride and meit our lawful King,
And bring him safe to Gilnockie.'

IV

'Make kinnen[1] and capon ready, then,
And venison in great plentie;
We'll welcum here our royal King;
I hope he'll dine at Gilnockie!'

V

They ran their horse on the Langholme howm,
And brak their spears wi' mickle main;
The ladies lukit frae their loft windows –
'God bring our men weel back agen!'

VI

When Johnie cam before the King,
W' a' his men sae brave to see,
The King he movit his bonnet to him;
He ween'd he was a King as weel as he.

VII

'May I find grace, my sovereign liege,
Grace for my loyal men and me?
For my name it is Johnie Armstrang,
And subject of yours, my liege,' said he.

VIII

'Away, away, thou traitor strang!
Out o' my sight soon mayst thou be!
I grantit nevir a traitor's life,
And now I'll not begin wi' thee.'

IX

'Grant me my life, my liege, my King!
And a bonny gift I'll gie to thee –
Full four-and-twenty milk-white steids,
Were a' foaled in ae yeir to me.

X

'I'll gie thee a' these milk-white steids,
That prance and nicker[2] at a speir;
And as mickle gude Inglis gilt,[3]
As four of their braid backs dow[4] bear.'

XI

'Away, away, thou traitor strang!
Out o' my sight soon mayst thou be!
I grantit nevir a traitor's life,
And now I'll not begin wi' thee!'

XII

'Grant me my life, my liege, my King!
And a bonny gift I'll gie to thee –
Gude four-and-twenty ganging⁵ mills,
That gang thro' a' the yeir to me.

XIII

'These four-and-twenty mills complete,
Sall gang for thee thro' a' the yeir;'
And as mickle of gude reid wheit,
As a' their happers dow to bear.'

XIV

'Away, away, thou traitor strang!
Out o' my sight soon mayst thou be!
I grantit nevir a traitor's life,
And now I'll not begin wi' thee.'

XV

'Grant me my life, my liege, my King!
And a great gift I'll gie to thee –
Bauld four-and-twenty sisters' sons,
Sall for thee fecht, tho' a' should flee!'

XVI

'Away, away, thou traitor strang!
Out o' my sight soon mayst thou be!
I grantit nevir a traitor's life,
And now I'll not begin wi' thee.'

XVII

Grant me my life, my liege, my King!
And a brave gift I'll gie to thee –
All between heir and Newcastle town
Sall pay their yeirly rent to thee.'

XVIII

Away, away, thou traitor strang!
Out o' my sight soon mayst thou be!
I grantit nevir a traitor's life,
And now I'll not begin wi' thee.'

XIX

'Ye lied,[6] ye lied, now, King,' he says,
'Altho' a King and Prince ye be!
For I've luved naething in my life,
I weel dare say it, but honesty –

XX

'Save a fat horse, and a fair woman,
Twa bonny dogs to kill a deir;
But England suld have found me meal and mault,
Gif I had lived this hundred yeir!

XXI

'She suld have found me meal and mault,
And beif and mutton in a' plentie;
But nevir a Scots wyfe could have said,
That e'er I skaith'd her a pure flee.

XXII

'To seik het water beneith cauld ice,
Surely it is a great folie –
I have asked grace at a graceless face,
But there is nane for my men and me!

XXIII

'But, had I kenn'd ere I cam frae hame,
How thou unkind wadst been to me!
I wad have keepit the Border syde,
In spite of all thy force and thee.

XXIV

Wist England's King that I was ta'en,
O gin a blythe man he wad be!
For anes I slew his sister's son,
And on his breist bane brak a trie.'

XXV

John wore a girdle about his middle,
Imbroidered ower wi' burning gold,
Bespangled wi' the same metal;
Maist beautiful was to behold.

XXVI

There hang nine targats[7] at Johnie's hat,
And ilk ane worth three hundred pound –
'What wants that knave that a King suld have,
But the sword of honour and the crown!

XXVII

'O whair got thou these targats, Johnie,
That blink sae brawly[8] abune thy brie?'
'I gat them in the field fechting,
Where, cruel King, thou durst not be.

XXVIII

'Had I my horse, and harness gude,
And riding as I wont to be,
It suld have been tauld this hundred yeir,
The meeting of my King and me!

XXIX

'God be with thee, Kirsty,[9] my brother!
Lang live thou Laird of Mangertoun!
Lang mayst thou live on the Border syde,
Ere thou see thy brother ride up and down!

XXX

'And God be with thee, Kirsty, my son,
Where thou sits on thy nurse's knee!
But and thou live this hundred yeir,
Thy father's better thou'lt nevir be.

XXXI

'Farewell! my bonny Gilnock hall,
Where on Esk side thou standest stout!
Gif I had lived but seven yeirs mair,
I wad hae gilt thee round about.'

XXXII

John murdered was at Carlinrigg,
And all his gallant cumpanie;
But Scotland's heart was ne'er sae wae,
To see sae mony brave men die –

XXXIII
Because they saved their countrey deir
Frae Englishmen! Nane were sae bauld,
While Johnie lived on the Border syde,
Nane of them durst cum neir his hauld.

1 *Kinnen*, rabbits
2 *Nicker*, neigh
3 *Gilt*, gold
4 *Dow*, able to
5 *Ganging*, going
6 *Lied*, lie

7 *Targats*, tassels
8 *Blink sae brawly*, glance so bravely
9 Kirsty Christopher [The name of the Laird of Mangerton at this time was Thomas]

The Murder of Rizzio

PATRICK RUTHVEN, 3rd LORD RUTHVEN (c. 1520–1566)

In the field of Scottish political crimes there are few more dramatic incidents than the murder of David Rizzio or Riccio, the Italian musician, secretary and favourite of Mary Queen of Scots. The murder was carried out by a group of courtiers on 9th March 1566 at the Palace of Holyrood in front of the Queen, who was at the time six months' pregnant with the future James VI.

Riccio had come to Scotland in the suite of the ambassador of Savoy and his musical talents had brought him to the attention of the Queen. His relationship with the Queen seems to have been innocent but the Queen's husband, Henry Stewart, Lord Darnley, an erratic and inadequate personality, became obsessed with the idea that Mary and Riccio were lovers and that Riccio's influence over the Queen was harmful and powerful. Mary, brought up at the cultured and sophisticated French court, doubtless enjoyed the company of a talented and amusing cosmopolitan figure like Riccio, finding few congenial spirits at the Scottish court and becoming increasingly isolated there by reason of her Catholicism.

Darnley managed to recruit various disaffected nobles to his cause. Some, like James Douglas, 4th Earl of Morton, and Patrick Ruthven, were supporters of the Reformation and were suspicious of the Catholic Riccio and potential foreign influence in the state. However the Riccio assassination was an attempt to destabilise the state and can also be seen as yet another example of groups of Scottish nobles attempting to create a position where they controlled the Crown. As will be seen in the text, Darnley and the nobles carried out the common Scottish practice of signing 'articles' – in effect subscribing a mutual bond pledging the parties to take certain actions.

After the murder, Ruthven fled to England, where he wrote this vivid, if perhaps not entirely reliable account of the crime. Its intended audience seems to have been Queen Elizabeth of England and Ruthven accordingly emphasises the accusation that Mary had been unfaithful to Darnley with Riccio (or Davie as he usually refers to him) – the only possible grounds that Elizabeth might have considered to have excused the crime.

Ruthren died at Newcastle in June 1566. Henry Darnley was murdered in his own turn, being killed in mysterious and controversial circumstances at Kirk o' Field, Edinburgh, in February 1567 – the degree of *foreknowledge of the murder which the Queen had being still a matter of debate. (See* The Murder of Darnley *in this section for an account of this incident.)*

In Ruthven's 'relation' of the events, he refers consistently to Darnley as the King. Although Henry Stewart, Lord Darnley, married the Queen in July 1565, he never formally was recognised as King This indeed was, Ruthven tells us, one of his complaints against Riccio, who:

> *... lately had stayed the Queen's Majesty from giving him the crown matrimonial of Scotland, which her Majesty had promised to him divers times before ...*

Ruthven's account is vivid and clear, the only terms that may cause doubt are his references to the Queen's 'utter chamber' – a version of outer chamber, and to a 'whiniard' – this is a short stabbing sword, the word is often rendered in the Scots of the period as a 'whinger'

The Ruthven family had a somewhat chequered history – Patrick's son William was created 1st Earl of Gowrie in 1581. He led a group of extreme Protestants who captured the sixteen-year-old James VI in August 1582 and held him prisoner at Castle Ruthven for ten months. After being pardoned for this, William was executed for his involvement in another conspiracy in 1582. His heir, John, was killed along with his younger brother, the Master of Ruthven, in the Gowrie Conspiracy in 1600 – another plot against James VI. Hardly surprisingly, the Gowrie Earldom was then forfeited.

✝

The author of this relation, Lord Ruthven, at the age of forty-six, was visited by the hand of God with great trouble and sickness, whereby he kept his bed continually by the space of three months, and was under the cure of physicians, as of the Queen's French doctor, Dr Preston, and Thomas Thompson, apothecary; and was so feebled and weakened through the sickness and medicines, that scarcely he might walk twice the length of his chamber unsitting down. During this time the King conceived hatred against an Italian called David Riccio: and about the 10th day of February, sent his dear friend and kinsman, George Douglas, son to Archibald, sometime Earl of Angus and declared to Lord Ruthven, how that the said David Riccio, had abused him in many sorts, and lately had stayed the Queen's Majesty from giving him the crown matrimonial of Scotland, which her Majesty had promised to him divers times before: besides many other wrongs that David had done to him, which he could not bear with longer, and behoved to be revenged thereof. And because the Lord Ruthven was one of the nobility that he confided and trusted most unto, in respect that his children and he were sisters' children; therefore he desired his counsel and advice what way was best to be revenged on David. The Lord Ruthven, hearing the message aforesaid, gave answer to George Douglas, that he could give no counsel in that matter, in respect he knew the King's youth and facility; for he had sundry of the nobility that had given him counsel for his own honour and weal, and immediately be revealed the same again to the Queen's Majesty, who reproved them with great anger and contumelious words; so that he would have no meddling with the King's proceedings until the time he could keep his own counsel. The said George departed with the answer about 12th of February. The King, hearing the answer, was very miscontented and said, it is a sore case that I can get none of the nobility that will assist me against yonder false villain Davie. George Douglas answered, the fault was in yourself, that cannot keep your own counsel. Then the King took a book and swore thereon, that what counsel soever the Lord Ruthven should give him, he would not reveal, neither to the Queen's Majesty, nor to any others, and immediately directed George to him again, declaring what oath the King hath made. Notwithstanding, the Lord Ruthven was eight days after ere he would give any counsel therein; howbeit, the King sent George Douglas to him every day three or four times. After eight days were past, which was toward the 20th day of February, the Lord Ruthven, perceiving that the King's whole intent was but only the slaughter of Davie, resolved in his mind, and considered that he had a good time to labour for certain of the nobility, his brethren that were banished in the realm of England and in Argyle; and specially the Earls of Argile, Murray, Glencarn, and Rothes; the Lords Boyd and Ocheltrie, and the Lairds of Pittarro and Grange, with many other gentlemen and barons. Wherefore so soon as the said George was directed again from the King to him, he answered, that he could not meddle with the King's affairs, without that he would bring home the noblemen before rehearsed, who were banished only for the Word of God. And after long reasoning, and divers days travelling, the King was contented they should come home into the realm of Scotland; so that the Lord Ruthven would make him sure that they would be his, and set forward all his affairs. He gave answer to the King, and bad him make his own security, and that he should cause it to be subscribed by the aforesaid Earls, Lords, and Barons. Immediately thereafter the King directed George Douglas to Lord Ruthven with certain articles, which he desired him to put in form of writing, to be subscribed by the Lords banished;

the which he caused to be put in form. And having consideration that the King desired them to be bound to him, he caused to be drawn certain articles in the said Lords' names for the King's part towards them; which the King himself reformed with his own hand.

The articles being penned for both parties, and the King reading and considering the same, he was contented therewith, and subscribed his part, and delivered it to the Lord Ruthven, who sent the other articles to the Earl of Murray, and the remanent being within England; and to the Earl of Argile, and the remanent being with him in the west, who subscribed the same, and sent them to Lord Ruthven to be kept till their meeting with the King, and every one to have their own part; the tenour whereof followeth

• • •

Certain Articles to be fulfilled by James, Earl of Murray; Archibald, Earl of Argile; Alexander, Earl of Glencarne; Andrew, Earl of Rothes; Robert, Lord Boyd; Andrew, Lord Ochiltree; and their Complices, to the Noble and Mighty Prince Henry, King of Scotland, husband to our Sovereign Lady: which Articles the said Persons offer with most humility, lowliness, and service to the said Noble Prince, for whom to God they pray, &c.

Imprimis. The said Earls, Lords, and their complices, shall become, and by the tenour hereof become, true subjects, men and servants, to the noble and mighty Prince Henry, by the grace of God King of Scotland, and husband to our Sovereign Lady; that they, and all others that will do for them, shall take a loyal and true part with the said noble Prince in all his actions, causes, and quarrels, against whomsoever, to the uttermost of their powers; and shall be friends to his friends, and enemies to his enemies, and neither spare their lives, lands, goods, nor possessions.

2. *Item,* The said Earls, Lords, and their complices shall, at the first Parliament, and other Parliaments that shall happen to be after their returning within this realm, by themselves and others that have voice in Parliament, consent, and by these presents do consent now as then, and then as now, to grant and give the crown matrimonial to the said noble Prince for all the days of his life. And if any person or persons withstand or gainsay the same, the said Earls, Lords, and their complices shall take such part as the said noble Prince taketh, in whatsoever sort, for the obtaining of the said crown, against all, and whatsoever that let or deny, as shall best please the said noble Prince.

3. *Item,* The said Earls, Lords, and their complices shall fortify and maintain the said noble Prince to his just title to the Crown of Scotland, failing of succession of our Sovereign Lady, and shall justify and set

forward the same at their utmost powers. And if any manner of person will usurp or gainsay the just title, then the said Earls, Lords, and their complices shall maintain, defend, and set forwards the same, as best shall please the said noble Prince, without fear of life or death; and shall seek and pursue them the usurpers, as shall please the said noble Prince to command, to extirp them out of the realm of Scotland, or take or slay them.

4. *Item*, As to the religion which was established by the Queen's Majesty our Sovereign, shortly after her arrival in this realm, whereupon Acts and Proclamation was made, and now again granted by the said noble Prince to the said Earls, Lords, and their complices; they, and every of them, shall maintain and fortify the same at their uttermost powers, by the help, supply, and maintenance of the said noble Prince. And if any person or persons will gainsay the same, or any part thereof, or begin to make tumult or uproar for the same, the said Earls, Lords, and their complices to take a full, true, and plain part with the said noble Prince, against the said contemners and usurpers, at their uttermost.

5. *Item*, As they are become true subjects, men and servants, to the said noble Prince, so shall they be loyal and true to his Majesty, as becometh true subjects to their natural Prince; and as true and faithful servants serve their good master with their bodies, lands, goods, and possessions; and shall neither spare life nor death in setting forward all things, that may be to the advancement and honour of the said noble Prince.

6. *Item*, The said Earls, Lords, and their complices, shall labour at the Queen of England's hands for the relief of the said noble Prince, his mother, and brother, by themselves and such others as they may procure, to the uttermost of their power, that they may be relieved out of ward, or remain in England freely, or repair into Scotland, as they shall think most expedient, without stop or impediment to herself, her son, their servants and moveables.

7. *Item*, The said Earls, Lords, and their complices, shall, by themselves and others that will do for them, labour and procure, at the Queen of England's hands, that the said noble Prince may have her kindness, good-will, and assistance in all his Majesty's honourable and just causes, against whatsoever foreign Prince.

• • •

Certain Articles to be fulfilled by the Noble and Mighty Prince Henry, King of Scotland, husband to our Sovereign Lady, of his Majesty's mere clemency and good-will, to James, Earl of Murray; Archibald, Earl of Argile;

*Alexander, Earl of Glencarne; Andrew, Earl of Rothes; Robert, Lord Boyd;
Andrew, Lord Stewart, of Ocheltrie, remaining in England, &c.*

Item, First, The said noble Prince shall do his good-will, to obtain them one remission, if they require the same, for all faults and crimes by-past, of whatsoever quality or condition they be. And if that cannot be obtained at the first time, shall persevere in suing of the same until it be obtained; and at the last shall give them a free remission of all crimes so soon as we are placed, by their help and supply to the crown matrimonial: And in the mean time shall stop and make impediments, so much as lieth in us, that they be not called nor accused for whatsoever crime: And presently remits and forgives the aforesaid Earls, Lords, and their complices, all crimes committed against us of whatsoever quality or condition they be; and do bury and put the same in oblivion, as they had never been: And shall receive them at their returning, thankfully, and with heartiness, as others our true and faithful subjects and servants.

2. *Item*, We shall not suffer, by our good wills, the foresaid Lords and their complices, to be called or accused in parliament, nor suffer any forfeitures to be laid against them, but shall stop the same at our uttermost power: And if any person or persons pretend otherwise, we shall neither consent to the holding the parliament, nor yet shall grant to their forfeiture willingly, but shall stop the same to our uttermost power, as said is.

3. *Item*, That the said Earls, Lords, and their complices, returning within the realm of Scotland, we shall suffer or permit them to use and enjoy all their lands, tackes, steedings, and benefices, that they or any of them had before their passage into England. And if any manner of persons do make them impediments in the peaceable enjoying of the said lands, steedings, tackes, benefices and possessions, it being made known to us, we shall fortify and maintain them to the uttermost of our powers, to the obtaining of the same.

4. *Item*, As to the said Earls, Lords, and their complices religion, we are contented and consent that they use the same, conform to the Queen's Majesty's act and proclamation made thereupon, shortly after her Highness's return out of France. And if any person or persons pretend to make them impediment thereunto, or to trouble them for using the same religion, we shall take part with the aforesaid Earls, Lords and their complices, at our utmost power. And after their returning upon their good bearing and service to be done to the said noble Prince, shall, by their advice, consent to the stablishing the religion now professed, and shall concur with them, if any persons do withstand them.

5. *Item*, We shall fortify and maintain the said Earls, Lords, and their complices, as a natural Prince should do to his true and obedient subject; and as one good master should fortify and maintain his true and natural servants against whatsoever, in all their just causes, actions, and quarrels.

All this while the King kept secret from the Queen's Majesty the whole proceedings; and as her Majesty sought by subtil means to learn of him what was in his mind, so crafted he with her to seek out her mind: And in the same time he daily sent to the Lord Ruthven, saying that he could not abide Davie any longer and if his slaughter was not hastened, he would slay him himself, yea, though it were in the Queen's Majesty's own chamber. The Lord Ruthven counselled him to the contrary, and thought it not decent that he should put hand on such a mean person: yet always the King could not be content, without the Lord Ruthven affixed a day when Davie should be slain. The said Lord considering with himself that it was not convenient nor honourable to slay Davie, notwithstanding the offences he had made; but rather to take him, and give him judgment by the nobility, the King's Majesty answered, it was cumbersome to tarry in such a cause; but always he could be contented that he were taken and hanged, or dispatched otherwise. In the mean time the King and Queen's Majesties rode to Seaton; the King so burning in his desire towards the slaughter of David, that he sent divers privy writings written in his own hand, and also messages by tongue to George Douglas, to be shewed to the Lord Ruthven, to have all things in readiness against his repairing to Edinburgh towards the slaughter of David, or otherwise he would put the same in execution with his own hands. In the mean time Lord Ruthven was practising with the Earl of Morton, who was the King's near kinsman, and with the Lord Lindsey, because his wife was a Douglas, and of consanguinity to the King; and with a great number of barons, gentleman, and freeholders, to assist the King in such affairs as he had to do; and then they should have their religion freely established conformable to Christ's book and to the articles the King had subscribed to the Lords. And after the King's return out of Seaton, he directed George Douglas to the Earl of Morton and Lord Ruthven, to see what day should be appointed, with place and time, for the performance of the enterprise against David. The said Earl and Lord sent answer to the King, and declared they should have a sufficient number ready against Friday or Saturday the 8th or 9th of March, to do what he pleased; and enquired of the King what time he would have it the ratherest performed; for, according to their opinion, they thought it best to take them when David should be in his own chamber in the morning, or in passing through the close: which the King refused simpliciter, and said he could not be well taken in his own chamber, nor no time in the morning, by reason that at night he tarried late with the Queen's Majesty: he lay in the over cabinet, and other whiles in Signor Francisco's chamber, and sometimes in his own, to which he had sundry back doors and windows that he might escape at, and if so it were, all were lost. Therefore he would have him taken at the time of the supping, sitting with her Majesty at the table, that he might be taken in her own presence; because she had not entertained him, her husband according to her accustomed manner, nor as she ought of duty. To the which the said Earl and Lords were very loth to grant, and gave many reasons to the contrary, that it was better to have been done out of her presence, not in the same. Notwithstanding no reason might avail, but the King would have him taken in her Majesty's presence, and devised the manner himself, as after followeth: That upon the Saturday, at supper time, the Earl of Morton, Lord Ruthven, and Lord Lindsey should have ready so many as would be assistants and partakers with the King, in their houses, against he should send them word: and so soon as he sent them word, that the Earl of Morton should come in, and come up to the Queen's utter chamber, and a company with him; and the Lord Ruthven was to come through the King's secret chamber; and that the King would pass up before by a privy passage to the Queen's chamber, and open the door, through which the Lord Ruthven and his company might enter; and that the King himself should be speaking with the Queen's Majesty sitting at supper; the remanent barons and gentlemen to be in the court of the palace for keeping of the gates, and defending of the close in case any of the Lords or officers would endeavour to gainstand the King's enterprise. The Earl of Morton and Lord Ruthven having consideration of the King's desire towards the taking of Davie in the Queen's Majesty's chamber, were loth to grant thereto; yet the King would not otherwise, but have it done as he had devised. The Earl and Lords considering he was a young Prince, and having a lusty Princess to lie in his arms afterwards, who might persuade him to deny all that was done for his cause, and to allege that others persuaded him to the same, thought it necessary to have security thereupon: and a bond was made in the King's name to the Earls, Lords, Barons, freeholders, merchants, and craftsmen, declaring all that was to be done was his own devise, invention, and fact; and bound and obliged himself, his heirs and successors, to them, their heirs and successors, to keep them skathless, and unmolested or troubled for the taking and executing of Davie in the Queen's presence or otherwise, like as the bond specified hereafter word by word.

'Be it Kend to all men by these present letters: We, Henry by the grace of God King of Scotland, and Lieutenant to the Queen's Majesty; for so much we having consideration of the gentle and good nature, with many other good qualities in her Majesty, we have thought pity, and also think it great conscience to us that are her husband, to suffer her to be abused or reduced by certain privy persons, wicked and ungodly, not regarding her Majesty's honour ours, nor the nobility thereof, nor the common-weal of the same, but seeking their own commodity and privy gains, especially a stranger Italian called Davie: which may be the occasion of her Majesty's destruction, ours, the nobility, and common-weal, without hasty remedy be put thereto, which we are willing to do: and to that effect we have devised to take these privy persons, enemies to her Majesty, us, the nobility, and common-wealth, to punish them according to their demerits; and in case of any difficulty, to cut them off immediately, and to take and slay them wherever it happeneth. And because we cannot accomplish the same without the assistance of others, therefore have we drawn certain of our nobility, Earls, Lords, Barons, freeholders, gentlemen, merchants, and craftsmen, to assist us in our enterprise, which cannot be finished without great hazard. And because it may chance that there be sundry great personages present, who may endeavour to gainstand our enterprise, where-through some of them may be slain, and likewise of ours, where-through a perpetual feud may be contracted betwixt the one and the other; therefore we bind and oblige us our heirs, and successors, to the said Earls, Lords, Barons, gentlemen, freeholders, merchants, and craftsmen, their heirs and successors, that we shall accept the same feud upon us, and fortify and maintain them at the uttermost of our power, and shall be friend to their friends, and enemy to their enemies; and shall neither suffer them nor theirs to be molested nor troubled in their bodies, lands, goods, nor possessions, so far as lieth in us. And if any person would take any of the said Earls, Lords, Barons, gentlemen, freeholders, merchants, or craftsmen, for enterprizing and assisting with us for the achieving of our purpose, because it may chance to be done in presence of the Queen's Majesty, or within her Palace of Holyrood House, we, by the word of a Prince, shall accept and take the same on us now as then, and then as now, and shall warrant and keep harmless the foresaid Earls, Lords, Barons freeholders, gentlemen, merchants, and craftsmen, at our utter power. In witness whereof we have subscribed this with our own hand at Edinburgh, the 1st of March 1565.'

Upon Saturday the 9th day of March, as is conform to the King's ordinance and device the Earl Morton, Lords Ruthven and Lindsey, having their men and friends in readiness, abiding for the King's advertisement; the King having supped and the sooner for that cause, and the Queen's Majesty being in her cabinet within her inner chamber at the supper, the King sent to the said Earl and Lords, and their complices; and desired them to make haste and come into the Palace, for he should have the door of the privy passage open, and should be speaking with the Queen before their coming, conform to his device rehearsed before. Then the Earl of Morton, Lord Ruthven and Lord Lindsey, with their complices, passed up to the Queen's utter chamber, and the Lord Ruthven passed in through the King's chamber, and up through the privy way to the Queen's chamber, as the King had learned him, and through the chamber to the cabinet, where he found the Queen's Majesty sitting at her supper, at the middest of a little table, the Lady Argile sitting at one end, and Davie at the head of the table with his cap on his head, the King speaking with the Queen's Majesty, and his hand about her waist.

The Lord Ruthven at his coming in said to the Queen's Majesty, 'It would please your Majesty to let yonder man Davie come forth of your presence, for he hath been over-long here.' Her Majesty answered, 'What offence hath he made?' The said Lord replied again, that he had made great offence to her Majesty's honour, the King her husband, the nobility and commonweal of the realm. 'And how?' saith she, 'It will please your Majesty,' said he, 'he hath offended your Majesty's honour, which I dare not be so bold to speak of: As to the King your husband's honour, he hath hindred him of the crown matrimonial; which your grace promised him, beside many other things which are not necessary to be expressed. And as to the nobility, he hath caused your Majesty to banish a great part and most chief thereof, and fore-fault them at this present Parliament, that he might be made a lord. And as to your commonweal, he hath been a common destroyer thereof, in so far as he suffered not your Majesty to grant or give anything but that which passed through his hands, by taking of bribes and goods for the same: and caused your Majesty to put out the Lord Ross from his whole lands, because he would not give over the lordship of Melvin to the said Davie; besides many other inconveniences that he solicited your Majesty to do.'

Then the Lord Ruthven said to the King, 'Sir, take the Queen's Majesty your sovereign and wife to you,' who stood all amazed, and wyst not what to do: Then her Majesty rose on her feet and stood before Davie he holding her Majesty by the plates of the gown, leaning back over in the window, his whiniard drawn in his hand. Arthur Erskine and the Abbot of Holyroodhouse, the Laird of Creech, master of the household, with the French apothecary, and one of the Grooms of the Chamber, began to lay hands upon the Lord Ruthven, none of the King's party being present.

Then the said Lord pulled out his whiniard, and freed himself while more came in, and said to them, 'Lay not hands on me, for I will not be handled;' and at the incoming of others into the cabinet, the Lord Ruthven put up his whiniard. And with the rushing in of men the board fell to the wallwards, with meat and candles being thereon; and the Lady of Argile took up one of the candles in her hand: and in the same instant Lord Ruthven took the Queen in his arms, and put her into the King's arms, beseeching her Majesty not to be afraid; for there was no man there that would do her Majesty's body more harm than their own hearts; and assured her Majesty, all that was done was the King's own deed and action. Then the remanent gentlemen being in the cabinet, took Davie out of the window; and after that they had him out in the Queen's chamber, the Lord Ruthven followed, and bad take him down the privy way to the King's chamber; and the said Lord returned to the cabinet again, believing that Davie had been had down to the King's chamber, but the press of the people hurled him forth to the utter chamber, where there was a great number standing, who were so vehemently moved against the said Davie, that they would not abide any longer, but slew him at the Queen's far door in the utter chamber. Immediately the Earl of Morton passed forth of the Queen's Majesty's utter chamber to the inner court for keeping of the same and the gates, and deputed certain barons to keep David's chamber till he knew the Queen's Majesty's pleasure and the King's.

Shortly after their Majesties sent the Lord Lindsey and Arthur Erskine to the said Earl of Morton, to pass to David's chamber to fetch a black coffer with writings and cyphers, which the said Earl of Morton delivered to them, and gave the chamber in keeping to John Semple, son to the Lord Semple, with the whole goods there; gold, silver, and apparel being therein.

In this meantime the Queen's Majesty and the King came forth of the cabinet to the Queen's chamber, where her Majesty began to reason with the King, saying, 'My Lord, why have you caused to do this wicked deed to me, considering I took you from a base estate, and made you my husband? What offence have I made you, that ye should have done me such shame?' The King answered and said, 'I have good reason for me; for since yon fellow Davie fell in credit and familiarity with your Majesty ye regarded me not, neither treated me nor entertained me after your wonted fashion; for every day before dinner, and after dinner, ye would come to my chamber and pass time with me, and this long time ye have not done so; and when I come to your Majesty's chamber ye bear me little company, except Davie had been the third marrow; and after supper your Majesty hath a use to set at the cards with the said Davie, till one or two of the clock after midnight; and this is the entertainment I have had of you this long time.'

Her Majesty's answer was, it was not gentlewomen's duty to come to their husband's chamber, but rather the husband to come to the wive's chamber, if he had anything to do with her. The King answered, 'How came ye to my chamber at the beginning, and ever, till within these few months that Davie fell in with familiarity with you? or am I failed in any sort? or what disdain have you at me? or what offence have I made you, that you should not use me at all times alike? seeing that I am willing to do all things that becometh a good husband to do to his wife, for since you have chose me to be your husband, suppose I be of the baser degree, yet I am your head, and ye promised obedience at the day of our marriage, and that I should be equal with you, and participant in all things. I suppose you have used me otherwise by the persuasions of Davie.' Her Majesty answered, and said, 'that all the shame that was done to her, that my Lord, ye have the weight thereof; for the which I shall never be your wife nor lie with you; nor shall never like well, till I gar you have as sore a heart as I have presently.'

Then the said Lord Ruthven made answer, and besought her Majesty to be of good comfort, and to treat herself and the King her husband, and to use the counsel of the nobility, and he was assured her government should be as well guided as ever it was in any King's days. The said Lord being so feebled with his sickness, and wearied with his travel, that he desired her Majesty's pardon to sit down upon a coffer, and called for a drink for God's sake; so a French man brought him a cup of wine, and after that he had drunken, the Queen's Majesty began to rail against the said Lord: 'Is this your sickness, Lord Ruthven?' The said Lord answered, God forbid that your Majesty had such a sickness; for I had rather give all the moveable goods that I have. Then, said her Majesty, if she died, or her bairn or common-weal perished, she should leave the revenge thereof to her friends to revenge the same upon the Lord Ruthven and his posterity; for she had the King of Spain her great friend, the Emperor likewise, and the King of France, her good brother, the Cardinal of Lorrain, and her uncles in France, besides the Pope's Holiness, with many other Princes in Italy. The said Lord answered, that these noble Princes were over-great personages to meddle with such a poor man as he was, being her Majesty's own subject: and where her Majesty said, that if either she, her bairn, or the common-weal perished, the Lord Ruthven should have the weight thereof; he answered, that if any of the three perished, her Majesty's self and her particular counsel should have the weight thereof, and should be accused as well before God as the world: for there was no man there within that palace, but they that would honour and serve her Majesty, as becometh true subjects; and would suffer no manner of harm to be done to her Majesty's body than to their own hearts; and if anything be done this night that your Majesty mislikes, charge the King your husband, and none of us your subjects; which the King confessed was of verity.

In the same instant one came knocking fast at the Queen's chamber door, declaring that the Earls Huntly, Athol, Bothwell, Caithness and Sutherland, with the Lords Fleming, Levingstone, secretary, Tillibarn, the comptroller, and the Laird of Grant, with their own servants and officers of the palace, were fighting in the close against the Earl of Morton and his company, being on the King's party. The King hearing the same, would have gone down, and the Lord Ruthven staid him, and desired him to intreat the Queen Majesty, and he would go down and take order amongst them. So he passed to the close, borne under the arm; and before his coming the officers were among into their houses; and the Lords were holden in at the gallery door by the Earl of Morton and others being with him, and were constrained to pass up to the gallery and to their chambers. So the said Lord Ruthven passed up to the Earl Bothwell's chamber, where he found the Earls of Huntley, Sutherland, Caithness, the Laird of Grant, and divers others, to whom he shewed that the whole proceeding that was done that night, was done and invented by the King's Majesty's own devise, like as his hand-written was to shew thereupon; and how he had sent for the Lords that were banished in England and Argyle, who would be there before day: And because there was some enmity unreconciled betwixt the Earls of Huntley and Bothwell, and the Earls of Argyle and Murray, and their colleagues, the said Lords promised in their names, that it should be mended at the sight of two or three of the nobility, they doing such like to them; whereupon the said Earls of Huntly and Bothwell gave the Lord Ruthven their hands, and received his for the other part: and after they had drunken, the Lord Ruthven took his leave of them, and passed to the Earl of Athol's chamber, accompanied with the Earls of Caithness, Sutherland, and the Laird of Grant; and found with the said Earl the comptroller, secretary, Mr James Balfour, and diverse others: and because of the familiarity and kindness betwixt the Earl of Athol and the Lord Ruthven, the Earl began to be angry with the said Lord, for that he would not shew him what enterprise soever that he had to do; whose answer was, that it was the King's action and the King's devise, and that none of them had further meddling therewith than the King had commanded, like as his handwritten did testify. Yet the Earl enquired further upon the Lord Ruthven, why he would not let him know thereof: he answered, it was the King's secret; and feared if he had given knowledge thereof, he would have revealed it to the Queen's Majesty, which might have been a hindrance of the purpose, and caused the King to have holden me unhonest for my part. The Earl perceiving that all that was done was the King's own deed, desired the said Lord Ruthven to pass to the King, and get him leave to pass to his country, and so many as were presently in the chamber with him.

In this meantime the Earls of Bothwell and Huntley, taking a fear of the other Lords returning out of England and Argyle, and because they were hardly imprisoned before, thought it better to escape too than to remain; so they went out at a low window, and passed their ways. In the meantime, while the Lord Ruthven was with the Earl of Athol, the King declared to the Queen's Majesty that he had sent for the Lords to return again; whereunto she answered, she was not in the blame that they were so long away, for she could have been content to have brought them home at any time, had it not been for angering the King; and to verify the same, when her Majesty gave a remission to the Duke, the King was very miscontent therewith: whereto the King answered, that it was true that he was miscontented then, but now he was content, and doubted not but she would also be content to persevere in the good mind to them as she had done before. At the same time came the Provost of Edinburgh, and a great number of men of the town with him, in arms, to the utter court of the Palace of Holyrood House, where the King called out of the window to them, commanding them to return to their houses, like as they did; for he declared to them that the Queen's Majesty and he were in good health. The Lord Ruthven being come up to the Queen's chamber again, where the King was beside her, he shewed them that there was no hurt done, and that the Lords and all others were merry, and no harm done. Then her Majesty enquired what was become of Davie. The said Lord Ruthven answered, that he believed he was in the King's chamber; for he thought it not good to shew her as he died, for fear of putting her Majesty in greater trouble presently. Then the Queen's Majesty enquired of the said Lord what great kindness was betwixt the Earl of Murray and him, that rather than he and the remanent should be forfaulted that he would be forfault with them. 'Remember ye not,' said she, 'what the Earl of Murray would have had me done to you for giving me the ring?' The Lord Ruthven answered, 'That he would bear no quarrel for that cause, but would forgive him and all others for God's sake; and as to that ring, it had no more virtue than another, and was one little ring with a pointed diamond in it.' 'Remember ye not,' said her Majesty, 'that ye said it had a virtue to keep me from poisoning?' 'Yea, Madam, I said so much, that the ring had that virtue, only to take that evil opinion out of your head of poisoning, which you conceived that the Protestants would have done; which the said Lord knew the contrary, that the Protestants would have done no more harm to your Majesty's body than to their own hearts; but it was so imprinted in your Majesty's mind, that it could not be taken away without a contrary impression.'

'Then,' said her Majesty, 'what fault or offence have I made to be handled in this manner?' 'Inquire,' said he, 'of the King your husband.' 'Nay, but I will enquire of you,' who answered, 'Madam, ye well remember that ye have had this long time a few number of privy persons, and most special Davie, a stranger Italian, who have guided and ruled you contrary to the advice of your nobility and counsel; and especially against those noblemen that were banished.' 'But were ye not one of my council? What is the cause that ye should not have declared if I had done anything amiss against them that became me not?' 'Because your Majesty would hear no such thing: for all the time that your Majesty was in Glasgow or Dumfriese, let see if ever ye caused your council to sit, or to reason upon anything, but did all things by your Majesty's self and your privy persons, albeit the nobility bare the pains and expences.' 'Well,' said her Majesty, 'ye find great fault with me, I will be contented to set down my crown before the Lords of the articles; and if they find I have offended, to give it where they please.' 'God forbid, madam, that your crown should be in such hazard; but yet, madam, who chose the Lords of the articles?,' 'Not I,' said she, 'saving your Majesty's reverence,' said the Lord Ruthven, 'ye chose them all in Seaton, and nominated them: And as for your Majesty's council, it hath not been suffered to wait freely this long time, but behoved to say what was your pleasure. And as to the Lords of the articles, your Majesty chose such as would say whatsoever you thought expedient to the forfaulters of the Lords banished: And now when the Lords of the articles have sitten fourteen days reasoning on the summons of treason, have ye found a just head wherefore they ought to be forfaulted? No, madam, not so much as one point, without false witness be brought in against them.' Whereunto she gave no answer.

The Lord Ruthven perceiving that the Queen's Majesty was weary, said to the King, 'Sir, it is best ye take your leave at the Queen's Majesty, that she may take rest.' So the King took his goodnight, and came forth of the Queen's chamber, and we with him, and left none there but the ladies, gentlewomen, and the grooms of the Queen's Majesty's chamber. And as soon as the King came to his own chamber, the Lord Ruthven declared the message he had from the Earl of Athol to the King, that he might have license to return home to Athol: Which the King was loth to do without he gave him a bond that he should be his. The Lord Ruthven answered, that he was a true man of his promise, and would keep the thing he said, as well as others would do their handwriting and seal. Then the King desired him to fetch the Earl of Athol to him, which he did: And after the King and Earl of Athol had talked together, he desired the Earl to be ready to come whensoever he should send for him. His answer was, that whensoever it pleased the Queen's Grace and him to send for him, that he would come gladly: And the Earl desired the King that he might speak with the Queen's Majesty, which the King refused. And then the Earl took his good-night, and passed to his chamber, and the Lord Ruthven with him, where he made him ready and his company to pass forth, like as they did; and in his company were the Earls of Sutherland and Cathness, the Master of Caithness, the secretary, and controller, Mr James Balfour, the Laird of Grant, with divers others.

Immediately the King directed two writings, subscribed with his hand, on Saturday after the slaughter of Davie, to certain men of Edenburg bearing office for the time, charging them to convene men in arms, and make watch within the town upon the Calsay; and to suffer none others to be seen out of their houses, except Protestants, under all highest pain and charge that after may follow. And on the morrow after, which was Sunday the 10th of March, the King directed a letter, subscribed with his hand, making mention that it was not his will that the Parliament should hold, for divers causes, but discharged the same by the tenor thereof And therefore commanding all Prelats Earls, Lords, Barons, Commissioners, and Barrowis, and others that are warned to the said parliament, to depart from Edenburg within three hours next after that charge, under the pain of life, lands, and goods, except so many as the King by his special command caused to remain; which letter was openly proclaimed at the market-cross, and fully obeyed. The gates being locked, the King being in his bed, the Queen's Majesty walking in her chamber, the said Lord Ruthven took air upon the lower gate, and the privy passages; and at the King's command, in the mean time, Davie was hurled down the steps of the stairs from the place where he was slain, and brought to the porter's lodge; where the porter's servant taking off his clothes, said, 'This hath been his destiny; for upon this chest was his first bed when he entered into this place; and now here he lieth again, a very ingrate and misknowing knave.' The King's whiniard was found sticking in Davie's side after he was dead; but always the Queen inquired of the King where his whiniard was? who answered, that he wit not well: Well, said she, it will be known afterwards.

The King rose at eight of the clock, and passed to the Queen's chamber, where he and she fell to reasoning of the matter proceeded the night afore, the one grating on the other till it was ten o'clock, then the King came down to his chamber; and at his coming from her, she desired him to let all the ladies and gentlewomen come unto her, which the King granted, and at his coming down shewed the same to the Earl of Morton and Lord Ruthven, who were not contented with the same: and shewed the King, that they feared that the Queen's Majesty would traffick by them with the Lords, and all other that would do for her, like as it followed indeed: For instantly her Majesty wrote some writing, and caused them to write others in her name to the Earls of Argile, Huntley, Bothwell, Athol, and others. After that the King had dined, he passed up to the Queen's Majesty's chamber, where the Queen made as she would have parted with bairn, and caused the midwife to come and say the same. So her Majesty complained that she could get none of the gentlewomen to come up to her, Scots nor French. The King sending this word to the Earl of Morton and Lord Ruthven, all were let in that pleased. At the same time the Queen's Majesty thought that the Lord Ruthven would do her body harm, and sent John Semple to Lord Ruthven to enquire what her Majesty might lippen unto in that behalf: Whose answer was, that he would do no more harm to her body, than to his own heart; if any man intended to do otherwise, he should defend her Majesty's body at the uttermost of his power. And further said, her Majesty had experience of his mind in that night's proceeding, when he suffered none to come near her Majesty to molest and trouble her. John Semple brought this message to the Lord Ruthven at two of the clock afternoon, sitting then in the King's utter chamber at his dinner. At four of the clock the King came down to his chamber, where the Lord Ruthven shewed him that the Queen's Majesty was to steal out among the throng of the gentlewomen in their down coming, as he said he was advertised. So the King commanded him to give attendance thereto; which he did, and put certain to the door, and let no body nor gentlewomen pass forth undismuffled.

After, about seven or eight of the clock, the Earls of Murray and Rothes, with their complices, came out of England, and lighted at the Abbey, and were thankfully received of the King; and after certain communing, the Earl of Murray took his good night of the King, and passed to the Earl of Morton's house to supper. Immediately thereafter, the Queen's Majesty sent one of her ushers, called Robert Phirsell, for the Earl of Murray; who passed to her Majesty, whom she received pleasantly, as appeared; and after communing, he passed to the Earl of Morton's house again, where he remained that night. At this time the King remained communing with the Queen's Majesty, and after long reasoning with her, she granted to lie with him all night, he coming to her chamber, and putting all men out of his utter chamber, except the waiters of the chamber, and made a complaint that her gentlewomen could not go forth at the door undismuffled at the King's coming down. He shewed the Earl of Morton and Lord Ruthven the whole manner of his proceedings with the Queen's Majesty, which they liked no way, because they perceived the King grew effeminate again; and said to him, we see no other but ye are able to do that thing that will gar you and us both repent. Always he would have the said Earl and Lord to rid all the house, conform to the Queen's Majesty's desire; which they did, and the Lord Ruthven passed and lay in the King's wardrobe: and after he was lien down, George Douglas came to him, and shewed him that the King was fallen asleep. He caused George to go to wake the King; and after that he had gone in twice or thrice, finding him sleeping so sound, he would not awake him. Thereat the said Lord was very miscontented, the King slept still till six in morning, that the Lord Ruthven came and reproved him, that he had not kept his promise to the Queen's Majesty, in lying with her all that night. His answer was, that he was fallen on such a dead sleep that he could not awaken; and put the blame to William Tellor, one of his servants, that permitted him to sleep. But always, said he, 'I will take my nightgown and go up to the Queen.' The Lord Ruthven answered, 'I trust she shall serve you in the morning as you did her at night.'

Always the King passed up, being Monday the 11th of March, at six of the clock, to her Majesty's chamber, and sat down on the bed-side, she being sleeping, or at least made herself so, and sat there by the space of one hour e're she spoke word to him. Then when her Majesty waked, she enquired of the King, why he came not up yesterday night conform to his promise? He answered, he fell in so dead a sleep, that he awaked not afore six. Now, saith he, am I come, and offered to lie down beside her Majesty; but she would not suffer him, for she said she was sick, and would ride incontinent. Then the King fell in reasoning with her Majesty towards the returning of the said Lords that were banished, and forgiving of them all offences, and likewise for the slaughter of Davie: and as appeared to him her Majesty was content; for the King came down to his own chamber at eight of the clock very merrily, and shewed the Earl of Morton and Lord Ruthven the proceedings betwixt him and the Queen's Majesty: who answered him, and said, 'all was but words that they heard'. For look how ye intend to persuade her Majesty; we fear she will persuade you to follow her will and desire, by reason she hath been trained up from her youth in the court of France, as well in the affairs of France as Scotland, in the privy council. 'Well,' said the King, 'will yet let me alone, and I will warrant to dress all things well.'

And after that the King had put on his clothes, he passed at nine to the Queen's chamber, where he reasoned of many things with her Majesty: and at his returning to his dinner at eleven, he declared to the Earls of Murray and Morton, Lords Ruthven and Lindsay, that he had addressed the Queen's Majesty: that the said two Earls and Lord Ruthven, should come to the presence of the Queen's Majesty, that she would forgive, and put in oblivion all things by past, and bury them out of her Majesty's mind, as they had never been. The said Earls and Lords answered, 'that all that speaking was but policy; and suppose it were promised, little or nothing would be kept.' Always the King took freely in hand, and had them make such security as they pleased, and the Queen's Majesty and he should subscribe the same. And then after dinner the King passed up again to the Queen's chamber, where the midwife was made to come to him, and said, 'that the Queen would not fail to part with bairn, if her Majesty went not to some other place where there were more freer air:' and in like manner divers of the Lords said the same.

And the King returning to his chamber at three afternoon, declared the same to the Earls and Lord Ruthven: And in the meantime in came the French doctor, who declared to the King, that it was unable to the Queen's Majesty to eschew a fever; which, if she take, she will not fail to part with bairn, without she were transported from that place to some better aired place. After they were departed, the King inquired of the said Earls and Lords, what they thought of their speaking? Who answered, 'they feared all was but craft and policy that was spoken and done'. Always the King would not trow the same, and said, 'that she was a true Princess, and that thing she promised, he would set his life for the same'. And between four and five afternoon, the King passed to the Queen's chamber, and took the Earls of Morton, Murray and Lord Ruthven with him; and after they had come to the Queen's utter chamber, the King went and left the Lords, to know her pleasure, whether her Majesty would come out of her utter chamber, or if the Lords should come in to her Majesty. She took purpose, and came out of the utter chamber, led by the King; the said Earls and Lords sitting down upon their knees, made their general oration by the Earl of Morton, chancellor, and after, their particular orations by themselves. And after that her Majesty had heard all, her answer was, that it was not unknown to the Lords, that she was never bloodthirsty, nor greedy upon their lands and goods, sithence her coming into Scotland; nor yet would be upon theirs that were present, but would remit the whole number that was banished, or were at the last deed; and bury and put all things in oblivion as if they had never been; and so caused the said Earls, Lords, and Barons to arise on their feet. And afterwards her Majesty desired them to make their own security in that sort they pleased best, and she should subscribe the same. Thereafter her Majesty took the King by the one hand, and the Earl of Murray by the other, and walked in her said utter chamber the space of one hour; and then her Majesty passed into her inner chamber, where she and the King appointed that all they that were on the King's party, should go forth of the place after supper. The King coming down to his chamber afore six of the clock, the articles which were the security that were on the King's party, were given by the Earls of Ruthven and Morton, and Lords Ruthven and Lindsey to the King, to be subscribed by the Queen, which the King took in hand so soon as he had supped to be done; and he desired the said Lords to remove themselves out of the palace, to that effect, that her Majesty's guard and servants might order all as they pleased. The Lords' answer was to the King, 'You may well cause us to do that thing that is your pleasure, but it is sore against our wills; for we fear all this is but deceit that is meant towards us, and that the Queen's Majesty will pass away secretly, and take you with her, either to the castle of Eeinburg, or else Dunbar. And here the Lord Ruthven protested, that what end followed thereupon, or what blood was shed for the same, that it should come upon the King's head and posterity, and nought upon theirs. The King said, 'he should warrant all'. So they departed, and took their leave of the King, and passed all forth of the Palace of Holyroodhouse to the Earl of Morton's house, where they supped; and after supper directed Mr Archibald Douglas to the King, to see if the Queen's Majesty had subscribed the articles of the Lords' and Barons' security. The King gave answer, that he had let the Queen's Majesty see them, who found them very good; and because she was sick and going to her bed, she delayed the subscribing of them to the morning; and immediately after Mr Archibald returned to the Lords with answer. The Laird of Traquair, master of the guard, made an errant to the Earl of Murray, to see what the Lords were doing, and after he was departed, the whole Earls, Lords, and Barons, with gentlemen, passed to the town of Edenburg to their beds, believing surely the Queen's Majesty's promise, and the King's.

The same night about one o'clock after midnight, the Queen's Majesty and the King with her, went out at a back-door that passed through the wine-cellar; where Arthur Erskin, the captain of the guard, and other six or seven persons, met her Majesty with her horses, and rode towards Dunbar; and on the morrow, which was Tuesday the 12th of March, the Lords hearing how the Queen's Majesty was departed, and taken the King with her, convened the Earls, Lords, Barons, and gentlemen, and after the matter was appointed, enquired every man's opinion, which concluded all to remain in the town of Edenburg, till such time they might send some noblemen to her Majesty for performance of the articles promised for their security; and to that effect sent for the Lord Semple, and desired him that he would pass to Dunbar, with a writing of the Lords, which he granted to do, and received the same with a copy of the articles that the King received before, and promised to do his utter diligence to get the same immediately sped, if it were the King and Queen's Majesties pleasure so to do. After the Lord Semple's coming to Dunbar, having presented the Lords' writing to their Majesties, he was evil taken with the Queen's Majesty, who caused him to remain three days: he reported at his returning, that there was no good way to be looked for there, but extremity to the Earls, Lords, and gentlemen, who had been at the slaughter of David, notwithstanding her Majesty's promise made before.

At that time her Majesty being in Dunbar, wrote to all Earls, Lords, and Barons to meet her in Haddington town the 17th or 18th of March, and likewise directed universal letters, charging all maner of men betwixt sixty and sixteen to be there, day and place aforesaid, being in arms in fear of war; and also sent divers charges to the Lord Erskine, captain of the castle of Edinburgh, to shut up the town unless the Lords departed out of it. In this time it was declared to the Earl of Murray, that if he would sue address to the Queen's Majesty, he would obtain the same, who shewed it to the Lords, who counselled him to write to her Majesty to that effect; which he did, and received her Majesty's answer with certain articles. In this time the Earls of Glencairn and Rothes took their appointment of the Queen's Majesty. The Earl of Morton, Lord Ruthven, and the remanent their complices, perceiving that the Queen was willing to remit the Lords banished into England and Argyle, and bare her Majesty's whole rage against them that were with the King at the slaughter of Davie, thought best to retire themselves into England, under the Queen's Majesty of England's protection, till such time as the nobility of Scotland, their peers, understood their cause; for they have done nothing without the King's command, as is before mentioned, and doubt not but their cause shall be found just and honest whatsoever the same be tried; and lament the extream handling contrary to order and justice, that they may not compear for fear of their lives; in respect that her Majesty hath caused a band to be made, and all Earls, Lords, and Barons, that resorted to her Majesty, to subscribe the same, that they shall pursue the said Earl Morton, Lord Ruthven, and Lindsay, and their complices with fire and sword; which is against all order of the law: And on Saturday, the 22d of March, her Majesty hath caused to be summoned the Earl of Morton,

Lords Ruthven and Lindsay, the Master of Ruthven, Lairds of Ormyston, Brinston, Halton, Elveston, Calder; Andrew Carr of Faldomside, Alexander Ruthven, brother to the Lord Ruthven, Patrick Murray of Tippermure, William Douglas of Whittingham, Archibald Douglas his brother, George Douglas, Lyndsay of Prystone, Thomas Scott of Cambysmichet, William Douglas of Loch Leven, James Jeffert of Shreffal, Adam Erskine, commendator of Camskinnel, Mentershfear of Kars, Patrick Ballenden of Stenehouse, brother to Justice Clerk, Patrick Wood of Conyton, Mr James Magil, Clerk of Registers, with others, to compear before her Majesty and secret council within six days, under the pain of rebellion, and putting them to her horn, and eschetting and bringing of all their moveable goods, the which like order is not used in any Christian realm; nor is it the law of Scotland of old, but new cropen in, and invented by them that understand no law nor yet good practice: and how her Majesty hath handled the Barons of Lothian our brothers, it is known; and in likewise our poor brethren of Edinburgh, merchants and craftsmen, and how they are oppressed by the men of war, God knoweth, who will put remedy hereto when it pleaseth him best: and how the Lords' and Barons' wives are oppressed in spoiling of their places, robbing of their goods without any fine for the same, it would pity a godly heart. And where her Majesty alledgeth, that night that Davie was slain, some held pistols to her Majesty; some stroke whiniards so near her, that she felt the coldness of the iron, with many other such like sayings, which we take God to record was never meant nor done; for record was never meant nor done; for the said Davie received never a stroke in her Majesty's presence, nor was not stricken till he was at the farthest door of her Majesty's utter chamber, as is before rehearsed. Her Majesty makes all these allegations to draw the Earl Morton the Lords Ruthven and Lindsay, and their complices, in greater hatred with other foreign princes, and with the nobility and commonalty of the realm, who have experience of the contrary, and know that there was no evil meant to her Majesty's body. The eternal God who hath the rule of Princes' hearts in his hands, send her his Holy Spirit, to instruct her how she should rule and govern with clemency and mercy over her subjects.

'The Murder of Darnley'

from Traditions of Edinburgh

ROBERT CHAMBERS (1802–1871)

Robert Chambers, born in Peebles, was a publisher, printer and bookseller in Edinburgh. He founded, with his brother William (1800–1883), the famous firm which published such works as Chambers's Encyclopaedia. *William became heavily involved in public affairs, eventually becoming Lord Provost of the city, while Robert concentrated more on literary activities – his* Biographical Dictionary of Eminent Scotsmen *(1832–4) being still a valuable reference work.*

His Traditions of Edinburgh *(first published 1822, revised 1868) is an entertaining mixture of anecdote and legend and Chambers was fortunate enough to be able to draw on many unpublished sources, including sixteen pages of reminiscences from Sir Walter Scott, in the compilation of his book.*

One of Chambers' virtues, well demonstrated in this extract, is a concern to fix the exact location of the incidents he describes. Although Kirk o' Fields, the site of the murder of Henry Stewart, Lord Darnley, the husband of Mary Queen of Scots, has been swept away, Chambers' description allows a visitor to present-day Edinburgh to identify the place where the deed occurred.

✝

While this event is connected with one of the most problematical points in our own history, or that of any other nation, it chances that the whole topography of the affair is very distinctly recorded. We know not only the exact spot where the deed was perpetrated, but almost every foot of the ground over which the perpetrators walked on their way to execute it. It is chiefly by reason of the depositions and confessions brought out by the legal proceedings against the inferior instruments, that this minute knowledge is attained.

The house in which the unfortunate victim resided at the time was one called the Prebendaries' Chamber, being part of the suite of domestic buildings connected with the collegiate church of St-Mary-in-the-Fields (usually called the Kirk o' Field). Darnley was brought to lodge here on the 30th of January 1566–7. He had contracted the smallpox at Glasgow, and it was thought necessary, or pretended to be thought necessary, to lodge him in this place for air, as also to guard against infecting the infant prince, his son, who was lodged in Holyrood House. The house, which then belonged, by gift, to a creature of the Earl of Bothwell, has been described as so very mean, as to excite general surprise. Yet, speaking by comparison, it does not appear to have been a bad temporary lodging for a person in Darnley's circumstances. It consisted of two storeys, with a *turnpike* or spiral staircase behind. The gable adjoined to the town-wall, which there ran in a line east and west, and the cellar had a postern opening through that wall. In the upper floor were a chamber and closet, with a little gallery having a window also through the town-wall.[1] Here Darnley was deposited in an old purple travelling-bed. Underneath his room was an apartment in which the Queen slept for one or two nights before the murder took place. On the night of Sunday, February 9, she was attending upon her husband in his sick-room, when the servants of the Earl of Bothwell deposited the powder in her room, immediately under the king's bed. The Queen afterwards took her leave, in order to attend the wedding of two of her servants at the palace.

It appears, from the confessions of the wretches executed for this foul deed, that, as they returned from depositing the powder, they saw 'the Queenes grace gang and before thame with licht torches up the Black Frier Wynd'. On their returning to Bothwell's lodging at the palace, that nobleman prepared himself for the deed, by changing his gay suit of 'hose, stockit with black velvet, passemented with silver, and doublett of black satin of the same manner', for 'ane uther pair of black hose[2] and ane canves doublet white, and tuke his syde [long] riding-cloak about him, of sad English claith, callit the new colour'. He then went, attended by Paris, the queen's servant, Powry, his own porter, Pate Wilson, and George Dalgliesh, 'downe the turnepike altogedder, and along the bak of the Queenes garden, till you come to the bak of the cunyie-house [mint], and the bak of the stabbillis, till you come to the Cannogate fornent the Abbey zett'. After passing up the Canongate, and gaining entry with some difficulty by the Netherbow Port, 'thai gaid up abone Bassentyne's hous on the south side of the gait[3] and knockit at ane door beneath the sword slippers, and callit for the laird of Ormistounes, and one within answerit he was not thair; and thai passit down a cloiss beneath the Frier Wynd [apparently Toddrick's Wynd], and enterit in at the zett of the Black Friers, till thay came to the back wall and dyke of the town-wall, whair my lord and Paris past in over the wall'. The explosion took place soon after, about two in the morning. The earl then came back to his attendants at this spot, and 'thai past all away togidder out at the Frier zett, and sinderit in the Cowgait'. It is here evident that the alley now called the High School Wynd was the avenue by which the conspirators approached the scene of their atrocity. Bothwell himself, with part of his attendants, went up the same wynd 'be east the Frier Wynd', and crossing the High Street, endeavoured to get out of the city by leaping a broken part of the town-wall in Leith Wynd, but finding it too high, was obliged to rouse once more the porter at the Netherbow. They then passed – for every motion of the villains has a strange interest – down St Mary's Wynd, and along the south back of the Canongate, to the earl's lodgings in the palace.

The house itself, by this explosion, was destroyed, 'even' as the Queen tells in a letter to her ambassador in France, 'to the very grund-stane'. The bodies of the King and his servant were found next morning in a garden or field on the outside of the town-wall. The buildings connected with the Kirk o' Field were afterwards converted into the College of King James, now our Edinburgh university. The hall of the Senatus in the new building occupies nearly the exact site of the Prebendaries' Chamber, the ruins of which are laid down in De Witt's map of 1648.

1 About seventy paces to the east of the site of the Prebendaries' Chamber, and exactly opposite to the opening of Roxburgh Place, was a projection in the wall, which has been long demolished, and the wall altered. Close, however, to the west of the place, and near the ground, are some remains of an arch in the wall, which Malcolm Laing supposes to have been a gun-port connected with the projection at this spot. It certainly has no connection, as Arnot and (after him) Whitaker have supposed, with the story of Darnley's murder.

2 Hose, in those days, covered the whole of the lower part of the person.

3 This indicates pretty nearly the site of the house of Bassendyne, the early printer. It must have been opposite, or nearly opposite, to the Fountain Well.

The Bonnie House o' Airlie

ANONYMOUS

The ancient tradition of feud and foray between Scottish magnates continued well into supposedly 'modern' and 'civilised' times and the civil wars of the seventeenth century provided many splendid opportunities for personal scores to be redressed under the cloak of national policy or religious doctrine.

In the Bishops' War of 1640 Archibald Campbell, 8th Earl of Argyll, known throughout the Highlands as 'Gilleasbuig Gruamach' – Archibald the Grim – was a leading commander on the Covenanting side and obtained letters of fire and sword to harry the rich Angus lands of the Royalist Ogilvie Earls of Airlie. This commission was more than usually welcome to Argyll because there had been a history of conflict between the Campbells and Airlies dating back to the previous century.

James Graham, Marquis of Montrose, a friend and neighbour of the Earl of Airlie, who at this stage in his varied career was fighting for the Covenant forces, attempted to forestall his Campbell ally by securing the castle. However this plan failed to preserve 'The Bonnie House o' Airlie' and in July 1640 Argyll and 4,000 men arrived and laid waste to it and the lands of the Ogilvie tenants. An old account of the sacking of Airlie suggests that the Earl of Argyll took a more than usually active part in the assault:

> *... hammer in hand and knocking down the hewed work of doors and windows until he did sweat for heat at his work.*

The ballad version, interesting as it is, does confuse several details. Argyll had, of course, considerably more than the hundred men, even a hundred 'harnessed rarely', the ballad writer speaks of, and although the ballad tells of Argyll taking the Countess of Airlie by 'the middle so small', Professor Edward Cowan in his life of Montrose points out that the lady was in an advanced state of pregnancy and was allowed to depart quietly. However the crops were ruined, cattle slaughtered, horses driven off to Argyllshire and the Countess's dowry, 'the planting o' Airlie' – the rich timber plantations, destroyed. In all, some £7,000 of damage was done – a sum which could comfortably be multiplied by a hundred to get a twenty-first century equivalent.

The year after the destruction of Airlie, Argyll was reconciled to King Charles I and was raised a step in the peerage, to a Marquis, for his pains. When the English Civil War broke out he joined the Parliamentary side

*and had his town of Inveraray sacked by his erstwhile comrade in arms,
the Marquis of Montrose, in 1644, before suffering a major defeat at the
hands of Montrose and one of his clan's hereditary enemies, Alastair
Macdonald, at Inverlochy in 1645. After the execution of Charles I he
proclaimed Charles II as king and crowned him at Scone in 1651.
Following Charles II's flight into exile Argyll submitted to Cromwell – a
decision which, after Charles II's restoration in 1660, led to his execution
in Edinburgh in 1661.*

THE BONNIE HOUSE O' AIRLIE

It fell on a day, and a bonnie simmer day,
When green grew aits and barley,
That there fell out a great dispute
Between Argyll and Airlie.

Argyll has raised an hundred men,
An hundred harness'd rarely,
And he 's awa' by the back o' Dunkell,
To plunder the bonnie house o' Airlie.

Lady Ogilvie looks o'er her bower-window;
And oh, but she looks weary!
And there she spied the great Argyll,
Come to plunder the bonnie house o' Airlie.

'Come down, come down, my Lady Ogilvie,
Come down, and kiss me fairly':
'O I winna kiss the fause Argyll,
If he shouldna leave a standing stane in Airlie.'

He hath taken her by the left shoulder,
Says, ' Dame, where lies thy dowry?'
'It's up and it's down by the bonnie bank-side,
Amongst the planting o' Airlie.'

They hae sought it up, they hae sought it down,
They hae sought it baith late and early;
And they hae found it in the bonnie plum-tree,
That shines on the bowling-green o' Airlie.

He hath taken her by the middle sae small,
And oh, but she grat sairly!
He hath laid her down by the bonnie burn-side,
Till he hath plundered the bonnie house o' Airlie.

'Gif my gude lord were here this night,
As he is with Prince Charlie,
Neither you, nor no Scottish lord
Durst have set a foot on the bowling-green o' Airlie.

'Ten bonnie sons I have borne unto him,
The eleventh ne'er saw his daddie,
But though I had an hundred mair,
I'd gie them a' to Prince Charlie.'

The Tears of Scotland

TOBIAS SMOLLETT (1721–1771)

The Jacobite Rising of 1745–46 was by definition a crime against the state, but the brutal suppression of the clans after Culloden was equally certainly a crime against humanity.

Tobias Smollett, who was born in Renton, Dumbartonshire, was working as a doctor in London in 1746, when the word came that the Duke of Cumberland had defeated the Jacobite forces at Culloden. As Alexander 'Jupiter' Carlyle, later to be the minister of Inveresk, who was in London at that time observed:

> *Smollett, though a Tory, was not a Jacobite, but he had the feelings of a Scotch gentleman on the reported cruelties that were said to be exercised after the battle of Culloden.*

Smollett himself commented on the behaviour of the jubilant London mob when the news of the victory reached the capital:

> *. . . John Bull is as haughty and insolent tonight as he was abject and cowardly on the Black Wednesday the Highlanders were at Derby.*

When this deeply felt poem was first written it had only six verses. Friends of Smollett suggested that the poem might give offence and that it was too strongly expressed. Smollett's reaction was to sit down and add the seventh verse, even more vehemently phrased.

The Tears of Scotland was Smollett's first published work, he went on to become a noted novelist, historian and travel-writer.

> Mourn, hapless Caledonia, mourn
> Thy banish'd peace, thy laurels torn!
> Thy sons, for valour long renown'd,
> Lie slaughter'd on their native ground;
> Thy hospitable roofs no more
> Invite the stranger to the door;
> In smoky ruins sunk they lie,
> The monuments of cruelty.
>
> The wretched owner sees afar
> His all become the prey of war;

Bethinks him of his babes and wife,
Then smites his breast and curses life.
Thy swains are famish'd on the rocks
Where once they fed their wanton flocks;
Thy ravish'd virgins shriek in vain;
Thy infants perish on the plain.

What boots it then, in ev'ry clime,
Through the wide-spreading waste of time,
Thy martial glory, crown'd with praise,
Still shone with undiminish'd blaze?
Thy tow'ring spirit now is broke,
Thy neck is bended to the yoke:
What foreign arms could never quell,
By civil rage and rancour fell.

The rural pipe and merry lay
No more shall cheer the happy day;
No social scenes of gay delight
Beguile the dreary winter night;
No strains but those of sorrow flow,
And nought be heard but sounds of woe,
While the pale phantoms of the slain
Glide nightly o'er the silent plain.

O baneful cause, O fatal morn,
Accurs'd to ages yet unborn!
The sons against their fathers stood,
The parent shed his children's blood.
Yet, when the rage of battle ceas'd',
The victor's soul was not appeas'd;
The naked and forlorn must feel
Devouring flames, and murd'ring steel!

The pious mother, doom'd to death,
Forsaken, wanders o'er the heath;
The bleak wind whistles round her head,
Her helpless orphans cry for bread:
Bereft of shelter, food, and friend,
She views the shades of night descend;
And, stretch'd beneath th' inclement skies,

Weeps o'er her tender babes, and dies.

While the warm blood bedews my veins,
And unimpair'd remembrance reigns,
Resentment of my country's fate
Within my filial breast shall beat;
And, spite of her insulting foe,
My sympathising verse shall flow:
'Mourn, hapless Caledonia, mourn
Thy banish'd peace, thy laurels torn!'

The Adventure of the Spectacled Roadman

from The Thirty-Nine Steps

JOHN BUCHAN (1875–1940)

For some readers coming to it for the first time, The Thirty-Nine Steps *presents a quite unusual difficulty. The vivid and abiding association in many people's minds of* The Thirty-Nine Steps, *thanks to the Alfred Hitchcock film adaptation of 1935, is of the fugitive's train crossing the Forth Bridge – and it therefore comes as something of a shock to find that Buchan says nothing of the 'Flying Scotsman', the London and North Eastern Railway, or an escape on the Forth Bridge. Buchan has his fugitive fleeing from London, courtesy of St Pancras Station and the Midland Railway, to South-West Scotland rather than to Edinburgh and Fife and thus rather obscurely to Perthshire, as Hitchcock filmed it.*

Set in the last summer of peace before the First World War The Thirty-Nine Steps *marks the first appearance of Richard Hannay, whose later adventures provided Buchan with material for another four of what he himself described as 'shockers':* Greenmantle, Mr Standfast, The Three Hostages! *and* The Island of Sheep.

Hannay, a Scots-born mining engineer, has unwittingly become caught up in the dastardly machinations of the Black Stone gang, a German espionage ring. Scudder, an American secret agent, had got on the track of the Black Stone but had been killed by them in Hannay's flat in London's Portland Place. Hannay, newly arrived in England from South Africa and without anyone to vouch for him, convinced that his only chance of escaping the gang and the police and foiling the plot is to disappear from London, travels to Scotland. However the police and, more dangerously, the gang are quickly on his trail and pursue him by aeroplane and motor car around the quiet uplands of Galloway (a part of Scotland which figures extensively in Buchan's novels and short stories).

Our extract has Hannay still on the run on the bare moors. He is surrounded by the forces of the Black Stone when he comes on the once familiar figure of a country roadman. In the days before tarmacadam had spread over the length and breadth of the land, country roads were maintained by roadmen, each assigned a stretch of highway, who repaired, maintained and surfaced the road with graded stone – much as the Romans had done.

First published in 1915, The Thirty-Nine Steps *marked something of a departure for Buchan, who had previously been known for his historical novels such as* John Burnet of Barns *and* A Lost Lady of Old Years, *although he had, in 1913, published a thriller about an anarchist conspiracy,* The Power House, *in* Blackwood's Magazine.

The enduring appeal of The Thirty-Nine Steps – *with its isolated hero struggling against a conspiracy of dark forces (a staple theme in Buchan's thrillers) – is testified to by the regularity with which it has been adapted for film. Apart from the Hitchcock version (masterly, if not particularly faithful to Buchan's story), starring Robert Donat, there were less inspired versions by Ralph Thomas in 1959 (starring Kenneth More) and Don Sharp in 1978 (starring Robert Powell).*

Buchan was born in Perth, the son of a Free Church minister and brought up in Glasgow and Peebles. After a brilliant academic career at Glasgow and Oxford he was called to the English Bar and went on to combine politics, literature and business in a quite remarkable way. As a young man he went out to South Africa on the staff of Lord Milner, the High Commissioner. Africa and Scotland were to be regularly recurring themes in his work, sometimes combined, as in the story of Prester John *and indeed in the figure of Scots–South African Hannay.*

Perhaps driven by a need for success in everything he touched Buchan wrote thirty novels and over sixty works of non-fiction, including admirable biographies of Sir Walter Scott and James Graham, the Marquis of Montrose. His public career also flourished, he became Member of Parliament for the Scottish Universities seat, Chancellor of Edinburgh University and was twice appointed Lord High Commissioner to the General Assembly of the Church of Scotland. He was appointed as Governor General of Canada in 1935, a post he continued to hold until his death in February 1940.

I sat down on the very crest of the pass and took stock of my position.

Behind me was the road climbing through a long cleft in the hills, which was the upper glen of some notable river. In front was a flat space of maybe a mile, all pitted with bog-holes and rough with tussocks, and then beyond it the road fell steeply down another glen to a plain whose blue dimness melted into the distance. To left and right were round-shouldered green hills as smooth as cakes, but to the south – that is, the left hand – there was a glimpse of high heathery mountains, which I remembered from the map as the big knot of hill which I had chosen for my sanctuary. I was on the central boss of a huge upland country, and could see everything moving for miles. In the meadows below the road half a mile back a cottage smoked, but it was the only sign of human life. Otherwise there was only the calling of plovers and the tinkling of little streams.

It was now about seven o'clock, and as I waited I heard once again that ominous beat in the air. Then I realized that my vantage-ground might be in reality a trap. There was no cover for a tomtit in those bald green places.

I sat quite still and hopeless while the beat grew louder. Then I saw an aeroplane coming up from the east. It was flying high, but as I looked it dropped several hundred feet and began to circle round the knot of hill in narrowing circles, just as a hawk wheels before it pounces. Now it was flying very low, and now the observer on board caught sight of me. I could see one of the two occupants examining me through glasses.

Suddenly it began to rise in swift whorls, and the next I knew it was speeding eastward again till it became a speck in the blue morning.

That made me do some savage thinking. My enemies had located me, and the next thing would be a cordon round me. I didn't know what force they could command, but I was certain it would be sufficient. The aeroplane had seen my bicycle, and would conclude that I would try to escape by the road. In that case there might be a chance on the moors to the right or left. I wheeled the machine a hundred yards from the highway, and plunged it into a moss-hole, where it sank among pond-weed and water-buttercups. Then I climbed to a knoll which gave me a view of the two valleys. Nothing was stirring on the long white ribbon that threaded them.

I have said there was not cover in the whole place to hide a rat. As the day advanced it was flooded with soft fresh light till it had the fragrant sunniness of the South African veld. At other times I would have liked the place, but now it seemed to suffocate me. The free moorlands were prison walls, and the keen hill air was the breath of a dungeon.

I tossed a coin – heads right, tails left – and it fell heads, so I turned to the north. In a little I came to the brow of the ridge which was the containing wall of the pass. I saw the highroad for maybe ten miles, and far down it something that was moving, and that I took to be a motorcar. Beyond the ridge I looked on a rolling green moor, which fell away into wooded glens. Now my life on the veld has given me the eyes of a kite, and I can see things for which most men need a telescope . . . Away down the slope, a couple of miles away, men were advancing like a row of beaters at a shoot.

I dropped out of sight behind the sky-line. That way was shut to me, and I must try the bigger hills to the south beyond the highway. The car I

had noticed was getting nearer, but it was still a long way off with some
very steep gradients before it. I ran hard, crouching low except in the
hollows, and as I ran I kept scanning the brow of the hill before me. Was
it imagination, or did I see figures – one, two, perhaps more – moving in a
glen beyond the stream?

If you are hemmed in on all sides in a patch of land there is only one
chance of escape. You must stay in the patch, and let your enemies search
it and not find you. That was good sense, but how on earth was I to
escape notice in that table-cloth of a place? I would have buried myself to
the neck in mud or lain below water or climbed the tallest tree. But there
was not a stick of wood, the bog-holes were little puddles, the stream was
a slender trickle. There was nothing but short heather, and bare hill bent,
and the white highway.

Then in a tiny bight of road, beside a heap of stones, I found the
Roadman.

He had just arrived, and was wearily flinging down his hammer. He
looked at me with a fishy eye and yawned.

'Confoond the day I ever left the herdin'!' he said, as if to the world at
large. 'There I was my ain maister. Now I'm a slave to the Goavernment,
tethered to the roadside, wi' sair een, and a back like a suckle.'

He took up the hammer, struck a stone, dropped the implement with
an oath, and put both hands to his, ears. 'Mercy on me! My heid's burst
in!' he cried.

He was a wild figure, about my own size but much bent, with a week's
beard on his chin, and a pair of big horn spectacles.

'I canna dae't,' he cried again. 'The Surveyor maun just report me. I'm
for my bed.'

I asked him what was the trouble, though indeed that was clear
enough.

The trouble is that I'm no sober. Last nicht my dochter Merran was
waddit, and they danced till fower in the byre. Me and some ither chiels
sat down to the drinkin', and here I am. Peety that I ever lookit on the
wine when it was red!'

I agreed with him about bed.

'It's easy speakin',' he moaned. 'But I got a postcaird yestreen sayin'
that the new Road Surveyor would be round the day. He'll come and he'll
no find me, or else he'll find me fou, and either way I'm a done man. I'll
awa back to my bed and say I'm no weel, but I doot that'll no help me, for
they ken my kind o' no-weel-ness.'

Then I had an inspiration. 'Does the new Surveyor know you?' I asked.

'No him. He's just been a week at the job. He rins about in a wee motor-cawr, and wad speir the inside oot o' a whelk.'

'Where's your house?' I asked, and was directed by a wavering finger to the cottage by the stream.

'Well, back to your bed,' I said, 'and sleep in peace. I'll take on your job for a bit and see the Surveyor.'

He stared at me blankly; then, as the notion dawned on his fuddled brain, his face broke into the vacant drunkard's smile.

'You're the billy,' he cried. 'It'll be easy eneuch managed. I've finished that bing o' stanes, so you needna chap ony mair this forenoon. Just take the barry, and wheel eneuch metal frae yon quarry doon the road to mak anither bing the morn. My name's Alexander Trummle, and I've been seeven year at the trade, and twenty afore that herdin' on Leithen Water. My freens ca' me Ecky, and whiles Specky, for I wear glesses, being weak i' the sicht. Just you speak the Surveyor fair, and ca' him Sir, and he'll be fell pleased. I'll be back or midday.'

I borrowed his spectacles and filthy old hat; stripped off coat, waistcoat and collar, and gave him them to carry home; borrowed, too, the foul stump of a clay pipe as an extra property. He indicated my simple tasks, and without more ado set off at an amble bedwards. Bed may have been his chief object, but I think there was also something left in the foot of a bottle. I prayed that he might be safe under cover before my friends arrived on the scene.

Then I set to work to dress for the part. I opened the collar of my shirt – it was a vulgar blue-and-white check such as ploughmen wear – and revealed a neck as brown as any tinker's. I rolled up my sleeves, and there was a forearm which might have been a blacksmith's, sunburnt and rough with old scars. I got my boots and trouser legs all white from the dust of the road, and hitched up my trousers, tying them with string below the knee. Then I set to work on my face. With a handful of dust I made a watermark round my neck, the place where Mr Turnbull's Sunday ablutions might be expected to stop. I rubbed a good deal of dirt also into the sunburn of my cheeks. A roadman's eyes would no doubt be a little inflamed, so I contrived to get some dust in both of mine, and by dint of vigorous rubbing produced a bleary effect.

The sandwiches Sir Harry had given me had gone off with my coat, but the roadman's lunch, tied up in a red handkerchief, was at my disposal. I ate with great relish several of the thick slabs of scone and cheese and drank a little of the cold tea. In the handkerchief was a local paper tied with string and addressed to Mr Turnbull – obviously meant to solace his midday leisure. I did up the bundle again, and put the paper conspicuously beside it.

My boots did not satisfy me, but by dint of kicking among the stones I reduced them to the granitelike surface which marks a roadman's footgear. Then I bit and scraped my finger nails till the edges were all cracked and uneven. The men I was matched against would miss no detail. I broke one of the bootlaces and retied it in a clumsy knot, and loosed the other so that my thick grey socks bulged over the uppers. Still no sign of anything on the road. The motor I had observed half an hour ago must have gone home.

My toilet complete, I took up the barrow and began my journeys to and from the quarry a hundred yards off.

I remember an old scout in Rhodesia, who had done many queer things in his day, once telling me that the secret of playing a part was to think yourself into it. You could never keep it up, he said, unless you could manage to convince yourself that you were *it*. So I shut off all other thoughts and switched them on to the road-mending. I thought of the little white cottage as my home. I recalled the years I had spent herding on Leithen Water, I made my mind dwell lovingly on sleep in a box-bed and a bottle of cheap whisky. Still nothing appeared on that long white road.

Now and then a sheep wandered off the heather to stare at me. A heron flopped down to a pool in the stream and started to fish, taking no more notice of me than if I had been a milestone. On I went, trundling my loads of stone, with the heavy step of the professional. Soon I grew warm and the dust on my face changed into solid and abiding grit. I was already counting the hours till evening should put a limit to Mr Turnbull's monotonous toil.

Suddenly a crisp voice spoke from the road, and looking up I saw a little Ford two-seater, and a roundfaced young man in a bowler hat.

'Are you Alexander Turnbull?' he asked. 'I am the new County Road Surveyor. You live at Blackhopefoot, and have charge of the section from Laidlaw-byres to the Riggs? Good! A fair bit of road, Turnbull, and not badly engineered. A little soft about a mile off, and the edges want cleaning. See you look after that. Good morning. You'll know me the next time you see me.'

Clearly my get-up was good enough for the dreaded Surveyor. I went on with my work, and as the morning grew towards noon I was cheered by a little traffic. A baker's van breasted the hill, and sold me a bag of ginger biscuits which I stowed in my trousers pocket against emergencies. Then a herd passed with sheep, and disturbed me somewhat by asking loudly, 'What had become o' Specky?'

'In bed wi' the colic,' I replied, and the herd passed on . . .

Just about midday a big car stole down the hill, glided past and drew up a hundred yards beyond. Its three occupants descended as if to stretch their legs, and sauntered towards me.

Two of the men I had seen before from the window of the Galloway inn – one lean, sharp, and dark, the other comfortable and smiling. The third had the look of a countryman – a vet perhaps, or a small farmer. He was dressed in ill-cut knickerbockers, and the eye in his head was as bright and wary as a hen's.

'Morning,' said the last. 'That's a fine easy job o' yours.'

I had not looked up on their approach, and now, when accosted, I slowly and painfully straightened my back, after the manner of roadmen; spat vigorously, after the manner of the low Scot; and regarded them steadily before replying. I confronted three pairs of eyes that missed nothing.

'There's waur jobs and there's better,' I said sententiously. 'I wad rather hae yours, sittin' a' day on your hinderlands on thae cushions. It's you and your muckle cawrs that wreck my roads! If we a' had oor richts, ye sud be made to mend what ye break.'

The bright-eyed man was looking at the newspaper lying beside Turnbull's bundle.

'I see you get your papers in good time,' he said.

I glanced at it casually. 'Aye, in gude time. Seein' that that paper cam out last Setterday I'm just sax days late.'

He picked it up, glanced at the superscription, and laid it down again. One of the others had been looking at my boots, and a word in German called the speaker's attention to them.

'You've fine taste in boots,' he said. 'These were never made by a country shoemaker.'

'They were not,' I said readily. 'They were made in London. I got them frae the gentleman that was here last year for the shootin'. What was his name now?' And I scratched a forgetful head.

Again the sleek one spoke in German. 'Let us get on,' he said. 'This fellow is all right.'

They asked one last question.

'Did you see any one pass early this morning? He might be on a bicycle or he might be on foot.'

I very nearly fell into the trap and told a story of a bicyclist hurrying past in the grey dawn. But I had the sense to see my danger. I pretended to consider very deeply.

'I wasna up very early,' I said. 'Ye see, my dochter was merrit last nicht, and we keepit it up late. I opened the house door about seeven and there was naebody on the road then. Since I cam up here there has just been the baker and the Ruchill herd, besides you gentlemen.'

One of them gave me a cigar, which I smelt gingerly and stuck in Turnbull's bundle. They got into their car and were out of sight in three minutes.

My heart leaped with an enormous relief, but I went on wheeling my stones. It was as well, for ten minutes later the car returned, one of the occupants waving a hand to me. Those gentry left nothing to chance.

I finished Turnbull's bread and cheese, and pretty soon I had finished the stones. The next step was what puzzled me. I could not keep up this road-making business for long. A merciful Providence had kept Mr Turnbull indoors, but if he appeared on the scene there would be trouble. I had a notion that the cordon was still tight round the glen, and that if I walked in any direction I should meet with questioners. But get out I must. No man's nerve could stand more than a day of being spied on.

I stayed at my post till about five o'clock. By that time I had resolved to go down to Turnbull's cottage at nightfall and take my chance of getting over the hills in the darkness. But suddenly a new car came up the road, and slowed down a yard or two from me. A fresh wind had risen, and the occupant wanted to light a cigarette.

It was a touring car, with the tonneau full of an assortment of baggage. One man sat in it, and by an amazing chance I knew him. His name was Marmaduke Jopley, and he was an offence to creation. He was a sort of blood stockbroker, who did his business by toadying eldest sons and rich young peers and foolish old ladies. 'Marmie' was a familiar figure, I understood, at balls and polo-weeks and country houses. He was an adroit scandalmonger, and would crawl a mile on his belly to anything that had a title or a million. I had a business introduction to his firm when I came to London, and he was good enough to ask me to dinner at his club. There he showed off at a great rate, and pattered about his duchesses till the snobbery of the creature turned me sick. I asked a man afterwards why nobody kicked him, and was told that Englishmen reverenced the weaker sex.

Anyhow there he was now, nattily dressed, in a fine new car, obviously on his way to visit some of his smart friends. A sudden daftness took me, and in a second I had jumped into the tonneau and had him by the shoulder.

'Hullo, Jopley,' I sang out. 'Well met, my lad!'

He got a horrid fright. His chin dropped, as he stared at me. 'Who the devil are you?' he gasped.

'My name's Hannay,' I said. 'From Rhodesia, you remember.'

'Good God, the murderer!' he choked.

'Just so. And there'll be a second murder, my dear, if you don't do as I tell you. Give me that coat of yours. That cap, too.'

He did as he was bid, for he was blind with terror. Over my dirty trousers and vulgar shirt I put on his smart driving-coat, which buttoned high at the top and thereby hid the deficiencies of my collar. I stuck the cap on my head, and added his gloves to my get up. The dusty roadman in a minute was transformed into one of the neatest motorists in Scotland. On Mr Jopley's head I clapped Turnbull's unspeakable hat, and told him to keep it there.

Then with some difficulty I turned the car. My plan was to go back the road he had come for the watchers, having seen it before, would probably let it pass unremarked, and Marmie's figure was in no way like mine.

'Now, my child,' I said, 'sit quite still and be a good boy. I mean you no harm. I'm only borrowing your car for an hour or two. But if you play me any tricks, and above all if you open your mouth, as sure as there's a God above me I'll wring your neck. *Savez?*'

I enjoyed that evening's ride. We ran eight miles down the valley, through a village or two, and I could not help noticing several strange-looking folk lounging by the roadside. These were the watchers who would have had much to say to me if I had come in other garb or company. As it was, they looked incuriously on. One touched his cap in salute, and I responded graciously.

As the dark fell I turned up a side glen which, as I remember from the map, led into an unfrequented corner of the hills. Soon the villages were left behind, then the farms, and then even the wayside cottages. Presently we came to a lonely moor where the night was blackening the sunset gleam in the bog pools. Here we stopped, and I obligingly reversed the car and restored to Mr Jopley his belongings.

'A thousand thanks,' I said. 'There's more use in you than I thought. Now be off and find the police.'

As I sat on the hillside, watching the tail lights dwindled I reflected on the various kinds of crime I had now sampled. Contrary to general belief I was not a murderer, but I had become an unholy liar, a shameless impostor, and a highwayman with a marked taste for expensive motor-cars.

4
THE BLOODY DEED
Introduction

†

Whiles I threat, he lives;
Words to the heat of deeds too cold breath gives.
I go and it is done; the bell invites me.
Hear it not, Duncan, for it is a knell
That summons thee to heaven or to hell. [*Exits*]

In Act Two, Scene I, Macbeth 'psyches himself up' as we might say today, into carrying out the murder of the king – this is the moment when the resolution is complete and action begins. He exits and when he returns the deed is done. We have selected pieces for this chapter in which Scots writers contemplate and describe ways in which evil influences criminals' actions. To be fascinated with the details of a crime is an experience common to many; detailed and preferably lurid descriptions of criminal deeds, especially murder, assault and rape, have always found an avid readership. This is as true of the popular press as it is of crime novels or whatever is the modern equivalent of 'penny dreadfuls' – Robert Burns made a nice quip about the fascination of crime reports in the newspapers of his day in a note he sent to a neighbour from Ellisland Farm:

> To Captain Riddel, Glenriddel (Extempore Lines on Returning a Newspaper)
>
> > Your news and review, sir,
> > I've read through and through, sir,
> > With little admiring or blaming:
> > The papers are barren
> > Of home-news or foreign,
> > No murders or rapes worth the naming.

Of course Burns himself gives us in *Tam o' Shanter*, in the passage where Tam rides across a landscape strewn with scenes of crimes, a succession of quick descriptions with unmatched deftness and energy reminiscent of the ballads of old. And in speaking of that earlier age – the fascination, the seductiveness of crime and of unspeakable deeds and horrific actions can be imagined in the minds of the listeners to the ballad makers. Our first item in this chapter is just such a ballad, *Edward*. This is the story of a doomed *ménage à trois*, the bare plot of which could serve for the script of a soap opera, but which in compactness of language and dramatic power is almost without equal. No ballad about the murder of the Red Comyn by Robert the Bruce is known, but we can imagine what it would be like. It would have the same dramatic impact as other ballads, illuminated by action, as when the Bruce's companion resolves to 'mak siccar' – that is to make sure that the deed is done.

One famous historical murder for which we do have a first-rate literary account is the 'Appin Murder', the killing in 1752 of a government factor of estates in Appin, one Colin Campbell of Glenure – the account is given by Robert Louis Stevenson in his historical romance *Kidnapped*. This murder, the whole truth about which has never been revealed, is at the heart of the novel and inspired *Kidnapped* and the sequel, *Catriona*. Our chosen chapter, *The Death of the Red Fox* (the 'Red Fox' is Glenure), pictures the moment of the assassination in this way:

> But just as he turned there came the shot of a firelock from higher up the hill; and with the very sound of it Glenure fell upon the road.

One of Stevenson's later works about a criminal deed is a short story, *The Body Snatcher* (not included here), about the resurrection men of the nineteenth century. We have, however, an extract which deals with that murky period of Scottish history. It comes from William Roughead's collection *Riddle of the Ruthvens, and Other Studies* and deals with the most infamous of the body-snatchers, Burke and Hare. Many would argue that such crimes and criminals are the products of social conditions, of slums, poverty and disease. As Jimmy Boyle, the twentieth-century convicted murderer and artist, put it: crime is 'the inarticulate expression of the inequalities of life'. This may be true, but it is interesting that the real villains in Stevenson's tale, mentioned above, were quite different from Burke and Hare – there were middle class medical students and doctors, and not the 'unclean and desperate interlopers who supplied the [dissecting] table'.

Social injustice on a scale equivalent to a crime is the subject of the next extract. It is a letter taken from Donald MacLeod's *Gloomy Memories of the Highlands*, which was a sustained barrage of criticism in the pages of the Edinburgh *Weekly Chronicle* directed at those responsible for the Sutherland Clearances around 1807. In this letter we encounter the demonic figure of Patrick Sellar, a factor to the Sutherland estates. Sellar was never charged with the murders that MacLeod and others believed he had committed, and was acquitted of the charges for which he was brought to trial.

A famous crime with quite a different ambience is the subject of a short poem, *Heaven Knows*, by Janet Hamilton. Here the setting is Glasgow in 1857, and a young woman of good family, Madeleine Smith, is facing a charge of murder. The trial proves to be incredibly sensational and has remained so, partly because the murder was carried out by means of poison, the most melodramatic of all methods. The case is also memorable because of the final verdict of 'Not Proven'. In her poem, Hamilton is sympathetic towards the deceased, Smith's lover Emile L'Angelier; equally, her attitude to Smith is made clear in the first verse, when she is described as 'the fair, false syren'.

Lastly in this chapter, *The Dark of Summer* was Eric Linklater's version of a murder mystery with a historical dimension. It is in a way similar to the Josephine Tey story, *The Daughter of Time*, an extract from which appears elsewhere in this anthology.

Edward

A Ballad

ANONYMOUS

*The ballads were, in origin, part of the culture of a society which was
essentially non-literate. They are believed to have flourished from about
the fourteenth up to the end of the seventeenth century, especially in areas
of political, linguistic and social tension, such as the marches with England
and the frontier between the Highlands and the Scots-speaking North
East. The process of oral (sung) transmission of the ballads, handed down
'from lip to ear', was surely amazing but can only be guessed at, because
today we usually know them only in written form. David Buchan in* The
Ballad and the Folk *explains that the balladeer in a pre-literate society had
no concept of a ballad text. 'He has none of the sophisticated literate
mind's word-fixation; he makes no attempt to render the actual words of
the story as he heard it, but he does make a strenuous effort to render the
story itself exactly as he heard it. For him, the story's the thing.'*

And the story in Edward *is an enormously direct and powerful
revelation of a crime – the crime being patricide.*

*None more than this, ballads can take on a dramatic form, made up of a
series of scenes lit by flashes of action and revelations of what is happening
or, as in this case, has already happened. It is a domestic tragedy the layers
of which are unpeeled bit by bit, until the tragic Edward reveals why he is
clutching his bloodstained 'brand' or sword, in a scene which is strangely
reminiscent of* Macbeth. *Finally we learn that he has killed his father, and
worse still, he has done so at the prompting of his mother. The doleful
figure of the mother is common to a number of the ballads and the ghastly
psychology of the commission of the deed and its consequences for the rest
of the family is an example of, as Maurice Lindsay says, 'horrible
happenings which today would merit a paragraph or two in . . . one of the
less salubrious newspapers'.*

✝

I

'Why does your brand sae drop wi' blude,
Edward, Edward?
Why does your brand sae drop wi' blude,
And why sae sad gang ye, O?' –
'O I hae kill'd my hawk sae gude,
Mither, mither;
O I hae kill'd my hawk sae gude,
And I had nae mair but he, O.'

II

'Your hawk's blude was never sae red,
Edward, Edward;
Your hawk's blude was never sae red,
My dear son, I tell thee, O.' –
'O I hae kill'd my red-roan steed,
Mither, mither;
O I hae kill'd my red-roan steed,
That erst was sae fair and free, O.'

III

'Your steed was auld, and ye hae got mair,
Edward, Edward;
Your steed was auld, and ye hae got mair;
Some other dule ye dree, O.' –
'O I hae kill'd my father dear,
Mither, mither;
O I hae kill'd my father dear,
Alas, and wae is me, O!'

IV

'And whatten penance will ye dree for that,
Edward, Edward?
Whatten penance will ye dree for that?
My dear son, now tell me, O.' –
'I'll set my feet in yonder boat,
Mither, mither;
I'll set my feet in yonder boat,
And I'll fare over the sea, O.'

V

'And what will ye do wi' your tow'rs and your ha',
Edward Edward?
And what will ye do wi' your tow'rs and your ha',
That were sae fair to see, O?' –
'I'll let them stand till they doun fa',
Mither, mither;
I'll let them stand till they doun fa',
For here never mair maun I be, O.'

VI

'And what will ye leave to your bairns and your wife,
Edward, Edward?
And what will ye leave to your bairns and your wife,
When ye gang owre the sea, O?' –
'The warld's room: let them beg through life,
Mither, mither;
The warld's room: let them beg through life;
For them never mair will I see, O.'

VII

'And what will ye leave to your ain mither dear,
Edward, Edward?
And what will ye leave to your ain mither dear,
My dear son, now tell me, O?' –
'The curse of hell frae me sall ye bear,
Mither, mither;
The curse of hell frae me sall ye bear:
Sic counsels ye gave to me, O!'

'The Appin Murder'

from Kidnapped

ROBERT LOUIS STEVENSON (1850–1894)

In the aftermath of the '45 Rising the forfeited estates of Jacobite leaders were administered by government factors. One such factor was Colin Campbell of Glenure, nicknamed 'The Red Fox', who in May 1752 was shot by a hidden marksman while collecting rents on the Appin estates of Clan Cameron and Stewart of Ardshiel. One James Stewart – 'James of the Glens' – was arrested and charged with being an accessory to the murder. The actual murderer was never arrested, although a soldier in French service, Alan Breck Stewart, was the prime suspect among many. James of the Glens was tried at Inveraray ('the Campbells' head place'), executed and for years after his body hung from a gibbet at Ballachulish.

The Appin Murder was the inspiration for two of Stevenson's best-loved a historical romances: Kidnapped *and the sequel* Catriona. *This extract is taken from the former novel and deals with the involvement of the (fictional) narrator, David Balfour, in the case and 'his misfortunes anent the Appin Murder' as the title plate of the book put it. In* Kidnapped *David witnesses the assassination of Glenure and is restored to his fortune at the end of that novel; in* Catriona *he attempts (unsuccessfully) to bring about the acquittal of James Stewart. Stevenson wrote this in Bournemouth – it echoes his complete immersion in Scotland's cultural past at the same time as it provides a gripping tale and what Walter Allen called in* The English Novel *the 'birth of the novel of action as we know it'. Together with its sequel,* Catriona *it has claims to be one of the earliest of note in that genre.*

The next day Mr Henderland found for me a man who had a boat of his own and was to cross the Linnhe Loch that afternoon into Appin, fishing. Him he prevailed on to take me, for he was one of his flock; and in this way I saved a long day's travel and the price of the two public ferries I must otherwise have passed.

It was near noon before we set out; a dark day, with clouds, and the sun shining upon little patches. The sea was here very deep and still, and had scarce a wave upon it; so that I must put the water to my lips before I could believe it to be truly salt. The mountains on either side were high, rough and barren, very black and gloomy in the shadow of the clouds, but all silver-laced with little watercourses where the sun shone upon them. It seemed a hard country, this of Appin, for people to care as much about as Alan did.

There was but one thing to mention. A little after we had started, the sun shone upon a little moving clump of scarlet close in along the waterside to the north. It was much of the same red as soldiers' coats; every now and then, too, there came little sparks and lightning, as though the sun had struck upon bright steel.

I asked my boatman what it should be; and he answered he supposed it was some of the red soldiers coming from Fort William into Appin, against the poor tenantry of the country. Well, it was a sad sight to me; and whether it was because of my thoughts of Alan, or from something prophetic in my bosom, although this was but the second time I had seen King George's troops, I had no good will to them.

At last we came so near the point of land at the entering in of Loch Leven that I begged to be set on shore. My boatman (who was an honest fellow and mindful of his promise to the catechist) would fain have carried me on to Balachulish; but as this was to take me farther from my secret destination, I insisted, and was set on shore at last under the wood of Lettermore (or Lettervore, for I have heard it both ways) in Alan's country of Appin.

This was a wood of birches, growing on a steep, craggy side of a mountain that overhung the loch. It had many openings and ferny howes; and a road or bridle track ran north and south through the midst of it, by the edge of which, where was a spring, I sat down to eat some oat-bread of Mr Henderland's, and think upon my situation.

Here I was not only troubled by a cloud of stinging midges, but far more by the doubts of my mind. What I ought to do, why I was going to join myself with an outlaw and a would-be murderer like Alan, whether I should not be acting more like a man of sense to tramp back to the south country direct, by my own guidance and at my own charges, and what Mr Campbell or even Mr Henderland would think of me if they should ever learn my folly and presumption: these were the doubts that now began to come in on me stronger than ever.

As I was so sitting and thinking, a sound of men and horses came to me through the wood; and presently after, at a turning of the road, I saw four travellers come into view. The way was in this part so rough and narrow that they came single and led their horses by the reins. The first was a great, redheaded gentleman, of an imperious and flushed face, who carried his hat in his hand and fanned himself, for he was in a breathing heat. The second, by his decent black garb and white wig, I correctly took to be a lawyer. The third was a servant, and wore some part of his clothes in tartan, which showed that his master was of a Highland family, and either an outlaw or else in singular good odour with the Government, since the wearing of tartan was against the Act. If I had been better versed in these things, I would have known the tartan to be of the Argyle (or Campbell) colours. This servant had a good-sized port-manteau strapped on his horse, and a net of lemons (to brew punch with) hanging at the saddle-bow; as was often enough the custom with luxurious travellers in that part of the country.

As for the fourth, who brought up the tail, I had seen his like before, and knew him at once to be a sheriff's officer.

I had no sooner seen these people coming than I made up my mind (for no reason that I can tell) to go through with my adventure; and when the first came alongside of me, I rose up from the bracken and asked him the way to Aucharn.

He stopped and looked at me, as I thought, a little oddly; and then, turning to the lawyer, 'Mungo,' said he, 'there's many a man would think this more of a warning than two pyats. Here am I on my road to Duror on the job ye ken; and here is a young lad starts up out of the bracken, and speers if I am on the way to Aucharn.'

'Glenure,' said the other, 'this is an ill subject for jesting.'

These two had now drawn close up and were gazing at me, while the two followers had halted about a stone-cast in the rear.

'And what seek ye in Aucharn?' said Colin Roy Campbell of Glenure; him they called the Red Fox; for he it was that I had stopped.

'The man that lives there,' said I.

'James of the Glens,' says Glenure, musingly; and then to the lawyer: 'Is he gathering his people, think ye?'

'Anyway,' says the lawyer, 'we shall do better to bide where we are, and let the soldiers rally us.'

'If you are concerned for me,' said I, 'I am neither of his people nor yours, but an honest subject of King George, owing no man and fearing no man.'

'Why, very well said,' replies the Factor. 'But if I may make so bold as ask, what does this honest man so far from his country? and why does he come seeking the brother of Ardshiel? I have power here, I must tell you. I am King's Factor upon several of these estates, and have twelve files of soldiers at my back.'

'I have heard a waif word in the country,' said I, a little nettled, 'that you were a hard man to drive.'

He still kept looking at me, as if in doubt.

'Well,' said he, at last, 'your tongue is bold; but I am no unfriend to plainness. If ye had asked me the way to the door of James Stewart on any other day but this, I would have set ye right and bidden ye God speed. But today – eh, Mungo?' And he turned again to look at the lawyer.

But just as he turned there came the shot of a firelock from higher up the hill; and with the very sound of it Glenure fell upon the road.

'Oh, I am dead!' he cried, several times over.

The lawyer had caught him up and held him in his arms, the servant standing over and clasping his hands. And now the wounded man looked from one to another with scared eyes, and there was a change in his voice that went to the heart.

'Take care of yourselves,' says he. 'I am dead.'

He tried to open his clothes as if to look for the wound, but his fingers slipped on the buttons. With that he gave a great sigh, his head rolled on his shoulder, and he passed away.

The lawyer said never a word, but his face was as sharp as a pen and as white as the dead man's; the servant broke out into a great noise of crying and weeping, like a child; and I, on my side, I stood staring at them in a kind of horror. The sheriff's officer had run back at the first sound of the shot, to hasten the coming of the soldiers.

At last the lawyer laid down the dead man in his blood upon the road, and got to his own feet with a kind of stagger.

I believe it was his movement that brought me to my senses; for he had no sooner done so than I began to scramble up the hill, crying out, 'The murderer! the murderer!'

So little a time had elapsed, that when I got to the top of the first steepness, and could see some part of the open mountain, the murderer was still moving away at no great distance. He was a big man, in a black coat, with metal buttons, and carried a long fowling-piece.

'Here!' I cried. 'I see him!'

At that the murderer gave a little, quick look over his shoulder, and began to run. The next moment he was lost in a fringe of birches; then he came out again on the upper side, where I could see him climbing like a jackanapes, for that part was again very steep; and then he dipped behind a shoulder, and I saw him no more.

All this time I had been running on my side, and had got a good way up, when a voice cried upon me to stand.

I was at the edge of the upper wood, and so now, when I halted and looked back, I saw all the open part of the hill below me.

The lawyer and the sheriff's officer were standing just above the road, crying and waving on me to come back; and on their left, the red-coats, musket in hand, were beginning to struggle singly out of the lower wood.

'Why should I come back?' I cried. 'Come you on!'

'Ten pounds if ye take that lad!' cried the lawyer. 'He's an accomplice. He was posted here to hold us in talk.'

At that word (which I could hear quite plainly, though it was to the soldiers and not to me that he was crying it) my heart came in my mouth with quite a new kind of terror. Indeed, it is one thing to stand the danger of your life, and quite another to run the peril of both life and character. The thing, besides, had come so suddenly, like thunder out of a clear sky, that I was all amazed and helpless.

The soldiers began to spread, some of them to run, and others to put up their pieces and cover me; and still I stood.

'Jouk in here among the trees,' said a voice, close by.

Indeed, I scarce knew what I was doing, but I obeyed; and as I did so, I heard the firelocks bang and the balls whistle in the birches.

Just inside the shelter of the trees I found Alan Breck standing, with a fishing-rod. He gave me no salutation; indeed it was no time for civilities; only 'Come!' says he, and set off running along the side of the mountain towards Balachulish; and I, like a sheep, to follow him.

Now we ran among the birches; now stooping behind low humps upon the mountain side; now crawling on all fours among the heather. The pace was deadly; my heart seemed bursting against my ribs; and I had neither time to think nor breath to speak with. Only I remember seeing with wonder, that Alan every now and then would straighten himself to his full height and look back; and every time he did so, there came a great faraway cheering and crying of the soldiers.

Quarter of an hour later, Alan stopped, clapped down flat in the heather, and turned to me.

'Now,' said he, 'it's earnest. Do as I do for your life.'

And at the same speed, but now with infinitely more precaution, we traced back again across the mountain side by the same way that we had come, only perhaps higher; till at last Alan threw himself down in the upper wood of Lettermore, where I found him at the first, and lay, with his face in the bracken, panting like a dog.

My own sides so ached, my head so swam, my tongue so hung out of my mouth with heat and dryness that I lay beside him like one dead.

'The Body Snatchers'

from Burke and Hare

WILLIAM ROUGHEAD (1870–1952)

William Roughead was an Edinburgh lawyer who early in his career developed a fascination with murder cases and the darker recesses of Scottish legal history. He edited ten volumes in the Notable British Trials *series as well as over a hundred other accounts of criminal cases collected in fourteen volumes of his work.*

In his preface to this 1921 volume about 'one of the most extraordinary episodes in our social and legal history', Roughead observed that there were 'many books about Burke and Hare', but his was 'the first to combine an account of the whole circumstances with a verbatim legal report of the case.' Other works about the illicit supply of dead bodies by the 'Resurrectionists' include Stevenson's short story, The Body Snatcher *and the play,* The Anatomist, *by James Bridie. These both show how the horror and depravity of grotesques like Burke and Hare existed cheek by jowl with medical establishment figures like Dr Knox, whom Stevenson refers to simply, in unconscious anticipation of Kafka, as 'K'.*

The extract from Roughead is selected from his preliminary description of the 'whole circumstances' of the case, which are such as to make it difficult for him to live up to his intention not to 'make anyone's flesh creep'. What is most surprising of course is the realisation that although the two are inextricably linked in the imaginations of people around the world, only William Burke was found guilty and hanged for the 'West Port Murders', while Hare escaped by turning King's evidence. Here are a few of the closing remarks to the jury of Burke's defence counsel, the Dean of Faculty, Sir James Moncrieff:

> You must have legal evidence in this as well as in all other cases that the crime was committed, and that the prisoner was the person who committed it. Gentlemen, if it were otherwise, what would the condition of any man in this country be? If a man's life, or liberty, or character, were to hang on the breath of such witnesses as Hare and his wife, what security could any man have for his existence in society for a single hour!

✝

In the Anatomical Museum of the University of Edinburgh may be seen, appropriately suspended in a show case, a short thick-set skeleton, bearing upon its exiguous frame a label inscribed with the laconic legend, 'William Burke, The Murderer'. The tall gentleman with the fine teeth who supports him on the left is, as his card succinctly announces, 'Howison, The Cramond Murderer, and last person to be hanged and dissected'. But Burke is the doyen of the collection; his companion, though interesting enough in his own way, is a personage of lesser note.

Confronted by these suggestive relics, the observer is moved to reflect how strangely the evil that men do may yet tend indirectly to the general good; for, indeed, Burke is to be considered as in some sort a patron of that great school of surgery in which his bones are thus piously preserved. Were it not for his atrocious doings the Anatomy Act had not passed when it did, nor the followers of a noble science been so early freed from the reproach of trafficking for the subjects of their study with the villainous violators of graves. Burke was a maker of history. With him died what was known as the Resurrectionist system, the fell shadow of which had long darkened the land, though neither he nor his partner Hare, despite the popular belief to the contrary, was ever himself a body snatcher in the technical sense of that picturesque term. He has enriched our language by a new metonomy, and his name is writ for all time in the English dictionary. By the unlettered he is sometimes confounded with his Right Honourable namesake – a vulgar error from which even so shrewd a man as Mr Jorrocks did not escape.

That Burke is entitled to rank high in the calendar of crime is indisputable. His trial is the most famous in the judicial annals of Scotland, by reason of the world-wide interest which the case created, the complicated atrocity of the crimes and the ingenious manner of their commission, the importance of the legal principles involved, and the eminence of the judges and counsel engaged upon its conduct. In an imperfect world we cannot get everything as we would wish it, and in one respect the proceedings were glaringly defective; the absence from the bar of Burke's fiendish associate Hare, whose arraignment would have conduced not only to the ends of justice, but to the uniformity of the series in which the present volume appears. Finally, the literature of the West Port murders inspired that grisliest of Robert Louis Stevenson's tales, *The Body Snatcher*, wherein, granting the subject to be legitimate matter of fiction – 'This talk fit for a charnel,' as the Duchess of Malfi says in the play – we are given the very atmosphere of that horrid business, and share in all the terrors of the time. Perhaps the somewhat macabre pleasantries of *The Wrong Box* derive from the same source.

While the circumstances of Burke's case are gruesome beyond the common run of murders, and few would care to have attended the trial when the dreadful tale was first unfolded by the very actors in the tragedy, there are many who find in the written records of such affairs a curious attraction. Thus Edward Fitzgerald, writing of his 'wonderful museum' of out-of-the-way matter, remarks 'But my chief article is murderers; I am now having a Newgate Calendar from London. I don't ever wish to see and hear these things tried; but when they are in print I like to sit in Court then, and see the judges, counsel, prisoners, crowd; hear the lawyers' objections, the murmur in the Court, &c. –

> The Charge is prepar'd; the Lawyers are met,
> The Judges all rang'd (a terrible Show!)'[2]

It is pleasant to find, by the way, that the Gilbertian humours of *The Beggar's Opera*, so dear to Deacon Brodie, were appreciated by the inspired translator of Omar.

Then Lockhart informs us that Sir Walter Scott had a passion for reading murder trials, and kept a collection of such in his library, with the contemporary ballads and broadsheets relating to them, some of these annoted with his own hand. And has not Mr H.B. Irving recorded how Tennyson and Jowett once sat up a whole night discussing – murders? To such, therefore, as share these great men's taste the following report of Burke's trial affords an opportunity to participate, at a convenient remove, in a case of high interest and importance.

Visitors to the older Edinburgh graveyards must have noted their strange resemblance to zoological gardens, the rows of iron cages suggesting rather the dens of wild animals than the quiet resting places of the dead. And, in fact, these barred and grated cells were designed as a protection against human wolves who nightly prowled about such places in quest of prey, and furnish very real testimony to the fears by which our forbears were beset respecting the security of sepulchres. The Resurrectionist drama, of which Scotland in general and her capital in particular were the theatre, was produced under conditions the most adverse. Not only was its performance illegal, which, as in the case of smuggling, might have mattered little, but it was intensely unpopular, and in sustaining their rôles the players ran, in the fullest sense, grave risks. Belief in the resurrection of the body had ever been held in a strictly literal and material way by the Scots, who, regarding with superstitious veneration the mortal remains of their kindred, were apt to take summary vengeance on the disturbers of their repose. Thus the natural repugnance to dissections of the human body, fortified by religious sentiment, opposed for centuries an insuperable barrier to anatomical research.

The earliest provision for dissection in Edinburgh was made in 1505, when the Town Council granted a charter to the Incorporation of Surgeons and Barbers, whereby it was provided that every intrant should 'knaw anatomea nature and complexioun of every member In manis bodie,' for which purpose 'We [the surgeons] may have anis in the yeir ane condampnit man efter he be deid to mak anatomea of, quhairthrow we may have experience Ilk ane to instruct uthers, And we sall do suffrage for the soule'. Though one malefactor's body per annum, however piously commemorated, would not go very far, the surgeons had to rest content with such provision till 1694, when an effort was made to found a school of anatomy in Edinburgh, and the available subjects were augmented by a further grant of 'those bodies that dye in the correction-house; the bodies of fundlings who dye betwixt the tyme that they are weaned and their being put to schools or trades; also the dead bodies of such as are stiflet in the birth, which are exposed, and thir have none to owne them; as also the dead bodies of such as are *felo de se*; likewayes the bodies of such as are put to death by sentence of the magistrat.' In 1705 the first Professor of Anatomy was appointed with the munificent yearly salary of £15, and in 1720 Alexander Monro, *primus*, succeeded to the duties and emoluments of the Chair. Under him and his son Alexander, *secundus*, appointed in 1754, the anatomical school of Edinburgh was finally and firmly established. In 1798 Alexander, *tertius*, ascended the hereditary rostrum as Professor Monro – 'also, but not likewise', according to the nice distinction drawn by John Clerk in the case of the two Lords Meadowbank. The Monro dynasty endured for the long period of 126 years, but, though the first and second had it all their own way, the supremacy of the last ruler was challenged by a succession of extramural lecturers, of whom the most brilliant were John Barclay and Robert Knox.

It is obvious that the lawful supply of subjects was wholly inadequate to meet the growing needs of the new school, and even before the reign of the Monros the surgeons' and barbers' apprentices had been in use diligently to till the soil and reap the harvest of what has been finely called 'Death's mailing'. Complaints of rifled graves were frequent, and in 1711 the College of Surgeons demurely records that 'of late there has been a violation of sepulchres in the Greyfriars churchyard' – then the chief city burying-ground – 'by some who most unchristianly have been stealing the bodies of the dead'. In view of the spread of this profane practice due to the success which attended the first Monro's teaching, the Surgeons in 1721 passed the self-denying ordinance that their apprentices' indentures should in future contain a clause forbidding the violation of churchyards. That this restriction was regarded by the students merely as 'a scrap of paper' appears from the fact that four years later the continued robbing of graves led to a formidable riot, when Monro's rooms were well-nigh demolished by the mob. At first zealous apprentices were the only body snatchers, but owing to the popularity of the Edinburgh medical school and the great increase of students, there arose a class of men who, adopting as a business the raising of the dead, became known as Resurrectionists. These 'honest tradesmen' of whom Mr Jeremiah Cruncher is in letters the typical example, did not confine their activities to Scotland. A brisk export trade was driven in London, the Leith smack sometimes including in her cargo as many as twelve bodies, consigned to Edinburgh surgeons; while in Ireland the industry was developed by the well-known commercial enterprise of Glasgow. It was unfortunate, and, as the sequel will show, disastrous, that anatomists were thus brought to depend for their supplies upon ruffians of the most abandoned character, instead of being able to meet their wants by justifiable methods.

The penalties for exhumation were stringently enforced; in one year there were fourteen convictions in England, but fines, imprisonment, and even transportation could not counter the equally inexorable laws of supply and demand. Proper skill in practical anatomy was enforced by the Legislature upon every medical man, while the means of securing its pursuit rendered him liable to disgrace and punishment. In this respect, as has been observed, the law resembled that of Venice as interpreted by Portia – exacting the pound of flesh, it forbade the operation necessary for its removal. In Scotland the increasing boldness of the body snatchers was met by the public with equal vigour; anyone suspected of the act was roughly entreated, and such as fell into the hands of justice were severely punished. Certain cases occuring in the year 1742 may be instanced. On 9th March the body of a man which had been buried in the West Kirkyard was discovered in the house of a surgeon, Dr Martin Eccles; the mob, roused, as in the affair of Porteous, by tuck of the Portsburgh drum, wrecked Eccles' premises, and attacked the houses of other surgeons. The riot was with difficulty suppressed; the surgeon was charged before the magistrates as accessory to the raising of dead bodies, but owing to lack of proof was liberated. On the 13th the Incorporation of Surgeons, met 'to testify their abhorrence of so wicked a crime', enacted that any apprentice guilty of the practice should forfeit his indentures, and offered 100 merks for discovery of every such offence. On the 15th the mob fell upon the house of the West Kirk beadle, 'calling it Resurrection Hall', and razed it to the ground, despite the owner's protest of innocence, previously published in the newspapers. On the 18th at Inveresk, the house of one Richardson, a gardener, believed to ply his trade illegitimately in the local graveyard, was burnt by the parishioners. On the 26th, two Edinburgh chairmen were banished the city for being found at the Nether Bow Port in possession of a dead body seated in a chair. In the following July a gardener at Grangegateside was sentenced by the High Court to whipping and transportation, having been caught at the Potter-row Port with a bag containing the body of a child which he had lifted from Pentland kirkyard. Prior to the proceedings against Burke the leading case in this connection was that of Helen Torrence and Jean Waldie in February, 1752, cited by Counsellor Pleydell in *Guy Mannering*, which is the sole instance of 'Resurrection-women' on record. They were charged with *plagium* (man-stealing) and murder, in respect that, having failed to obtain for a surgeon the body of a dead child, they stole a live one, which they slew and sold to him for 2s. 6d. and the price of a dram. Both these hags, employing Burke's ritual, suitably shared his doom.

'A Highland Clearance'

from Gloomy Memories of the Highlands

DONALD MACLEOD

The attempted sale of the Black Cuillin on the Island of Skye brings to mind ancient memories of the series of events over a period of more than a hundred years from the 1740s, known collectively as the Clearances. Of course, the greater part of the Cuillin is so inhospitable that it never supported a population, even in the days before the clearances on Skye. And the Macleods of Dunvegan were not reviled in the way that, for example, the Sutherland landowners were reviled. (At a time of great famine in 1850 the then Macleod brought himself to ruin in an attempt to help his people.)

This extract deals with the Sutherland Clearances and is one of a series of letters written by a journalist, coincidentally bearing the Macleod name, which appeared in the Edinburgh Weekly Chronicle *around 1820. The 'Gloomy Memories' were political journalism which amounted to polemic and provoked a reaction and debate which have lasted to the present day; and especially when the letters were recovered and published in 1883 by Alexander Mackenzie in his* History of the Highland Clearances. *That was at a time when the 'Battle of the Braes' in Skye had reawakened controversy about land ownership.*

The letter (No. IV) is one of twenty-five written by Macleod which introduced to the world the demonic, or possibly demonised, figure of Patrick Sellar, factor of the Countess of Sutherland's estates, who was held responsible for the forced eviction of many of the tenants. A flavour of the full-blown nature of the polemic can be gained from a famous sentence in the first letter, which speaks in a curiously modern way about 'asylum seekers':

> The country was darkened by the smoke of the burnings, and the descendants of those who drew their swords at Bannockburn, Sheriffmuir and Killiecrankie – the children and nearest relatives of those who sustained the glory of the British name in many a bloody field – the heroes of Egypt, Corunna, Toulouse, Salamanca, and Waterloo – were ruined, trampled upon, dispersed, and compelled to seek an asylum across the Atlantic; while those who remained from inability to emigrate, deprived of all the comforts of life, became paupers – beggars – a disgrace to the nation whose freedom and honour many of them had maintained by their valour and cemented with their blood.

Sellar was unanimously acquitted as the British Establishment closed ranks. Evictions and emigration continued as slowly observers came to realise that the post '45 order in the Highlands had abolished the chief's traditional role and forcibly introduced an alien form of cash economy.

In the month of March, 1814, a great number of the inhabitants of the parishes of Farr and Kildonan were summoned to give up their farms at the May term following, and, in order to ensure and hasten their removal with their cattle, in a few days after, the greatest part of the heath pasture was set fire to and burnt, by order of Mr Sellar, the factor, who had taken these lands for himself. It is necessary to explain the effects of this proceeding. In the spring, especially when fodder is scarce, as was the case in the above year, the Highland cattle depend almost solely on the heather. As soon, too, as the grass begins to sprout about the roots of the bushes, the animals get a good bite, and are thus kept in tolerable condition. Deprived of this resource by the burning, the cattle were generally left without food, and this being the period of temporary peace, during Buonaparte's residence in Elba, there was little demand for good cattle, much less for these poor starving animals, who roamed about over their burnt pasture till a great part of them were lost, or sold for a mere trifle. The arable parts of the land were cropped by the outgoing tenants, as is customary, but the fences being mostly destroyed by the burning, the cattle of the incoming tenant were continually trespassing throughout the summer and harvest, and those who remained to look after the crop had no shelter; even watching being disallowed, and the people were hunted by the new herdsmen and their dogs from watching their own corn! As the spring had been severe, so the harvest was wet, cold, and disastrous for the poor people, who, under every difficulty, were endeavouring to secure the residue of their crops. The barns, kilns, and mills, except a few necessary to the new tenant, had, as well as the houses, been burnt or otherwise destroyed and no shelter left, except on the other side of the river, now overflowing its banks from the continual rains; so that, after all their labour and privations, the people lost nearly the whole of their crops, as they had already lost their cattle, and were thus entirely ruined.

But I must now go back to the May term and attempt to give some account of the ejection of the inhabitants; for to give anything like an adequate description I am not capable. If I were, its horrors would exceed belief.

The houses had been all built, not by the landlord as in the low country, but by the tenants or by their ancestors, and, consequently, were their property by right, if not by law. They were timbered chiefly with bog fir, which makes excellent roofing but is very inflammable: by immemorial usage this species of timber was considered the property of the tenant on whose lands it was found. To the upland timber, for which the laird or the factor had to be asked, the laird might lay some claim, but not so to the other sort, and in every house there was generally a part of both.

In former removals the tenants had been allowed to carry away this timber to erect houses on their new allotments but now a more summary mode was adopted, by setting fire to the houses! The able-bodied men were by this time away after their cattle or otherwise engaged at a distance, so that the immediate sufferers by the general house-burning that now commenced were the aged and infirm, the women and children. As the lands were now in the hands of the factor himself, and were to be occupied as sheep-farms, and as the people made no resistance, they expected at least some indulgence, in the way of permission to occupy their houses and other buildings till they could gradually remove, and meanwhile look after their growing crops. Their consternation, was, therefore, the greater when, immediately after the May term day, and about two months after they had received summonses of removal, a commencement was made, to pull down and set fire to the houses over their heads! The old people, women, and others, then began to try to preserve the timber which they were entitled to consider as their own. But the devastators proceeded with the greatest celerity, demolishing all before them, and when they had overthrown the houses in a large tract of country, they ultimately set fire to the wreck. So that timber, furniture, and every other article that could not be instantly removed, was consumed by fire, or otherwise utterly destroyed.

These proceedings were carried on with the greatest rapidity as well as with most reckless cruelty. The cries of the victims, the confusion, the despair and horror painted on the countenances of the one party, and the exulting ferocity of the other, beggar all description. In these scenes Mr Sellar was present, and apparently (as was sworn by several witnesses at his subsequent trial) ordering and directing the whole. Many deaths ensued from alarm, from fatigue, and cold; the people being instantly deprived of shelter, and left to the mercy of the elements. Some old men took to the woods and precipices, wandering about in a state approaching to, or of absolute insanity, and several of them, in this situation, lived only a few days. Pregnant women were taken with premature labour, and several children did not long survive their sufferings. To these scenes I was an eye-witness, and am ready to substantiate the truth of my statements, not only by my own testimony, but by that of many others who were present at the time.

In such a scene of general devastation it is almost useless to particularise the cases of individuals – the suffering was great and universal. I shall, however, just notice a very few of the extreme cases which occur to my recollection, to most of which I was an eye-witness. John MacKay's wife, Ravigill, in attempting to pull down her house, in the absence of her husband, to preserve the timber, fell through the roof. She was, in consequence, taken with premature labour, and in that state, was exposed to the open air and the view of the bystanders. Donald Munro, Garvott, lying in a fever, was turned out of his house and exposed to the elements. Donald Macbeath, an infirm and bedridden old man, had the house unroofed over him, and was, in that state, exposed to wind and rain till death put a period to his sufferings. I was present at the pulling down and burning of the house of William Chisholm, Badinloskin, in which was lying his wife's mother, an old bedridden woman of near 100 years of age, none of the family being present. I informed the persons about to set fire to the house of this circumstance, and prevailed on them to wait till Mr Sellar came. On his arrival I told him of the poor old woman being in a condition unfit for removal. He replied, 'Damn her, the old witch, she has lived too long; let her burn.' Fire was immediately set to the house, and the blankets in which she was carried were in flames before she could be got out. She was placed in a little shed, and it was with great difficulty they were prevented from firing it also. The old woman's daughter arrived while the house was on fire, and assisted the neighbours in removing her mother out of the flames and smoke, presenting a picture of horror which I shall never forget, but cannot attempt to describe. She died within five days.

I could multiply instances to a great extent, but must leave to the reader to conceive the state of the inhabitants during this scene of general devastation, to which few parallels occur in the history of this or any other civilised country. Many a life was lost or shortened, and many a strong constitution ruined; – the comfort and social happiness of all destroyed; and their prospects in life, then of the most dismal kind, have, generally speaking, been unhappily realised.

Heaven Knows

JANET HAMILTON (1795–1873)

These 'Lines on the trial of Madeleine Smith for the Murder of L'Angelier'
were written at the time of the trial in 1857. The story is well known. The
city of Glasgow was shocked by the news of the extraordinary trial for
murder of Madeleine Smith, twenty-two-year-old daughter of a leading
architect. Madeleine was accused of murdering her lover, Pierre Emile
L'Angelier, by poisoning his cocoa – poison, the infamous 'woman's
method' – and the newspaper reading public were agog with daily
revelations, not least the reading of Madeleine's uninhibited love letters.
The West of Scotland Magazine and Review could hardly contain itself:

> *What a putrefying layer of debasement, lust, and hypocrisy, festering under*
> *the smooth-skinned surface of society in moral-living, church-going,*
> *theatre-hating, Sabbath-keeping Glasgow do the occurrences present out of*
> *which arose the trial of Madeleine Smith!*

The evidence was circumstantial, though strong. Madeleine was shown to
have purchased arsenic and she clearly had a motive for ridding herself of
L'Angelier – her desire to replace the affair with her engagement to a more
suitable person. However, her defence was in the skilful hands of John
Inglis, whose efforts secured a verdict of 'Not Proven'.

The poem clearly sides with those who saw this as a travesty of justice,
but Madeleine Smith lived on until 1928 in her adopted home of the USA,
resisting all offers to play herself in a silent movie.

Shade of the hapless stranger, lost L'Angelier,
Whose life's young light was quenched in guilt and shame,
Say, haunt'st thou still the lane, the fatal gate,
Where to thy arms the fair, false syren came?

We seek not now thy 'merits to disclose,
Or draw thy frailties from their dread abode';
We would not sit in judgment on the man
Whose soul hath stood before the bar of God.

'Not proven' was thy thrice-repeated deed,
Thou of the stony heart and dauntless eye:

Smile not; in Heaven's high court thou yet shalt hear
The unerring proven verdict of the sky.

A lovely isle lies cradled in the deep,
Its flowery glades embowered in fruitful trees,
A weeping mother wanders on the beach
And pours her sorrows on the seaward breeze.

Ah! to her widowed heart her only son
She last had clasped upon that island shore;
He came, he saw, he loved, he sinned, he died –
We wait till Heaven and time shall tell us more.

'Ancient Murder'

from The Dark of Summer

ERIC LINKLATER (1899–1974)

Eric Linklater's first spell of literary popularity came in the years before the Second World War. His big successes in a prolific career were the light-hearted satire Juan in America *and* Magnus Merriman. *After the War he wrote an anti-war comedy,* Private Angelo, *which was made into a successful film, another literary satire* The Merry Muse *and* The Dark of Summer (1957) *which has been hailed as his masterpiece. Its unusual and complex structure takes the reader to locations and settings which include several parts of Europe, North Africa and the Western Desert, and Korea, and in time, from the immediate past back to the eighteenth century and the Jacobite Risings. Carefully interwoven into the story are two long extracts taken from an old volume of family history dating from that period. The work is called* The Wishart Inheritance; *it vividly recreates episodes in the past of the Wisharts, ancestors of the family that the novel's hero, Tony Chisholm, has become involved with in present-day Shetland. The opening chapter of the novel, which we include here, describes the unearthing of a long-dead corpse which has been partly preserved in a peat bog, and which, it seems, is the remains of one of these ancestors, who has been murdered.*

Linklater, as an Orcadian, knew these northern isles well, the Faroes as well as the Shetlands, and here he distinguishes the latter – 'long, dark and narrow, poor and picturesque' – from the 'squat and prosperous' Orkneys and the 'wild, abruptly rising, cloud-hung' Faroes. This murder, the menace of this ancient mystery, is at the outset contrasted with the eerie quality of life and light in the northern isles: ' "the summer dim" – the dimness, or twilight, at midnight, that is – in which can be seen beauty enough for happiness.'

Where I shall live when I retire – where I am living now, on leave from the great watershed – there is, at the top of summer, no darkness at midnight. The day puts on a veil, the light is screened, and a landscape that, in fine weather, appears at noon to be almost infinite – in which long roads and little houses are luminously drawn – becomes small and circumscribed, and the hills and the shore, the sheep in the fields and the glinting sea, are visible, as it were, through a pane of slightly obscuring glass. The landscape becomes an image of the world in which we live. It is not dark, but nothing can be seen as plainly and decisively as the light of noon pretends – noon flatters and deludes us – yet all that can be seen is solid, solid enough for faith, and if one's heart is whole one can enjoy the beauty inherent in our mystery – a beauty that is, paradoxically, more visible in half-light.

That night – the night of our discovery – my heart was whole, as for nearly a twelvemonth it had been whole, in spite of my duty that made me a sort of tightrope-walker, treading a narrow crest in history. In spite, also, of my previous waste of life, much of which I had spent in a cold mechanism of existence. For almost a year I had been happy. Within the limits of my own imagination, within the scope of my consciousness, I had been fulfilled. I was skin-tight with love, God's grace perhaps, and animal joy. My arm – my only arm – was round my lovely wife's young body, my fingers, the only set I had, were outspread beneath her breast and as we walked, and looked towards the sea, I recognised the long tentacles of land, reaching round a silver-dappled firth, as a symbol of communion; as my remnant arm was with her bright candour and her beauty.

I could see, and not see. What I saw was transmuted by the diminished light of the sun that lay an inch or two below the horizon; and what I could not see was made real by an expansion of my faith in the solid substance of the nearer view. I had no complaint against a distant invisibility. Is it an insufferable boast, in our world, to say I was content? Though it be intolerable, it was true then, and still is. And partly the blame (if blame is necessary) must lie on the quality of light that in these northern islands is called 'the summer dim' – the dimness, or twilight, at midnight, that is – in which can be seen beauty enough for happiness. Not enough, nor nearly enough, for comprehension; yet enough to make comprehension unnecessary. But most of the blame, and none of the twilight, falls on Gudrun. Gudrun has her own illumination, and it was she who had given me faith in the realities of the foreground and distance too.

We had been married for less than a year, and to touch was still a flicker of fire that could blaze and consume us. We stopped on the road, and kissed, and if I had had my way we would have gone no farther. There was a patch of gorse there, smelling of honey and coconut, and the roadside turf was warm and dry. 'But no,' she said, 'you mustn't be foolish,' and her soft Shetland voice in its nonsensical rhythm went up and down, up and down, like the little clapping waves that strike a green-fringed jetty in the sea when a quick motor boat passes. 'Be sensible,' she said, 'and wait till we get home. I want to see the new road.'

So we walked on to the cart-track that turns abruptly to the right, and the brand-new, black continuation of the road that would presently go down to the beach. With a bulldozer hired from the County Council I had begun, that morning, to cut a path through a belt of peat, a long tongue of peat and dingy heather, that lay athwart the hard foundation of the hill between the house and the narrow, green, serpentine firth a hundred feet below it. Most of our work on the property had had a good economic motive, but the new road was designed for pleasure: it would take us down from the garden gate to a little sandy cove bounded on either side by black rocks, through which, to the north, a narrow stream tumbled, with yellow irises on its banks, and on the other side rose low cliffs where we had found a wren nesting not far from the white-splashed untidiness of a cormorant's roost . . .

So much for the setting: for the scene which is the end (so far as I can see) of my story, and in one respect was where it began. I am not a professional writer, and I cannot be sure of telling the story as it should be told: there may be devices and tricks of the trade by which a man of letters could magnify certain episodes and give to the whole more 'effect' – but even without these additions (or, perhaps, subtractions) the story is, I think, worth telling, and that for two reasons.

I am, in the first place, very much a man of my own times; and this, God knows, is not boastfully said, though a conclusion shot through with gratitude may to some look too much like boasting – I grew up in the knowledge that 'we had come down in the world'; and by 'we' I mean, quite simply, all of us who by birth are British. I was born on July 1st, 1916, when the battle of the Somme began, that cost us sixty thousand casualties in a single day and destroyed the great army of volunteers with which we began that war; and in the years of my boyhood and my youth I read and was told, again and again, of the vanity of that sacrifice. The Britain to which I was born was in every way shabbier and poorer – materially, spiritually, in political influence – than the Britain my parents had known; and what I found particularly depressing was my mother's repeated assertion that the very best, the cream and the pride, of a generation had been lost. She herself, it appeared, had known a vast number of young men distinguished by the brilliance of their intellect, their personal courage, or their beauty – and all, all had gone. 'All but your father,' she would say, 'and he, thank God, remains to let you see the sort of men whom our politicians threw away!'

To an early appreciation of my mental and physical inferiority was added, therefore, a deep distrust of the politicians whose authority, it seemed, we must still acknowledge. Many of my contemporaries grew up under a like influence, and very few of us were unaffected by the endemic fears and anxieties of our time. We heard – at second or third hand for the most part, because we did not live with intellectuals – of the chaos that Marx had made of history, Freud of the human mind – and, perhaps, Einstein of the universe. We saw for ourselves the chaos in our economy that a money famine in America had made. And we in Britain, who had long since reduced patriotism to a small, enjoyable emotion, and never had any faith in messianic politics, watched with bewilderment and increasing fear the dreadful, the inexplicable growth of mass emotion, regimented nationalism, and apocalyptic leadership in Russia, Italy, and Germany.

That was the world in which my generation grew to something like manhood, and then, for six years, our scrap of manhood was tested in another war. To have survived so much is, I think, something of an achievement, and I admit a persistent sense of wonder about the why and the how of survival. But my own small part in so large a miracle would not, of itself, justify my attempt to write of it; nor, by itself, would it make a story.

The story I am trying to tell springs from my connection – I being so much the product of my time – with a succession or string of events that began more than two hundred years ago. My connection was in part accidental, in part deliberate; and my life was entangled in the string. I became involved in the affairs and death of a man called Mungo Wishart, a landed proprietor in Shetland, whose mind, to a singular degree, had been shaped, or misshaped, by a family history of long unhappiness: a history that started from sedition, murder, and dark uncertainties, and was continued through purposeless and wasteful litigation to no better end than the deformity of a man's reason and a new project of sedition.

If I was a product of my own time and a world in chaos, Mungo Wishart was the offspring of a remembered time when human weakness, enormity of human greed, and extreme of passion had convulsed a little, extinct society of rather stupid, often drunken lairds in one of the remotest parishes of Britain – and time past had done worse for him than time present for me. . . .

I have admitted that I cannot tell my story as neatly as, I daresay, a professional author would tell it; but I have begun it where I mean to end it – and so, if I am lucky, I may draw a full circle – and I have said as clearly, I think, as is necessary, that it springs from my involvement with the affairs of Mungo Wishart. I have admitted also that the story's end will leave me happy – clean-contrary, I suppose, to what is expected of a story nowadays – and to that I shall add a claim to have laid, at long last, the ghost that bedevilled the poor tormented mind of Mungo. It is for that purpose I have begun my narrative with the tale of our evening walk – Gudrun and I, enlaced in love, walking to see the new road – for the ghost of an old injustice had had a corporal essence, and we discovered it. We found, in the peat, the body of a dead man.

The bulldozer was in the blind alley of the new road. An eight-foot-high rampart of peat stood in front of it, and shining black walls confined it. We scrambled up the lower side to admire the view, to consider the descending line of the road, and on the ledge of the cutting a table-top of heather was dislodged by our weight, and slid down. We had time to step on to firmer ground, but when the great clod had fallen away it left a break in the peat, and in the break there was a little surface of something different. The surface of something that had a different texture.

We went down again, Gudrun helping me, and stood beside it. The surrounding peat was smooth and damp, a yielding solidity, but the foreign surface had the slimy hardness of an old rope left and lost in the sea. It was strangely but certainly something made by human hands and, as though the vegetable peat had resisted total marriage with the human body inside the coat, there was a little cleft about its head and shoulders. We had no doubt as to what it was, and leaping conjecture told us who.

I remember Gudrun breathing, as it seemed, through a congested whistle, and though I had less cause for emotion I felt, under the quickness of astonishment, a sudden need to protect her against what might emerge from this uncovering of an old mystery – of old rascality, perhaps – and I would not let her look closely at the body. I told her we must wait for the morning to make a proper examination, and I took her back to the house. She came readily enough, and said nothing till we stood at the front door, when she asked, 'Do you think it's Old Dandy? It must be, mustn't it?'

'Not necessarily. I don't suppose Dandy was the only old scamp in Shetland to die of exposure – of drink and exposure –'

'Or to be murdered,' she said.

'Yes, perhaps he was murdered. But it was a long time ago – it was two hundred years ago – and even murder doesn't mean much after a couple of centuries.'

'It does,' she said. 'You can't forgive murder.'

'Wait till the morning, and then perhaps we'll find out more about it.'

'But I'm sure it's Dandy! So near the house, and for you and me to find him at last! Oh, I'm sure of it.'

We went to bed and she lay beside me, holding my hand, but almost as separate as some thin, carved effigy on a medieval tomb of man and wife. I knew what thoughts possessed her – I had seen the havoc they made of her father's mind – but I knew also that she was not haunted, that her mind was not deformed, as his had been, by an old twisted tale of a family so united in hatred that its two bitter branches had clung together in costly dispute that impoverished both of them, and left in both a brooding resentment because the one side still maintained, the other privily suspected, that the lawyers' judgment had been wrong.

But Gudrun had inherited neither their bitterness nor shame. She could not forget the story, but it had not darkened her mind nor disabled her judgment. Her father had prevented that. She had turned in revulsion from his bitter spirit, and gone wilfully into exile from all his people and their history. Her mother came of a different – a stronger, simpler stock of crofters and fishermen – and because her mother's character had a placid strength, an untroubled sweetness, and Gudrun had inherited enough of her mother for contentment, her exile from the better blood of her spear-side was untouched by regret. She remembered, with a strong dislike for him, her angry father; but if the old story still teased her, it was only because she had the quick, gossiping curiosity of a country girl and wanted to know what had happened. I had no fear that her excitement and distress would last more than a day or two. Perhaps the night would cure it; for it was not the distress of someone born to unhappiness, but only the shock of dark discovery and a girl's excitement, ordinary and natural enough.

If we could find proof, moreover, that it was Dandy who lay in the peat – the drunken, distressed old Jacobite whose death was still a mystery – then the unsolved and teasing parts of the story might show more clearly. Supposition might be strengthened. It depended on the state of the body, and I began, with Gudrun still awake beside me, to try and remember the effect of peat on human tissues. Did it preserve or dissolve them? But I fell asleep before I could remember, and when I woke Gudrun was sleeping like a child in summer, exhausted under a haycock, so I got up quietly, and dressed and went out.

The men were late as usual, and it was half past eight before they came down to the cutting in the peat. The driver of the bulldozer, who was employed by the County Council, knew nothing of Old Dandy, but my own two men (we shared a fishing-boat and they worked my small farm for me) jumped to identification as quickly as Gudrun, and for twenty minutes or so, while they rehearsed the story, and argued about its details and gave their own explanations of it, no one laid a finger on him. But then, with care and respect in their hands, they began to remove the peat that was so curiously moulded about his body.

I am no expert on costume of the eighteenth century, but his coat and breeches! – hard and well-preserved and a little slimy – were certainly the carefully made dress of a gentleman, not the haphazard clothing of a peasant. 'Old Dandy!' said my men. 'No doubt of that!' But when we tried to lift him from his grave, we were disconcerted by the lack of substance within his coat. His body, it seemed, had collapsed. He was lying on his face, and the men did not know what to do and were reluctant to handle him, and grew a little shamefaced about their reluctance.

I knelt and put my solitary arm under his chest, and felt for a solid hold, and like the others admitted a sensation of nausea at the yielding emptiness of the coat. But I tried to raise him, and then, with a little cry of pain, quickly drew back my hand; and that was foolish. For whatever had pierced my finger – my middle finger, at the base – scored a deep cut to the tip of it, and my hand, when I pulled it out, was a mess of blood oozing on black peat.

I am a little ashamed of my behaviour after that, though I had some excuse for it. It was, after all, my only hand, and in the circumstances it was not unnatural to think of sepsis, of septicaemia, and the total loss of my hand. But I need not have been so precipitate. It was my old habit of fear long buried, but buried alive, I suppose – that made me exclaim, in too high a voice, 'O God, look at that! I must see a doctor.'

'It is deep,' said one of my men.

'It will be poisonous,' said the other.

'That's what I'm frightened of. Don't touch him, or be very careful. There's something in his chest, it may be a dagger. I'm going to Lerwick to have my hand dressed.'

'You will be needing a driver,' said the younger man.

'My wife will take me. And don't touch him till I come back – or be careful if you do.'

I left them, and in a nervous hurry went back to the house and put my hand under the kitchen tap, and saw the cut finger open pinkly and show pale edges. There Gudrun found me, and I told her what had happened.

'He was murdered,' she said. 'I always knew it! And you must go straight to the surgeon.'

Gudrun was calm and swiftly efficient. It was her turn now to be sensible, as I had been the night before; and I still found common sense miraculous in her, who seemed too young and soft and wild to have any hardness in her mind. She bandaged my finger, she made breakfast for us, and because she was so lovely I thought it a marvel of womanhood that she could do these simple things.

We drove to Lerwick, down the twisted spine of the island – the long road running from tip to tip of the Mainland of Shetland, that is sixty miles long and no broader than a lizard – and because my fear had gone, leaving only a nervous excitement, I felt, not for the first time, that we were riding on a sort of aery bridge – on a parallel of longitude flying above the natural earth – and indeed the view, now on this side, now on the other, of cliffs dropping suddenly to the white crumbling of a bright blue sea, gave to hallucination a shred of reality. I remembered, in my excitement that was darkened by only a small foreboding, my first coming to the islands, and how I had hated them; and when I looked back at the angry years it seemed that my happiness had been trodden out of me by their iron-shod feet as wines of great quality used to be trodden out by the horny feet of lean, sour smelling, hungry peasants. It was in the year of touch-and-go, the year of the great alliance, that I first saw the islands that lie in three groups in the Atlantic north of Britain.

The nearest are the Orkneys, squat and prosperous, divided from Scotland only by the swollen tides of the Pentland Firth; then the Shetlands, long, dark and narrow, poor and picturesque, bearing good sailors and small brown sheep; and lastly, far out to the north-west, the wild, abruptly rising, cloud-hung Faeroes, breeding also sheep and sailors, as if in her extremity nature could rear only what was born with a good coat or a bold heart – and to two of these archipelagos I went, for the first time, in 1941 – twice in the same year, in spring and winter – and hated them all for their wind-swept nakedness. But now, because time had had its way with me, I took delight in their nakedness, having eyes to see how comely and how gentle it was.

I thought too – and when I looked at my bandaged finger a little *frisson* of superstition sharpened my pleasure – that time had shown its purpose very clearly by using Old Dandy to wound me. I, married with such contentment to the daughter of the man whose life had been deformed by a hatred that sprang, in part, from the death of Dandy, was now related to her more closely than by arms in bed and the conjunctive light of minds in love. I had become a member of her story, and my marriage was dignified by a purpose bred of time. There was in it so much of joy that I looked for, and longed to find, a deeper reason for its happiness than the satisfaction of mortal bodies; and on our flying parallel of longitude, high above common earth, I saw my wounded finger as proof of time's ordination and my relevance to its purpose.

Intent on driving, and the turning road, Gudrun was silent. She has the gift of companionable silence, and drives well. She does not withdraw into silence, but spreads it like a rug, and in the safety of her comfort I was free to traverse memory and play with fancy. I left responsibility to her, and when we reached the hospital she took me, without question or hesitation, to the surgeon's private room, where we found him, having done half his morning's work, drinking a cup of coffee and signing letters that a quiet, primly dressed secretary put before him. We knew him – we were friends in the second degree of friendship – and when Gudrun described what we had found, and what had happened to me, he grew interested at once, not so much in my mishap, as in the possible *éclaircissement* of a story that, in his five years' service in Shetland, he had heard more than once. He told us that we must let the police know of our discovery, and promised to come out in the afternoon, as soon as he had finished his work, to see the body for himself. Then, still talking of Old Dandy, he looked at my finger and, summoning his theatre sister to bring dressings, cleaned and rebandaged the wound.

'And to give you full insurance,' he said, 'I'll pump some penicillin into you. You haven't had an injection lately, have you? That's good. Now come in here' – he led me behind a blue-curtained screen, and because, with only one set of fingers, I am a little clumsy with buttons and so forth, he helped me unfasten and take down my trousers – 'and that, though you'll be uncomfortable for the next hour or two when you sit down, will put your mind at rest,' he said. 'You can stop thinking about septicaemia.'

I dressed again, with a slight feeling of numbness in my right buttock, and we rejoined my wife. The surgeon – a lively, sturdy, interested man – demanded more details of our discovery, and then, turning to the theatre sister, inquired, 'I've plenty of time, haven't I? There's Mrs Johnson's kidney, and that boy's appendix. Nothing else before lunch, is there? All right, come and see my new theatre equipment. I'm very proud of it.'

I had no wish to look at surgical apparatus, but to refuse would have been churlish, and we followed him along a brown-footed corridor to a room of staring and expert simplicity – a room of white enamel, chromium steel, and brilliant weapons against the indiscipline of nature – and with a naïve pleasure in the forces at his command, he exclaimed, 'But put on the light, Sister. The overhead light.'

The light went on – a pure, dry, anatomical light – and I who, for the past hour and more, had been exploring memory as well as fancy, was suddenly and fully reminded of the very beginning – not of story, indeed, for that lay with the dead man in the peat – but of my association with it: my involvement with life and death in Shetland. That began in very different surroundings, in London – under a London pavement – and so vivid was the recollection that I had no ear for what the surgeon said, but in the staring light in which we stood I remembered the wound I had suffered, under a light that in memory seemed comparable, a dozen years before . . .

More than a dozen years; but years dissolve in their own flux, and little remains of them but the scars they leave, or sometimes, but not often, the beatitudes they bring.

5
CATCH THE THIEF!
Introduction

✝

As eager runs the market-crowd,
When 'Catch the thief!' resounds aloud.

The simile is from *Tam o' Shanter*; it compares the pursuit of Tam by
Cutty Sark and the other members of the 'hellish legion' of witches to a
market-crowd, most of whom, it seems, are prepared to 'have a go' at
stopping the fugitive. This provides us with a glimpse of the kind of rough
justice which existed in eighteenth-century towns like Ayr before the
introduction of paid police forces. Pickpockets and cutpurses, dips and
lifters are all candidates for the kind of thief who would set the pursuit off
and running.

We must imagine that apart from the sheer enjoyment of behaving like
a mob it was the chance of a reward that motivated the crowd. But, as
Cunninghame Graham put it, 'rewards of any kind are but vulgarities',
and the astonishing thing is that in the Scotland of the past a remarkable
number of forms of theft, such as poaching and smuggling, enjoyed a
measure of tacit public support and at times a degree of active complicity.
Even in the Scotland of today, although, for example, poaching is not so
common among country folk as it once was, the laws relating to such
matters as recording music or videotape are regularly evaded by many. In
some circles, also, the dislike of 'clyping' or 'grassing' remains as high as
ever.

These peccadilloes aside, there is no doubt that many laws have been
'planted' in the land in order to secure the rights of property against those
who, generally from an inferior class, would seek to take such property
away from its owners. For a clear statement of the position we need look
no further than Lord Braxfield, the Court of Session judge, who is quoted
elsewhere in this anthology:

Hang a thief when he's young and he'll no steal when he's auld.

Perhaps because so many took Lord Braxfield's advice, actual accounts of
simple thieving, of breaking and entering and burglary seem pretty thin

on the ground when we turn to look at the output of Scottish writers. Of course, there was one fairly notable case of 'theft' in the year of 1296, which has had repercussions down through the centuries. In this case the accused standing at the bar of history is one Edward I of England, alias the 'Hammer of the Scots'. Apart from a small matter of rape and pillage and the seizure of much land and many castles, he also purloined the Stone of Destiny from Scone, a portion of the Records of Scotland, assorted plate and jewels, and the relic, St Margaret's portion of the True Cross. Here is Thomas Pennant's somewhat inaccurate description – it was of course the Stone which was taken south to be placed under Edward the Confessor's Chair:

> Till the destruction of the abbey, the kings of Scotland were crowned here, sitting in the famous wooden chair, which Edward I transported to Westminster Abbey, much to the mortification of the Scots, who esteemed it as their palladium.

Our first four extracts in this chapter have to do with a much less grand crime – that of smuggling. We have already remarked about the general tolerance that many Scots had for what might be called family-friendly criminal activities, and of these smuggling was pre-eminent. All around the coasts of Scotland the illicit importation of goods on which no duty had been paid was a crime carried on by many and blinked at by many more. Smuggling had existed for centuries – it was known as the 'national vice of the Scots' – and was the cause of an immense amount of friction with England in the years leading up to the Union of 1707. After the Union it grew to enormous limits and was particularly prevalent in the south-west and on the coasts of Fife. The goods which were smuggled included at various times salt, textiles and sugar, but the classic products with which smugglers sought to evade the forces of the crown, in the shape of the customs and excise, were spirits, wine and tobacco.

Throughout the eighteenth century the forces of the government, the excisemen or 'gaugers', became more and more effective in dealing with the problem, despite the connivance, as we learn in almost all of the extracts, of many otherwise honest citizens. Walter Scott, though a lawyer and a Tory, could concede in *The Heart of Midlothian* that the people were unaccustomed to duties and regarded them 'as an unjust aggression upon their ancient liberties'.

The first extract is Robert Burns's *The Deil's Awa' Wi' Th'Exciseman*. It seems to share this common point of view in that it is sung by those who are happy to see the exciseman 'danc'd awa' with the 'meikle black deil'. The delicious joke is of course that Burns was himself an exciseman at the time – and in fact relied on the income from his excise post when he gave up farming. Appended to the song is a short account of the poet's most famous exploit in relation to the work of the excise.

Scott's *Heart of Midlothian* begins with the events leading up to the Porteous Riots, earlier in the eighteenth century. As we learn in an extract there was a deep involvement by smugglers in these events, and in particular a character known as Wilson. The smugglers' great popularity among elements of the famous Edinburgh mob was an important factor in the riot itself, which followed on from the execution of Wilson for his smuggling activities. In a note to the novel Scott wrote of a group of sympathisers:

> ... whose animosity against Porteous, on account of the execution of Wilson, was so extreme, that they resolved to execute vengeance on him with their own hands, rather than he should escape punishment. With this resolution they crossed the Forth at different ferries, and rendezvoused at the suburb called Portsburgh, where their appearance in a body soon called numbers around them. The public mind was in such a state of irritation, that it only wanted a single spark to create an explosion.

The extract from *Guy Mannering*, also by Walter Scott, stresses the same kind of approach to this particular crime and illustrates some of the romanticism which surrounded it, even in the minds of minor gentry like Bertram.

A very different set of circumstances surround the next extract, which deals with that variety of theft known as forgery – in this case literary forgery. William Roughead's *Antique Smith* is an amusing account of a celebrated case in the early nineteenth century where a forger cleverly produced numerous skilful facsimiles of important historical documents and original pieces which included a poem by Burns. Forgery, or rather its first cousin plagiarism, is akin to piracy, according to Roget, so perhaps there is a tinge of romanticism in this crime too. Stevenson, who has something to say about every crime it seems, urges the reader in his foreword to *Underwood*:

> Of all my verse, like not a single line;
> But like my title, for it is not mine.
> That title from a better man I stole;
> Ah, how much better, had I stol'n the whole!

The last three extracts take us into a territory where writers once more seem to treat of crime in a benevolent fashion – that is in the area of poaching. Poaching, for many, summons up images of poacher's moons and kindly men with strangely bulging pockets. Firstly, we include a chapter from John Buchan's *John Macnab*, his much-loved 1925 novel that is constructed on the amusing premise that something of the thrill and excitement of crime, in this case poaching (although rejecting that simple description), can be shared by gentlemen just as much as by the lower orders. The subtitle of Chapter I reads, 'In Which Three Gentlemen Confess Their Ennui', and the plot takes them through a series of challenges involving game like deer and salmon and flirtations with the laws of property. Elsewhere in the novel, Buchan gives a remarkable description of one of his characters, Lord Lamancha, which shows the quintessential aristocrat and High Tory challenging his own property laws. This is an insight into Buchan's view of the British class system, in a book which is perhaps as much about politics as it is about crime and evading retribution. Lamancha has been caught shooting a stag on another's land in the guise of the amazing composite poacher, John Macnab.

> It is a melancholy fact which exponents of democracy must face that, while all men may be on a level in the eyes of the State, they will continue in fact to be preposterously unequal. Lamancha had been captured in circumstances of deep suspicion which he did not attempt to explain; he had been caught on Johnson's land, by Johnson's servants; the wounded man was in Johnson's pay, and might reasonably be held to be at Johnson's orders. Yet this outrageous trespasser was not only truculent and impenitent; he was taking it upon himself to give orders to gillies and navvies, and to dictate the use of an expensive automobile. The truth is, that if you belong to a family which for a good many centuries has been accustomed to command and to take risks, and if you yourself, in the forty-odd years of your life, have rather courted trouble than otherwise and have put discipline into Arab caravans, Central African natives and Australian mounted brigades – well when you talk about wringing necks your words may carry weight.

Neil Munro's ever-popular character, Para Handy, certainly takes a relaxed view of the laws relating to game and its ownership. We include a story *Para Handy – Poacher*, in which he and Dougie, the mate of the puffer, the *Vital Spark*, elude not only the game keeper and the river watchers of a particular beat on Loch Fyne, but also the local police force. Still in humorous vein, we finally include a poem, *Poaching In Excelsis* by G.K. Menzies.

The Deil's Awa' Wi' th'Exciseman

ROBERT BURNS (1759–1796)
and 'Burns and the Smugglers'

from an account by Walter Crawford, Revenue Officer

The poet became an exciseman in 1788, soon after his belated marriage to Jean Armour and when the expectation of poor returns from the 'cold bottom' of the backbreaking land of Ellisland Farm was becoming all too apparent. With a wife and a ready-made family to keep, the extra money was useful. As he wrote to Robert Ainslie:

> *I do not know how the word 'exciseman', or still more opprobrious 'gauger', will sound on your ears. I have seen the day when my auditory nerves would have felt very delicately on the subject; but a wife and children are things which have a wonderful power in blunting these kind of sensations.*

The job was for the most part not very exciting and involved much trudging around the highways and byways of Nithsdale. The Excise Commission given to Burns runs to several pages and is largely taken up with the minutiae of a laborious tax-gathering exercise, which included the 'receipt and management' of dozens of duties and 'gauging, weighing, measuring, etc.' of goods and commodities. It drew from him An Extemporaneous Effusion:

> *Searching auld wives' barrels*
> *Och-hon! The day!*
> *That clarty barm should stain my laurels;*
> *But – what'll ye say!*
> *These muvin' things ca'd wives and weans*
> *Wad muve the very hearts o' stanes!*

More excitingly, a few years later, in 1792, Burns was caught up in an episode involving actual criminals – who attempted something more than a spot of illicit brewing This involved the interception in the Solway Firth of a sizeable brig, called the Rosamond, *which was engaged in large-scale smuggling; it gave the poet a flavour of the virtual state of war which for many years existed between smugglers and officers of the excise, backed up by the military and even the Royal Navy. The second extract is a somewhat unreliable account of the incident given by another officer present, one Walter Crawford.*

This makes it clear that the excise were often actively hampered in their work by local people, particularly in the coastal communities, in a way which was akin to the activities of the wreckers. Burns, as a man who, according to another story, tried to send the Rosamond's *guns to the Revolutionary Convention in Paris, maintained an ambivalent attitude to some, more domestic, evasions of taxation. This is apparent in our first extract, the splendidly anarchic 'Deil's Awa', where clearly everyone is free to 'laugh, sing, and rejoice . . . thanks to the meikle black deil'. The song comes from the fourth volume of Johnson's* Scots Musical Museum.

THE DEIL'S AWA', WI' TH' EXCISEMAN

The deil cam fiddling thro' the town,
And danc'd awa' wi' th' Exciseman;
And ila wife cries auld Malhoun,
I wish you luck o' the prize, man.

CHORUS

The deil's awa', the deil's awa',
The deil's awa' wi' th' Exciseman;
He's danc'd awa', he's danc'd awa',
He's danc'd awa' wi' th' Exciseman.

We'll mak our maut, and we'll brew our drink,
We'll laugh, sing, and rejoice, man;
And mony braw thanks to the meikle black deil,
That danc'd awa' wi' th' Exciseman.
The deil's awa', &c.

There's threesome reels, there's foursome reels,
There's hornpipes and strathspeys, man,
But the ae best dance e'er cam to the land,
Was the deil's awa' wi' th' Exciseman.
The deil's awa', &c.

BURNS AND THE SMUGGLERS

. . . We approached with . . . Dragoons in all forty-four fully accoutered and on horseback. The vessel having fallen down the Solway Firth about a mile from where she was yesterday, and being about a mile within sea mark, most of which space being covered with water and a very heavy current running between us and the vessel, we deemed it impossible to get at her, either on foot or on horseback, so we agreed to search the coast for boats in which to board her. But the country people, guessing our design, got the start of us and staved every boat on the coast before we could reach them; the vessel in the mean time keeping up a fire of grape shot and musquetry, we resolved as [a] last resource to attempt the passage on foot, as the quick sands made the ridding on horseback dangerous, or rather impossible.

We drew up the Military in three divisions, determined to approach an attac[k] her if the s[t]ream was foardable, one part fore and aft, and the third on her broadside, the first party being commanded by Quarter Master Manly, the second by my self, and the third by Mr Burns.

Our orders to the Military were to reserve their fire till within eight yards of the vessel, then to pour a volley and board her with sword and pistol. The vessel kept on firing, tho' without any damage to us, as from the situation of the ship, they could not bring their great guns to bear on us, we in the mean time wading breast high, and in justice to the party under my command I must say with great alacrity; by the time we were within one hundred yeards of the vessel, the crew gave up the cause, got over [the] side towards England, which shore was for a long, long way dry sand. As I still supposed that there were only country people they were putting ashore, and that the crew was keeping under cover to make a more vigorous immediate resistance, we marched up as first concerted, but found the vessel completely evacuated both of crew and every moveable on board, expect as per inventory, the smugglers as their last instance of vengen[c]e having poured a six-pounder Carronade through her broadside. She proved to be the *Rosamond* of Plymouth, Alexander Patty Master, and about one hundred tons burthern, schooner r[igged].

'Scott's Smugglers'

from The Heart of Midlothian *and* Guy Mannering

WALTER SCOTT (1771–1832)

The two following extracts are taken from the novels of Walter Scott and each has a connection with the crime of smuggling. The Heart of Midlothian, *which comes from the second series of* Tales of My Grandfather *is one of Scott's finest novels and is set at the time of the Porteous Riots in 1736. Our selected passage is taken from near the beginning and sets the scene for the execution in the Grassmarket of Edinburgh of a historical figure, Andrew Wilson, a notorious smuggler from the Kingdom of Fife. Scott has created an additional character, Robertson, who is assisted to escape by his accomplice Wilson. Wilson, however, is hanged, much to the displeasure of the vast crowd of citizens who attend the execution.*

Robertson plays an important part in the development of the novel's plot, as he is the lover of Effie Deans, whose sister Jeanie is the splendid heroine. The tolerance which many Scots had for any flouting of the excise laws is already apparent in this scene – when Captain Porteous of the City Guard orders his men to fire on the crowd, the ease with which protest could become disorder becomes clearer still.

Guy Mannering, *written three years earlier in 1815, is less firmly rooted in historical fact; Scott gives the time of the events as 17— and the setting is near the Solway Firth. This yarn (written in a space of six weeks) has a plot which revolves around the stealing away of young Harry Bertram, heir to the Laird of Ellangowan, by a smuggler, Dirk Hatteraick. The novel was popular in much the same way as* Rob Roy; *it, too, was adapted for the stage as* An Operatic drama in Three Acts, *by Isack Pocock, with immense popular success.*

In this extract, we are introduced to Harry Bertram's father, the Laird, along with the soldier, Colonel Guy Mannering, who will in due course encounter young Harry again under another name, and one of the novelist's inimitable Scots-speaking characters, Harry's tutor, Dominie Sampson, whose catch-phrase is 'Prodigious'. Another memorable character is Meg Merrilies, the gypsy. In what is probably a humorous touch by Scott, it turns out that Hatteraick, the smuggler, is not so much a villain as another character, one Glossin, who is in fact a lawyer.

✝

THE HEART OF MIDLOTHIAN

In former times, England had her Tyburn, to which the devoted victims of justice were conducted in solemn procession up what is now called Oxford Road. In Edinburgh, a large open street, or rather oblong square, surrounded by high houses, called the Grassmarket, was used for the same melancholy purpose. It was not ill chosen for such a scene, being of considerable extent, and therefore fit to accommodate a great number of spectators, such as are usually assembled by this melancholy spectacle. On the other hand, few of the houses which surround it were, even in early times, inhabited by persons of fashion; so that those likely to be offended or over deeply affected by such unpleasant exhibitions were not in the way of having their quiet disturbed by them. The houses in the Grassmarket are, generally speaking, of a mean description; yet the place is not without some features of grandeur, being overhung by the southern side of the huge rock on which the castle stands, and by the moss-grown battlements and turreted walls of that ancient fortress.

It was the custom, until within these thirty years, or thereabouts, to use this esplanade for the scene of public executions. The fatal day was announced to the public by the appearance of a huge black gallows-tree towards the eastern end of the Grassmarket. This ill-omened apparition was of great height, with a scaffold surrounding it and a double ladder placed against it, for the ascent of the unhappy criminal and the executioner. As this apparatus was always arranged before dawn, it seemed as if the gallows had grown out of the earth in the course of one night, like the production of some foul demon; and I well remember the fright with which the schoolboys, when I was one of their number, used to regard these ominous signs of deadly preparation. On the night after the execution the gallows again disappeared, and was conveyed in silence and darkness to the place where it was usually deposited, which was one of the vaults under the Parliament House, or courts of justice. This mode of execution is now exchanged for one similar to that in front of Newgate – with what beneficial effect is uncertain. The mental sufferings of the convict are indeed shortened. He no longer stalks between the attendant clergymen, dressed in his grave-clothes, through a considerable part of the city, looking like a moving and walking corpse, while yet an inhabitant of this world; but, as the ultimate purpose of punishment has in view the prevention of crimes, it may at least be doubted, whether in abridging the melancholy ceremony, we have not in part diminished that appalling effect upon the spectators which is the useful end of all such inflictions, and in consideration of which alone, unless in very particular cases, capital sentences can be altogether justified.

On the 7th day of September, 1736, these ominous preparations for execution were descried in the place we have described, and at an early hour the space around began to be occupied by several groups, who gazed on the scaffold and gibbet with a stern and vindicate show of satisfaction very seldom testified by the populace, whose good-nature, in most cases, forgets the crime of the condemned person, and dwells only on his misery. But the act of which the expected culprit had been convicted was of a description calculated nearly and closely to awaken and irritate the resentful feelings of the multitude. The tale is well known, yet it is necessary to recapitulate its leading circumstances, for the better understanding what is to follow, and the narrative may prove long, but I trust not uninteresting, even to those who have heard its general issue. At any rate, some detail is necessary, in order to render intelligible the subsequent events of our narrative.

Contraband trade, though it strikes at the root of legitimate government, by encroaching on its revenues – though it injures the fair trader, and debauches the minds of those engaged in it – is not usually looked upon, either by the vulgar or by their betters, in a very heinous point of view. On the contrary, in those counties where it prevails, the cleverest, boldest, and most intelligent of the peasantry, are uniformly engaged in illicit transactions, and very often with the sanction of the farmers and inferior gentry. Smuggling was almost universal in Scotland in the reigns of George I and II; for the people, unaccustomed to imposts, and regarding them as an unjust aggression upon their ancient liberties, made no scruple to elude them whenever it was possible to do so.

The county of Fife, bounded by two firths on the south and north, and by the sea on the east, and having a number of small seaports, was long famed for maintaining successfully a contraband trade; and, as there were many seafaring men residing there, who had been pirates and buccaneers in their youth, there were not wanting a sufficient number of daring men to carry it on. Among these, a fellow called Andrew Wilson, originally a baker in the village of Pathhead, was particularly obnoxious to the revenue officers. He was possessed of great personal strength, courage, and cunning, was perfectly acquainted with the coast, and capable of conducting the most desperate enterprises. On several occasions he succeeded in baffling the pursuit and researches of the king's officers, but he became so much the object of their suspicious and watchful attention, that at length he was totally ruined by repeated seizures. The man became desperate. He considered himself as robbed and plundered; and took it into his head, that he had a right to make reprisals, as he could find opportunity. Where the heart is prepared for evil, opportunity is seldom long wanting. This Wilson learned that the Collector of the Customs at Kirkcaldy had come to Pittenweem, in the course of his official round of duty, with a considerable sum of public money in his custody. As the amount was greatly within the value of the goods which had been seized from him, Wilson felt no scruple of conscience in resolving to reimburse himself for his losses, at the expense of the Collector and the revenue. He associated with himself one Robertson, and two other idle young men, whom, having been concerned in the same illicit trade, he persuaded to view the transaction in the same justifiable light in which he himself considered it. They watched the motions of the Collector; they broke forcibly into the house where he lodged – Wilson, with two of his associates, entering the Collector's apartment, while Robertson, the fourth, kept watch at the door with a drawn cutlass in his hand. The officer of the customs, conceiving his life in danger, escaped out of his bedroom window, and fled in his shirt, so that the plunderers, with much ease, possessed themselves of about two hundred pounds of public money. This robbery was committed in a very audacious manner, for several persons were passing in the street at the time. But Robertson, representing the noise they heard as a dispute or fray betwixt the Collector and the people of the house, the worthy citizens of Pittenweem felt themselves no way called on to interfere in behalf of the obnoxious revenue officer; so, satisfying themselves with this very superficial account of the matter, like the Levite in the parable, they passed on the opposite side of the way. An alarm was at length given, military were called in, the depredators were pursued, the booty recovered, and Wilson and Robertson, tried and condemned to death, chiefly on the evidence of an accomplice.

Many thought that, in consideration of the men's erroneous opinion of the nature of the action they had committed, justice might have been satisfied with a less forfeiture than that of two lives. On the other hand, from the audacity of the fact, a severe example was judged necessary; and such was the opinion of the Government. When it became apparent that the sentence of death was to be executed, files, and other implements necessary for their escape, were transmitted secretly to the culprits by a friend from without. By these means they sawed a bar out of one of the prison windows, and might have made their escape, but for the obstinacy of Wilson, who, as he was daringly resolute, was doggedly pertinacious of his opinion. His comrade, Robertson, a young and slender man, proposed to make the experiment of passing the foremost through the gap they had made, and enlarging it from the outside, if necessary, to allow Wilson free passage. Wilson, however, insisted on making the first experiment, and being a robust and lusty man, he not only found it impossible to get through betwixt the bars, but, by his struggles, he jammed himself so fast, that he was unable to draw his body back again. In these circumstances discovery became unavoidable, and sufficient precautions were taken by the jailor to prevent any repetition of the same attempt. Robertson uttered not a word of reflection on his companion for the consequences of his obstinacy; but it appeared from the sequel, that Wilson's mind was deeply impressed with the recollection that, but for him, his comrade, over whose mind he exercised considerable influence, would not have been engaged in the criminal enterprise which had terminated thus fatally; and that now he had become his destroyer a second time, since, but for his obstinacy, Robertson might have effected his escape. Minds like Wilson's, even when exercised in evil practices, sometimes retain the power of thinking and resolving with enthusiastic generosity. His whole thoughts were now bent on the possibility of saving Robertson's life, without the least respect to his own. The resolution which he adopted, and the manner in which he carried it into effect, were striking and unusual.

GUY MANNERING

When the boat which carried the worthy Captain on board his vessel had accomplished that task, the sails began to ascend, and the ship was got under way. She fired three guns as a salute to the house of Ellangowan, and then shot away rapidly before the wind, which blew off shore, under all the sail she could crowd.

'Aye, aye,' said the Laird, who had sought Mannering for some time, and now joined him, 'there they go – there go the free-traders – there goes Captain Dirk Hattaraick, and the Yungfrow Hagenslaapen, half Manks, half Dutchman, half devil! run out the boltsprit, up main-sail, top and top-gallant sails, royals, and skyscrapers, and away – follow who can! That fellow, Mr Mannering, is the terror of all the excise and customs cruisers; they can make nothing of him; he drubs them or distances them; – and, speaking of excise, I come to bring you to breakfast; and you shall have some tea, that' –

Mannering, by this time, was aware that one thought linked strangely on to another in the concatenation of worthy Mr Bertram's ideas,

Like orient pearls at random strung

and, therefore, before the current of his associations had drifted farther from the point he had left, he brought him back by some enquiry about Dirk Hattaraick.

'O he's a – a – good sort of blackguard fellow enough – no one cares to trouble him – smuggler, when his guns are in ballast – privateer, or pirate, faith, when he gets them mounted. He has done more mischief to the revenue folk than any rogue that ever came out of Ramsay.'

'But, my good sir, such being his character, I wonder he has any protection and encouragement on this coast.'

'Why, Mr Mannering, people must have brandy and tea, and there's none in this country but what comes this way – and then there's short accounts, and maybe a keg or two, or a dozen pounds left at your stable door at Christmas, instead of a d—d lang account from Duncan Robb, the grocer at Kippletringan, who has aye a sum to make up, and either wants ready money, or a short-dated bill. Now, Hattaraick will take wood, or he'll take barley, or he'll take just what's convenient at the time. I'll tell you a good story about that. There was ance a laird – that's Macfie of Gudgeonford – he had a great number of kain hens – that's hens that the tenants pay to the landlord – like a sort of rent in kind – They aye feed mine very ill; Luckie Finniston sent up three that were a shame to be seen only last week, and yet she has twelve bows sowing of victual; indeed her goodman, Duncan Finniston – that's him that's gone (we must all die, Mr Mannering, that's ower true) and, speaking of that, let us live in the meanwhile, for here's breakfast on the table, and the Dominie ready to say grace.'

The Dominie did accordingly pronounce a benediction, that exceeded in length any speech which Mannering had yet heard him utter. The tea, which of course belonged to the noble Captain Hattaraick's trade, was pronounced excellent. Still Mannering hinted, though with due delicacy, at the risk of encouraging such desperate characters: 'Was it but in justice to the revenue, I should have supposed –'

'Ah, the revenue-lads' – for Mr Bertram never embraced a general or abstract idea, and his notion of the revenue was personified in the commissioners, surveyors, comptrollers, and riding officers, whom he happened to know – 'the revenue-lads can look sharp enough out for themselves – no one needs to help them – and they have all the soldiers to assist them besides. And as to justice – you'll be surprised to hear it, Mr Mannering – but I am not a justice of peace.'

Mannering assumed the expected look of surprise, but thought within himself that the worshipful bench suffered no great deprivation from wanting the assistance of his good-humoured landlord. Mr Bertram had now hit upon one of the few subjects on which he felt sore, and went on with some energy.

'No, sir, the name of Godfrey Bertram of Ellangowan is *not* in the last commission, though there's scarce a carle in the country that has a plough-gate of land, but what he must ride to quarter sessions, and write J.P. after his name. I ken full well who I am obliged to – Sir Thomas Kittlecourt as good as told me he would sit in my skirts, if he had not my interest at the last election, and because I chose to go with my own blood and third cousin, the Laird of Balruddery, they keepit me off the roll of freeholders, and now there comes a new nomination of justices, and I am left out – And whereas they pretend it was because I let David MacGuffog, the constable, draw the warrants, and manage the business his own gate, as if I had been a nose o' wax, it's a main untruth; for I never granted but seven warrants in my life, and the Dominie wrote every ane of them – and if it had not been that unlucky business of Sandy MacGruthar's, that the constables should have keepit for two or three days up yonder at the auld castle, just till they could get conveniency to send him to the county jail – and that cost me aneugh of siller– But I ken what Sir Thomas wants very well – it was just sick and sicklike about the seat in the Kirk of Kilmagirdle – was I not entitled to have the front gallery facing the minister, rather than MacCrosskie of Creochstone, the son of Deacon MacCrosskie the Dumfries weaver?'

Mannering expressed his acquiescence in the justice of these various complaints.

'And then, Mr Mannering, there was the story about the road, and the fauld dike – I ken Sir Thomas was behind the curtain there, and I said plainly to the clerk to the trustees that I saw the cloven foot, let them take that as they like – Would any gentleman, or set of gentlemen, go and drive a road right through the corner of a fauld-dike, and take away, as my agent observed to them, like two roods of good moorland pasture? – And there was the story about chusing the collector of the cess' –

'Certainly, sir, it is hard you should meet with any neglect in a country, where, to judge from the extent of their residence, your ancestors must have made a very important figure.'

'Very true, Mr Mannering – I am a plain man, and do not dwell on these things; and I must needs say, I have little memory for them; but I wish you could have heard my father's stories about the old fights of the MacDingawaies – that's the Bertrams that now is – wi' the Irish, and wi' the Highlanders, that came here in their berlings from Ilay and Cantire – and how they went to the Holy Land – that is, to Jerusalem and Jericho, wi' a' their clan at their heels – they had better have gaen to Jamaica, like Sir Thomas Kittlecourt's uncle – and brought home reliques, like what Catholics have, and a flag that's up yonder in the garret – if they had been casks of Muscovado, and puncheons of rum, it would have been better for the estate at this day – But there's little comparison between the auld keep at Kittlecourt and the castle of Ellangowan – I doubt if the keep's forty feet of front – But ye make no breakfast, Mr Mannering; ye're no eating your meat; allow me to recommend some of the kipper – It was John Hay that catched it Saturday was three weeks down at the stream below Hempseed ford,' &c. &c. &c.

The Laird, whose indignation had for some time kept him pretty steady to one topic, now launched forth into his usual roving stile of conversation, which gave Mannering ample time to reflect upon the disadvantage attending the situation, which, an hour before, he had thought worthy of so much envy. Here was a country gentleman, whose most estimable quality seemed his perfect good nature, secretly fretting himself and murmuring against others for causes which, compared with any real evil in life, must weigh like dust in the balance. But such is the equal distribution of Providence. To those who lie out of the road of great afflictions, are assigned petty vexations, which answer all the purpose of disturbing their serenity; and every reader must have observed, that neither natural apathy nor acquired philosophy can render country gentlemen insensible to the grievances which occur at elections, quarter sessions, and meetings of trustees.

Curious to investigate the manners of the country, Mannering took the advantage of a pause in good Mr Bertram's string of stories, to enquire what Captain Hattaraick so earnestly wanted with the gypsey woman.

'O to bless his ship, I suppose – you must know, Mr Mannering, that these free-traders, whom the law calls smugglers, having no religion, make it all up in superstition, and they have as many spells, and charms, and nonsense' –

'Vanity and waur,' said the Dominie, 'it is a trafficking with the Evil One. Spells, periapts, and charms, are of his device – choice arrows out of Apollyon's quiver.'

'Hold your peace, Dominie – you're speaking for ever – (by the way it was the first words the poor man had uttered that morning, excepting that he said grace, and returned thanks) Mr Mannering cannot get in a word for you – And so, Mr Mannering, talking of astronomy, and spells, and these matters, have you been so kind as to consider what we were speaking about last night?'

'I begin to think, Mr Bertram, with your worthy friend here, that I have been rather jesting with edge-tools; and although neither you nor I, nor any sensible man, can put faith in the predictions of astrology, yet, as it has sometimes happened that enquiries into futurity undertaken in jest, have in their results produced serious and unpleasant effects both upon actions and characters, I wish you would dispense with my replying to your question.

It was easy to see that this evasive answer only rendered the Laird's curiosity more uncontrollable. Mannering was, however, determined in his own mind not to expose the infant to the inconveniences which might have arisen from his being supposed the object of evil prediction. He therefore delivered the paper into Mr Bertram's hand, and requested him to keep it for five years with the seal unbroken. When the month of November was expired, after that date had intervened, he left him at liberty to examine the writing, trusting that the first fatal period being then safely over-passed, no credit would be paid to its further contents. This Mr Bertram was content to promise, and Mannering, to ensure his fidelity, hinted at misfortunes which would certainly take place if his injunctions were neglected.

The rest of the day, which Mannering by Mr Bertram's invitation spent at Ellangowan, past over without any thing remarkable; and on the morning of that which followed, the traveller mounted his palfrey, bade a courteous adieu to his hospitable landlord, and to his clerical attendant, repeated his good wishes for the prosperity of the family, then, turning his horse's head towards England, disappeared from the sight of the inmates of Ellangowan. He must also disappear from that of our readers, for it is to another and later period of his life that the present narrative relates.

Antique Smith

from Riddle of the Ruthvens and Other Studies

WILLIAM ROUGHEAD (1870–1952)

William Roughead was an Edinburgh lawyer who early in his career developed a fascination with murder cases and the darker recesses of Scottish legal history. He edited ten volumes in the Notable British Trials *series as well as over a hundred other accounts of criminal cases collected in fourteen volumes of his work.*

In this essay he gives an account of a rather different, more harmless, kind of case. Not murder, grave-robbing, or treason on this occasion but forgery, and again, not forgery of the currency or coin of the realm but literary forgery. In the year 1892 the Edinburgh Evening Dispatch *broke the story of the discovery of a series of forged documents and literary papers. These were mainly historical, in particular from the Jacobite era, and others came allegedly from the pens of Robert Burns and Sir Walter Scott. The forger was eventually shown to be Alexander Howland Smith, a legal copying clerk, who had produced for sale over some time, spurious copies of such diverse documents as the seventeenth-century 'Solemn League and Covenant' and a song by Burns,* The Rosebud. *Smith was tried by jury and was unanimously found guilty, but 'on the grounds of the unusual character of the crime' leniency was recommended, so Smith was sentenced to imprisonment for twelve months.*

Literary forgery in Scotland may be associated with, firstly, Mary, Queen of Scots, because of the famous Casket Letters, the authorship of which was never proven satisfactorily, and with James Macpherson, translator of the Gaelic verse of Ossian, which dated, he claimed, from the third century AD. *According to others, of course, like Samuel Johnson, 'there never were any' originals of these epic poems. Smith's production of previously unknown verses by Burns may have provided some inspiration for Eric Linklater in his 1959 novel,* The Merry Muse, *which is about the discovery of a manuscript of Burns's erotic* Merry Muses of Caledonia.

✝

Some men has plenty money and no brains, and some men has plenty
brains and no money. Surely men with plenty money and no brains were
made for men with plenty brains and no money.

Aphorism of the Tichborne Claimant

There is something singularly base in the fabrication of personal written
relics of the illustrious dead. Duncan is in his grave; treason has done its
worst, nothing, says the poet, can touch him further; yet your literary
ghoul will violate upon occasion the last silence, and furnish for a pound
or two the acceptance of Lady Macbeth's invitation to spend a night at
Cawdor. For the acquirer of autographs to whom these are worth merely
their market price, the discovery that, through lack of skill or knowledge,
his wares include some sample of the forger's art, is sufficiently painful –
he suffers in a tender place; but the worshipper of heroes who buys an old
letter of a few lines in faded ink, bearing to be written by the object of his
homage, is in a harder case. The busy hand that traced, as he believes,
those characters upon the frail and perishable page has long since turned
to dust. Its works, mayhap, in noble and permanent form survive, and
that is much, but this is intimately more; here is some part of the man
himself, a peculiar possession and delight. And to foist for gain upon the
unwary enthusiast a heartless travesty of his treasure is surely the
meanest of despicable deeds. But the forger is doubtless well advised thus
to rob the living only at the expense of the dead; should he imitate the
handwriting of some butcher or baker in being, his punishment, on
detection, will be a very different one from that awarded in respect of
such fraudulent traffic in the immortal names of Burns and of Scott.
Verily, in his case, a dead lion is better (and safer) prey than a living dog.

On 22nd November 1892 the *Evening Dispatch*, an Edinburgh
newspaper, presented to its readers the first of a series of articles which
forms a notable chapter in the history of literary forgeries. In introducing
the subject it was remarked that the question then publicly raised was one
of national, even international, importance, which had long exercised a
section of the literary world, namely, the authenticity of a mass of old
MSS, chiefly Burns, Scott, and Jacobite, recently placed with amazing
prodigality upon the market. The genuineness of these documents, it was
said, had long been a subject of fierce contention among collectors, and
the time and opportunity were ripe for tracing them to their source and
determining once for all their truth or falsity.

This was the first intimation the general public received of the
existence in Edinburgh of a manufactory of spurious autographs on a
large scale, but the fact seems to have been well known to experts. Indeed,
on reading the contemporary account of the exposure of these elaborate

and extensive frauds one is struck by the circumstance that, although many dealers and collectors were aware of the wholesale forgeries and of the thriving trade long driven therein with impunity, but for the enterprise and public spirit of the *Dispatch* the career of the forger might have been indefinitely prolonged. Some of those concerned were doubtless wilfully blind; others having been, as the phrase is, 'had', preferred rather to suffer in silence than publish their losses to an unsympathetic world; and another class, who by their attitude delayed the day of reckoning, honestly believed genuine what they had paid for, and struggled against the light as an imputation either on their judgment or good faith. Scotland, too, had been singularly free from a form of crime of which the forged letters of Byron and Shelley, detected in 1852, was in England the last example, and the very effrontery of the fraud helped for a time to disarm suspicion.

It is here proposed briefly to recount the unmasking of the forger as effected by the agency of the *Dispatch*.

On 26th May 1891 there appeared in the *Scotsman* an account of the sale by auction in Edinburgh of certain letters of Burns and other documents, known as the Rillbank Crescent Manuscripts, being the collection of one Mr James Mackenzie, FSA (Scot.). Before beginning the sale the auctioneer stated that while some people said they were forgeries and he said they were not, yet his word must not be taken for it; purchasers must judge for themselves. As the result of this depressing exordium the prices realised were disappointing. Five autograph letters of Burns, including a poem, brought between one and two guineas. A song in his handwriting sold for thirty shillings, a discharge granted and signed by him, thirty-two shillings, and so forth. In the course of the subsequent controversy Mr Mackenzie stated that the MSS were perfectly genuine; 'that they were not warranted *was for a purpose*, which proved that some who pretended to be judges of such were not so', on the analogy of the new sovereigns offered for 14s 6d on London Bridge, of which purchasers were shy – in both cases, it would seem, rather too costly a way of backing one's opinion.

This sale, however, did not exhaust Mr Mackenzie's collection, for in August following there was printed in the *Cumnock Express*, an Ayrshire newspaper, an unpublished letter of Burns, the property of that gentleman, whom the editor vouched for as an industrious and intelligent collector of MSS. The letter, which was addressed 'Mr John Hill, weaver, Cumnock' – apparently an old friend of the bard – concluded with the curious expression, 'Believe me, I did not intend to go beyond anything that was unfriendly *(sic)*, and your communication has shown me that.' So effectually had Mr John Hill shuffled off this mortal coil that no trace or tradition of his ever having existed upon earth could anywhere be found, and a correspondent in the *Express* threw strong doubts upon the authenticity of the letter, which he challenged Mr Mackenzie to submit to the British Museum authorities. He further referred to the Rillbank Crescent MSS, and asked for the history of that remarkable collection. The correspondent, as afterwards appeared, was Mr Craibe Angus of Glasgow, an eminent authority on Burns. To this Mr Mackenzie replied, characterising the anonymous correspondent as a dealer whose craft was in danger, and maintaining that the John Hill letter was genuine, having been 'attested fully by those who are thoroughly competent to judge, including a respected descendant of the author'. Mr Colvill-Scott, the well-known expert, next took a hand in the game, warning the public that the number of Burns and Scott forgeries in Scotland was then considerable and urging that the letter be submitted to the British Museum; and the correspondent followed suit, offering to give a guinea to the Kilmarnock Burns Federation if the letter was pronounced genuine by those authorities. Mr Mackenzie, in answer, denied that there was a large quantity of spurious MSS upon the market – he had not seen one yet nor could he find one; the letter had been submitted to the most experienced critic known to exist, who was prepared to give his oath that Robert Burns wrote it; and for a change he proposed this time to have a song 'which may be followed by something more substantial'. The song 'To the Rosebud', commencing 'All hail to thee, thou bawmy bud', failed to convince the correspondent. He pressed for the history of its acquisition, and gave a concrete instance of a '£40 lot' of Burns MSS recently bought in Edinburgh by a bookseller, who sold it in good faith to a customer, which was afterwards discovered to be spurious and as such returned.

The critics having proved less bawmy than the belated bud, Mr Mackenzie, for their confusion, produced in the *Express* two other unpublished poems by Burns, to wit, 'The Poor Man's Prayer', and certain verses written after hearing a sermon preached in Tarbolton Church, beginning 'The Sophist spins his subtle thread', both of which he claimed were the genuine productions of our national poet, and as such would stand the strictest tests. The publication of two unknown poems by Burns attracted much attention, but, regrettably for Mr Mackenzie, 'The Poor Man's Prayer' was found, on research, to have already appeared above the name of 'Simon Hedge, Labourer', in the *London Magazine*, September 1766, at which date Robert Burns was a child of seven. After making every allowance for the earliest possible development of his genius, it was difficult to believe that the bard, however precocious, wrote in his seventh year the line 'No lawless passion swelled my even breast', while a reference to his prattling children playing round his knees seemed equally premature. Further, it appeared the Sophist had not spun his subtle thread fine enough to elude the tracing of his verses to a volume of poems by Dr Roberts, Provost of Eton College, published in London in 1774; thus, unless he stole them, Burns had no more connection with the lines – really addressed to Jacob Bryant, Esq. – than they had with Tarbolton Church. Nay, more, the pseudonymous 'Poor Man's Prayer', addressed to the Earl of Chatham, was itself included by Dr Roberts among the other poems as his own work, without acknowledgement to the infant author.

Meanwhile Mr James Stillie, a veteran Edinburgh bookseller who dealt largely in Burns MSS, and enjoyed some local celebrity as a link with Sir Walter Scott, wrote to the *Express* that he had examined the John Hill letter, as to the genuiness of which he had no doubt. This was the prophet in his own country whom Mr Mackenzie honoured above the English experts. How far his judgment justified that gentleman's confidence we shall see later.

Specialists were naturally anxious to inspect the mine from which such curious gems had been unearthed, and as Mr Mackenzie had said the manuscripts could be seen at his address, Mr Craibe Angus and Mr Colvill-Scott, accepting this informal invitation, called together for that purpose. They took with them specimens of spurious Burns MSS, borrowed by them for the occasion from two respected Edinburgh firms. These Mr Mackenzie inclined to think authentic – 'We were not so complimentary to those he showed us,' says Mr Craibe Angus. There is, regrettably, a direct conflict of evidence between the parties as to what occurred at this interview. The visitors stated that when pressed to disclose the source of his Burns MSS Mr Mackenzie said he had found them in a secret drawer of an old cabinet; his version was that the MSS thus discovered by him were not Burns MSS, but merely old medical MSS, and that he had told Messrs Angus and Scott so at the time, which those gentlemen denied. Enlightened later by the revelations of the *Dispatch*, which included the fact that a permit presented by him to Edinburgh Town Council, purporting to have been granted by Prince Charles at Holyrood in 1745, was pronounced spurious, Mr Mackenzie wrote to the press that he had dealt with the residue of his collection 'as such documents deserve to be treated'; and so ended the episode known as the Cumnock Correspondence.

The publicity given to the matter by the *Dispatch* articles brought forth many interesting and instructive facts. It appeared that a familiar old-book shop in George IV Bridge, Edinburgh, had been for some years the happy hunting-ground of an eccentric customer. His concern was mainly with ancient folios having fair and ample fly-leaves, while books bound in vellum had also for him an attraction quite irrespective of the quality of their contents. Though his purchasers were necessarily bulky it was his homely habit, after paying for them on the spot, to carry them off himself; no persuasion of the obliging shopman could induce him to have them sent to an address in the ordinary way. The unusual consideration for others thus evinced by the amiable unknown created remark.

In 1886 a gentleman called one day at the shop in Bristo Place kept by Mr Andrew Brown, a bookseller with whom he was in the way of dealing. This bookseller is to be distinguished from his eminent *confrère*, the late Mr William Brown of Princes Street. Mr Brown exhibited an album containing a number of letters and autographs, including those of Sir Walter Scott, Admiral autographs, including those of Sir Walter Scott, Admiral Cochrane (Viscount Dundonald), Thackeray, and other great men, which he said had just been offered him for sale. After a cursory glance at the treasures in which the album abounded the gentleman inquired its price, and being told £1, instantly closed the bargain, believing he had chanced upon one of those finds whereby the hopes of the collector are too rarely crowned. A man standing in the shop during this conversation, who, it appeared, was the owner of the album, then observed that he ought now to get more than the fifteen shillings he had asked for, whereupon the customer gladly paid a few further shillings, and departed with his prize. On another occasion Mr Brown showed this fortunate customer certain historical documents, which he said he had obtained from the former owner of the album; but as these papers, if genuine, were obviously of great value, the gentleman very properly inquired how that person had become possessed of them, and the explanation furnished not commending itself to his mind, he, luckily for himself, declined to purchase.

The mysteriously low-priced album disclosed upon a closer inspection many points of interest. The pencilled descriptions of the items in the collector's autograph showed a striking similarity to the handwriting of the great names represented, and it was equally remarkable that the same family likeness pervaded the writing of men of characters so diverse as Scott, Hogg, Cochrane, and John Bright. Apart from this general resemblance there were other peculiarities common to collector and collected; Thackeray, for instance, having by a strange oversight omitted from the word 'philosophical' the second 'i', that the writer of the docquet should make the same mistake was a curious coincidence. In short, one and all of the autographs were plainly spurious.

The methods of the forger in disposing of his wares ingeniously varied. Sometimes he submitted them personally or by letter to likely purchasers, sold them to booksellers of inexperienced judgment, or left them for sale with more cautious members of the tribe; sometimes he sent his goods to public auction-rooms, or when times were bad and the supply exceeded the demand, pawned them for what he could get. As he did not trouble himself to redeem his literary pledges, in due time they found their way into the sale-room. At one of these sales in 1890, a well-known Edinburgh bookseller bought in the ordinary course of business a parcel of such pledges, including Burns, Scott, and Jacobite MSS, letters of Oliver Cromwell and divers great men, together with certain books of no intrinsic value, but enriched with autograph inscriptions by Scott, Carlyle, and other authors. After the sale the various lots were carefully examined by their new owner, who was forced to the painful conclusion that he had indeed purchased, as the phrase is, a pig in a poke, with the results proverbially attending that transaction. Many of the lots were docqueted as having been bought at the Whitefoord Mackenzie sale, with the prices there paid for them. Now the sale at Chapman's Rooms in 1886 of the library of the late Mr John Whitefoord Mackenzie, WS, was a very different affair from that of the Rillbank Crescent Manuscripts. The library was one of the finest and most valuable ever offered by public sale in Scotland; the sale lasted twenty-eight days, and the catalogue – a portly volume containing 8935 lots, many of great rarity and price – became a handbook for collectors. It need not surprise us to learn that on reference to this authority the bookseller found in every case the docquets impudently lied; no such items had been included in that sale. But certain of the documents and books indubitably bore the familiar Whitefoord Mackenzie bookplate. This was explained by the fact that in so large a library were many volumes of minor value which sold for a few shillings; these contained the bookplate, which the forger removed and affixed to his own works, to give, in the phrase of the distinguished Japanese official, Pooh-Bah, artistic verisimilitude to a bald and unconvincing narrative of their acquisition.

Some of the spurious documents had attached to them cuttings from catalogues descriptive of their pretended character and value. One of these corroborative details, affixed to a proclamation by the Earl of Mar issued during the Rising of 1715, by a curious chance led to more light being thrown upon the dark business in question. The cutting was recognised as from the catalogue of a sale at Chapman's Rooms in 1887 (of which we shall hear again), and the auctioneer, on inquiry referring to his books, found that the item had been purchased for £3, 10s by Mr James Stillie, the veteran voucher for the John Hill letter. The *Dispatch* promptly challenged Mr Stillie to state whether he still held the document, or, if not, to whom he sold it, as they believed and averred that the MS was not, though purporting to be, the one bought by him in 1887. That gentleman, however, declined to be drawn; doubtless he was much occupied at the time by a matter of more importance. Mr John Stewart Kennedy, the wealthy American banker whose name is remembered in connection with the *Murthly Estate* case, had purchased from the patriarch for £750 a quantity of alleged Burns and important historical MSS for presentation to the Lenox Library, New York. Their authenticity had never been impugned, but the recent revelations caused a very natural anxiety on the point. Accordingly, the collection was sent by Mr Kennedy to this country for examination by the British Museum experts, who, having inspected upwards of two hundred documents of which it consisted, reported that only one was genuine, all the rest being manifest forgeries. It was interesting to find from the historical MSS that Mary, Queen of Scots, Rob Roy, and Claverhouse all used the same make of paper.

This was not the first occasion on which Mr Stillie had the misfortune to differ in judgment from the London authorities regarding the genuineness of the manuscripts in which he dealt, and he had issued a leaflet headed 'Manuscripts – English Experts', denouncing those gentlemen in unmeasured terms. Upwards of three hundred original MSS of Burns alone, he said, had in the course of business passed through his hands – for his customers' sake it is to be hoped that these included a larger proportion of genuine documents than those which he sold to Mr Kennedy. In the case of a sale by him to Mr W. W. Caddell of Manchester in 1889 of certain Burns and Scott letters, these were, on later scrutiny by experts of repute, pronounced to be palpable forgeries; yet Mr Stillie refused to refund the money, on the ground that having known Sir Walter Scott for upwards of fifty years he was a better judge of his handwriting than any professional expert. Mr Caddell, in the course of the correspondence which ensued, remarked that to have enjoyed the friendship of Scott for so long a period the veteran must have known him since he was ten or eleven years old, and must himself be at that time upwards of 107. This is the longest link with Sir Walter of which we have any record. No legal steps were taken by Mr Caddell to enforce repayment; Mr Kennedy, however went further. He raised in the Court of Session an action against Mr Stillie for recovery of the price paid by him for the Burns and other MSS. The defender denied that he had represented the documents to be genuine, and also denied that they were forgeries. Mr Kennedy, yielding to repeated appeals addressed to him by Mr Stillie on the ground of his advanced years and the state of his health, and considering his protestations of entire good faith and strict honesty in the transaction, authorised his law agents to drop the action, which was accordingly done.

The publication by the *Dispatch* of facsimiles of some of the MSS pawned by the forger furnished an important clue. A reader recognised the writing of the false docquets as bearing a striking resemblance to that of a clerk named Smith whom he casually employed, and specimens of this person's penmanship supplied to and published in the *Dispatch* left little doubt that the same hand was responsible for both. Alexander Howland Smith, the man in question, who lodged at 87 Brunswick Street, Edinburgh, was, it appeared, thirty-one years of age. His ostensible occupation was that of a copying clerk, in which capacity he was occasionally engaged in various law offices in the city. He was described as of dull appearance, but plausible and insinuating address, and as possessing an intimate acquaintance with the lives and works of Burns and Scott. Among his friends he was known as 'Antique' Smith, from the fact that he had constantly about him old documents or other curiosities for sale. In the course of an interview with a *Dispatch* reporter Smith frankly explained how he acquired his literary and historic treasures. He was at one time clerk in the office of the late Thomas Henry Ferrier, WS, whose father had been agent for several great families. In such a business a large quantity of old papers had accumulated, and, according to Smith, Mr Ferrier told him to clear these out and destroy them. Instead of doing so, however, Smith took the papers home, and discovering among them many documents of value, he from time to time converted these into cash. He was content to dispose of his documents to certain booksellers at prices ranging from one to fifteen shillings on the spot, rather than wait for the larger return to be obtained by dealing personally with collectors. Finding a ready market for genuine MSS Smith, when the original store became exhausted, replenished his stock by providing counterfeits. He claimed that on due notice he could supply any kind of ancient MS; the demand was constant, but he was able easily to meet it. Such was his own account of the transactions. The scene of his literary labours was a little summer-house connected with some model gardens situated behind Hope Crescent in Leith Walk. 'He is said to dread prosecution for his part in the traffic,' wrote the *Dispatch*; 'though he doubts if positive proof that he manufactured MSS can be adduced.' These doubts the subsequent trial and conviction must have gone far to remove. Whether or not Smith ever had in his possession any genuine MSS at all is uncertain; probably on this, as on other points, he lied. In view of the circumstances in which he left Mr Ferrier's employment in 1883 – he was charged with stealing two cheques from the office – that gentleman would doubtless think Smith had already taken documents enough.

On 5th December, within a fortnight of the *Dispatch*'s 'First Blaste' against the scandalous prevalence of forgery, the authorities – not those alien ones of the British Museum, contemned by Messrs Stillie and Mackenzie, but the local experts of the Criminal Investigation Department – at last intervened in the controversy by arresting Smith on a magistrate's warrant, and next morning that ingenious gentleman was in the Police Court formally remitted upon the charge of uttering forged documents as genuine.

The columns of the *Dispatch* continued open to the discussion of how far the collecting public had been duped, and many interesting sidelights were thrown upon the methods of the forger and the extent of his practice, of which considerations of space here forbid an account. The *Athenaeum*, in an article dealing with the mischievous and widespread effects of the fraud, observed: 'Spurious documents including letters of Queen Mary, Claverhouse, Jacobite chiefs, Walter Scott, and Thackeray, inedited poems by Burns, etc., have been for the last five years scattered broadcast over Scotland and England, the United States, and the Colonies. The *Dispatch* will probably reprint in some separate form the whole story, together with numerous facsimiles of the documents and of Smith's handwriting. It will form a useful *vade mecum* for the amateur collector of literary curiosities.' Unfortunately this was not done, and the only separate account of the matter, so far as known to the present writer, is the chapter entitled 'Wholesale Forgeries Perpetrated in Edinburgh', contained in Dr Scott's valuable work, *Autograph Collecting* (London, 1894). The treatment of the subject there is necessarily brief, and the ashes of the controversy still remain buried in the files of the *Dispatch*. It is satisfactory to note that Dr Scott, who personally examined many of the forged MSS remarks, 'There is no evidence whatever to show that a person of common sense possessing the most elementary knowledge of autographs need have been deceived, or anything that should cause the average collector to be at all nervous about his treasures.' The author gives some useful hints respecting the characteristics of genuine autographs of Burns and Scott as contrasted with those of the laboured and clumsy imitations.

Although the *Dispatch* had picturesquely described the spurious MSS as executed with a skill compared with which the forgeries of Chatterton and Ireland were but infants' efforts, it is plain that the view expressed of the forger's executive ability is much too favourable. He displayed upon occasion a kind of cynical carelessness. One of the Burns letters, for instance, had been sealed, and attached to the wax was a piece of paper, apparently torn from the sheet when the letter was opened; on examination, however, this was found too large to fit the place from which it should have been torn, and was, moreover, of quite a different texture. By a curious coincidence numbers of letters written by all sorts of distinguished people from 1757 to 1858 began and ended with the same form of words. A copy of the Solemn League and Covenant on parchment, bearing to be two hundred years old, was pronounced by Dr Joseph Anderson, secretary to the Society of Antiquaries of Scotland, obviously to have been 'written yesterday'. The Kennedy and other historical MSS were by persons learned in Scottish history proved on internal evidence false, by reason of the gross and ignorant blunders, chronological and factual, in which they abounded: and this apart altogether from technical questions of age, handwriting, etc., with regard to which it was also found by scientific tests that documents ranging from 1644 to 1793 were written in similar ink and with a steel pen!

On 14th December the prisoner, having emitted a declaration, was committed for trial, and on the 16th a petition was presented on his behalf to the High Court of Justiciary, craving the Court to restrain the *Dispatch* from publishing further articles on the subject until after the trial. Mr Dewar, advocate, in support of the application, stated that since 22nd November a series of articles had been published by the *Dispatch*, entitled 'Great Forgeries of Old MSS', in which Smith was named as the forger; his methods and appearance were described, and his address and photograph given, together with representations of his handwriting as compared with the writing of the forged MSS. Notwithstanding his apprehension and committal the *Dispatch* still continued to publish articles similar in their nature and tendency, and calculated to prejudice the prisoner in his defence. On 9th December an article appeared, headed 'The MSS Forgeries', and similar articles had been published every evening since that date. The continued publication of these was highly injurious to the accused, and he asked the Court to prohibit the *Dispatch* from circulating any further statements relative to the alleged forgeries until the prisoner should be tried. The Court ordered the petition to be intimated to the respondents – the editor, the publishers, and the proprietors of the *Dispatch* – and ordained them to appear by counsel at the Bar next day.

Accordingly, on 17th December, Mr F. T. Cooper, advocate, appeared for the respondents, the prisoner being represented by Mr Dewar. Mr

Cooper objected to the form of the application as incompetent, and disputed the right of the Court to interfere with the publication of anything that a newspaper chose to publish, so long as it did not amount to contempt. It would be contempt if the *Dispatch* criticised the evidence against the petitioner and insinuated that he was guilty, but since the date of his arrest they had been careful to omit his name from all discussion of the MSS frauds. Mr Dewar contended that in this matter the Court had jurisdiction, and found on the case of *Edmond* (7th December 1829, Shaw's *Justiciary Reports*, p. 229). Such articles as 'The Forger and His Prey', published on 9th December, and 'The Investigations of a Chemical Expert', on the 16th, though not referring to Smith by name, must, if read by persons who should sit upon the jury, unfairly prejudice his case. The Lord Justice-Clerk (Macdonald), in giving judgement, observed that the application was plainly competent. Apart from the clear precedent in the case of *Edmond*, his Lordship had no doubt that so soon as a person was placed by a magistrate in the hands of the authorities to be tried for an offence, he was under the protection of the court, and was entitled to ask the Court to secure him against anything which might prejudice the public mind and prevent him having a fair trial. After referring to the very important service rendered by the recent discussion in the *Dispatch*, his Lordship said that once a person was charged and committed for trial with reference to matters which a newspaper had brought to light, all that ought to be effected by the work of a public journal was at an end; the investigation was then in responsible official hands. His Lordship therefore proposed to pronounce such an order as would prevent any further comments which might be prejudicial to the prisoner. Lords Trayner and Kincairney concurred, and the Court pronounced an interlocutor prohibiting the respondents from publishing or circulating statements relative to MSS or signatures alleged to have been forged by the petitioner, until the proceedings against him had been brought to a conclusion.

On Monday, 26th June 1893, Alexander Howland Smith was placed at the Bar of the High Court of Justiciary, charged with selling and pawning spurious MSS as genuine. The Lord Justice-Clerk presided, Messrs R. U. Strachan and J. A. Reid, Advocates-Depute, conducted the prosecution, and the prisoner was represented by Messrs Dewar and Grainger Stewart, advocates. The trial is reported in the first volume of Adam's *Justiciary Reports*. The indictment bore that the panel had formed a fraudulent scheme of obtaining money from others by fabricating manuscripts of apparent historic or literary interest, and disposing of these as genuine to parties who might purchase the same or take them in pledge. There were four separate charges against the panel, namely – (1) on various occasions between 1st January and 31st August 1892, pretending to Andrew Brown, bookseller, 15 Bristo Place, Edinburgh, that fifty-three manuscripts were genuine and that he had obtained the same from the office of the late Thomas Henry Ferrier, WS, and thus inducing Brown to purchase them at various prices to the prosecutor unknown, he (Smith) knowing the documents to be false and fabricated by himself, and appropriating the proceeds to his own use; (2) on certain dates between 18th August 1888 and 31st May 1889, pretending to George Tait, manager of the Equitable Loan Company of Scotland, Milne Square, Edinburgh, that thirty-two manuscripts were genuine, and that they had been bequeathed to him by his uncle, Mr Ferrier, and thus inducing Tait to take the same in pledge and advance £24, 9s on security thereof; (3) on certain dates in August 1889, pretending to James Williamson & Sons, pawnbrokers, 98 Rose Street, Edinburgh, that ten manuscripts were genuine, and thus inducing him to advance £6 on security thereof; and (4) on certain dates in September, 1889, obtaining by similar means from James Mullan, pawnbroker, 35 South Bridge Edinburgh, 15s on security of three manuscripts. Annexed to the indictment was a list of 170 productions, chiefly MSS, and a list of forty-seven witnesses cited for the Crown. Among the productions were four volumes of *The Autographic Mirror* – a useful text-book for students of forgery – and an extensive collection of ink-bottles, penholders, and other literary requisites, from the prisoner's rural retreat behind Leith Walk.

When the diet was called counsel for, the prisoner stated the following objections to the relevancy of the indictment: – Failure to specify the amount received under the first charge; in the pawnbroking charges, no allegation that the security was inadequate; it should have been stated that the accused had no intention of repaying the loan, and, in all the charges, that the value of the documents was not equivalent to the sum obtained, and that loss had been sustained by those who gave money for them. Mr Strachan, for the Crown, replied that false representation to induce payment of money was the crime charged. The genuineness of the documents was essential to the transaction, and there was a distinct averment that they were spurious and had been represented as genuine. His Lordship repelled the objections, the prisoner pleaded Not Guilty, a jury was empannelled, and the prosecutor adduced his proof.

The first witness was Andrew Brown. He stated that he became acquainted with the prisoner in 1886, when Smith brought him the album of autographs already mentioned. Some months later he bought from Smith certain Mar and Argyll documents, upon the representation that these had come from Mr Ferrier's office. To verify the statement he called upon Mr Ferrier, who said there were a lot of such things in his office which were of no legal value, and that he did not know where Smith had ferreted out the other autographs, but he (Ferrier) might find it difficult to identify them and would leave them alone. After Mr Ferrier's death witness continued to buy documents from Smith, as he found a ready sale for them. He sold to Mr Buchanan in 1887 twenty-two of the documents produced, nine to Mr Moir Bryce in 1887 or 1888, seven to Mr Mackenzie in 1890, and others to various customers. He showed to purchasers a letter from Smith, dated 8th April 1887, giving an account of how he came by the documents. He kept no record of his transactions with Smith, which lasted from 1886 to 1892. In November 1887, having heard many stories about the authenticity of the MSS, he sent some of these to Chapman's Rooms for public sale, where the Duke of Argyll's agent claimed certain documents as the property of His Grace – which, by the way, were afterwards found to be forged and were accordingly destroyed. The prices obtained at the sale ran from ten to fifteen shillings. In cross-examination, Mr Brown said he believed the panel's statement as to the acquisition of the MSS, but he sold them without a guarantee. He declined to say what was his present opinion about the documents. If he had made a profit on them, his business as a whole had suffered by the transactions. The following letter was read to witness, who admitted that he might have written it to Smith: –

> 26th November, 1890. – If you could bring up anything more on the Covenanters or the Covenant; you spoke of a large thing you had; also items I am specially wanting – the following as on other side, if you have them. You might please call tonight (Friday) at, say, quarter past seven.
>
> Sanquhar Declaration and Testimony, 22nd June 1680.
>   Do.   Do.   28th May 1685.
> Hamilton Declaration, June 1679.
> Also the large parchment things you spoke of.
> Also any important man.
> Also Graham of Claverhouse.
> And any other variety. If you drop a postcard I would get it, for fear I might be out.

Mr Brown's faith in the richness of the Ferrier *trouvaille* was apparently as inexhaustible as that treasure itself.

The next witness, Mr Buchanan, spoke to his purchase from Mr Brown of some of the documents libelled. He paid £50 for them. 'When did you discover they were bad?' asked the prisoner's counsel. 'About five minutes after I bought them,' was the reply. Mr Moir Bryce and Mr Mackenzie gave similar evidence; they had paid Mr Brown £70 and £50 respectively for MSS bought from him. Mr George Tait described the pawning of the MSS by the prisoner. At the time he believed the documents genuine, but had his suspicions that Smith himself was spurious. These however, were allayed on production by the latter of Mr Ferrier's will, bequeathed to him as his nephew the whole of his valuable MSS. It seems superfluous to add that the will was forged. The documents pawned were sold as unredeemed pledges on 3rd April 1890. Mr George Thin deponed that he purchased certain lots at the sale for £12. He afterwards found these to be forgeries and handed them later to the Procurator-Fiscal. After further evidence as to the other pawnbroking charges, Mr Chapman, auctioneer, stated that none of the documents libelled had been included in the Whitefoord Mackenzie sale in 1886, while Mr Dowell gave similar evidence regarding the Gibson Craig sale in 1887, some of the MSS purporting to have been bought at those sales.

Several other witnesses having been examined, one of whom stated that Mr Stillie was too old and feeble to come to Court, Mr G. F. Warner, assistant-keeper of MSS in the British Museum, deponed that at the request of the Procurator-Fiscal he had inspected the documents produced in the case. His conclusion was that the whole were spurious, and that they were all written by the same hand. They were of four classes: – Burns, Scott, miscellaneous letters, and historical papers. The Burns MSS were written upon paper such as Robert Burns never used. In some cases it had plainly been torn out of old books, in others, artificially tinted to give the appearance of age. All the signatures had been formed on one model. As to the Scott letters, these were folded in a different manner from that employed by Sir Walter, the paper was not such as he used, and the handwriting continually lapsed into that which appeared on the docquets. The handwriting of the miscellaneous letters was totally unlike that of the supposed writers. With regard to the historical documents, in some instances the dates were impossible, in all the imitation of the handwriting was bad, the signatures defective, and the paper of a different character from that used for official purposes. It being then seven o'clock the Court at this stage rose.

Next day, Tuesday, 27th June, on the resumption of the sitting, Mr G. S. Inglis, expert in handwriting, was examined, who concurred in the evidence given by Mr Warner. The handwriting of the docquets was, he said, unmistakably that of Smith. This closed the Crown case. For the defence, Miss Agnes Smith, sister to the prisoner, stated that in 1884 her brother showed her in Mr Ferrier's office a room, the floor of which was covered with documents and papers. She remembered him bringing a lot of papers home to their house in Albany Street. When they removed in the preceding September she burned a basketful of these, as she was destroying all the rubbish in the house. It is a pity that the lady's reforming zeal was satisfied with the sacrifice of a single basketful. J. H. Dobbie, gunner, Royal Artillery, said that he had lived with the prisoner for eighteen months, beginning in 1889. During that time he never saw Smith preparing spurious documents.

The evidence for the defence concluded, Mr Strachan addressed the jury for the prosecution. With reference to the first charge, the question was, he said, whether the documents delivered by the accused to Mr Brown were received by him on the strength of Smith's representation that they were genuine. He expressed surprise at the line taken by the defence, namely, that Mr Brown himself knew that they were not genuine, of which there was no evidence. At an early stage of the transactions some doubts certainly were cast upon the authenticity of the MSS, and in order to test that Mr Brown offered some of them to public sale at Chapman's, where they fetched good prices. There was, no doubt, a difference of opinion as to their being genuine, but Mr Brown honestly believed in them and continued to do business with the accused on that footing till the very end. The defence insinuated that the letter from Mr Brown, put in by the prisoner, was an order as from a merchant to a manufacturer, but its terms were explained by Mr Brown's belief in the existence of a large collection of documents in Smith's hands. Mr Brown paid throughout substantial prices for what he bought. With respect to the pawnbroking charges, the fraud was committed the moment Smith pledged the MSS, whether the pawnbrokers lost by advancing money on them or not. That all the documents produced were spurious and fabricated by the accused admitted of no doubt. The evidence of Mr Warner, one of the greatest authorities, was on that point conclusive. He therefore asked for a verdict of guilty upon all the charges.

Mr Dewar then addressed the jury for the defence. The Crown, he said, sought to prove that the accused had swindled four men. One, Brown, had been driven to admit that he had been a substantial gainer; the other three had in the box admitted that they made money out of Smith. The essence of the crime charged was that someone had been deceived and by that deception was induced to part with money. Did the jury believe that Brown was the injured innocent he pretended? If Mr Buchanan, an amateur, speedily detected forgery, why was it not equally apparent to Brown, who was in the trade? He was a very unsuspicious man when cross-examined, but not quite so simple when making a bargain – he stuck to the £50. After narrating the connection of Mr Brown with the series of documents, counsel observed, 'That is the man who says, "I was a simple dupe for seven years"! He ordered these manuscripts from Smith as he would order a pair of trousers or a sack of coals; the jury, however, would not make Smith the scapegoat. The pawnbroking charges were in an entirely different position, the witnesses being all perfectly reputable and honest men, who told the truth. Williamson took the documents on Stillie's representation that they were genuine, and Mullan took them as a speculation. If they afterwards became the innocent medium of deceiving the public, Smith was not charged with that, but with deceiving the pawnbrokers. In conclusion, counsel threw doubts upon the expert testimony, skilled witnesses as to handwriting being, he said, notoriously unreliable. Finally, he argued that no crime had been committed and no injury done to anybody, upon both of which grounds the accused was entitled to a verdict.

The Lord Justice-Clerk, in charging the jury, remarked upon the novel features of the case. With regard to its legal aspect, his Lordship said that if the prisoner fabricated these documents for the purpose of selling them as of literary and historic interest to persons who bought them on his representation, that undoubtedly was a crime in the law of Scotland. The question was whether or not the documents were spurious. Counsel for the prisoner first argued that Brown knew that they were forgeries, and then contended that they were genuine; he could not have it both ways. As for the expert testimony, that evidence went much further than mere similarity of writing; apart altogether from comparison of handwriting there was the question of the paper used and the character of the contents. After reviewing the evidence upon these points, his Lordship observed that it was for the jury to say if even a plausible case had been made out that the prisoner got the documents from Mr Ferrier's office. In respect to the first charge, if the prisoner's case was that Brown knew the documents were spurious, the prisoner himself must also have known. If the jury were satisfied that these two were concerned together in a fraudulent scheme, then, of course, the first charge must fall; but that would be a very strong step to take. It was more than judging of Brown's credibility if they found that he was a party to a criminal scheme. Even if they held that Brown, having at first believed the story, came to know later that he was buying fictitious documents, they could convict the prisoner under that charge. As to the pawnbroking charges, if Mr Tait advanced money to the prisoner, relying upon the fictitious will of Mr Ferrier, and if Williamson and Mullan respectively did so on false representations made to them by him regarding the documents, that was sufficient to entitle the jury to convict. Whether or not anyone had suffered loss by the prisoner's guilt, if proved, might be considered in awarding his punishment, but had no bearing upon the question which they had to determine. The crime was a very serious and uncommon one; if their deliberations led to a conviction his Lordship would consider any recommendation as to punishment which, as common-sense citizens, they might see fit to make.

The jury then retired, and after an interval of half an hour brought in a unanimous verdict of guilty on all the charges, but by a majority they recommended the prisoner to the leniency of the Court, on the grounds of the unusual character of the crime and the facility afforded him for disposing of spurious documents. The Lord Justice-Clerk said that in view of that recommendation he would abstain from pronouncing sentence of penal servitude; and the prisoner, having been sentenced to imprisonment for twelve calendar months, was removed, and the Court rose.

This, professionally, was the end of 'Antique' Smith; but the evil that men do lives after them – of the truth of which saying the present case is a primary example. The forged manuscripts recovered and produced by the Crown were but the gleanings of the nefarious field in which for over seven years Smith had so discreditably laboured, and there is reason to fear that, as some at least of his literary tares must still survive among the genuine grain, unwary amateurs may yet be tempted to give their money for that which is not bread. The contemporary autograph collector – that badly-burnt child – after the revelations of the trial naturally fought somewhat shy of Burns. But a new generation has arisen which knew not Joseph and his Edinburgh brethren; for such this narrative of the forgotten facts may, like the moral pocket handkerchiefs described by Mr Stiggins, be found to combine amusement with instruction.

Desperate Characters in Council

from John Macnab

JOHN BUCHAN (1875–1946)

The three participants in this elaborate 'thriller as game' are of course not 'desperate' at all. Nor are they representatives of the sorts of anarchic forces who generally provide the villains in Buchan's 'shockers', as he called the novels like The Thirty-Nine Steps *and* Greenmantle. *They are all firmly establishment figures in the usual Buchan mould – Lord Lamancha is a member of the Cabinet (need one enquire which party?) and a great landowner, Sir Edward Leithen is a 'great lawyer' and (plain, untitled) John Palliser-Yeates is an 'eminent banker'! Their host at the shooting lodge is another respectable figure, Sir Archie Roylance, flying ace and general good egg. He and Leithen make appearances in other Buchan novels.*

Prior to the events described in the following extract, the three aforementioned who collectively make up the fictitious gentlemanly poacher, 'John Macnab', have issued their challenge to three different neighbouring landowners:

> *Sir, I have the honour to inform you that I propose to kill a stag – or a salmon as the case may be – on your ground between midnight on – and midnight on – The animal, of course, remains your property and will be duly delivered to you . . .*

Sir Archie is the Conservative candidate for the Highland constituency where this drama is played out. And drama it is, because in John Macnab *Buchan has created a marvellously balanced tale, carefully constructed almost like a board game or fantasy computer game. Each of the participants is allocated certain advantages and handicaps and each plays the game in a different environment or landscape. The separate stories fit together beautifully and by the end the reader has learned a great deal about the Highlands and about the class structure of Britain in the Twenties.*

Poaching in stories has always been a bit of a joke, as other extracts will illustrate. But there were occasions when it was far from funny. Punitive game laws in some parts of Scotland once meant loss of lives or livelihood. The Highlander may have felt that 'a branch from the wood, a trout from the pool, a deer from the forest were three thefts of which Highlanders are never ashamed', but infringement of the laird's rights to hunt and kill his own beasts was not always viewed so indulgently.

So what we have in the novel are the descendants of the hunting aristocracy. They have their own code and rules. The book is ostensibly about poaching, but in the end they are not really poachers, at least not criminal poachers. When Wattie the stalker suggests that he might 'sniggle a salmon in one of the deep pots' (i.e. not on rod and line), Leithen replies, 'No, we must play the game by the rules. We're not poachers.' And here is Buchan on one of the landowners targeted by John Macnab –

> Colonel Raden could be emphatic enough on the rights of property, but no Highlander can ever grow excited about trespass. 'The fellow has made a sporting offer and is willing to risk a pretty handsome stake . . . I might have done the same thing as a young man, if I had had the wits to think of it.'

In the way that the respective landowners reply to the challenge, we see how close they approach to the author's ideal of gentlemanliness. And yet one of the best speeches in a very good book comes from the same Wattie, when Lord Lamancha has shot his beast. Wattie is moved to pronounce Trestag's epitaph:

> It's yoursel, ye auld hero, and ye've come by a grand end. Ye've had a braw life traivellin' the hills, and ye've been a braw beast, and the fame of ye gaed through a' the countryside; Ye micht have dwined awa' in the cauld winter and dee'd in the wame o' a snawdrift. Or ye micht have been massacred by ane o' thae Haripol sumphs wi' ten bullets in the big bag But ye've been killed clean and straucht by John Macnab, and that is a gentleman's death whatever.

Crask – which is properly Craoisg, and is so spelled by the Ordnance Survey – when the traveller approaches it from the Larrig Bridge has the air of a West Highland terrier, *couchant* and *regardant*. You are to picture a long tilt of moorland running east and west, not a smooth lawn of heather, but seamed with gullies and patched with bogs and thickets and crowned at the summit with a low line of rocks above which may be seen peeping the spikes of the distant Haripol hills. About three-quarters of the way up the slope stands the little house, whitewashed, slated, grey stone framing the narrow windows, with that attractive jumble of masonry which belongs to an adapted farm. It is approached by a road which scorns detours and runs straight from the glen highway, and it looks south over broken moorland to the shining links of the Larrig, and beyond them to the tributary vale of the Raden and the dark mountains of its source. Such is the view from the house itself, but from the garden behind there is an ampler vista, since to the left a glimpse may be had of the policies of Strathlarrig and even of a corner of that monstrous mansion, and to the right of the tidal waters of the river and the yellow sands on which in the stillest weather the Atlantic frets. Crask is at once a sanctuary and a watch-tower; it commands a wide countryside and yet preserves its secrecy, for, though officially approached by a road like a ruler, there are a dozen sheltered ways of reaching it by the dips and crannies of the hillside.

So thought a man who about five o'clock on the afternoon of the 24th of August was inconspicuously drawing towards it by way of a peat road which ran from the east through a wood of birches. Sir Edward Leithen's air was not more cheerful than when we met him a month ago, except that there was now a certain vigour in it which came from ill-temper. He had been for a long walk in the rain, and the scent of wet bracken and birches and bog myrtle, the peaty fragrance of the hills salted with the tang of the sea, had failed to comfort, though, not so long ago, it had had the power to intoxicate. Scrambling in the dell of a burn, he had observed both varieties of the filmy fern and what he knew to be a very rare cerast, and, though an ardent botanist, he had observed them unmoved. Soon the rain had passed, the west wind blew aside the cloud-wrack, and the Haripol tops had come out black against a turquoise sky, with Sgurr Dearg, awful and remote, towering above all. Though a keen mountaineer, the spectacle had neither exhilarated nor tantalised him. He was in a bad temper, and he knew that at Crask he should find three other men in the same case, for even the debonair Sir Archie was in the dumps with a toothache.

He told himself that he had come on a fool's errand, and the extra absurdity was that he could not quite see how he had been induced to come. He had consistently refused: so had Palliser-Yeates; Archie as a prospective host had been halting and nervous; there was even a time when Lamancha, the source of all the mischief, had seemed to waver. Nevertheless, some occult force – false shame probably – had shepherded them all here, unwilling, unconvinced, cold-footed, destined to a preposterous adventure for which not one of them had the slightest zest . . . Yet they had taken immense pains to arrange the thing, just as if they were all exulting in the prospect. His own clerk was to attend to the forwarding of their letters, including any which might be addressed to 'John Macnab'. The newspapers had contained paragraphs announcing that the Countess of Lamancha had gone to Aix for a month, where she would presently be joined by her husband, who intended to spend a week drinking the waters before proceeding to his grouse-moor of Leriot on the Borders. The *Times*, three days ago, had recorded Sir Edward Leithen

and Mr John Palliser-Yeates as among those who had left Euston for
Edinburgh, and more than one social paragrapher had mentioned that the
ex-Attorney-General would be spending his holiday fishing on the Tay,
while the eminent banker was to be the guest of the Chancellor of the
Exchequer at an informal vacation conference on the nation's precarious
finances. Lamancha had been fetched under cover of night by Archie from
a station so remote that no one but a lunatic would think of using it.
Palliser-Yeates had tramped for two days across the hills from the south,
and Leithen himself, having been instructed to bring a Ford car, had had a
miserable drive of a hundred and fifty miles in the rain, during which he
had repeatedly lost his way. He had carried out his injunctions as to secrecy
by arriving at two in the morning by means of this very peat road. The
troops had achieved their silent concentration, and the silly business must
now begin. Leithen groaned, and anathematized the memory of Jim Tarras.

As he approached the house he saw, to his amazement, a large closed
car making its way down the slope. Putting his glass on it, he watched it
reach the glen road and then turn east, passing the gates of Strathlarrig, till
he lost it behind a shoulder of hill. Hurrying across the stable-yard, he
entered the house by the back-door, disturbing Lithgow the keeper in the
midst of a whispered confabulation with Lamancha's man, whose name
was Shapp. Passing through the gun-room he found, in the big smoking-
room which looked over the valley, Lamancha and Palliser-Yeates with
the crouch of conspirators flattening their noses on the window-panes.

The sight of him diverted the attention of the two from the landscape.

'This is an infernal plant,' Palliser-Yeates exclaimed. 'Archie swore to
us that no one ever came here, and the second day a confounded great car
arrives. Charles and I had just time to nip in here and lock the door, while
Archie parleyed with them. He's been uncommon quick about it. The
brutes didn't stay for more than five minutes.'

'Who were they?' Leithen asked.

'Only got a side glance at them. They seemed to be a stout woman and
a girl – oh, and a yelping little dog. I expect Archie kicked him, for he was
giving tongue from the drawing room.'

The door opened to admit their host, who bore in one hand a large
whisky-and-soda. He dropped wearily into a chair, where he sipped the
beverage. An observer might have noted that what could be seen of his
wholesome face was much inflamed, and that a bandage round chin and
cheeks which ended in a top-knot above his scalp gave him the
appearance of Riquet with the Tuft in the fairy tale.

'That's all right,' he said, in the tone of a man who has done a good
piece of work. 'I've choked off visitors at Crask for a bit, for the old lady

will put it all round the countryside.'

'Put what?' said Leithen, and 'Who is the old lady?' asked Lamancha, and 'Did you kick the dog?' demanded Palliser-Yeates.

Archie looked drearily at his friends. 'It was Lady Claybody and a daughter – I think the second one – and their horrid little dog. They won't come back in a hurry – nobody will come back – I'm marked down as a pariah. Hang it, I may as well chuck my candidature. I've scuppered my prospects for the sake of you three asses.'

'What has the blessed martyr been and done?' asked Palliser-Yeates.

'I've put a barrage round this place, that's all. I was very civil to the Claybodys, though I felt a pretty fair guy with my head in a sling. I bustled about, talking nonsense and offerin' tea, and then, as luck would have it. I trod on the hound. That's the worst of my game leg. The brute nearly had me over, and it started howlin' – you must have heard it. That dog's a bit weak in the head, for it can't help barkin' just out of pure cussedness – Lady Claybody says it's high-strung because of its fine breedin'. It got something to bark for this time, and the old woman had it in her arms fondlin' it and lookin' very old-fashioned at me. It seems the beast's name is Roguie, and she called it her darlin' Wee Roguie, for she's pickin' up a bit of Scots since she came to live in these parts . . . Lucky Mackenzie wasn't at home. He'd have eaten it . . . Well, after that things settled down, and I was just going to order tea, when it occurred to the daughter to ask what was wrong with my face. Then I had an inspiration.'

Archie paused and smiled sourly.

'I said I didn't know, but I feared I might be sickenin' for smallpox. I hinted that my face was a horrid sight under the bandage.'

'Good for you, Archie,' said Lamancha. 'what happened then?'

'They bolted – fairly ran for it. They did record time into their car – scarcely stopped to say good-bye. I suppose you realise what I've done, you fellows. The natives here are scared to death of infectious diseases, and if we hadn't our own people we wouldn't have a servant left in the house. The story will be all over the countryside in two days, and my only fear is that it may bring some medical officer of health nosin' round . . . Anyhow, it will choke off visitors.'

'Archie, you're a brick,' was Lamancha's tribute.

'I'm very much afraid I'm a fool, but thank Heaven I'm not the only one. Sime,' he shouted in a voice of thunder, 'what's happened to tea?'

The shout brought the one-armed butler and Shapp with the apparatus of the meal, and an immense heap of letters all addressed to Sir Archibald Roylance.

'Hullo! The mail has arrived,' cried the master of the house. 'Now let's see what's the news of John Macnab?'

He hunted furiously among the correspondence, tearing open envelopes and distributing letters to the others with the rapidity of a conjurer. One little sealed packet he reserved to the last, and drew from it three missives bearing the same superscription.

These he opened, glanced at, and handed to Lamancha. 'Read 'em out, Charles,' he said. 'It's the answers at last.'

Lamancha read slowly the first document, of which this is the text:

Glenraden Castle,
Strathlarrig,
Aug.— 19—.

'Sir,

'I have received your insolent letter. I do not know what kind of rascal you may be, except that you have the morals of a bandit and the assurance of a halfpenny journalist. But since you seem in your perverted way to be a sportsman, I am not the man to refuse your challenge. My reply is, sir, damn your eyes and have a try. I defy you to kill a stag in my forest between midnight on the 28th of August and midnight of the 30th. I will give instructions to my men to guard my marches, and if you should be roughly handled by them you have only to blame yourself.

Yours faithfully,
Alastair Raden'
'John Macnab, Esq.'

'That's a good fellow,' said Archie with conviction. 'Just the sort of letter I'd write myself. He takes things in the proper spirit. But it's a blue look-out for your chances, my lads. What old Raden doesn't know about deer isn't knowledge.'

Lamancha read the second reply:

Strathlarrig House,
Strathlarrig,
Aug.—, 19—.

'My dear Sir,

Your letter was somewhat of a surprise, but as I am not yet familiar with the customs of this country, I forbear to enlarge on this point, and since you have marked it 'Confidential' I am unable to take advice. You state that you intend to kill a salmon in the Strathlarrig water between midnight on September 1 and midnight on September 3, this salmon, if killed, to remain my property. I have consulted such books as might give me guidance, and I am bound to state that in my view the laws of Scotland are hostile to your suggested enterprise. Nevertheless, I do not take my stand on the law, for I presume that your proposition is conceived in a sporting spirit, and that you dare me to stop you. Well, sir, I will see you on that hand. The fishing is not that good at present that I am inclined to quarrel about one salmon. I give you leave to use every method that may occur to you to capture that fish, and I promise to use every method that may occur to me to prevent you. In your letter you undertake to use only "legitimate means". I would have pleasure in meeting you in the same spirit, but I reckon that all means are counted legitimate in the capture of poachers.

Cordially,
Junius Theodore Bandicott'
'Mr J. Macnab.'

'That's the young 'un,' Archie observed. 'The old man was christened "Acheson", and don't take any interest in fishin'. He spends his time in lookin' for Norse remains.'

'He seems a decent sort of fellow,' said Palliser-Yeates, 'but I don't quite like the last sentence. He'll probably try shooting, same as his countrymen once did on the Beauly. Whoever gets this job will have some excitement for his money.'

Lamancha read out the last letter:

227 North Melville Street,
Edinburgh,
Aug.—, 19—.

'Sir,

Re: *Haripol Forest*

Our client, the Right Honourable Lord Claybody, has read to us on the telephone your letter of Aug.—, and has desired us to reply to it. We are instructed to say that our client is at a loss to understand how to take your communication, whether as a piece of impertinence or as a serious threat. If it is the latter, and you persist in your intention, we are instructed to apply to the Court for a summary interdict to prevent your entering upon his lands. We would also point out that, under the Criminal Law of Scotland, any person whatsoever who commits a trespass in the daytime by entering upon any land without leave of the proprietor, in pursuit of, *inter alia*, deer, is liable to a fine of £2, while, if such person have his face blackened, or if five or more persons acting in concert commit the trespass, the penalty is £5 (2 & 3 William IV, c. 68).

We are, sir,
Your obedient servants,
Prosser, McKelpie, and Maclymont
'John Macnab, Esq'

Lamancha laughed. 'Is that good law, Ned?'

Leithen read the leter again. 'I suppose so. Deer being *ferae naturae*, there is no private property in them or common law crime in killing them, and the only remedy is to prevent trespass in pursuit of them or to punish the trespasser.'

'It seems to me that you get off pretty lightly,' said Archie. 'Two quid is not much in the way of a fine, for I don't suppose you want to black your faces or march five deep into Haripol . . . But what a rotten sportsman old Claybody is!'

Palliser-Yeates heaved a sigh of apparent relief. 'I am bound to say the replies are better than I expected. It will be a devil of a business, though, to circumvent that old Highland chief, and that young American sounds formidable. Only, if we're caught out here, we're dealing with sportsmen and can appeal to their higher nature, you know. Claybody is probably the easiest proposition so far as getting a stag is concerned, but if we're nobbled by him we needn't look for mercy. Still, it's only a couple of pounds.'

'You're an ass, John,' said Leithen. 'It's only a couple of pounds for John Macnab. But if these infernal Edinburgh lawyers get on to the job, it will be a case of producing the person of John Macnab, and then we're all in the cart. Don't you realise that in this fool's game we simply cannot afford to lose – none of us?'

'That,' said Lamancha, 'is beyond doubt the truth, and it's just there that the fun comes in.'

The reception of the three letters had brightened the atmosphere. Each man had now something to think about, and, till it was time to dress for dinner, each was busy with sheets of the Ordnance maps. The rain had begun again, the curtains were drawn, and round a good fire of peats they read and smoked and dozed. Then they had hot baths, and it was a comparatively cheerful and very hungry party that assembled in the dining-room. Archie proposed champagne, but the offer was unanimously declined. 'We ought to be in training,' Lamancha warned him. 'Keep the Widow for the occasions when we need comforting. They'll come all right.'

Palliser-Yeates was enthusiastic about the food. 'I must say, you do us very well,' he told his host. 'These haddocks are the best things I've ever eaten. How do you manage to get fresh sea-fish here?'

Archie appealed to Sime. 'They come from Inverlarrig, Sir Erchibald,' said the butler. 'There's a wee laddie comes up here sellin' haddies verra near every day.'

'Bless my soul, Sime. I thought no one came up here. You know my orders.'

'This is just a tinker laddie, Sir Erchibald. He sleeps in a cairt down about Larrigmore. He just comes wi' his powny and awa' back, and doesna bide twae minutes. Mistress Lithgow was anxious for haddies, for she said gentlemen got awfu' tired of saumon and trout.'

'All right, Sime. I'll speak to Mrs Lithgow. She'd better tell him we don't want any more. By the way, we ought to see Lithgow after dinner. Tell him to come to the smoking-room.'

When Sime had put the port on the table and withdrawn, Leithen lifted up his voice.

'Look here, before we get too deep into this thing, let's make sure that we know. We've all three turned up here – why, I don't know. But there's still time to go back. We realise now what we're in for. Are you clear in your minds that you want to go on?'

'I am,' said Lamancha doggedly. 'I'm out for a cure. Hang it, I feel a better man already.'

'I suppose your profession makes you take risks,' said Leithen dryly. 'Mine doesn't. What about you, John?'

Palliser-Yeates shifted uneasily in his chair. 'I don't want to go on. I feel no kind of keenness, and my feet are rather cold. And yet – you know – I should feel rather ashamed to turn back.'

Archie uplifted his turbanned head. 'That's how I feel, though I'm not on myself in this piece. We've given hostages, and the credit of John Macnab is at stake. We've dared old Raden and young Bandicott, and we can't decently cry off. Besides, I'm advertised as a smallpox patient, and it would be a pity to make a goat of myself for nothing. Mind you, I stand to lose as much as anybody, if we bungle things.'

Leithen had the air of bowing to the inevitable. 'Very well, that's settled. But I wish to Heaven I saw myself safely out of it. My only inducement to go on is to score off that bounder Claybody. He and his attorney's letter put my hackles up.'

In the smoking-room Lamancha busied himself with preparing three slips of paper and writing on them three names.

'We must hold a council of war,' he said. 'First of all, we have taken measures to keep our presence here secret. My man Shapp is all right. What about your people, Archie?'

'Sime and Carfrae have been warned, and you may count on them. They're the class of lads that ask no questions. So are the Lithgows. We've no neighbours, and they're anyway not the gossiping kind, and I've put them on their Bible oath. I fancy they think the reason is politics. They're a trifle scared of you, Charles, and your reputation, for they're not accustomed to hidin' Cabinet Ministers in the scullery. Lithgow's a fine crusted old Tory.'

'Good. Well, we'd better draw for beats, and get Lithgow in.'

The figure that presently appeared before them was a small man, about fifty years of age, with a great breadth of shoulder and a massive face decorated with a wispish tawny beard. His mouth had the gravity and primness of an elder of the Kirk, but his shrewd blue eyes were not grave. The son of a Tweeddale shepherd who had emigrated years before to a cheviot farm in Sutherland, he was in every line and feature the Lowlander, and his speech had still the broad intonation of the Borders. But all his life had been spent in the Highlands on this and that deer forest, and as a young stalker he had been picked out by Jim Tarras for his superior hill-craft. To Archie his chief recommendation was that he was a passionate naturalist, who was as eager to stalk a rare bird with a field-glass as to lead a rifle up to deer. Other traits will appear in the course of this narrative; but it may be noted here that he was a voracious reader and in the long winter nights had amassed a store of varied knowledge, which was patently improving his master's mind. Archie was accustomed to quote him for most of his views on matters other than ornithology and war.

'Do you mind going over to that corner and shuffling these slips? Now, John, you draw first.'

Mr Palliser-Yeates extracted a slip from Lithgow's massive hand.

'Glenraden,' he cried. 'Whew! I'm for it this time.'

Leithen drew next. His slip read Strathlarrig.

'Thank God, I've got old Claybody,' said Lamancha. 'Unless you want him very badly, Ned?'

Leithen shook his head. 'I'm content. It would be a bad start to change the draw.'

'Sit down, Wattie,' said Archie. 'Here's a dram for you. We've summoned you to a consultation. I daresay you've been wonderin' what all this fuss about secrecy has meant. I'm going to tell you. You were with Mr Tarras, and you've often told me about his poachin'. Well, these three gentlemen want to have a try at the same game. They're tired of ordinary sport, and want something more excitin'. It wouldn't do, of course, for them to appear under their real names, so they've invented a *nom de guerre* – that's a bogus name, you know. They call themselves collectively, as you might say, John Macnab. John Macnab writes from London to three proprietors, same as Mr Tarras used to do, and proposes to take a deer or a salmon on their property within certain dates. There's a copy of the letter, and here are the replies that arrived tonight. Just you read 'em.'

Lithgow, without moving a muscle of his face, took the documents. He

nodded approvingly over the original letter. He smiled broadly at
Colonel Raden's epistle, puzzled a little at Mr Bandicott's, and wrinkled
his brows over that of the Edinburgh solicitors. Then he stared into the
fire, and emitted short grunts which might have equally well been
chuckles or groans.

'Well, what do you think of the chances?' asked Archie at length.

'Would the gentlemen be good shots?' asked Lithgow.

'Mr Palliser-Yeates, who has drawn Glenraden, is a very good shot,'
Archie replied, 'and he has stalked on nearly every forest in Scotland.
Lord Lamancha – Charles, you're pretty good, aren't you?'

'Fair,' was the answer. 'Good on my day.'

'And Sir Edward Leithen is a considerable artist on the river. Now,
Wattie, you understand that they want to win – want to get the stags and
the salmon – but it's absolute sheer naked necessity that, whether they fail
or succeed, they mustn't be caught. John Macnab must remain John
Macnab, an unknown blighter from London. You know who Lord
Lamancha is, but perhaps you don't know that Sir Edward Leithen is a
great lawyer, and Mr Palliser-Yeates is one of the biggest bankers in the
country.'

'I ken all about the gentlemen,' said Lithgow gravely. 'I was readin' Mr
Yeates's letter in the *Times* about the debt we was owin' America, and I
mind fine Sir Edward's speeches in Parliament about the Irish
Constitution. I didna altogether agree with him.'

'Good for you, Wattie. You see, then, how desperately important it is
that the thing shouldn't get out. Mr Tarras didn't much care if he was
caught, but if John Macnab is uncovered there will be a high and holy
row. Now you grasp the problem, and you've got to pull up your socks
and think it out. I don't want your views tonight, but I should like to have
your notion of the chances in a general way. What's the bettin'? Twenty to
one against?'

'Mair like a thousand,' said Lithgow grimly. 'It will be verra verra
deeficult. It will want a deal o' thinkin'.' Then he added, 'Mr Tarras was
an awfu' grand shot. He would kill a runnin' beast at fower hundred
yards – aye, he could make certain of it.'

'Good Lord, I'm not in that class,' Palliser-Yeates exclaimed.

'Aye, and he was more than a grand shot. He could creep up to a
sleepin' beast in the dark and pit a knife in its throat. The sauvages in
Africa had learned him that. There was plenty o' times when him and me
were out that it wasna possible to use the rifle.'

'We can't compete there,' said Lamancha dolefully.

'But I wad not say it was impossible,' Lithgow added more briskly. 'It will want a deal o' thinkin'. It might be done on Haripol – I wadna say but it might be done, but yon auld man at Glenraden will be ill to get the better of. And the Strathlarrig water is an easy water to watch. Ye'll be for only takin' shootable beasts, like Mr Tarras, and ye'll not be wantin' to cleek a fish? It might be not so hard to get a wee staggie, or to sniggle a salmon in one of the deep pots.'

'No, we must play the game by the rules. We're not poachers.'

'Then it will be verra, verra deeficult.'

'You understand,' put in Lamancha, 'that, though we count on your help, you yourself mustn't be suspected. It's as important for you as for us to avoid suspicion, for if they got you it would implicate your master, and that mustn't happen on any account.'

'I ken that. It will be verra, verra deeficult. I said the odds were a thousand to one but I think ten thousand wad be liker the thing.'

'Well, go and sleep on it, and we'll see you in the morning. And tell your wife I don't want any boys comin' up to the house with fish. She must send elsewhere and buy 'em. Goodnight, Wattie.'

When Lithgow had withdrawn the four men sat silent and meditative in their chairs. One would I rise now and then and knock out his pipe, but scarcely a word was spoken. It is to be presumed that the thoughts of each were on the task in hand, but Leithen's must have wandered. 'By the way, Archie,' he said, 'I saw a very pretty girl on the road this afternoon, riding a yellow pony. Who could she be?'

'Lord knows!' said Archie. 'Probably one of the Raden girls. I haven't seen 'em yet.'

When the clock struck eleven Sir Archie arose and ordered his guests to bed.

'I think my toothache is gone,' he said, switching off his turban and revealing a ruffled head and scarlet cheek. Then he muttered: 'A thousand to one! Ten thousand to one! It can't be done, you know. We've got to find some way of shortenin' the odds!'

Para Handy – Poacher

from The Complete Para Handy

NEIL MUNRO (1863–1930)

It was in 1905, when he was writing the profile of the river Clyde, River & Firth, *that Neil Munro first delighted readers of his* Looker-On *column in the* Glasgow Evening News, *with the adventures of Para Handy and the crew of the steam lighter or puffer,* Vital Spark, *'the smertest boat in the coastin' tred'. Munro continued to record the adventures of Para Handy in the* News *for close on twenty years. The stories have never been out of print and their West Coast setting, charm, humour and wry social comment have continued to attract readers from every generation.*

Both in newspaper and book form, Munro's creation has become one of the enduring comic characters. The stories have been successfully translated into the television medium, have been adapted for the stage and were the inspiration for the 1954 film The Maggie. *Recently, some eighteen stories never before published in book form were rescued from the files of the* Evening News *(at the same time as a large number of Munro's two series of Glasgow tales about Erchie Macpherson and about Jimmy Swan) and published by Birlinn.*

The story chosen for this anthology, however, comes from Munro's first collection, The Vital Spark *(under the pseudonym 'Hugh Foulis'). It deals with the well-worn subject of poaching and the game laws, about which many Scots and certainly Highlanders like Para Handy and Dougie the mate held views at best indulgent and at worst ambivalent. Ranged against them are the vigilant defenders of property in shape of the river watchers, gamekeepers and the polis, but really, for those who know the redoubtable pair, there can be only one result.*

Like very many of the stories, this is set in Para's (and Munro's) beloved Loch Fyne. No specific parish or port is mentioned, perhaps because of the slightly risqué involvement of 'Fast Days' with Para's alibi. A Fast Day was a day kept as a local holiday in the week preceding the celebration of Holy Communion. At that time Communion services in the Highlands were held at very infrequent intervals – typically twice a year.

✝

The *Vital Spark* was lying at Greenock with a cargo of scrap-iron, on the top of which was stowed loosely an extraordinary variety of domestic furniture, from bird cages to cottage pianos. Para Handy had just had the hatches off when I came to the quayside, and he was contemplating the contents of his hold with no very pleasant aspect.

'Rather a mixed cargo!' I ventured to say.

'Muxed's no' the word for't,' he said bitterly. 'It puts me in mind of an explosion. It's a flittin' from Dunoon. There would be no flittin's in the *Fital Spark* if she wass my boat. But I'm only the captain, och aye! I'm only the captain, thirty-five shullin's a week and liberty to put on a pea-jecket. To be puttin' scrap-iron and flittin's in a fine smert boat like this iss carryin' coals aboot in a coach and twice. It would make any man use Abyssinian language.'

'Abyssinian language?' I repeated, wondering.

'Chust that, Abyssinian language – swearing, and the like of that, you ken fine, yoursel', withoot me tellin' you. Fancy putting' a flittin' in the *Fital Spark*! You would think think she wass a coal-laary, and her with two new coats of pent out of my own pocket since the New Year.'

'Have you been fishing?' I asked, desirous to change the subject, which was, plainly, a sore one with the Captain. And I indicated a small fishing-net which was lying in the bows.

'Chust the least wee bit touch,' he said, with a very profound wink. 'I have a bit of a net there no' the size of a pocket-naipkin, that I use noo and then at the river-mooths. I chust put it doon – me and Dougie – and whiles a salmon or a sea-trout meets wi' an accident and gets into't. Chust a small bit of a net, no' worth speakin' aboot, no' mich bigger nor a pocket-naipkin. They'll be calling it a splash-net, you ken yoursel' withoot me tellin' you.' And he winked knowingly again.

'Ah, Captain!' I said, 'that's bad! Poaching with a splash-net! I didn't think you would have done it.'

'It's no' me; it's Dougie,' he retorted promptly. 'A fair duvvle for high jeenks, you canna keep him from it. I told him many a time that it wasna right, because we might be found oot and get the jyle for't, but he says they do it on aal the smertest yats. Yes, that iss what he said to me – 'They do it on aal the first-cless yats; you'll be bragging the *Fital Spark* iss chust ass good ass any yat, and what for would you grudge a splash-net?" '

'Still it's theft, Captain,' I insisted. 'And it's very, very bad for the rivers.'

'Chust that!' he said complacently. 'You'll likely be wan of them fellows that goes to the hotels for the fushing in the rivers. There's more sport aboot a splash-net; if Dougie wass here he would tell you.'

'I don't see where the sport comes in,' I remarked, and he laughed contemptuously.

'Sport!' he exclaimed. 'The best going. There wass wan time yonder we were up Loch Fyne on a Fast Day, and no' a shop open in the place to buy onything for the next mornin's breakfast. Dougie says to me "What do you think yoursel' aboot takin' the punt and the small bit of net no' worth mentionin', and going doon to the river mooth when it's dark and seeing if we'll no' get a fush?"

' "It's a peety to be poaching on the Fast Day," I said to him.

' "But it's no' the Fast Day in oor parish" he said. "We'll chust give trial, and if there's no fush at the start we'll come away back again." Oh! a considerate fellow, Dougie; he saw my poseetion at wance, and that I wasna awfu' keen to be fushin' wi" a splash-net on the Fast Day. The end and the short of it wass that when it wass dark we took the net and the punt and rowed doon to the river and began to splash. We had got a fine haul at wance of six great big salmon, and every salmon Dougie would be takin' oot of the net he would be feeling it all over in a droll way, till I said to him, "What are you feel-feelin' for, Dougie, the same ass if they had pockets on them? I'm sure they're all right."

' "Oh, yes," he says, 'right enough, but I wass frightened they might be the laird's salmon, and I wass lookin' for the luggage label on them. There's none. It's all right; they're chust wild salmon that nobody planted."

'Weel, we had got chust ass many salmon ass we had any need for when somebody birled a whustle, and the river watchers put off in a small boat from a point outside of us to catch us. There wass no gettin' oot of the river mooth, so we left the boat and the net and the fush and ran ashore, and by-and-by we got up to the quay and on board the *Fital Spark*, and paaused and consudered things.

' "They'll ken it's oor boat," said Dougie, and his clothes wass up to the eyes in salmon scales.

' "There's no doo't aboot that," I says. 'If it wassna the Fast Day I wouldna be so vexed; it'll be an awful disgrace to be found oot workin' a splash-net on the Fast Day. And it's a peety aboot the boat, it wass a good boat, I wish we could get her back."

' "Ay, it's a peety we lost her," said Dougie; "I wonder in the wide world who could have stole her when we were doon the fo'c'sle at oor supper?" Oh, a smert fellow, Dougie, when he said that I saw at wance what he meant.

' "I'll go up this meenute and report it to the polis office," I said quite firm, and Dougie said he would go with me too, but that we would need to change oor clothes, for they were covered with fush-scales. We changed oor clothes and went up to the sercheant of polis, and reported that somebody had stolen oor boat.

He wass sittin' readin' his Bible, it bein' the Fast Day, wi' specs on, and he keeked up at us, and said, "You are very spruce, boys, with your good clothes on at this time of the night."

' "We aalways put on oor good clothes on the *Fital Spark* on a Fast Day," I says to him; "it's as little as we can do, though we don't belong to the parish."

'Next day there wass a great commotion in the place aboot some blackguards doon at the river mooth poachin' with a splash-net. The Factor wass busy, and the heid gamekeeper wass busy, and the polis wass busy. We could see them from the dake of the *Fital Spark* goin' aboot buzzin' like bum-bees.

' "Stop you!" said Dougie to me aal of a sudden. "They'll be doon here in a chiffy, and findin' us with them scales on oor clothes – we'll have to put on the Sunday wans again."

' "But they'll smell something if they see us in oor Sunday clothes," I said. "It's no' the Fast Day the day."

' "Maybe no' here," said Dougie, "but what's to hinder it bein' the Fast Day in oor own parish?"

'We put on oor Sunday clothes again and looked the Almanac to see if there wass any word in it of a Fast Day any place that day, but there wass nothing in the Almanac but tides, and the Battle of Waterloo, and the weather for next winter. That's the worst of Almanacs; there's nothing in them you want. We were fair bate for a Fast Day any place, when The Tar came up and asked me if he could get to the funeral of a cousin of his in the place at two o'clock.

' "A funeral!" said Dougie. "The very thing. The Captain and me'll go to the funeral too. That's the way we have on oor Sunday clothes." Oh, a smert, smert fellow, Dougie!

'We had chust made up oor mind it wass the funeral we were dressed for, and no' a Fast Day any place, when the polisman and the heid gamekeeper came doon very suspeecious, and said they had oor boat. "And what's more," said the gamekeeper, "there's a splash-net and five stone of salmon in it. It hass been used, your boat, for poaching."

' "Iss that a fact?" I says. "I hope you'll find the blackguards," and the gamekeeper gave a grunt, and said somebody would suffer for it, and went away busier than ever. But the polis sercheant stopped behind. "You're still in your Sunday clothes, boys," said he; "what iss the occasion today?'

' "We're going to the funeral," I said.

' "Chust that! I did not know you were intimate with the diseased," said the sercheant.

' "Neither we were," I said, "but we are going oot of respect for Colin." And we went to the funeral, and nobody suspected nothin', but we never got back the boat, for the gamekeeper wass chust needin' wan for a brother o' his own. Och, ay! there's wonderful sport in a splash-net.'

Poaching 'In Excelsis'

G. K. MENZIES (1869–1954)

This little poem is a nice summing up of the indulgent and humorous view of poaching which was prevalent in Scotland until very recently. Concealment of the poached animal and then getting it off the scene or 'off the hill' isn't all that easy for anyone engaged in the 'play' that is poaching – so something as big as a rhinoceros, the poacher imagines, would present unimaginable problems. It would be even bigger than a 'royal' stag – that is one with a full spread of antlers of twelve points. The stolen 'paitricks' or partridges can be concealed about the person, and the 'licht o' mune an' star' will not be too bright, but the 'rhinocerious' is a different matter altogether.

Apart from the fact that big-game poaching in Africa nowadays hardly qualifies as humorous, it is probably true that the technology of large-scale slaughter has taken the edge off the jokes in Scotland as well.

✝

('Two men were fined £120 apiece for poaching a white rhinoceros.' –
South African Press)

I've poached a pickle paitricks when the leaves were turnin' sere,
I've poached a twa-three hares an' grouse, an' mebbe whiles a deer,
But ou, it seems an unco thing, an' jist a wee mysterious,
Hoo any mortal could contrive tae poach a rhinocerious.

I've crackit wi' the keeper, pockets packed wi' pheasants' eggs,
An' a ten-pun' saumon hangin' doun in baith my trouser legs,
But eh, I doot effects wud be a wee thing deleterious
Gin ye shuld stow intil yer breeks a brace o' rhinocerious.

I mind hoo me an' Wullie shot a Royal in Braemar,
An' brocht him doun tae Athol by the licht o' mune an' star.
An' eh, Sirs! but the canny beast contrived tae fash an' weary us –
Yet staigs maun be but bairn's play beside a rhinocerious.

I thocht I kent o' poachin' jist as muckle's ither men,
But there is still a twa-three things I doot I dinna ken;
An' noo I cannot rest, my brain is growin' that deleerious
Tae win awa' tae Africa an' poach a rhinocerious.

6
DETECTION
Introduction

✝

Policemen, detectives and private investigators are as old as crime, which is to say that they are as old as time. Formal police forces and private investigative agencies are however a great deal younger, and the literary genre of the detective story is younger still.

The classic detective story is generally considered to have its origins in the 1840s with Edgar Allan Poe and his brilliant investigator Dupin, as recounted in tales such as *The Murders in the Rue Morgue*. Wilkie Collins, in *The Moonstone* (1868), and his Sergeant Cuff, is another key influence. However the genre really came into its own with the Sherlock Holmes stories of Arthur Conan Doyle.

Doyle, Edinburgh-born and educated, having enjoyed a not terribly successful medical career, turned to fiction and in 1887 published his first Holmes novel *A Study in Scarlet*. Another three novels and five collections of short stories published between then and 1927 made Sherlock Holmes and his indispensable associate Dr John Watson among the most familiar fictional characters of all times. The Doyle stories, and the Doyle characters, have been translated into countless films, television and radio adaptations. The minutiae of life at 221B Baker Street and the recorded and unrecorded events of the lives of Holmes and Watson have inspired a vast secondary literature and form the staple diet of a huge body of devoted Sherlockians across the world. We include as our homage to this great Scottish literary creation a very typical story, and one which has clear roots in Doyle's Edinburgh medical training: *The Adventure of the Greek Interpreter* from the 1893 collection *The Memoirs of Sherlock Holmes*.

Doyle involved himself in a number of real-life problems of investigation and criminal justice – one which he took up was the Oscar Slater case. Slater had been convicted of murder in Glasgow in 1909 but strenuously protested his innocence. Doyle took up the cause and eventually Slater was freed and compensated for his nineteen years in prison. A sidelight on this case comes in a piece of journalism by Neil Munro. Taken from his weekly *Looker-On* column in the *Glasgow*

Evening News it discusses three Glasgow detectives known to Munro – the third of these was Lieutenant Trench who investigated the Slater case, became convinced of his innocence and released police documents to Slater's lawyers – an action that resulted in his dismissal from the Glasgow police force.

Neil Munro, in more familiar surroundings, the villages and mountains of his native Argyll, furnishes our oldest detective – oldest in terms of setting, that is. In the troubled Scotland between the 1715 and 1745 Jacobite Risings there was little organised policing and still less in the wild and unruly Highlands. Munro's character, Ninian Macgregor Campbell, is an undercover agent, a private eye, a spy, a detective, a special investigator working for the Duke of Argyll – he is known in Gaelic as the 'beachdair' and goes, if not down the Chandlerian 'mean streets', at least down some mean glens. Ninian amply fulfils Raymond Chandler's famous prescription for the private eye:

> Down these mean streets a man must go who is not himself mean, who is neither tarnished nor afraid.

The 'beachdair' features in Munro's finest historical novel *The New Road*.

Scotland produced one of the most famous of the private detective forces in the world. The Pinkerton Detective Agency was formed in 1850 by Allan Pinkerton, the son of a Glasgow police sergeant. The young Pinkerton, after training as a cooper, emigrated to the United States in 1842 and settled in Chicago where he swiftly rose to become Deputy Sheriff of Cook County. In 1850 he resigned from the official police force to set up the Pinkerton Agency which specialised in theft cases on the rapidity expanding US rail network. During the Civil War he worked for the military intelligence service of the Union against the Confederacy. In later years the Pinkerton Agency became associated with the struggle between employers and organised labour and the Pinkerton agents became notorious for their strike-breaking activities. One of the most notorious of these incidents happened, after Allan Pinkerton's death, at the Homestead Steel Mills in Pennsylvania – mills owned by another Scots emigrant to the United States, Andrew Carnegie. The Pinkerton Agency was also responsible for breaking up 'The Wild Bunch', the notorious outlaw gang headed by Butch Cassidy and the Sundance Kid. One of the pioneers of hard-boiled American detective fiction – Dashiel Hammett – spent eight years as a Pinkerton agent.

Patriotic Scots frequently remind their southern neighbours that the Bank of England was founded by a Scotsman; they less often remind them that the first uniformed police force in the world, London's Marine

Police Establishment, owes its creation to a Scot. Dr Patrick Colquhoun (1745–1820) was born in Dumbarton, became a Virginia merchant, was the Lord Provost of Glasgow from 1782–84, founded the city's Chamber of Commerce in 1783 and then moved to London, where he became a Stipendiary Magistrate in 1792, wrote his *Treatise on the Policing of the Metropolis* and set up the marine police force in 1798.

Detective fiction has always featured the activities of the non-official sleuth, whether the scientific investigator like Holmes, the hard-boiled private eye of the Philip Marlowe or Sam Spade type, or the inspired thinker like Hercules Poirot and his 'little grey cells'. The gentleman amateur is exemplified by Dorothy L. Sayers and Peter Death Bredon Wimsey: Lord Peter Wimsey, the younger son of the Duke of Denver. Fortunately for the Scottish crime anthologist, Lord Peter was in the habit of spending holidays in Galloway and on one occasion his vacation coincided with an interesting murder – we include an extract from *Five Red Herrings*, the account of this incident.

The official detective, more realistically, carries the bulk of the work of literary detection and we conclude with two very different examples of the genre. The first, by Josephine Tey, herself a Scot, is about Alan Grant, a detective of Scottish origins (even if his Scottishness does not seem particularly marked). Grant is an Inspector at Scotland Yard, the headquarters of London's Metropolitan Police. The London Police Force was formed in 1829 and its first public office faced onto Great Scotland Yard. Scotland Yard is traditionally said to owe its name to a piece of land where the Scottish Kings had a London residence – there is, however, no evidence for any such building. Another version attributes the name to a former owner of the site – a man named Adam Scot. Our Josephine Tey extract is from *The Daughter of Time* in which Inspector Grant investigates a historical mystery.

Our final detective is entirely Scottish built – John Rebus, the Edinburgh Detective Inspector created by Ian Rankin. Rebus's adventures in Edinburgh have been recorded in a very successful series of novels and a collection of short stories, and it is from the short story collection *A Good Hanging* that we take *Concrete Evidence*. The name *A Good Hanging* is explained in the title story as a quotation from Shakespeare's *Twelfth Night*: 'Many a good hanging prevents a bad marriage.' The phrase also has a very Scottish resonance, reminding us of that pithy phrase used by the eighteenth-century Scottish judge, Lord Braxfield, who we will meet in our section 'Judgement'. Braxfield told one offender brought before him:

Ye're a verra clever chiel, man but ye'd be nane the waur o'a hanging.

'The Beachdair'

from The New Road

NEIL MUNRO (1863–1930)

Guardians of the law come in many guises, few perhaps less conventional than Ninian Macgregor Campbell, one of the two central characters in Neil Munro's greatest historical novel The New Road *(1914). Ninian, 'a Campbell only for expedience', was by birth a member of the broken and proscribed Clan Gregor – the children of the mist. This ambiguous background fitted him for his role as 'beachdair' – scout, spy or observer for John Campbell, the second Duke of Argyll, 'Red John of the Battles', and his brother Lord Islay. Ninian is formally described as a messenger at arms but his real role is as an undercover agent of MacCailein Mor, the Duke of Argyll, and he is a key player in the Duke's strategy of keeping the lawless Highlands under control.*

The action of The New Road *takes place around 1733 against the background of continuing Jacobite unrest and the construction of the military roads, designed by General Wade, which give the book its name and its theme. Young Æneas MacMaster travels north, ostensibly on business for his uncle, an Inveraray merchant, but really hoping to find the truth about his father Paul's death in the 1719 Jacobite rising which ended at the Battle of Glenshiel. The 'beachdair' goes north to find the source of Jacobite unrest and investigate traffic in arms, and to consult with the other pillar of Government in the Highlands, the Lord Advocate, Duncan Forbes of Culloden.*

Æneas has just been suddenly dismissed as tutor to Margaret, the daughter of Sandy Duncanson and William Campbell, Duncanson's ward, the natural son of Lord Islay. Duncanson, in some mysterious way took over the estate of Drimdorran when Æneas' father vanished after Glenshiel.

The pairing of Æneas and Ninian may remind many of Robert Louis Stevenson's David Balfour and Alan Breck Stewart in Kidnapped *– but Æneas and Ninian are two Highlanders united as agents of change and order against the old Highlands of feudal power and brute force. The roads that Wade was building across the Highlands to facilitate military movement would also bring trade to the Highlands and open them up to new ideas – Ninian remarks:*

> *. . . that Road is goin' to be a rut that, once it is hammered deep enough, will be the poor Gael's grave.*

Later on Æneas says to Ninian's daughter Janet that the Road:

> ... means the end of many things, I doubt, not all to be despised – the last stand of Scotland, and she destroyed

while his merchant uncle, Alan-Iain-Alain Og says:

> Once the New Road is finished, and the troopers and the guns and my carts on it, it's an end to the dominion o' the chiefs.

This preoccupation with the process of change in the Highlands informs all Munro's historical novels, though perhaps never so well worked out as in this tale of undercover adventure and detection in the Highlands. Munro was evidently pleased with his wily Highland detective because Ninian Macgregor Campbell reappears in Munro's uncompleted and unpublished novel The Search, *set in the aftermath of the 1745 Rising.*

A CALL TO THE NORTH

The morning bell was ringing when he reached the town. Salt airs from sea were blowing through the lanes. Men at the harbour, dragging ropes, cried cheerfully. Oh, the bold, cold, hard, beautiful world! He felt like one that had come out from fever-rooms among the hearty bustle of the quay to which he went immediately to seek his uncle, who was there already at the loading of the *Good Intent* with timber baulks for Skye.

In half a dozen sentences he told his story, only keeping back Miss Margaret's prank with the forbidden keys, the meeting in the dovecote, and the shameful charge against himself to which her subterfuge had made him liable. Now that it was daylight, which brings caution and cools down the ardours of the night, he saw quite clearly that the girl was much to blame, deserving of no shelter, but he would be the very last to punish her. Rather would he stay silent, suffering Duncanson's suspicions if they went no further. The situation as presented to his uncle, too, was just in keeping with that gentleman's predictions.

'I told ye!' he declared when Æneas reported that the tutoring was ended, and that Drimdorran had some fancy that the pupil and her tutor had, between them, planned the missing of the evening lesson, 'I saw it coming! That girl a while ago was daft about ye; any one could see it in the kirk on Sundays! I would be much surprised if old Drimdorran didna notice. And that doesna fall in wi' his plans at all; he's set on having her for Campbell.'

'He's welcome so far as I am concerned,' said Æneas.

'Are ye sure, man?' said his uncle. 'Till last night I thought different. I didna tell your aunt nor say to you that Will's being on the quay at the hour he should be at his tasks looked gey and curious. For he was asking about you. He said he had been sent by Margaret to meet ye here, and that I couldna fathom, seeing you were gone as usual to Drimdorran House.'

'That was some caprice of Margaret's,' said Æneas. 'She herself had shirked the lesson.'

'Ye werena with her somewhere?' said the uncle drily, and Æneas looked blank to have the very keystone of his secret tapped so soon. He did not answer.

'Man!' cried his uncle, comprehending, as he fancied, 'ye have put your foot in it wi' Sandy! I knew if ye gave him the slightest reason to think ye were trifling wi' his girl and spoiling sport with Campbell, he would squeal. The man is fairly cankered wi' ambeetion; all his body's hoved wi' vanity since he became a laird and stepped into the property that should be yours. It's six-and-twenty years since he came here, no better than a packman, to be clerk to old Macgibbon. He played cuckoo wi' poor Macgibbon, and secured the factorship wi' Islay. Then he trafficked with your father, managing for him when he was off upon his silly escapades among the Jacobites, much against my will, and God be wi' him! No one better knew than old Drimdorran what your father was conniving at in France, and in the North wi' Glendaruel, and the damned old rogue, I'll swear, encouraged him, well knowing what the end would be. He leased Drimdorran from your father who could never stay at home after your mother died and got him in his debt for loans, the size of which gave me the horrors when I saw the bills. What your father did with all that money God Almighty knows! Unless, like Glendaruel, he scattered it among the disaffected clans. I couldna pay them off, whatever o't, when your father died; I wasna then in the position. When your father's name was plastered at the cross a rebel at the horn and outlawed – him a corp up yonder in Kintail – I went and saw the man that he had supped and drank wi', played the cartes and fished and worked at pigeons wi', and he was rowtin' like a bull about his loss. Not the loss o' his friend, ye'll mind, but of the money he had lent him. He staggered me by bringing out a deed in which your father pledged Drimdorran as the bond for Duncanson's accommodations, but he doubted, by his way o't, if the deed would hold against a property in danger of escheat for treason. Sly devil! Well he kent MacCailen could put that all right! And there he sits, this fourteen years – a son of Para-na-muic of Gunna – the Gentleman from Coll, and bonny on the gentleman! What will please him now but that Lord Islay's boy should get him grandsons! If it werena for Lord Islay – honest man! – ye wouldna dare have put a foot within Drimdorran's door! And on my soul, I'm glad ye're bye wi' him and his; I've something better for ye!'

For some time past the tutoring engagement had appeared scarcely worthy of his nephew to the Bailie. Æneas, to tell the truth, was something of a disappointment to his uncle who had reared him, sent him to the college with Lord knew what object, though the Law was mentioned, and some study of the same had sent him later on to Holland, where he met with Islay. But Æneas no more regarded Law than cutting breckans; his heart was all in pictures and poetry – very pretty things, no doubt, but scarcely with a living in them.

Many a time, since he came back, the Bailie spoke to Annabel about the possibility of giving him an interest in the business. She liked the notion well enough in some ways, but she had a hankering to keep the lad a gentleman, – a gentleman to her idea being one who lived in some ambiguous way without a shop or vulgar occupation.

'Do ye think, a'ghalaid! 'I'm no gentleman?' her man would ask.

'Ah! but you're different,' she would tell him. 'Æneas, by rights, should be Drimdorran, and nae Drimdorran ever fyled his hands wi' merchandise.'

'A sight better if they did, my dear,' said Alan-Iain-Alain Og, far sundered from his family traditions. 'It was better for Paul if he had dealt in stots and queys that's very good for folk, and profitable, rather than be scampering about the country herdin' French recruits and breeding trouble. What did he make of it, poor man? He's yonder in Kintail, and Duncanson, the man o' business, sleeping in his blankets. And as for me, myself, I'm proud to be a merchant! I owe no man a penny, and your gentlemen are in my books. There's some of the finest family gentlemen, as ye think them, canna sleep at night for thinking what I'm thinking o' their bills, and all the time I'm sleeping sound and never bothering. It's quite enough for me that they're harassed.'

The sudden termination, then of Æneas' office gave the very opportunity the Bailie wished for. It was so opportune that the occasion of it never caused him any feeling of annoyance; at the hour of breakfast he was full of schemes for launching Æneas on a career as merchant.

The Bailie's schemes had their dependence on the great New Road that Marshal Wade was cutting a rough the mountains. Hitherto the peaceful Lowland world – the machar of the Gall, the plains town-crowded, bartering with England, making money – was, in a fashion, sundered wholly from the world above the Forth. The Grampians, like ramparts, stood between two ages, one of paper, one of steel; on either side were peoples foreign to each other. Since roads had been in Scotland they had reached to Stirling, but at Stirling they had stopped, and on the castle rock the sentinel at nightfall saw the mists go down upon a distant land of bens and glens on which a cannon or a carriage wheel had never yet intruded. Only the bridle-paths to kirk and market, the drove-track on the shoulders of the hills!

Now was the furrow being made, as Ninian said, on which to drive the Gael like bridled oxen – smooth, street-wide, a soldier's road, cut straight across the country through the thickest-populated valleys, till it reached the shores of Moray and the forts that stretched from sea to sea.

In this New Road the merchant saw his opportunity. Always to the inner parts of Inverness it had been ill to get his goods in winter time with vessels weather-bound among the isles or staggering round Cape Wrath. Now he saw a chance of opening communication by a route as safe as the King's highway to London, and already was MacCailein talking of a branch into Argyll.

Annabel, in the nerves about her nephew's sudden stop as tutor, that day at least got little satisfaction for her curiosity; the big grey map of Blaeu that hung in the lobby was spread out upon the table; and her husband, stretched across it like a sailor, marked the track the New Road took through country in the chart set down without a line to break its rough ferocity.

'It may be a sodger's road,' he cried to Æneas, 'but it's just the very thing for merchant waggons. It's true we're off the line a bit, but I have the Red One's word that there's a lot of roads in view across the country, and in the meantime I could send my wintering straight from Leith to Stirling. And then what have I on the either hand of me for a hundred miles or more but the very pick o' people – Menzies, Robertsons, Stewarts, the Athole men, Clan Chattan, and the Frasers!'

'A bonny lot!' said Annabel. 'No' a pair o' breeks among them!'

'We'll soon put breeks on them, the Duke and me, *a' ghalaid!*' said her husband cheerily, plucking up the waistband of his trousers. 'Stop you!'

'It's not so much at first what I'll put into them,' he said to Æneas, 'it's only meal, eight merk the eight stone boll, and salt perhaps to start with; herring maybe, and an anker now and then of brandy for the gentry, but it's what I'll lift from them in beef. It's just a great big breeding-ground for stots! And look at all them Great Glen lochs and rivers – full o' salmon! There's a man in Inverness called Stuart has the pick just now of all their smoked fish, but I'll be learning him!'

'The only thing,' said Æneas, 'I know about it is that there's a lot of trouble on the Road at present.' And he told of Ninian's mission.

'Ye tell me Ninian's going!' cried his uncle. 'That is better still! My notion was to send ye round by Crieff, but what's to hinder ye to go with him? – Ye may be sure he'll take the nearest way for it: for all that he is tainted in his name, the man's an education.'

He dashed more heatedly than ever into Æneas' immediate occupation. If Ninian would take Æneas in his company they might be in the North by Michaelmas, or at the very latest by St Martin's Day, when lairds and tenantry alike were desperate for money. Æneas, in Inverness, would have the money, in *buinn oir* and bank notes – three hundred pounds of it, enough to make the Hielandmen run wild; the Bailie, for a wonder, had the cash that moment at his hand. Mackay, his correspondent in the town of Inverness, would give the lad an insight to the market situation, go about with him, and show him where to look for freights and either come to terms for barter or buy stuff for money down.

'Ye'll find a lot of them will want the money,' said his uncle in the Gaelic. 'Money is the boy in Gaeldom! It's seldom that they hear the cheery chink of it.'

Chinking his coin, then, Æneas was to spend a while in bargaining for salmon crops from Beauly, timber from Glen Moriston; if occasion offered, herring, cod, or mackerel for Spain. But what his uncle most insisted on was careful study of the Road, and what there might be in it for his trade.

It was but ruefully at first that Æneas spent that morning with the map and Alan-Iain-Alain Og's commercial dreams. It seemed to him a sad comedown in life from Caesar and the bards, but what was he to do? He looked across his uncle's back, and through the window, at the seagulls swooping in the wind above the ferry, and felt that what was here proposed was shackles for the spirit, mean engagements.

But one word of the Bailie's cleared away his vapours, and it was the word Adventure.

'It's just a bit of an adventure,' said the Bailie. 'That's the thing wi' me in business, otherwise it wasna worth a docken leaf!'

At that word Æneas took another look at Blaeu, and there at last he saw the marvel of the North as Blaeu had figured it – the mountains heaped like billows of the sea, the ranging bens, the glens with rivers coiling in them; great inland lochs and forests. He saw high-sounding names like Athole, Badenoch, and Brae Lochaber, Lorn and Spey; they moved him like a story. All his days had they been known to him, but mistily and more as things of fable than of actual nature – lands of the fancy only, like the lands of Ossian, figuring in winter songs and tales of old revenge.

Now, to his uncle's great astonishment, he leapt on Blaeu, and with his chest upon the parts he knew, he peered, transported, on that legendary region of the boisterous clans, still in the state of ancient Gaul, and with Gaul's customs. The very names of castles, passes, straths, misspelled, entranced him: everything was strange and beckoning. Moreover, it had been the country of his father's wanderings, somewhere there his father had been slain, somewhere there was buried. The reflection shook him.

'Where does it lie,' he asked in his mother tongue, 'the place of my father's changing? I do not see its name.' And someway all at once he felt the climate of his mind had altered, and the North was plucking at his bosom.

The other answered solemnly. 'Of what blood art thou, young Angus, that cannot hear the name cry grievously upon the paper! There it is – Kintail! Black be the end of that Kintail that finished him!' Not the merchant spoke but kinship; on the forehead of Macmaster swept the dark cloud of undying hate. His visage was convulsed; he smote upon the map; he seemed that moment like a man a million miles remote from the world of ledgers.

'Dear me!' cried Annabel, 'ye shouldna swear like that before a lady, even in the Gaelic.'

'I wasna swearing, *m'eudail*,' he assured her, scarcely cooling. 'I was only speaking of my brother Paul.' He turned again to Æneas. 'I'm not forgetting, mind,' says he, with bitterness. 'For me the claymore's by wi't but I'm fighting wi' MacCailein. These blackguards in the North brought out your father – the very men I'm selling meal and wine to; many a time I wish to heaven it would choke them! Do you think it's what I make of it in siller that's the pleasure of my trading wi' the North? If it was only siller I would never seek to sell an ounce beyond Loch Fyne. Na! na! there's more than that in it – *I'm smashing them*, the very men that led my brother Paul astray. MacCailein and me! MacCailein and me! And now there's Marshal Wade and his bonny Road that's going to make the North a land for decent folk to live in! I have the bills o' men like Keppoch and Glengarry flourishing about the Lowlands in the place o' paper money; they're aye gettin' a' the dreicher at the payin', but whatever comes o't I have got them in my grasp. It's no' the common people, mind – the poor and faithful clansmen – but their lairds and chiefs I'm after, them your father marched wi' in his folly, blind to their self-interest, thinking they were only out for James.'

'I'll go!' cried Æneas, almost lifted from his feet; the soul of him seemed filled with some dread pleasure.

'Of course ye'll go! That's what the Road's for – you and me and vengeance. Look at it!' – with a piece of keel he drew a line from Stirling far north on the map to Lovat's country. 'That's the Road the harrow is to go to level down the Hielands, and I have put a lot of seed in there already that is bound to come to crop. Once the New Road is finished, and the troopers and the guns and my carts on it, it's an end to the dominion o' the chiefs! The North, just now, might be in Africa, for all we ken about it; nobody dare venture there except wi' arms.'

'Does the law not run there?' Æneas asked.

'Law run!' the Bailie cried with mockery. 'It runs like fury – and the clansmen at its heels. Ask you Ninian! I'll no' say that he ever ran himsel', but many a time he had a smart bit step for it! Of course ye'll take a weapon, if it is nothing better than a wee Doune pistol, and at any rate it canna be so bad upon the Road – there's always sodgers back and forward from the barracks.'

'It's no' wi' my consent ye're goin', but I hope ye'll walk wi' caution,' said his aunt.

'Six years ago I darena send ye,' said his uncle. 'Ye might lie and rot for years in Castle Dounie dungeons and nobody would ken your fate except old Simon Lovat and his warders. That's the head and front of them – the fox! I ken him, and I've bought his fish – a double-dealing rogue that's married on a decent woman, Primrose Campbell, daughter of Mamore.'

'Poor Prim!' said Annabel, 'I'm vexed for her; I don't know what on earth possessed her to take up wi' such a man!'

'Nor I,' said the Bailie. 'Nor what on earth it was that made MacCailein and Lord Islay let her marry him. That's the sort o' man the Road's to put an end to; some day yet, if he is spared, ye'll see his head upon a stob and it no' very bonny! Mind I'm telling ye! There's no a roguery in the North for forty years he hasna had a hand in – one day wi' the Jacobites, the next day wi' the others. Many an honest man he hanged before his windows or sent to the plantations. God knows who he has in yon bastille o' his in irons! It's the only quarrel that I have with Himself here that he maintains a correspondence wi' the fellow. "Policy," says MacCailein wi' a cough, but any one that plays at politics wi' Lovat has a tarry stick to hold. And still, were it not for Simon's runners coming here wi' letters for Himself so often, we would ken no more about what's happening in the shire of Inverness than if it was Jerusalem, though every messenger he sends, as Ninian tells me, is as sly's himself. Far is the cry to Castle Dounie, and it's steep on Corryarrick! Not a whisper will come over Corryarrick that he doesna want. But the Road's going over Corryarrick, and the end of Sim's at hand, and of his kind! Perhaps when it is finished we will hear what happened to Lady Grange; since she was lifted near a twelvemonth since in Edinburgh nobody has found her whereabouts, and Lovat gets the blame for her trepanning. I wouldna put it past him! He's a dirty brock!'

The tutor's stipend came that afternoon to him from Duncanson, and with it came a little scrape of letter that confirmed his liberation from an office that had all at once become repugnant. It looked as if Drimdorran meant to have a plausible excuse for his suspension; the story, later in the day, went round that Islay's son was going to the college of St Andrews.

Æneas at once went to the Messenger-at-Arms to ask him when he meant to set out for the North.

'I'll soon can tell ye that!' said Ninian, and showed to him a knapsack. He turned it out upon a form. It held a shirt or two, some hose, a pair of brogues, a shagreen case of razors, a pot of salve, a Bible, and a dirk. 'The Bible,' he explained with gravity, 'is for the thing that is within us all, but the dirk is for my own particular skin; what else would any man be needing but his wits about him and a coin or two? Have ye the nut, my hero?'

Æneas had the nut.

'And now I'm all complete!' said Ninian, quite contented.

'It would be better, would it not, with a companion?' Æneas said to him.

'Ha, ha! You may be sure I thought of that,' said Ninian, 'and I've got him – there he is, the brave grey lad, and he not slender!' and with a movement of the haunch he brought to view the basket of a claymore, tucked away so sly below the skirts of him, its presence hitherto had been invisible.

'That's him,' he said, 'Grey Colin, sober as a wife and sharper in the tongue.'

'I was thinking of a man with you,' said Æneas.

'Another man's legs are no use for my travelling,' said Ninian; 'I'm better with my three fine comrades – courage, sense and foresight.'

'What I thought,' said Æneas, 'was you might take me: I'm finished with the tutoring, and my uncle wants me to go North on business.'

'Oh ho!' cried Ninian, sharp-looking at him. 'That's the way the wind blows, is it? I'll take the last thing in my mind the first, and tell ye this, that I'm the man that's willing, if you can have your pack made up tomorrow morning. I'm starting at the skirl of day myself, but whether you're to leave the town with me or not will have to be considered. Now for the first thing in my mind, and most important – what ails Drimdorran at ye?'

'Young Campbell's going to St Andrews,' said Æneas uneasily, and Ninian's eyes half shut.

He placed the plenishing of his knapsack back with some deliberation, whistling to himself the tune of 'Monymusk', then put the Molucca bean with care in a pouch he had inside his coat below his elbow, where was a small black knife; but all without a word, and Æneas felt mightily uncomfortable.

'What's in my mind,' at last said Ninian, turning on him quickly, 'is that if you're going with me, you'll need to be as open as the day. I'm deep enough for two of us whatever – that's my trade, and I want nothing muffled in my comrade. Stop, stop!' – for Æneas was about to blurt the truth – 'I'm asking nothing, mind! But at the very start ye try to blind me with this story of young Campbell going to St Andrews, and I'm not so easy blinded. *I asked what ailed Drimdorran at ye!* Last night the man was in a fury. What's more, he never put his head to pillow, and he sent for ye this morning at an hour when gentlemen are snoring. It's not for nothing that the falcon whistles – is he blaming ye for Margaret?'

''That's the truth,' admitted Æneas. 'I thought for her sake it was better not to mention it. But the man's mistaken; there is nothing in it.'

'Just that!' said Ninian dryly. 'Whether there is or not is none of my affair at all, at all; but it makes a difference in the way we'll have to start for Inverness. It would never do in the circumstances for the two of us to leave this town together like a cow and a veal at her tail. Myself I'm going by Glen Aray and the Orchy. I might have tried Glen Lochy, but I want to see some salmon in a linn that's close to Arichastlich, and forbye, I ken the folk that's in Glenorchy – decent people though they're no' Macgregors! It would not hinder you, now, to start on a road of your own. It might be that you would be going to the Lowlands, like,' and he gave a wink of great significance, and stuck his tongue out in the corner of his mouth. 'There's not a finer glen in Albyn than Glen Croe, and you would, let us be saying, take the track across Glen Croe down to Loch Lomond. But you would kind of shift your mind about the Lowlands when ye got to that fine water, and start up Glen Falloch, and who would I be seeing in the evening at the Bridge of Orchy change but young Macmaster! My welcome to him, I'll can swear, would be in grandeur and in splendour!'

'Very well; so be it!' said Æneas. 'You are riding?'

'Indeed and I'm not! said Ninian firmly. 'Only to the length of Bridge of Orchy, just to show my friends upon the road I'm not a man that needs to wear shoe-leather. From there I'm sending back the horse by a man that's coming that length with me. After that I'll stretch out like a warrior and take my shanks to it. Ye'll need a horse, so far, yourself, or else I'll have to wait a day for ye.'

'I'll take a horse to Bridge of Orchy too,' said Æneas, 'and send it back or sell it as my uncle may advise.'

'You see, a horse is not much use on my affairs,' said Ninian. 'It's something like two extra pair of legs – an awkward thing to have about ye; it looks too much like business in a hurry, and I like to give the notion that I'm daundering at my ease. Ye canna hide a horse behind a bush of juniper nor take it crawling wi' ye up a burn, and it's aye another thing to run the risk of losing. Nothing better than the shanks, my hero! and ye'll see a good deal more on them than cocked upon a saddle. Ye'll need a pickle money.'

'In that I'm likely to be well enough provided,' answered Æneas. 'I'll have three hundred pound about me.'

'What!' cried Ninian. 'Through Lochaber! God be about us! Am I to travel wi' a banker's vault? Ye havena robbed Drimdorran, have ye?'

'No,' said Æneas; laughing, and explained the nature of his mission to the North.

'Not a word about it then!' said Ninian. 'It's not that stealing money is a habit with the folk we're going among, poor bodies! They never touch a thing but bestial, and perhaps, at whiles, a web of clothing, but at this time o' the year, wi' Crieff Tryst comin' on, there's many a droll stravaiger stopping at the inns and changes we'll be sleeping in, if sleeping's going to be a thing we're going to waste much time on, and a man wi' all that money on him would be smelling like a spirit keg for their temptation.'

In the midst of their discussion, further, on the preparations for the journey, Janet entered, and at the sight of her, for Æneas the zest of the adventure flattened. It was not frosty wells she was today but ice itself, until her father told her Æneas was going with him, when she brightened.

'But why not all the way together?' she inquired, surprised to learn they were to take such devious ways into Breadalbane.

'Because, my lass, our friend here's leaving not in the friendliest trim with Mr Duncanson,' said Ninian, 'and I've no mind to vex that bonny gentleman until we have the width of two good parishes between us. He seems so little taken up, himself, with my bit jaunt on Islay's business, that he might be glad of any excuse to put it off. And indeed, forbye, it is a splendid chance for Æneas here to see Glen Falloch. It's a place I'm very fond of.'

'It seems a queer-like start,' she said with puzzled brows, 'but anyway I'm glad my father is to have your company.' She turned upon the young man rather warmer. 'You will find him,' she said, 'a kind of crooked stick to take the road with on the forests and the mountain moors.'

'It's ill to take the crook out of an old stick,' said Ninian blythly, 'but sometimes it's as good as any other for the business.'

'I hope you'll see that he will not go wandering about too much at night; that will always be the time when I'm most anxious for this man – this wild young dad of mine.'

'And that's the very time when I am surest of myself,' cried Ninian. 'My name's Macgregor and the fog's my friend! I'm thinking, too, you couldna send a better man wi' me to watch me in the night; he has that turn himsel'!' And there he gave a nudge to Æneas.

Æneas flushed before the level glance she gave him upon this.

'There's one thing I hope,' she said, 'and that is that you are not in a desperate hurry to get North or to get back again, for my father is a man who makes little speed through any country where there is a fish to catch.'

'I'll do my best,' said Æneas, 'to keep him from his angling.'

'It will be hard,' she said. 'A rod and a riverside for father, and the day slips by! It is like life itself and us, poor things, at playing.'

With a breast tumultuous Æneas went home, and with the help of Annabel prepared for a departure so precipitous she almost wept about it.

THE ANGLER

A better day for travel never shone, and Æneas rode through it till the gloaming with uplifted spirit on a track that, till he reached Loch Lomond, gave no trouble to his riding, for, so far, it was the trail to Lowland markets, and the very rock of it was stripped by feet of men and beast. The way was new to him; he saw the wild abyss below Ben Arthur and Ben Ime with wonder, gladdened in the salt breeze of the yellow beaches of Loch Long, and, having come to Tarbet, rested. His way was rougher in the afternoon – along Loch Lomond-side and through Glen Falloch, where Macfarlane crofts were thick upon the braes, and folks were harvesting, and it was not yet dusk when he passed through Tyndrum. There was he on the main route of the Appin drovers and the men from Skye; a change-house by the wayside hummed like a skep of bees with voices, and a field beside the change was occupied by big-horned shaggy cattle bellowing.

Two or three men came out and looked at him when he rode past, themselves no gentler-looking than their herds – thick, hairy fellows, wearing tartan, one of them at least in fier of war with a target on his back and a leather coat.

Æneas gave a wave in by-going.

'You're surely at the start of fortune, trim young lad, to be at the riding for't,' cried out the fellow of the targe: 'Come in and drop your weariness!' and Æneas looked at him again – he was so like a Roman, with bare knees!

But he went on, unheeding them, and by-and-by his track rose up among the heather for a bit above a plain all strewn with shingle of the winter storms, and there he saw the sun go down upon the wild turmoil of bens they called the Black Mount of Breadalbane. The dark was on when he came to the Bridge of Orchy, and the sky all shivering with stars.

There, too, were droves of cattle round the inn; no sooner had he clattered in upon the hamlet than a score of men were out upon him, even shaggier than the fellows of Tyndrum, and only reassured about the safety of their charges when they found he was a gentleman alone.

The inn was shabby to the point of scandal, no better than a common tavern, smoke-blackened, smelling of the reek of peat and mordants used in dyeing cloth; lit by cruisies, going like a fair with traffic. In the kitchen of it men were supping broth with spoons chained to the tables, and a lad with his head to the side as if in raptures at his own performance stood among the ashes with a set of braying bagpipes.

'*Failte!*' said the landlord courteously Æneas. 'Stick your horse in anywhere, just man, and what's your will for supper?'

'Cook for me a bannock and roast a cock,' said Æneas, like a traveller of the hero stories.

The landlord had the hue of drink upon him, and seemed in a merry key.

'Son,' said he (and he, too, thinking of the story), 'wouldst thou prefer the big bannock of my anger or the little wee bannock and my blessing?' and Æneas laughed. He took a squint at the baking-board upon the dresser, and said he, more wisely, 'I think we will not mind the bannock, big or little, but I have a friend who should be here by this time from Glen Orchy, and the bird will do between us.'

He had hardly put his horse into a stall when the company burst out again upon the house-front at a clack of hooves, and going out himself he heard the voice of Ninian. Before he could address him, Ninian was off the saddle at a jump, had ordered his attendant to put up the horses for the night, and dashed into the inn without the slightest notice of his friend.

'What is wrong?' asked Æneas, following him.

'Nothing at all,' said Ninian, cautiously in English, with a look about him at the drovers. 'But ye'll be better in your bed before the man that's with me there puts bye the beasts. I wouldn't for the world that he would see us here together.'

'I'm sorry to be such a bother to you,' said Æneas stiffly. 'I thought the width of two good parishes between you and Drimdorran made you master of yourself!'

'That's the best word ever I heard from ye!' said Ninian heartily. 'I'm glad to see ye have your tongue and I'm thinking we'll get on no' bad together. But still-and-on I'm serious about that fellow with me, and if we can get a chamber by ourselves I'll tell ye what's my reason.'

The only chamber they could get was that in which they were to sleep, and that not stately. Thither were they led by the landlord's wife, who said the fowl was now at plucking for their supper, and when the door was shut on her, Ninian turned on Æneas and looked him firmly in the eye.

'Ye didna tell me all, my lad,' says he, 'about Drimdorran's anger. I'm doubting you're a close one!'

'What else have you been hearing now?' asked Æneas, greatly downed.

'When I was coming up the glen this morning he was out upon the road with letters for my man to leave round here, but I was not long of learning that he knew you were away from Inveraray, and what he really wanted was to know if I could tell your destination. That, I'll assure ye, put me in a corner. But I was able for his lordship! "By all accounts," says I, "he is riding to the Lowlands." Then what in all the earth should happen but Drimdorran burst upon you for a thief –'

'Now is not that the swine!' cried Æneas, furious.

'Stop you! I knew the man was talking nonsense, and I was right, for in a bit the only thing he had against you was a snuffbox. But a body more concerned about a snuffbox never breathed the morning air of Scotland! He swore he would be even with you if ye ever set a foot again within the barony. You will see yourself, now, the position I was in – I had myself to think about as well as you, and if I was kent to be tramping through the North in company with the gentleman who stole the snuffbox, after telling Old Drimdorran yon about the Lowlands road, it would not look respectable.'

'Good God!' cried Æneas, 'you're surely not believing that I have the body's snuffbox!'

'Tach! What's the odds about a paltry snuffbox?' Ninian said lightly.

'But, man! I haven't got it! It's yonder in his house,' cried Æneas. 'Will you not believe me?'

'I believe every word of you,' said Ninian, 'but if there's not a snuffbox missing, what's the cause of yon one's tirravee?'

'I'll tell you that,' said Æneas, and straightaway laid before him all his tale without a word of reservation. Away from Janet Campbell's presence the dovecote incident now appeared quite innocent; he did not even baulk to tell Drimdorran's charge about the desk.

'If ye had told me this before,' said Ninian, 'I could have cleared the air for you. It's droll that my girl Janet should jalouse the truth before myself. She didna know, of course, about the doocot, but she guessed ye were with Margaret somewhere when ye should have been at your tasks whenever I said that Drimdorran had been angry looking for ye. Now I can tell ye something. When I was there colloguing with Drimdorran in his closet, he turned him from the window once as he was walking up and down the room, and with a changed complexion made a dash to look his desk; he went out of the room and in again like lightning. "Ye havena seen the young folk?" he inquired of me, and I had not but thought ye would be at your lessons. Ye werena there, he said, and out again and left me cooling twenty minutes, by my lone. I started wondering in the Gaelic what was bothering him, and walking to the window saw a thing that put me to my calculations. The window of his room, you may have noticed, shows the window of the doocot in between the branches of the thicket, and a light was there, the first time I have ever seen it. I watched it six or seven minutes, then the light went out.'

'Then after all it was her father!' cried out Æneas, 'and he knew that we were there.'

'Not a bit of doubt of it! I can see that now, although I thought when he came back he had not left the house, because he still had on his slippers. But there was something in his manner curious; he was a troubled man who found it hard to keep his mind upon our business. He asked me just the once again if I had seen you anywhere, and in a key that showed ye werena in his graces, and all the time was I not thinking it was just because of the neglected lessons?'

'There's no doubt it was he,' said Æneas. 'We thought at first it was, and then I was led astray by thinking he and you had been together all the time.'

'He had plenty of time to reach the doocot and be back,' said Ninian.

'But what,' said Æneas, 'was he lamenting for?'

'I would lament myself if I had any thought a girl of mine was yonder,' answered Ninian. 'It's aye a chancy thing a buzzard in a doocot. The difference with me is that the neck of ye would likely have been twisted. He's so keen on Campbell for the girl he wouldna risk that scandal. But that's all bye wi't; there's this business of the snuffbox; it's a handy story to give colour to his putting ye away without entangling the reputation of his daughter, and it's maybe just a pity that we're on the march together after that bit tale of mine about the Lowlands road. If this man with me takes the story back tomorrow that ye met me here, the tune is through the fiddle, and that's the way I want ye in your bed, or out of sight at least till he is gone.'

So Æneas took his supper in the bedded room, and Ninian kept his man engaged till he too went to bed, and in the morning got him off at break of day.

'All clear now; we'll have a bite of breakfast, and take our feet to it ourselves,' he said to Æneas, who had not slept a wink.

'First of all I have to send my horse back,' mentioned Æneas, and the other started.

'No other horse goes back from here!' he said with firmness. 'The man ye would send back wi't couldna hold his tongue. No, no, ye'll have to sell it. Some of these men there for the Tryst at Crieff will buy it from ye.'

To this was Æneas willing, since he had his uncle's consent to do what he thought best with the horse, and Ninian soon found among the drovers one who had a fancy for a bargain. They went together to the stable, and no sooner had the Messenger beheld the pony, dapple-grey, that carried Æneas from Inveraray, than he gave a cry.

'My grief! we're done for't now!' says he, and backed out of the stable, Aeneas behind him.

'What's the use of me telling lies if ye go and bring a horse like that with ye?' he asked, dejected. 'Ye might as well go round the country with a drum, to call attention. That speckled one is known to everybody in the seven parishes, and my man's off to Inveraray with the story that it's here. He couldna well mistake it, and in the stall next to his own! I thought there was something droll about his manner when we parted.'

For a while this new misfortune daunted Ninian, but he was not a man to nurse despair: they sold the horse, between them, for a sum of fifteen pounds shaken out of as many sporrans. They humped their pokes in which they put some cakes and cheese; Æneas cut for himself a hazel stick, to be upsides with Ninian who bore a curious thick rattan, and it seemed as if the world would fly below them till the dusk as they took up the waterside.

It was a mountain step that Ninian had – spanged out and supple, and the burgess of him left behind. He sniffed the air of gale and heather with applause, and searched the mounts before them and their corries with the eyes of birds that have come far from wandering and know their home. Now would he run upon a hillock with droll sounds of pleasure like a whinny, now leap the boulders and stretch flat among the thyme and thrift to peer into the dark, small pools of stream. 'Ah, now,' thought

Æneas, 'I have here with me but a child,' and yet it was, himself, a boy he felt, so bland and pleasant was the morning and his heart so strong, so sweet the thinking of the North before him, and the things that might befall. So he, too, stretched brave legs, and in the great wide moorland hollow of the upper Orchy looked ardently upon the massing clouds that floated silverly about the confines of the world.

They had walked but half an hour when Ninian all at once stopped short, and staring at a pool saw salmon leaping.

'*Mo chreach!*' said he, 'Look yonder!' and began to fidget with his stick. 'I was just thinking what two daft fellows we are to be taking the world for our pillow like this, as the saying goes, without first making up our minds together what's to be the tack we'll steer on.' And aye the corner of his eye was on the leaping fish.

'The nearest way is the best as far as I am concerned,' said Æneas.

'I would never take the nearest way anywhere,' said Ninian. 'Half the sport of life is starting and the other half is getting on the way, and everything is finished when it's done,' and he almost jumped as another fellow in the water splashed. 'Put we down our packs just here and be considering cautiously what airts we are to follow, for, thank God, there's many ways before us, every one as splendid as the other, like MacVurich's songs. To save the time when we're considering, I'll try a cast,' and in a second he had whipped the ferrule off his sturdy cane and out of it there came three parts, at sight of which the other smiled to have Miss Janet's reading of her father proved so soon.

Off went the poke from Ninian's back, and out of it he fetched some tackle ready busked with flies. He put the rod together, trembling with excitation, keeping up the while a constant chatter on their plans as if no other thing engaged his mind, and still and on his eye was aye upon the bonny fish.

'What we'll do, lad,' he said, 'is to put the night bye in a change-house yonder close on Buachaille Etive. It's only fourteen miles or thereabouts, but it's the only one between us and the Spean, and that is twice as far again. For a gentleman on my business there's many a bit of information to be picked up on a night in that inn beside the Moor of Rannoch. It's close enough on Glen Coe to learn what's stirring there among MacIan's folk I darena venture in among; forbye there's lochs beside it on the moor that's full of fish.'

'If it's fish we're out for it is not soon we will be at Inverness,' said Æneas ruefully, sitting down upon his pack and looking at the other stepping out already on the stones.

'Men and love! look at yon fellow!' cried Ninian in Gaelic over his shoulder. 'God's splendour! is he not the heavy gentleman! And me with this bit trifle of a stick not better than a wand.' All his wind seemed fighting in his breast; his very voice was changed with agitation. But still he kept up for a moment longer the pretence of interest in their route, and cried back to the lad upon the bank, 'Up Loch Laggan-side or through Glen Roy . . . Oh, Mary! Is not that the red one!'

For half an hour was not another word from him; he was a man bewitched, that crawled among the rushes of the bank and crouched in shadows of the boulders, and threw the lures across the linn among the playing fish, with eyes that seemed to grudge each moment that they were not on the water.

Æneas lay back and crushed the mint and thyme that gave the day a scent for ever after in his memory: fishing had never been a sport of his, and he but wondered at his comrade's patience. For long it looked as if the fisher worked in vain; great fishes surged and leaped about his hair-lines and his feathers, but they never touched them.

'Aren't they the frightened dirt!' cried Ninian at last. 'Not a bit of gallant spirit in them! And me so honest, striving wi' them! Stop you, though!' and he fixed another lure.

And Æneas, lying in his hollow, fell asleep. When he awoke the sun was straight above them, and his friend was still bent on the water-edge and whipping in the eddies where the fish still lay. An ear of Æneas was on the ground; he rather felt than heard a horseman galloping upon the track a little way above the river. Such furious haste was in the rider's manner that Æneas walked up the brae to watch him, and hailed him as he galloped past.

He got no answer. The horseman never even raised a hand, but swept upon his way as if some fiend were after him – a boorish fellow with a head like a two-boll bag of meal and a plaid upon him.

'We are in the land of poor manners, surely,' thought Æneas, and went down again beside his friend, and just as he got to him, saw him give a twitch. Ninian, crouched knee-deep now in the water, turned as he came nigh him with an aspect that astonished Æneas. All his face was puckered up with exaltation; in his eyes a curious glitter, proud and savage.

'*Tha e agam, a bhruide!* – I have him, the brute!' he screamed, and slowly backed out of the stream with his rod-point bent. Æneas watched him, fascinated, play the fish. It threw itself into the air, and fell with great commotion in the middle of the pool, and then the line went whirling out of the wooden pirn the whole length of the pool, which ended in a shallow narrow channel. Ninian, with his teeth clenched and his lips drawn back from them, all in a kind of a glorious agony, strained lightly on the rod and span the reel at every yard he gained upon his quarry. Repeatedly it burst away again and leaped until the pool was boiling with its fury.

'If I had only just a decent stick instead of this child's playock!' said the angler in anguish. 'I never had it in my mind to touch such big ones!'

He fought with it for near an hour; at last he had it close upon the bank; they saw it rolling at their feet blue-backed, and Æneas stretched a hand to grasp the line and lift it.

'Put a finger upon a hair of that and there is not a timber of your body but I'll break!' roared Ninian. 'I will take him to this stone and you must tail him. Catch him by the small and grip as if it were the very bars of heaven and you by God rejected!'

Æneas gripped. The fish moved mightily within his hand, writhed with extraordinary power, and breaking slimy from his grasp, snapped Ninian's line. It slowly turned a moment, and Ninian with a yell dropped rod, plucked out the knife below his elbow, threw himself upon the fish, and stabbed it through the gills.

'Sin thu!' he roared, and heaved it high upon the bank. 'Oh, Æneas!' he cried with brimming eyes, and, all dripping, put his arms about his friend and squeezed him to his breast. He skipped then, like a child, about the fish, and fondled it like one that loved it, saying the most beautiful things in death were a child, a salmon, and a woodcock. Then broke he into a curious Gaelic brag about his prey – he spoke of it as if it were leviathan.

'It is not so very big a fish as all that!' said Æneas, and at that the other looked again upon his prize, and his jaw fell.

'By the Books and you're right!' said he with some vexation. 'It's just a middling one, and red at that! And that is mighty droll, for I was sure this moment that he was a monster, and the side of him like a silver ship. But I think you'll must agree I played him pretty! Look you at this stick, that's only meant for catching trouts! But now we must be stretching. You were sleeping yonder like a headstone and I hadna the heart to waken you.

With two slashes of the small black knife he ripped the ends from off the salmon, and he shoved its middle, wrapped with ferns, into his knapsack.

'Whatever comes of it we have our dinner,' he exclaimed.

'That was a surly dog who passed,' said Æneas, as they turned to leave the river.

'Where? When?' cried Ninian, surprised; so keen had he been on the fish he had not heard nor seen the horseman.

'That's gey droll!' he said, when Æneas told him what had happened. 'A gentleman might pass like that without the word of day to you but not a common man in all Argyll; there's something curious in it – something curious! He wasna, was he, like a man in drink?'

'I think not,' answered Æneas.

'There's two or three things only sends a man at gallop through Breadalbane when he's sober – the ailment of bairns in women and the need for knee-wives; a bit of mischief in the rear to run away from, or a scheme ahead.'

'He might be just a man who went with letters,' said Æneas.

'Letters don't go at the gallop through this country yet,' said Ninian, 'whatever they may do when the Road is finished. They crawl. But still-and-on there's something in the notion; it might well be that the man had letters. And I don't like letters. They make trouble. They're sly and underhand. They may be going past ye in broad daylight and you not know. I never write a letter myself if I can help it; it's putting words in jail, and it's not the man alone who puts them in can get them out again; too many have the keys. I wish I had seen the fellow; there would certainly be something in him that you did not notice that would mean a lot to me.'

It seemed to Æneas that this was making far too much of what was, after all, a commonplace affair, but he was soon to find that everything that happened, night or day, set up this curious kind of speculation in his friend.

The Adventure of the Greek Interpreter

from The Memoirs of Sherlock Holmes

ARTHUR CONAN DOYLE (1859–1930)

Sherlock Holmes is surely the archetypal English detective, whether seated in his rooms at 221B Baker Street puffing away at a three-pipe problem, or rushing in a hansom cab through the fog-shrouded streets of London on the way to the scene of yet another mystery that has baffled Scotland Yard. So archetypically English that his essential Scottishness is all too often overlooked. While certainly not Scottish in ancestry – 'My ancestors were country squires' – he tells his chronicler Watson, he is undoubtedly Scottish in inspiration and formation, and the London setting of the stories (like the London setting of Robert Louis Stevenson's 'Strange Case of Dr Jekyll and Mr Hyde' – see Chapter 2 'The Criminal Mind' in this anthology – owes a surprising amount to Edinburgh, the city of his creator's birth.

Arthur Conan Doyle was born in Edinburgh of Irish parentage, and studied medicine at Edinburgh University where Dr Joseph Bell was one of his lecturers in surgery. Bell, something of a showman, made a practice of demonstrating to his classes lightning deduction based on close observation and acute reasoning. A great fictional figure like Holmes has, of course, many sources, but Joseph Bell was undoubtedly a major influence in the creation of the great detective. The conversation in The Adventure of the Greek Interpreter *between Sherlock Holmes and his brother Mycroft about the retired Sergeant in the Royal Artillery is pure Joseph Bell, as indeed was the conversation between Holmes and Watson in* A Study in Scarlet.

'You appeared to be surprised when I told you, on our first meeting, that you had come from Afghanistan.'

'You were told, no doubt.'

'Nothing of the sort. I knew you came from Afghanistan. From long habit the train of thoughts ran so swiftly through my mind that I arrived at the conclusion without being conscious of intermediate steps. There were such steps, however. The train of reasoning ran, "Here is a gentleman of a medical type, but with the air of a military man. Clearly an army doctor, then. He has just come from the tropics for his skin is dark, and that is not the natural tint of his skin for his wrists are fair. He has undergone hardship and sickness, as his haggard face says clearly. His left arm has been injured. He holds it in a stiff and unnatural manner. Where in the tropics could an English army doctor have seen such hardship and got his arm wounded? Clearly in Afghanistan".'

Doyle's medical training under Bell clearly stood him in good stead when he came to creating his fictional consulting detective and Holmes's essential companion, chronicler and sounding-board, John H. Watson, MD, late of the Army Medical Department. The rigorous Edinburgh training and the testing of each stage of a hypothesis before coming to a diagnosis helped create the detective who observed: 'It is a capital mistake to theorise before one has data.'

However, as Owen Dudley Edwards has argued in his fine biography of Doyle, The Quest for Sherlock Holmes, *the Edinburgh influence goes much further than this. Holmes identifies Dr Watson's movements around London by the colour of the mud-splashes on his shoes – a trick that Dr Bell is known to have demonstrated with the distinctive colour of the Bruntsfield Links soil. However, as Edwards points out:*

> Bell could speak with authority about Edinburgh, especially its small vital centre. Holmes really could not answer for a vast metropolis. Yet much of the appeal of the stories lies in an intimate and known London, very much more of a comfortable unity than the city really was. By putting so much of the intimacy of Edinburgh into it, Conan Doyle gave a sense of place to the dismaying anonymity of London and thereby won readers' identification.

It is perhaps remarkable that in the four novels and five collections of short stories in which he recounts Holmes's exploits, Dr Watson should leave us no record of any cases in Scotland. Holmes, though deeply rooted in London, did manage to travel widely, for example to the North of England to solve The Adventure of the Priory School, *to the West Country in search of* The Hound of the Baskervilles *and other cases, but we have no stories telling of work in Scotland, unless like the mysterious case of the giant rat of Sumatra, these were some of the stories 'for which the world is not yet prepared'.*

During my long and intimate acquaintance with Mr Sherlock Holmes I had never heard him refer to his relations, and hardly ever to his own early life. This reticence upon his part had increased the somewhat inhuman effect which he produced upon me, until sometimes I found myself regarding him as an isolated phenomenon, a brain without a heart, as deficient in human sympathy as he was pre-eminent in intelligence. His aversion to women and his disinclination to form new friendships were both typical of his unemotional character, but not more so than his complete suppression of every reference to his own people. I had come to believe that he was an orphan with no relatives living; but one day, to my very great surprise, he began to talk to me about his brother.

It was after tea on a summer evening, and the conversation, which had roamed in a desultory, spasmodic fashion from golf clubs to the causes of the change in the obliquity of the ecliptic, came round at last to the question of atavism and hereditary aptitudes. The point under discussion was, how far any singular gift in an individual was due to his ancestry and how far to his own early training.

'In your own case,' said I, 'from all that you have told me, it seems obvious that your faculty of observation and your peculiar facility for deduction are due to your own systematic training.'

'To some extent,' he answered thoughtfully. 'My ancestors were country squires, who appear to have led much the same life as is natural to their class. But, none the less, my turn that way is in my veins, and may have come with my grandmother, who was the sister of Vernet, the French artist. Art in the blood is liable to take the strangest forms.'

'But how do you know that it is hereditary?'

'Because my brother Mycroft possesses it in a larger degree than I do.'

This was news to me indeed. If there were another man with such singular powers in England, how was it that neither police nor public had heard of him? I put the question, with a hint that it was my companion's modesty which made him acknowledge his brother as his superior. Holmes laughed at my suggestion.

'My dear Watson,' said he, 'I cannot agree with those who rank modesty among the virtues. To the logician all things should be seen exactly as they are and to underestimate one's self is as much a departure from truth as to exaggerate one's own powers. When I say, therefore, that Mycroft has better powers of observation than I, you may take it that I am speaking the exact and literal truth.'

'Is he your junior?'

'Seven years my senior.'

'How comes it that he is unknown?'

'Oh, he is very well known in his own circle.'

'Where, then?'

'Well, in the Diogenes Club, for example.'

I had never heard of the institution, and my face must have proclaimed as much, for Sherlock Holmes pulled out his watch.

The Diogenes Club is the queerest club in London, and Mycroft one of the queerest men. He's always there from quarter to five to twenty to eight. It's six now, so if you care for a stroll this beautiful evening I shall be very happy to introduce you to two curiosities.'

Five minutes later we were in the street, walking towards Regent's Circus.

'You wonder,' said my companion, 'why it is that Mycroft does not use his powers for detective work. He is incapable of it.'

'But I thought you said –'

'I said that he was my superior in observation and deduction. If the art of the detective began and ended in reasoning from an armchair, my brother would be the greatest criminal agent that ever lived. But he has no ambition and no energy. He will not even go out of his way to verify his own solutions, and would rather be considered wrong than take the trouble to prove himself right. Again and again I have taken a problem to him, and have received an explanation which has afterwards proved to be the correct one. And yet he was absolutely incapable of working out the practical points which must be gone into before a case could be laid before a judge or jury.'

'It is not his profession, then?'

'By no means. What is to me a means of livelihood is to him the merest hobby of a dilettante. He has an extraordinary faculty for figures, and audits the books in some of the government departments. Mycroft lodges in Pall Mall, and he walks round the comer into Whitehall every morning and back every evening. From year's end to year's end he takes no other exercise, and is seen nowhere else, except only in the Diogenes Club, which is just opposite his rooms.'

'I cannot recall the name.'

'Very likely not. There are many men in London, you know, who, some from shyness, some from misanthropy, have no wish for the company of their fellows. Yet they are not averse to comfortable chairs and the latest periodicals. It is for the convenience of these that the Diogenes Club was started, and it now contains the most unsociable and unclubable men in town. No member is permitted to take the least notice of any other one. Save in the Stranger's Room, no talking is, under any circumstances, allowed, and three offences, if brought to the notice of the committee, render the talker liable to expulsion. My brother was one of the founders, and I have myself found it a very soothing atmosphere.'

We had reached Pall Mall as we talked, and were walking down it from the St James's end. Sherlock Holmes stopped at a door some little distance from the Carlton, and, cautioning me not to speak, he led the way into the hall. Through the glass panelling I caught a glimpse of a large and luxurious room, in which a considerable number of men were sitting about and reading papers, each in his own little nook. Holmes showed me into a small chamber which looked out into Pall Mall, and then, leaving me for a minute, he came back with a companion whom I knew could only be his brother.

Mycroft Holmes was a much larger and stouter man than Sherlock. His body was absolutely corpulent, but his face, though massive, had preserved something of the sharpness of expression which was so remarkable in that of his brother. His eyes, which were of a peculiarly light, watery gray, seemed to always retain that far-away, introspective look which I had only observed in Sherlock's when he was exerting his full powers.

'I am glad to meet you, sir,' said he, putting out a broad, fat hand like the flipper of a seal. 'I hear of Sherlock everywhere since you became his chronicler. By the way, Sherlock, I expected to see you round last week to consult me over that Manor House case. I thought you might be a little out of your depth.'

'No, I solved it,' said my friend, smiling.

'It was Adams, of course.'

'Yes, it was Adams.'

'I was sure of it from the first.' The two sat down together in the bow-window of the club. 'To anyone who wishes to study mankind this is the spot,' said Mycroft. 'Look at the magnificent types! Look at these two men who are coming towards us, for example.'

'The billiard-marker and the other?'

'Precisely. What do you make of the other?'

The two men had stopped opposite the window. Some chalk marks over the waistcoat pocket were the only signs of billiards which I could see in one of them. The other was a very small, dark fellow, with his hat pushed back and several packages under his arm.

'An old soldier, I perceive,' said Sherlock.

'And very recently discharged,' remarked the brother.

'Served in India, I see.'

'And a non-commissioned officer.'

'Royal Artillery, I fancy,' said Sherlock.

'And a widower.'

'But with a child.'

'Children, my dear boy, children.'

'Come,' said I, laughing, 'this is a little too much.'

'Surely,' answered Holmes, 'it is not hard to say that a man with that bearing, expression of authority, and, sun-baked skin, is a soldier, is more than a private, and is not long from India.'

'That he has not left the service long is shown by his still wearing his ammunition boots, as they are called,' observed Mycroft.

'He had not the cavalry stride, yet he wore his hat on one side, as is shown by the lighter skin on that side of his brow. His weight is against his being a sapper. He is in the artillery.'

'Then, of course, his complete mourning shows that he has lost someone very dear. The fact that he is doing his own shopping looks as though it was his wife. He has been buying things for children, you perceive. There is a rattle, which shows that one of them is very young. The wife probably died in childbirth. The fact that he has a picture-book under his arm shows that there is another child to be thought of.'

I began to understand what my friend meant when he said that his brother possessed even keener faculties than he did himself. He glanced across at me and smiled. Mycroft took snuff from a tortoise-shell box and brushed away the wandering grains from his coat front with a large, red silk handkerchief.

'By the way, Sherlock,' said he, 'I have had something quite after your own heart – a most singular problem – submitted to my judgment. I really had not the energy to follow it up save in a very incomplete fashion, but it gave me a basis for some pleasing speculations. If you would care to hear the facts –'

'My dear Mycroft, I should be delighted.'

The brother scribbled a note upon a leaf of his pocket-book, and, ringing the bell, he handed it to the waiter.

'I have asked Mr Melas to step across,' said he. 'He lodges on the floor above me, and I have some slight acquaintance with him, which led him to come to me in his perplexity. Mr Melas is a Greek by extraction, as I understand, and he is a remarkable linguist. He earns his living partly as interpreter in the law courts and partly by acting as guide to any wealthy Orientals who may visit the Northumberland Avenue hotels. I think I will leave him to tell his very remarkable experience in his own fashion.'

A few minutes later we were joined by a short, stout man whose olive face and coal black hair proclaimed his Southern origin; though his speech was that of an educated Englishman. He shook hands eagerly with

Sherlock Holmes, and his dark eyes sparkled with pleasure when he understood that the specialist was anxious to hear his story.

'I do not believe that the police credit me – on my word, I do not,' said he in a wailing voice. 'Just because they have never heard of it before, they think that such a thing cannot be. But I know that I shall never be easy in my mind until I know what has become of my poor man with the sticking-plaster upon his face.'

'I am all attention,' said Sherlock Holmes.

'This is Wednesday evening,' said Mr Melas. 'Well, then, it was Monday night – only two days ago, you understand – that all this happened. I am an interpreter as perhaps my neighbour there has told you. I interpret all languages – or nearly all – but as I am a Greek by birth and with a Grecian name, it is with that particular tongue that I am principally associated. For many years I have been the chief Greek interpreter in London, and my name is very well known in the hotels.

'It happens not unfrequently that I am sent for at strange hours by foreigners who get into difficulties, or by travellers who arrive late and wish my services. I was not surprised, therefore, on Monday night when a Mr Latimer, a very fashionably dressed young man, came up to my rooms and asked me to accompany him in a cab which was waiting at the door. A Greek friend had come to see him upon business, he said, and as he could speak nothing but his own tongue, the services of an interpreter were indispensable. He gave me to understand that his house was some little distance off, in Kensington, and he seemed to be in a great hurry, bustling me rapidly into the cab when we had descended to the street.

'I say into the cab, but I soon became doubtful as to whether it was not a carriage in which I found myself. It was certainly more roomy than the ordinary four-wheeled disgrace to London, and the fittings, though frayed, were of rich quality. Mr Latimer seated himself opposite to me and we started off through Charing Cross and up the Shaftesbury Avenue. We had come out upon Oxford Street and I had ventured some remark as to this being a roundabout way to Kensington when my words were arrested by the extraordinary conduct of my companion.

'He began by drawing a most formidable-looking bludgeon loaded with lead from his pocket, and swinging it backward and forward several times, as if to test its weight and strength. Then he placed it without a word upon the seat beside him. Having done this, he drew up the windows on each side, and I found to my astonishment that they were covered with paper so as to prevent my seeing through them.

' "I am sorry to cut off your view, Mr Melas," said he. "The fact is that I have no intention that you should see what the place is to which we are driving. It might possibly be inconvenient to me if you could find your way there again."

'As you can imagine, I was utterly taken aback by such an address. My companion was a powerful, broad-shouldered young fellow, and, apart from the weapon, I should not have had the slightest chance in a struggle with him.

' "This is very extraordinary conduct, Mr Latimer," I stammered. "You must be aware that what you are doing is quite illegal."

' "It is somewhat of a liberty, no doubt," said he, "but we'll make it up to you. I must warn you, however, Mr Melas, that if at any time tonight you attempt to raise an alarm or do anything which is against my interest, you will find it a very serious thing. I beg you to remember that no one knows where you are, and that, whether you are in this carriage or in my house, you are equally in my power."

'His words were quiet, but he had a rasping way of saying them, which was very menacing. I sat in silence wondering what on earth could be his reason for kidnapping me in this extraordinary fashion. Whatever it might be, it was perfectly clear that there was no possible use in my resisting, and that I could only wait to see what might befall.

'For nearly two hours we drove without my having the least clue as to where we were going. Sometimes the rattle of the stones told of a paved causeway, and at others our smooth, silent course suggested asphalt; but, save by this variation in sound, there was nothing at all which could in the remotest way help me to form a guess as to where we were. The paper over each window was impenetrable to light, and a blue curtain was drawn across the glasswork in front. It was a quarter past seven when we left Pall Mall, and my watch showed me that it was ten minutes to nine when we at last came to a standstill. My companion let down the window, and I caught a glimpse of a low, arched doorway with a lamp burning above it. As I was hurried from the carriage it swung open, and I found myself inside the house, with a vague impression of a lawn and trees on each side of me as I entered. Whether these were private grounds, however, or *bona fide* country was more than I could possibly venture to say.

'There was a coloured gas-lamp inside which was turned so low that I could see little save that the hall was of some size and hung with pictures. In the dim light I could make out that the person who had opened the door was a small, mean-looking, middle-aged man with rounded shoulders. As he turned towards us the glint of the light showed me that he was wearing glasses.

' "Is this Mr Melas, Harold?" said he.

' "Yes."

' "Well done, well done! No ill-will, Mr Melas, I hope, but we could not get on without you. If you deal fair with us you'll not regret it, but if you try any tricks, God help you!" He spoke in a nervous, jerky fashion, and with little giggling laughs in between, but somehow he impressed me with fear more than the other.

' "What do you want with me?" I asked.

' "Only to ask a few questions of a Greek gentleman who is visiting us, and to let us have the answers. But say no more than you are told to say, or –" here came the nervous giggle again – "you had better never have been born."

'As he spoke he opened a door and showed the way into a room which appeared to be very richly furnished, but again the only light was afforded by a single lamp half-turned down. The chamber was certainly large, and the way in which my feet sank into the carpet as I stepped across it told me of its richness. I caught glimpses of velvet chairs, a high white marble mantelpiece, and what seemed to be a suit of Japanese armour at one side of it. There was a chair just under the lamp, and the elderly man motioned that I should sit in it. The younger had left us, but he suddenly returned through another door, leading with him a gentleman clad in some sort of loose dressing-gown who moved slowly towards us. As he came into the circle of dim light which enabled me to see him more clearly I was thrilled with horror at his appearance. He was deadly pale and terribly emaciated, with the protruding, brilliant eyes of a man whose spirit was greater than his strength. But what shocked me more than any signs of physical weakness was that his face was grotesquely criss-crossed with sticking-plaster, and that one large pad of it was fastened over his mouth.

' "Have you the slate, Harold?" cried the older man, as this strange being fell rather than sat down into a chair. "Are his hands loose? Now, then, give him the a pencil. You are to ask the questions, Mr Melas, and he will write the answers. Ask him first of all whether he is prepared to sign the papers?"

'The man's eyes flashed fire.

' "Never!" he wrote in Greek upon the slate.

' "On no conditions?" I asked at the bidding of our tyrant.

' "Only if I see her married in my presence by a Greek priest whom I know."

The man giggled in his venomous way.

' "You know what awaits you, then?"

' "I care nothing for myself."

'These are samples of the questions and answers which made up our

strange half-spoken, half-written conversation. Again and again I had to
ask him whether he would give in and sign the documents. Again and
again I had the same indignant reply. But soon a happy thought came to
me. I took to adding on little sentences of my own to each question,
innocent ones at first, to test whether either of our companions knew
anything of the matter, and then, as I found that they showed no sign I
played a more dangerous game. Our conversation ran something like
this:

' "You can do no good by this obstinacy. *Who are you?*"
' "I care not. *I am a stranger in London.*"
' "Your fate will be on your own head. *How long have you been here?*"
' "Let it be so. *Three weeks.*"
' "The property can never be yours. *What ails you?*"
' "It shall not go to villains. *They are starving you?*"
' "You shall go free if you sign. *What house is this?*"
' "I will never sign. *I do not know.*"
' "You are not doing her any service. *What is your name?*"
' "Let me hear her say so. *Kratides.*"
' "You shall see her if you sign. *Where are you from?*"
' "Then I shall never see her. *Athens.*"

'Another five minutes, Mr Holmes, and I should have wormed out the
whole story under their very noses. My very next question might have
cleared the matter up, but at that instant the door opened and a woman
stepped into the room. I could not see her clearly enough to know more
than that she was tall and graceful, with black hair, and clad in some sort
of loose white gown.

' "Harold," said she, speaking English with a broken accent. "I could
not stay away longer. It is so lonely up there with only – Oh, my God, it
is Paul!"

'These last words were in Greek, and at the same instant the man with
a convulsive effort tore the plaster from his lips, and screaming out
"Sophy! Sophy!" rushed into the woman's arms. Their embrace was but
for an instant, however, for the younger man seized the woman and
pushed her out of the room, while the elder easily overpowered his
emaciated victim and dragged him away through the other door. For a
moment I was left alone in the room, and I sprang to my feet with some
vague idea that I might in some way get a clue to what this house was in
which I found myself. Fortunately, however, I took no steps, for looking
up I saw that the older man was standing in the doorway, with his eyes
fixed upon me.

' "That will do, Mr Melas," said he. "You perceive that we have taken you into our confidence over some very private business. We should not have troubled you, only that our friend who speaks Greek and who began these negotiations has been forced to return to the East. It was quite necessary for us to find someone to take his place, and we were fortunate in hearing of your powers."

'I bowed.

' "There are five sovereigns here," said he, walking up to me, "which will, I hope, be a sufficient fee. But remember," he added, tapping me lightly on the chest and giggling, "if you speak to a human soul about this – one human soul, mind – well, may God have mercy upon your soul!"

'I cannot tell you the loathing and horror with which this insignificant-looking man inspired me. I could see him better now as the lamp-light shone upon him. His features were peaky and sallow, and his little pointed beard was thready and ill-nourished. He pushed his face forward as he spoke and his lips and eyelids were continually twitching like a man with St Vitus's dance. I could not help thinking that his strange, catchy little laugh was also a symptom of some nervous malady. The terror of his face lay in his eyes, however, steel gray, and glistening coldly with a malignant, inexorable cruelty in their depths.

"We shall know if you speak of this," said he. "We have our own means of information. Now you will find the carriage waiting, and my friend will see you on your way."

'I was hurried through the hall and into the vehicle, again obtaining that momentary glimpse of trees and a garden. Mr Latimer followed closely at my heels and took his place opposite to me without a word. In silence we again drove for an interminable distance with the windows raised, until at last, just after midnight, the carriage pulled up.

' "You will get down here, Mr Melas," said my companion. "I am sorry to leave you so far from your house, but there is no alternative. Any attempt upon your part to follow the carriage can only end in injury to yourself."

'He opened the door as he spoke, and I had hardly time to spring out when the coachman lashed the horse and the carriage rattled away. I looked around me in astonishment. I was on some sort of a heathy common mottled over with dark clumps of furze-bushes. Far away stretched a line of houses, with a light here and there in the upper windows. On the other side I saw the red signal-lamps of a railway.

'The carriage which had brought me was already out of sight. I stood gazing round and wondering where on earth I might be, when I saw someone coming towards me in the darkness. As he came up to me I made out that he was a railway porter.

' "Can you tell me what place this is?" I asked.

' "Wandsworth Common," said he.

' "Can I get a train into town?"

' "If you walk on a mile or so to Clapham Junction," said he, "you'll just be in time for the last to Victoria."

'So that was the end of my adventure, Mr Holmes. I do not know where I was nor whom I spoke with, nor anything save what I have told you. But I know that there is foul play going on, and I want to help that unhappy man if I can. I told the whole story to Mr Mycroft Holmes next morning, and subsequently to the police.'

We all sat in silence for some little time after listening to this extraordinary narrative. Then Sherlock looked across at his brother.

'Any steps?' he asked.

Mycroft picked up the *Daily News*, which was lying on the side-table.

'Anybody supplying any information as to the whereabouts of a Greek gentleman named Paul Kratides, from Athens, who is unable to speak English, will be rewarded. A similar reward paid to anyone giving information about a Greek lady whose first name is Sophy. X 2473.'

'That was in all the dailies. No answer.'

'How about the Greek legation?'

'I have inquired. They know nothing.'

'A wire to the head of the Athens police, then?'

'Sherlock has all the energy of the family,' said Mycroft, turning to me. 'Well, you take the case up by all means and let me know if you do any good.'

'Certainly,' answered my friend, rising from his chair. 'I'll let you know, and Mr Melas also. In the meantime, Mr Melas, I should certainly be on my guard if I were you, for of course they must know through these advertisements that you have betrayed them.'

As we walked home together, Holmes stopped at a telegraph office and sent off several wires.

'You see, Watson,' he remarked, 'our evening has been by no means wasted. Some of my most interesting cases have come to me in this way through Mycroft. The problem which we have just listened to, although it can admit of but one explanation, has still some distinguishing features.'

'You have hopes of solving it?'

'Well, knowing as much as we do, it will be singular indeed if we fail to discover the rest. You must yourself have formed some theory which will explain the facts to which we have listened.'

'In a vague way, yes.'

'What was your idea, then?'

'It seemed to me to be obvious that this Greek girl had been carried off by the young Englishman named Harold Latimer.'

'Carried off from where?'

'Athens, perhaps.'

Sherlock Holmes shook in head. 'This young man could not talk a word of Greek. The lady could talk English fairly well. Inference – that she had been in England some little time, but he had not been in Greece.'

'Well, then, we will presume that she had once come on a visit to England, and that this Harold had persuaded her to fly with him.'

'That is more probable.'

'Then the brother – for that, I fancy, must be the relationship – comes over from Greece to interfere. He imprudently puts himself into the power of the young man and his older associate. They seize him and use violence towards him in order to make him sign some papers to make over the girl's fortune – of which he may be trustee – to them. This he refuses to do. In order to negotiate with him they have to get an interpreter, and they pitch upon this Mr Melas, having used some other one before. The girl is not told of the arrival of her brother and finds it out by the merest accident.'

'Excellent, Watson!' cried Holmes. 'I really fancy that you are not far from the truth. You see that we hold all the cards, and we have only to fear some sudden act of violence on their part. If they give us time we must have them.'

'But how can we find where this house lies?'

'Well, if our conjecture is correct and the girl's name is or was Sophy Kratides, we should have no difficulty in tracing her. That must be our main hope, for the brother is, of course, a complete stranger. It is clear that some time has elapsed since this Harold established these relations with the girl – some weeks, at any rate – since the brother in Greece has had time to hear of it and come across. If they have been living in the same place during this time, it is probable that we shall have some answer to Mycroft's advertisement.'

We had reached our house in Baker Street while we had been talking. Holmes ascended the stair first, and as he opened the door of our room he gave a start of surprise. Looking over his shoulder, I was equally astonished. His brother Mycroft was sitting smoking in the armchair.

'Come in, Sherlock! Come in, sir,' said he blandly, smiling at our surprised faces. 'You don't expect such energy from me, do you, Sherlock? But somehow this case attracts me.'

'How did you get here?'

'I passed you in a hansom.'

'There has been some new development?'

'I had an answer to my advertisement.'

'Ah!'

'Yes, it came within a few minutes of your leaving.'

'And to what effect?'

Mycroft Holmes took out a sheet of paper.

'Here it is,' said he, 'written with a J pen on royal cream paper by a middle-aged man with a weak constitution.

'Sir [he says]:

In answer to your advertisement of to-day's date, I beg to inform you that I know the young lady in question very well. If you should care to call upon me I could give you some particulars as to her painful history. She is living at present at The Myrtles, Beckenham.

Yours faithfully,
J. Davenport

'He writes from Lower Brixton,' said Mycroft Holmes. 'Do you not think that we might drive to him now, Sherlock, and learn these particulars?'

'My dear Mycroft, the brother's life is more valuable than the sister's story. I think we should call at Scotland Yard for Inspector Gregson and go straight out to Beckenham. We know that a man is being done to death, and every hour may be vital.'

'Better pick up Mr Melas on our way,' I suggested. 'We may need an interpreter.'

'Excellent,' said Sherlock Holmes. 'Send the boy for a four-wheeler, and we shall be off at once.' He opened the table-drawer as he spoke, and I noticed that he slipped his revolver into his pocket. 'Yes,' said he in answer to my glance, 'I should say, from what we have heard, that we are dealing with a particularly dangerous gang.'

It was almost dark before we found ourselves in Pall Mall, at the rooms of Mr Melas. A gentleman had just called for him, and he was gone.

'Can you tell me where?' asked Mycroft Holmes.

'I don't know, sir,' answered the woman who had opened the door, 'I only know that he drove away with the gentleman in a carriage.'

'Did the gentleman give a name?'

'No, sir.'

'He wasn't a tall, handsome, dark young man?'

'Oh, no, sir. He was a little gentleman, with glasses, thin in the face, but very pleasant in his ways, for he was laughing all the time that he was talking.'

'Come along!' cried Sherlock Holmes abruptly. 'This grows serious,' he observed as we drove to Scotland Yard. 'These men have got hold of Melas again. He is a man of no physical courage, as they are well aware from their experience the other night. This villain was able to terrorise him the instant that he got into his presence. No doubt they want his professional services, but, having used him they may be inclined to punish him for what they will regard as his treachery.'

Our hope was that, by taking the train, we might get to Beckenham as soon as or sooner than the carriage. On reaching Scotland Yard, however, it was more than an hour before we could get Inspector Gregson and comply with the legal formalities which would enable us to enter the house. It was a quarter to ten before we reached London Bridge, and half past before the four of us alighted on the Beckenham platform. A drive of half a mile brought us to The Myrtles – a large, dark house standing back from the road in its own grounds. Here we dismissed our cart and made our way up the drive together.

'The windows are all dark,' remarked the inspector. 'The house seems deserted.'

'Our birds are flown and the nest empty,' said Holmes.

'Why do you say so?'

'A carriage heavily loaded with luggage has passed out during the last hour.'

The inspector laughed. 'I saw the wheel-tracks in the light of the gate-lamp, but where does the luggage come in?'

'You may have observed the same wheel tracks going the other way. But the outward-bound ones were very much deeper – so much so that we can say for a certainty that there was a very considerable weight on the carriage.'

'You get a trifle beyond me there,' said the inspector, shrugging his shoulders. 'It will not be an easy door to force, but we will try if we cannot make someone hear us.'

He hammered loudly at the knocker and pulled at the bell, but without any success. Holmes had slipped away, but he came back in a few minutes.

'I have a window open,' said he.

'It is a mercy that you are on the side of the force, and not against it, Mr Holmes,' remarked the inspector as he noted the clever way in which my friend had forced back the catch. 'Well, I think that under the circumstances we may enter without an invitation.'

One after the other we made our way into a large apartment, which was evidently that in which Mr Melas had found himself. The inspector had lit his lantern, and by its light we could see the two doors, the curtain, the lamp, and the suit of Japanese mail as he had described them. On the table lay two glasses, an empty brandy-bottle, and the remains of a meal.

'What is that?' asked Holmes suddenly.

We all stood still and listened. A low moaning sound was coming from somewhere over our heads. Holmes rushed to the door and out into the hall. The dismal noise came from upstairs. He dashed up, the inspector and I at his heels, while his brother Mycroft followed as quickly as his great bulk would permit.

Three doors faced us upon the second floor, and it was from the central of these that the sinister sounds were issuing, sinking sometimes into a dull mumble and rising again into a shrill whine. It was locked, but the key had been left on the outside. Holmes flung open the door and rushed in, but he was out again in an instant, with his hand to his throat.

'It's charcoal,' he cried. 'Give it time. It will clear.'

Peering in, we could see that the only light in the room came from a dull blue flame which flickered from a small brass tripod in the centre. It threw a livid, unnatural circle upon the floor, while in the shadows beyond we saw the vague loom of two figures which crouched against the wall. From the open door there reeked a horrible poisonous exhalation which set us gasping and coughing. Holmes rushed to the top of the stairs to draw in the fresh air, and then, dashing into the room, he threw up the window and hurled the brazen tripod out into the garden.

'We can enter in a minute,' he gasped, darting out again. 'Where is a candle? I doubt if we could strike a match in that atmosphere. Hold the light at the door and we shall get them out, Mycroft, now!'

With a rush we got to the poisoned men and dragged them out into the well-lit hall. Both of them were blue-lipped and insensible, with swollen, congested faces and protruding eyes. Indeed, so distorted were their features that, save for his black beard and stout figure, we might have failed to recognize in one of them the Greek interpreter who had parted from us only a few hours before at the Diogenes Club. His hands and feet were securely strapped together, and he bore over one eye the marks of a violent blow. The other, who was secured in a similar fashion, was a tall man in the last stage of emaciation, with several strips of sticking-plaster arranged in a grotesque pattern over his face. He had ceased to moan as we laid him down, and a glance showed me that for him at least our aid had come too late. Mr Melas, however, still lived, and in less than an hour, with the aid of ammonia and brandy, I had the satisfaction of seeing him open his eyes, and of knowing that my hand had drawn him back from that dark valley in which all paths meet.

It was a simple story which he had to tell, and one which did but confirm our own deductions. His visitor, on entering his rooms, had drawn a life-preserver from his sleeve, and had so impressed him with the fear of instant and inevitable death that he had kidnapped him for the second time. Indeed, it was almost mesmeric, the effect which this giggling ruffian had produced upon the unfortunate linguist, for he could not speak of him save with trembling hands and a blanched cheek. He had been taken swiftly to Beckenham, and had acted as interpreter in a second interview, even more dramatic than the first, in which the two Englishmen had menaced their prisoner with instant death if he did not comply with their demands. Finally, finding him proof against every threat, they had hurled him back into his prison, and after reproaching Melas with his treachery, which appeared from the newspaper advertisement, they had stunned him with a blow from a stick, and he remembered nothing more until he found us bending over him.

And this was the singular case of the Grecian Interpreter, the explanation of which is still involved in some mystery. We were able to find out, by communicating with the gentleman who had answered the advertisement, that the unfortunate young lady came of a wealthy Grecian family, and that she had been on a visit to some friends in England. While there she had met a young man named Harold Latimer, who had acquired an ascendency over her and had eventually persuaded her to fly with him. Her friends, shocked at the event, had contented themselves with informing her brother at Athens, and had then washed their hands of the matter. The brother, on his arrival in England, had imprudently placed himself in the power of Latimer and of his associate, whose name was Wilson Kemp – a man of the foulest antecedents. These two, finding that through his ignorance of the language he was helpless in their hands, had kept him a prisoner, and had endeavoured by cruelty and starvation to make him sign away his own and his sister's property. They had kept him in the house without the girl's knowledge, and the plaster over the face had been for the purpose of making recognition difficult in case she should ever catch a glimpse of him. Her feminine perceptions, however, had instantly seen through the disguise when, on the occasion of the interpreter's visit, she had seen him for the first time. The poor girl, however, was herself a prisoner, for there was no one about the house except the man who acted as coachman, and his wife, both of whom were tools of the conspirators. Finding that their secret was out, and that their prisoner was not to be coerced, the two villains with the girl had fled away at a few hours' notice from the furnished house which they had hired, having first, as they thought, taken vengeance both upon the man who had defied and the one who had betrayed them.

Months afterwards a curious newspaper cutting reached us from Buda-Pesth. It told how two Englishmen who had been travelling with a woman had met with a tragic end. They had each been stabbed, it seems, and the Hungarian police were of the opinion that they had quarrelled and had inflicted mortal injuries upon each other. Holmes, however, is, I fancy, of a different way of thinking, and he holds to this day that, if one could find the Grecian girl, one might learn how the wrongs of herself and her brother came to be avenged.

'Three Thief-Catchers'

from The Looker-On

NEIL MUNRO (1863–1930)

The Looker-On *was Neil Munro's weekly column in the* Glasgow Evening News *– a column which gave him freedom to write what he liked, to reflect on life and to entertain and stimulate the Monday readers of the* News. *His evergreen comic creation Para Handy and the crew of the* Vital Spark *as well as his Glaswegian kirk beadle, Erchie, and the delightful commercial traveller, Jimmy Swan, first appeared in this column. Glasgow life was a staple theme of Munro's columns and in this piece, collected in George Blake's posthumous collection of Munro's journalism published as* The Looker-On *in 1933, Munro reminisces about his memories of three detective officer, – or 'thief-catchers' as he calls them – from three periods of the Glasgow city police force's history. The fact that the central figure of these Glasgow detectives was of Argyllshire origin of course confirms a popular belief about the markedly Highland character of the Glasgow 'polis'.*

Munro's first experience of an unnamed Glasgow thief catcher was as an Inveraray teenager on a visit to Glasgow. His guide to the Glasgow underworld was a former Glasgow policeman turned prison governor. Munro's stepfather, Malcolm Thomson, had been Governor of the Inveraray Jail and was in his seventies when Munro was in his mid-teens – although Munro doesn't identify the 'old gentleman' who introduced him to the 'splendour and misery' of Glasgow it seems very likely that his guide was Thomson.

The second thief-catcher, who flourished in the 1880s, by which time Munro was working as a young journalist in Glasgow, was Archibald Carmichael, a native of Kilbrandon parish, Argyll. In the 1881 Census he is recorded as being Sub Inspector of Detectives in Glasgow. Munro writes of 'the soft Gaelic accent of his native isle' which suggests he came from Seil or Luing, islands lying in that parish.

The third thief-catcher Munro reminisces about was to become the most famous – Detective Lieutenant John Thomson Trench, who was dismissed from the Glasgow police force for disclosing confidential information in the case of the murder of Marion Gilchrist, and the wrongful conviction for that murder of Oscar Slater.

Marion Gilchrist was robbed and savagely murdered in her Glasgow flat in December 1908 and Oscar Slater, who had a previous criminal record, was accused, on shaky evidence, of her murder and convicted and sentenced to death in one of the more flagrant miscarriages of justice in Scottish legal history. The sentence was commuted to life imprisonment.

Slater continued to protest his innocence and the case was taken up by, among others, Arthur Conan Doyle. A secret enquiry into the case was held in 1914 but no action was taken. At this time, Trench, who had doubts about Slater's guilt, passed on confidential information to the lawyers acting for Slater. Trench was accused of acting contrary to public policy and police practice and dismissed from the service. He died in May 1919 – Munro's column refers to him as the 'late Lieutenant Trench' and is obviously written after this time.

In 1928 Oscar Slater's conviction was overturned, when evidence emerged that Marion Gilchrist's nephew had probably been in her house on the night of the murder and that the police had persuaded a witness to identify Slater as the visitor and not the nephew. A £6000 'ex gratia' payment was made to compensate him for nearly 19 years' false imprisonment.

In 1998, the then Secretary of State for Scotland, Donald Dewar, went some way towards justifying Trench – a review of the case found that Trench had acted with 'moral conviction' but found no authority to issue a pardon or formally rehabilitate him.

'THREE THIEF-CATCHERS'

The first notability pointed out to me in the streets of Glasgow, on my first visit to that city in the middle of the Seventies, was a thief-catcher. If the term 'detective' was in use at the time I hadn't heard it. In any case, it would have failed to excite me so much as the word chosen by the old gentleman in whose company I was making a first acquaintance with the splendour and misery of a city he had not visited for many years.

His interest in it was almost wholly professional. Though now the governor of a Highland county prison, or, strictly speaking, but lately retired from that post on a pension, to be succeeded in his Highland bastile by the father of Sir John Lorne Macleod, of Edinburgh, he had served for years in the Glasgow force.

It was to old familiar places he was conducting me, for his own gratification – the portals of Duke Street Jail and the Rev. Evan Gordon's church; the exteriors of public houses that had been notorious in his youth, and were first to make him a bitter teetotaller; Jail Square, the

High Street, and the wynds off Trongate. No doubt for him they had the most thrilling associations, but to the youth who trudged beside him they had no important significance.

The Governor was startled when we got west as far as Hope Street and he discovered that the city, in his absence, had moved considerably west of that. He had promised me green fields and a sight of his first lodgings – both were gone. Somewhere, too, had been a dairy where one could see cows which were never let out of doors throughout their lives. I wanted to see the Broomielaw instead.

It was in Jamaica Street his eye caught sight of a man lounging along the pavement with his gaze intently fixed on a shop window across the street, where two or three loafers were looking in at the merchandise.

'Look! Look!' he said to me hurriedly, 'there's a thief-catcher!'

And I *knew* it was a thief-catcher though never hitherto had I heard of such a bird. The Governor's eyes had lit with expectant eagerness, as if in another moment he hoped to see the men at the window pounced on. And they were! This was something like a holiday!

Where we had come from thief-catchers were unknown, and thieves themselves were a rarity, though in his cage had been always a small collection of malefactors gathered from different parts of the county. When I got home a day or two after, I was the envy of my young companions. *They* would never have the luck to see a thief-catcher in operation. They knew nothing of the technique of it, for the art of the detective novel had not yet been perfected. For days I was in great demand for the narrative of my adventure, which became more sensational with every repetition.

Ten years later the most conspicuous thief-catcher in Glasgow was a man from my own county – Archibald Carmichael. His fame extended far beyond the city to which the exercise of his talents was confined. In the Highlands his name was almost as frequently heard as had been, earlier, that of Norman Macleod of the Barony, or John Anderson of the Polytechnic, or Macleod of the Waxworks.

I have not looked up the official records of his services as a criminal officer, but my impression is that the public importance of 'Archie Carmichael' was always considerably greater than his rank and designation would suggest. I could never imagine him in a helmet with a waterproof tippet on, yet for all I knew he may have started his career in Glasgow as undistinctively as that.

It took many years for the Glasgow Force to develop its organisation to the varied and intricate degree it has today, to decide that brawn and a baton were not sufficient to deal adequately with Scottish crime when

highly sophisticated as the result of modern School Board education. The
ideals and practice of Scotland Yard were far beyond us; indeed, it seemed
presumptuous when we first saw ordinary constables sent out in plain
clothes on the most delicate investigations.

Archie Carmichael was the most conspicuous thief-catcher of his time,
which might seem a handicap to his calling. There was not an intelligent
thief in Glasgow who did not know him by sight. Promoted for his brains
rather than for his avoirdupois in beef and boots, he was to a marked
degree, even among the slowly increasing squad of criminal investigators,
the perfect gentleman.

It was with wonder and admiration I used to watch him, a figure
debonair and somewhere ever present in the central streets of Glasgow.
Gentleness and good-breeding personified! He might be, to the casual
glance, a superior type of young magistrate not yet fattened, or a county
commissioner with a good tailor, who was only in town for the day to
buy fishing-flies or cartridges. Anything but a plain-clothes policeman!

Never were kindlier eyes! His smile was a benediction. I never saw him
pounce on any victim in the crafty manner of my first thief-catcher of
Jamaica Street – in any way at all, indeed, but I once saw him sorrowful in a
little hall filled with human shipwrecks of whose arrest he had been the
principal instrument. No stern official eye was there at the moment; in the
soft Gaelic accent of his native isle he was reminding me by how little,
possibly, they had missed being decent citizens. With a more conventional
education, Archie, it was said, would have risen much higher than he did in
the service.

For another type of thief-catcher – one who undoubtedly did his
ferreting with passion and could be terribly chagrined if baffled of his
prey – I must come down to a more recent period, and the late Lieutenant
Trench. That well-known Glasgow sleuth of pre-war years was of the
romantic spirit of Sherlock Holmes, and I suspect his practice in criminal
investigation was largely based on detective fiction. He would have
loved, I feel certain, to exercise all the artfulness and science which
popular fiction ascribes to the bigger men in Scotland Yard, and go about
his duties always in protean disguises, but criminal detection in Glasgow
even yet has not got the length of regularly employing 'make-up' and an
actor's wardrobe. In any case, it would have been difficult for Trench to
assume the guise of innocent benevolence which was natural to Archie
Carmichael.

But when he died the word 'mystery' was, I fancy, graven on his heart;
he was never happier than when he could take up a criminal case,
transparent to his colleagues as an innocent wife's attempt to conceal

some of his wages from a drunken husband, and discover in it features of the most baffling and sinister character.

In the West of Scotland, within a short period of years, there was a remarkable series of murders which have never been accounted for. One of them was in Glasgow, and though I was not resident there, I was, by a simple accident, dragged in to its investigation about a month afterwards, by which time 'The — Mystery' had exhausted itself in the newspapers.

It chanced that in a Glasgow club one Saturday I met the City Stipendiary, and in the course of conversation casually asked if this investigation had been abandoned.

'I'm afraid so,' he answered. 'But Trench has now been taken on, and he, as you know, is a keen one. He'll possibly find the tracks too cold.'

I had read everything that had been published about the mystery, one or two features of which had impressed me. 'Have the police never thought of inquiring round the neighbourhood of such-and-such a place?' I foolishly inquired, and the Stipendiary shut up like a clam.

Bright and early on Monday morning Trench was at my door, the first time I had ever seen him. He had, as I surmised immediately, got the hint from the Stipendiary. It took me less than ten minutes to convince him that by whomsoever 'The — Mystery' was to be unravelled, it was certainly not by me. My foolish query in the club was wholly inspired by a newspaper which he could read for himself.

'I know what you mean,' said Mr Trench, somewhat crestfallen. 'I have worked that out and gone over the ground repeatedly. But there's something wanting! I had just the faintest hope you could put me on to it.'

For an hour at least he sat with me traversing the whole circumstances as he knew them, not for my entertainment, as I could see quite well, but, more likely, to get a fresh mind and a literary imagination on his problem. He was, he said, sadly handicapped by being brought too late into the case, which was not in his division. He found that his forerunners on the job had overlooked or stupidly underestimated the importance of a clue which should have led them to the district I referred to. But in spite of that he had made the most surprising discoveries, including a double identification of the actual culprit.

'Then you haven't arrested him yet,' I remarked with surprise, for I had seen the alleged culprit the previous afternoon.

'Ah! Then you know who I mean!' said Trench. 'Yet you couldn't get *that* in a newspaper!'

He had me there! No suspect's name had been published, nor had the detective mentioned any.

Apparently unconcerned by this lapse of mine, he finished his narrative of the most convincing, circumstantial evidence I have ever heard or read of, and ended up with what for him was a catastrophic announcement: – 'And yet there's nothing in it!' While still convinced that his train of reasoning was absolutely right, he had been confronted by a hopelessly impregnable alibi; his suspect could not possibly have been anywhere near the scene at the time of the murder!

'An Artistic Murder'

from Five Red Herrings

DOROTHY L. SAYERS (1893–1957)

There can be few authors more obviously non-Scottish than Dorothy L. Sayers, nor few detectives more obviously non-Scottish than her aristocratic sleuth, Lord Peter Wimsey. Yet Five Red Herrings *(1931) has very good claims to be included in any anthology of Scottish crime.*

The setting – and Sayers' settings are always sharply observed and interesting – is the artistic community in and around Kirkcudbright and Gatehouse of Fleet in Galloway. Wimsey, like his creator, is a regular holiday-maker in Galloway and, with the usual ill-luck that attends fictional detectives, he finds himself involved in the murder of a remarkably unpopular artist. Much of the detection centres on painting techniques and railway timetables – the book was of course written at a period when there was a railway service in Galloway.

Although there is fortunately little real-life evidence of homicidal tendencies, the Kirkcudbright area became popular with artists from the 1880s, largely under the influence of the 'Glasgow Boys', George Henry (1859–1943) and E. A. Hornel (1864–1933). Broughton House, the latter artist's home in Kirkcudbright from 1901 until his death, is now a National Trust for Scotland property with an interesting collection of Hornel's, and other artists', works.

CHAPTER I

CAMPBELL QUICK

If one lives in Galloway, one either fishes or paints. 'Either' is perhaps misleading, for most of the painters are fishers also in their spare time. To be neither of these things is considered odd and almost eccentric. Fish is the standard topic of conversation in the pub and the post office, in the garage and the street, with every sort of person, from the man who arrives for the season with three Hardy rods and a Rolls Royce, to the man who leads a curious, contemplative life, watching the salmon-nets on the Dee. Weather, which in other parts of the Kingdom is gauged by the standards of the farmer, the gardener, and the weekender, is considered in Galloway in terms of fish and paint. The fisherman-painter has the best of the bargain as far as the weather goes, for the weather that is too bright for the trout deluges his hills and his sea with floods of radiant colour; the rain that interrupts picture-making puts water into the rivers and the lochs and sends him hopefully forth with rod and creel; while on cold dull days, when there is neither purple on the hills nor fly on the river, he can join a friendly party in a cosy bar and exchange information about Cardinals and March Browns, and practise making intricate knots in gut.

The artistic centre of Galloway is Kirkcudbright, where the painters form a scattered constellation, whose nucleus is in the High Street, and whose outer stars twinkle in remote hillside cottages, radiating brightness as far as Gatehouse-of-Fleet. There are large and stately studios, panelled and high, in strong stone houses filled with gleaming brass and polished oak. There are workaday studios – summer perching-places rather than settled homes – where a good north light and a litter of brushes and canvas form the whole of the artistic stock-in-trade. There are little homely studios, gay with blue and red and yellow curtains and odd scraps of pottery, tucked away down narrow closes and adorned with gardens, where old-fashioned flowers riot in the rich and friendly soil. There are studios that are simply and solely barns, made beautiful by ample proportions and high-pitched rafters, and habitable by the addition of a tortoise stove and a gas-ring. There are artists who have large families and keep domestics in cap and apron; artists who engage rooms, and are taken care of by landladies; artists who live in couples or alone, with a woman who comes in to clean, artists who live hermit-like and do their own charing. There are painters in oils, painters in water-colour, painters in pastel, etchers and illustrators, workers in metal; artists of every variety, having this one thing in common – that they take their work seriously and have no time for amateurs.

Into this fishing and painting community, Lord Peter Wimsey was received on friendly and even affectionate terms. He could make a respectable cast, and he did not pretend to paint, and therefore, though English and an 'incomer', gave no cause of offence. The Southron is tolerated in Scotland on the understanding that he does not throw his weight about, and from this peculiarly English vice Lord Peter was laudably free. True, his accent was affected and his behaviour undignified to a degree, but he had been weighed in the balance over many seasons and pronounced harmless, and when he indulged in any startling eccentricity, the matter was dismissed with a shrug and a tolerant, 'Christ, it's only his lordship'.

Wimsey was in the bar of the McClellan Arms on the evening that the unfortunate dispute broke out between Campbell and Waters. Campbell, the landscape painter, had had maybe one or two more wee ones than was absolutely necessary, especially for a man with red hair, and their effect had been to make him even more militantly Scottish than usual. He embarked on a long eulogy of what the Jocks had done in the Great War, only interrupting his tale to inform Waters in parenthesis that all the English were of mongrel ancestry and unable even to pronounce their own bluidy language.

Waters was an Englishman of good yeoman stock, and, like all Englishmen, was ready enough to admire and praise all foreigners except dagoes and niggers, but, like all Englishmen, he did not like to hear them praise themselves. To boast loudly in public of one's own country seemed to him indecent – like enlarging on the physical perfections of one's own wife in a smoking-room. He listened with that tolerant, petrified smile which the foreigner takes, and indeed quite correctly takes, to indicate a self-satisfaction so impervious that it will not even trouble to justify itself.

Campbell pointed out that all the big administrative posts in London were held by Scotsmen, that England had never succeeded in conquering Scotland, that if Scotland wanted Home Rule, by God, she would take it, that when certain specified English regiments had gone to pieces they had had to send for Scottish officers to control them, and that when any section of the front line had found itself in a tight place, its mind was at once relieved by knowing that the Jocks were on its left. 'You ask anybody who was in the War, my lad,' he added, acquiring in this way an unfair advantage over Waters, who had only just reached fighting age when the War ended, 'they'll tell you what they thought of the Jocks.'

'Yes,' said Waters, with a disagreeable sneer, 'I know what they said, "they skite too much".'

Being naturally polite and in a minority, he did not add the remainder of that offensive quotation, but Campbell was able to supply it for himself. He burst into an angry retort, which was not merely nationally, but also personally abusive.

'The trouble with you Scotch,' said Waters, when Campbell paused to take breath, 'is that you have an inferiority complex.'

He emptied his glass in a don't-careish manner and smiled at Wimsey.

It was probably the smile even more than the sneer which put the final touch to Campbell's irritation. He used a few brief and regrettable expressions, and transferred the better part of the contents of his glass to Waters' countenance.

'Och, noo, Mr Campbell,' protested Wullie Murdoch. He did not like these disturbances in his bar.

But Waters by this time was using even more regrettable language than Campbell as they wrestled together among the broken glass and sawdust.

'I'll break your qualified neck for this,' he said savagely, 'you dirty Highland tyke.'

'Here, chuck it, Waters,' said Wimsey, collaring him, 'don't be a fool. The fellow's drunk.'

'Come away, man,' said McAdam, the fisherman, enveloping Campbell in a pair of brawny arms. 'This is no way to behave. Be quiet.'

The combatants fell apart, panting.

'This won't do,' said Wimsey, 'this isn't the League of Nations. A plague on both your houses! Have a bit of sense.'

'He called me a —,' muttered Waters, wiping the whiskey from his face. 'I'm damned if I'll stand it. He'd better keep out of my way, that's all.' He glared furiously at Campbell.

'You'll find me if you want me,' retorted Campbell, '*I* shan't run away.'

'Now, now, gentlemen,' said Murdoch.

'He comes here,' said Campbell, 'with his damned sneering ways –'

'Nay, Mr Campbell,' said the landlord, 'but ye shuldna ha' said thae things to him.'

'I'll say what I damn well like to him,' insisted Campbell.

'Not in my bar,' replied Murdoch, firmly.

'I'll say them in any damned bar I choose,' said Campbell, 'and I'll say it again – he's a —.'

'Hut!' said McAdam, 'Ye'll be thinkin' better of it in the morning. Come away now – I'll give ye a lift back to Gatehouse.'

'You be damned,' said Campbell, 'I've got my own car and I can drive it. And I don't want to see any of the whole blasted lot of ye again.'

He plunged out, and there was a pause.

'Dear, dear,' said Wimsey.

'I think I'd best be off out of it too,' said Waters, sullenly.

Wimsey and McAdam exchanged glances.

'Bide a bit,' said the latter. 'There's no need to be in sic a hurry. Campbell's a hasty man, and when there's a wee bit drink in him he says mair nor he means.'

'Ay,' said Murdoch, 'but he had no call to be layin' them names to Mr Waters, none at all. It's a verra great pity – a verra great pity indeed.'

'I'm sorry if I was rude to the Scotch,' said Waters, 'I didn't mean to be, but I can't stand that fellow at any price.'

'Och, that's a'richt,' said McAdam. 'Ye meant no harm, Mr Waters. What'll ye have?'

'Oh, a double Scotch,' replied Waters, with rather a shamefaced grin.

'That's right,' said Wimsey, 'drown remembrance of the insult in the wine of the country.'

A man named McGeoch, who had held aloof from the disturbance, rose up and came to the bar.

'Another Worthington,' he said briefly. 'Campbell will be getting into trouble one of these days, I shouldn't wonder. The manners of him are past all bearing. You heard what he said to Strachan up at the golf course the other day. Making himself out the boss of the whole place. Strachan told him if he saw him on the course again, he'd wring his neck.'

The others nodded silently. The row between Campbell and the golf-club secretary at Gatehouse had indeed become local history.

'And I would not blame Strachan, neither,' went on McGeoch. 'Here's Campbell only lived two seasons in Gatehouse, and he's setting the whole place by the ears. He's a devil when he's drunk and a lout when he's sober. It's a great shame. Our little artistic community has always got on well together, without giving offence to anybody. And now there are nothing but rows and bickerings – all through this fellow Campbell.'

'Och,' said Murdoch, 'he'll settle down in time. The man's no a native o' these parts and he doesna verra weel understand his place. Forbye, for all his havers, he's no a Scotsman at a', for everybody knows he's fra' Glasgow, and his mother was an Ulsterwoman, by the name of Flanagan.'

'That's the sort that talks loudest,' put in Murray, the banker, who was a native of Kirkwall, and had a deep and not always silent contempt for anybody born south of Wick. 'But it's best to pay no attention to him. If he gets what is coming to him, I'm thinking it'll no be from anybody here.'

He nodded meaningly.

'Ye'll be thinking of Hugh Farren?' suggested McAdam.

'I'll be naming no names,' said Murray, 'but it's well known that he has made trouble for himself with a certain lady.'

'It's no fault of the lady's,' said McGeoch, emphatically.

'I'm not saying it is. But there's some gets into trouble without others to help them to it.'

'I shouldn't have fancied Campbell in the rôle of a home-breaker,' said Wimsey, pleasantly.

'I shouldn't fancy him at all,' growled Waters, 'but he fancies himself quite enough, and one of these days –'

'There, there,' said Murdoch, hastily. 'It's true he's no a verra popular man, is Campbell, but it's best to be patient and tak' no notice of him.'

'That's all very well,' said Waters.

'And wasn't there some sort of row about fishing?' interrupted Wimsey. If the talk had to be about Campbell, it was better to steer it away from Waters at all costs.

'Och, ay,' said McAdam. 'Him and Mr Jock Graham is juist at daggers drawn aboot it. Mr Graham will be fishing the pool below Campbell's hoose. Not but there's plenty pools in the Fleet wi'out disturbin' Campbell, if the man wad juist be peaceable aboot it. But it's no his pool when a's said and dune – the river's free – and it's no to be expectit that Mr Graham will pay ony heed to his claims, him that pays nae heed to onybody.'

'Particularly,' said McGeoch, 'after Campbell had tried to duck him in the Fleet.'

'Did he though, by Jove?' said Wimsey, interested.

'Ay, but he got weel duckit himsel',' said Murdoch, savouring the reminiscence. 'And Graham's been fushin' there every nicht since then, wi' yin or twa of the lads. He'll be there the nicht, I wadna wonder.'

'Then if Campbell's spoiling for a row, he'll know where to go for it,' said Wimsey. 'Come on, Waters, we'd better make tracks.'

Waters, still sulky, rose and followed him. Wimsey steered him home to his lodgings, prattling cheerfully, and tucked him into bed

'And I shouldn't let Campbell get on your nerves,' he said, interrupting a long grumble, 'he's not worth it. Go to sleep and forget it, or you'll do no work tomorrow. That's pretty decent, by the way,' he added, pausing before a landscape which was propped on the chest of drawers. 'You're a good hand with the knife, aren't you, old man?'

'Who, me?' said Waters. 'You don't know what you're talking about. Campbell's the only man who can handle a knife in this place – according to him. He's even had the blasted cheek to say Gowan is an out-of-date old blunderer.'

'That's high treason, isn't it?'

'I should think so. Gowan's a real painter – my God, it makes me hot when I think of it. He actually said it at the Arts Club in Edinburgh, before a whole lot of people, friends of Gowan's.'

'And what did Gowan say?'

'Oh, various things. They're not on speaking terms now. Damn the fellow. He's not fit to live. You heard what he said to me?'

'Yes, but I don't want to hear it again. Let the fellow dree his own weird. He's not worth bothering with.'

'No, that's a fact. And his work's not so wonderful as to excuse his beastly personality.'

'Can't he paint?'

'Oh, he can paint – after a fashion. He's what Gowan calls him – a commercial traveller. His stuff's damned impressive at first sight, but it's all tricks. Anybody could do it, given the formula. I could do a perfectly good Campbell in half an hour. Wait a moment, I'll show you.'

He thrust out a leg from the bed. Wimsey pushed him firmly back again.

'Show me some other time. When I've seen his stuff. I can't tell if he imitation's good till I've seen the original, can I?'

'No. Well, you go and look at his things and then I'll show you. Oh Lord, my head's fuzzy like nothing on earth.'

'Go to sleep,' said Wimsey. 'Shall I tell Mrs McLeod to let you sleep in, as they say? And call you with a couple of aspirins on toast?'

'No; I've got to be up early, worse luck. But I shall be all right in the morning.'

'Well, cheerio, then, and sweet dreams,' said Wimsey.

He shut the door after him carefully and wandered thoughtfully back to his own habitation.

Campbell, chugging fitfully homewards across the hill which separates Kirkcudbright from Gatehouse-of-Fleet, recapitulated his grievances to himself in a sour monotone, as he mishandled his gears. That damned, sneering, smirking swine Waters! He'd managed to jolt him out of his pose of superiority, anyhow. Only he wished it hadn't happened before McGeoch. McGeoch would tell Strachan, and Strachan would redouble his own good opinion of himself. 'You see,' he would say, 'I turned the man off the golf course and look how right I was to do it. He's just a fellow that gets drunk and quarrels in public houses.' Curse Strachan, with his perpetual sergeant-major's air of having you on the mat. Strachan, with his domesticity and his precision and his local influence, was at the base of all the trouble, if one came to think of it. He pretended to say nothing, and all the time he was spreading rumours and scandal and setting the whole place against one. Strachan was a friend of that fellow Farren too. Farren would hear about it, and would jump at the excuse to make himself still more obnoxious. There would have been no silly row that night at all if it hadn't been for Farren. That disgusting scene before dinner! That was what had driven him, Campbell, to the McClellan Arms. His hand hesitated on the wheel. Why not go back straight away and have the thing out with Farren?

After all, what did it matter? He stopped the car and lit a cigarette, smoking fast and savagely. If the whole place *was* against him, he hated the place anyhow. There was only one decent person in it, and she was tied up to that brute Farren. The worst of it was, she was devoted to Farren. She didn't care twopence for anybody else, if Farren would only see it. And he, Campbell, knew it as well as anybody. He wanted nothing wrong. He only wanted, when he was tired and fretted, and sick of his own lonely, uncomfortable shack of a place, to go and sit among the cool greens and blues of Gilda Farren's sitting-room and be soothed by her slim beauty and comforting voice. And Farren, with no more sense or imagination than a bull, must come blundering in, breaking the spell, putting his own foul interpretation on the thing, trampling the lilies in Campbell's garden of refuge. No wonder Farren's landscapes looked as if they were painted with an axe. The man had no delicacy. His reds and blues hurt your eyes, and he saw life in reds and blues. If Farren were to die, now, if one could take his bull-neck in one's hands and squeeze it till his great staring blue eyes popped out like – he laughed – like bull's eyes – that was a damned funny joke. He'd like to tell Farren that and see how he took it.

Farren was a devil, a beast, a bully, with his artistic temperament, which was nothing but inartistic temper. There was no peace with Farren about. There was no peace anywhere. If he went back to Gatehouse, he knew what he would find there. He had only to look out of his bedroom window to see Jock Graham whipping the water just under the wall of the house – doing it on purpose to annoy him. Why couldn't Graham leave him alone? There was better fishing up by the dams. The whole thing was sheer persecution. It wasn't any good, either, to go to bed and take no notice. They would wake him up in the small hours, banging at his window and bawling out the number of their catch – they might even leave a contemptuous offering of trout on his window-sill, wretched little fish like minnows, which ought to have been thrown back again. He only hoped Graham would slip up on the stones one night and fill his waders and be drowned among his infernal fish. The thing that riled him most of all was that this nightly comedy was played out under the delighted eye of his neighbour, Ferguson. Since that fuss about the garden-wall, Ferguson had become absolutely intolerable.

It was perfectly true, of course, that he had backed his car into Ferguson's wall and knocked down a stone or two, but if Ferguson had left his wall in decent repair it wouldn't have done any damage. That great tree of Ferguson's had sent its roots right under the wall and broken up the foundations, and what was more, it threw up huge suckers in Campbell's garden. He was perpetually rooting the beastly things up. A man had no right to grow trees under a wall so that it tumbled down at the slightest little push, and then demand extravagant payments for repairs. He would not repair Ferguson's wall. He would see Ferguson damned first.

He gritted his teeth. He wanted to get out of this stifle of petty quarrels and have one good, big, blazing row with somebody. If only he could have smashed Waters' face to pulp – let himself go – had the thing out, he would have felt better. Even now he could go back – or forward – it didn't matter which, and have the whole blasted thing right out with somebody.

He had been brooding so deeply that he never noticed the hum of a car in the distance and the lights flickering out and disappearing as the road dipped and wound. The first thing he heard was a violent squealing of brakes and an angry voice demanding.

'What the bloody hell are you doing, you fool, sitting out like that in the damn middle of the road right on the bend?' And then, as he turned, blinking in the glare of the headlights, to grapple with this new attack, he heard the voice say, with a kind of exasperated triumph.

'Campbell. Of course. I might have known it couldn't be anybody else.'

CHAPTER II

CAMPBELL DEAD

'Did ye hear aboot Mr Campbell?' said Mr Murdoch of the McClellan Arms, polishing a glass carefully as a preparation for filling it with beer.

'Why what further trouble has he managed to get into since last night?' asked Wimsey. He leaned an elbow on the bar and prepared to relish anything that might be offered to him.

'He's deid,' said Mr Murdoch.

'Deid?' said Wimsey, startled into unconscious mimicry.

Mr Murdoch nodded.

'Och, ay; McAdam's juist brocht the news in from Gatehouse. They found the body at two o'clock up in the hills by Newton Stewart.'

'Good heavens!' said Wimsey. 'But what did he die of?'

'Juist tummled intae the burn,' replied Mr. Murdoch, 'an' drooned himself, by what they say. The pollis'll be up there now tae bring him doon.'

'An accident, I suppose.'

'Ay, imph'm. The folk at the Borgan seed him pentin' there shortly after ten this morning on the wee bit high ground by the brig, and Major Dougal gaed by at two o'clock wi' his rod an' spied the body liggin' in the burn. It's slippery there and fou o' broken rocks. I'm thinkin' he'll ha' climbed doon tae fetch some watter for his pentin', mebbe, and slippit on the stanes.'

'He wouldn't want water for oil-paints,' said Wimsey, thoughtfully, 'but he might have wanted to mix mustard for his sandwiches or fill a kettle or get a drop for his whiskey. I say, Murdoch, I think I'll just toddle over there in the car and have a look at him. Corpses are rather in my line, you know. Where is this place exactly?'

'Ye maun tak' the coast-road through Creetown to Newton Stewart,' said Mr Murdoch, 'and turn to the richt over the brig and then to the richt again at the signpost along the road to Bargrennan and juist follow the road till ye turn over a wee brig on the richt-hand side over the Cree and then tak' the richt-hand road.'

'In fact,' said Wimsey, 'you keep on turning to the right. I think I know the place. There's a bridge and another gate, and a burn with salmon in it.'

'Ay, the Minnoch, whaur Mr Dennison caught the big fish last year. Well, it'll be juist afore ye come to the gate, away to your left abune the brig.'

Wimsey nodded.

'I'll be off then,' he said, 'I don't want to miss the fun. See you later, old boy. I say – I don't mind betting this is the most popular thing Campbell ever did. Nothing in life became him like the leaving it, eh, what?'

It was a marvellous day in late August, and Wimsey's soul purred within him as he pushed the car along. The road from Kirkcudbright to Newton-Stewart is of a varied loveliness hard to surpass, and with a sky full of bright sun and rolling cloud-banks, hedges filled with flowers, a well-made road, a lively engine and the prospect of a good corpse at the end of it, Lord Peter's cup of happiness was full. He was a man who loved simple pleasures.

He passed through Gatehouse, waving a cheerful hand to the Proprietor of the Anwoth Hotel, climbed up beneath the grim blackness of Cardoness Castle, drank in for the thousandth time the strange Japanese beauty of Mossyard Farm, set like a red jewel under its tufted trees on the blue sea's rim, and the Italian loveliness of Kirkdale, with its fringe of thin and twisted trees and the blue Wigtownshire coast gleaming across the bay. Then the old Border keep of Barholm, surrounded by white-washed farm buildings; then a sudden gleam of bright grass, like a lawn in Avalon, under the shade of heavy trees. The wild garlic was over now, but the scent of it seemed still to hang about the place in memory, filling it with the shudder of vampire wings and memories of the darker side of Border history. Then the old granite crushing mill on its white jetty, surrounded by great clouds of stone-dust, with a derrick sprawled across the sky and a tug riding at anchor. Then the salmon-nets and the wide semi-circular sweep of the bay, rosy every summer with sea-pinks, purple-brown with the mud of the estuary, majestic with the huge hump of Cairnsmuir rising darkly over Creetown. Then the open road again, dipping and turning – the white lodge on the left, the cloud-shadows rolling, the cottages with their roses and asters clustered against white and yellow walls; then Newton Stewart, all grey roofs huddling down to the stony bed of the Cree, its thin spires striking the sky-line. Over the bridge and away to the right by the kirkyard, and then the Bargrennan road, curling like the road to Roundabout, with the curves of the Cree glittering through the tree-stems and the tall blossoms and bracken golden by the wayside. Then the lodge and the long avenue of rhododendrons – then a wood of silver birch, mounting, mounting to shut out the sunlight. Then a cluster of stone cottages – then the bridge and the gate, and the stony hill-road, winding between mounds round as the hill of the King of Elf-land, green with grass and purple with heather and various with sweeping shadows.

Wimsey pulled up as he came to the second bridge and the rusty gate, and drew the car on to the grass. There were other cars there, and glancing along to the left he saw a little group of men gathered on the edge of the burn forty or fifty yards from the road. He approached by way of a little sheep-track, and found himself standing on the edge of a scarp of granite that shelved steeply down to the noisy waters of the Minnoch. Beside him, close to the edge of the rock, stood a sketching easel, with a stool and a palette. Down below, at the edge of a clear brown pool fringed with knotted hawthorns, lay something humped and dismal, over which two or three people were bending.

A man, who might have been a crofter, greeted Wimsey with a kind of cautious excitement.

'He's doon there, sir. Ay, he'll juist ha' slippit over the edge. Yon's Sergeant Dalziel and Constable Ross, mekkin' their investigation the noo.'

There seemed little doubt how the accident had happened. On the easel was a painting, half, or more than half finished, the paint still wet and shining. Wimsey could imagine the artist getting up, standing away to view what he had done – stepping farther back towards the treacherous granite slope. Then the scrape of a heel on the smooth stone, the desperate effort to recover, the slither of leather on the baked short grass, the stagger, the fall, and the bump, bump, bump of the tumbling body, sheer down the stone face of the ravine to where the pointed rocks grinned like teeth among the chuckling water.

'I know the man,' said Wimsey. 'It's a very nasty thing, isn't it? I think I'll go down and have a look.'

'Ye'll mind your footing,' said the crofter.

'I certainly will,' said Wimsey, clambering crablike among the stones and bracken. 'I don't want to make another police exhibit.'

The Sergeant looked up at the sound of Wimsey's scrambling approach. They had met already, and Dalziel was prepared for Wimsey's interest in corpses, however commonplace the circumstances.

'Hech, my lord,' said he, cheerfully. 'I dooted ye'd be here before verra long. Ye'll know Dr Cameron, maybe?'

Wimsey shook hands with the doctor – a lanky man with a non-committal face and asked how they were getting on with the business.

'Och, well, I've examined him,' said the doctor. 'He's dead beyond a doubt – been dead some hours, too. The rigor, ye see, is well developed.'

'Was he drowned?'

'I cannot be certain about that. But my opinion – mind ye, it is only my opinion – is that he was not. The bones of the temple are fractured, and I would be inclined to say he got his death in falling or in striking the stones in the burn. But I cannot make a definite pronouncement, you understand, till I have had an autopsy and seen if there is any water in his lungs.'

'Quite so,' said Wimsey. 'The bump on the head might only have made him unconscious, and the actual cause of death might be drowning.'

'That is so. When we first saw him, he was lying with his mouth under water, but that might very well come from washing about in the scour of the burn. There are certain abrasions on the hands and head, some of which are – again in my opinion – post-mortem injuries. See here – and here.'

The doctor turned the corpse over, to point out the marks in question. It moved all of a piece, crouched and bundled together, as though it had stiffened in the act of hiding its face from the brutal teeth of the rocks.

'But here's where he got the big dunt,' added the doctor. He guided Wimsey's fingers to Campbell's left temple, and Wimsey felt the bone give under his light pressure.

'Nature has left the brain ill-provided in those parts,' remarked Dr Cameron. 'The skull there is remarkably thin, and a comparatively trifling blow will crush it like an egg-shell.'

Wimsey nodded. His fine, long fingers were gently exploring head and limbs. The doctor watched him with grave approval.

'Man,' he said, 'ye'd make a fine surgeon. Providence has given ye the hands for it.'

'But not the head,' said Wimsey, laughing. 'Yes, he's got knocked about a bit. I don't wonder, coming down that bank full tilt.'

'Ay, it's a dangerous place,' said the Sergeant. 'Weel, noo, doctor, I'm thinkin' we've seen a' that's to be seen doon here. We would better be getting the body up to the car.'

'I'll go back and have a look at the painting,' said Wimsey, 'unless I can help you with the lifting. I don't want to be in the way.'

'Nay, nay,' said the Sergeant. 'Thank you for the offer, my lord, but we can manage fine by oorsel's.'

The Sergeant and a constable bent over and seized the body. Wimsey waited to see that that they required no assistance, and then scrambled up to the top of the bank again.

He gave his first attention to the picture. It was blocked in with a free and swift hand, and lacked the finishing touches, but it was even so a striking piece of work, bold in its masses and chiaroscuro, and strongly laid on with the knife. It showed a morning lighting – he remembered that Campbell had been seen painting a little after ten o'clock. The grey stone bridge lay cool in the golden night, and the berries of a rowan tree, good against witchcraft, hung yellow and red against it, casting splashes of red reflection upon the brown and white of the tumbling water beneath. Up on the left, the hills soared away in veil on veil of misty blue to meet the hazy sky. And splashed against the blue stood the great gold splendour of the bracken, flung in by spadefuls of pure reds and yellows.

Idly, Wimsey picked up the palette and painting-knife which lay upon the stool. He noticed that Campbell used a simple palette of few colours, and this pleased him, for he liked to see economy of means allied with richness of result. On the ground was an aged satchel, which had evidently seen long service. Rather from habit than with any eye to deduction, he made an inventory of its contents.

In the main compartment he found a small flask of whiskey, half-full, a thick tumbler and a packet of bread and cheese, eight brushes, tied together with a dejected piece of linen which had once been a handkerchief but was now dragging out a dishonoured existence as a paint-rag, a dozen loose brushes, two more painting-knives and a scraper. Cheek by jowl with these were a number of tubes of paint. Wimsey laid them out side by side on the granite, like a row of little corpses.

There was a half-pound tube of vermilion spectrum, new, clean and almost unused, a studio-size tube of ultramarine No. 2, half-full, another of chrome yellow, nearly full, and another of the same, practically empty. Then came a half-pound tube of viridian, half-full, a studio-size cobalt three-quarters empty, and then an extremely dirty tube, with its label gone, which seemed to have survived much wear and tear without losing much of its contents. Wimsey removed the cap and diagnosed it as crimson lake. Finally, there was an almost empty studio-size tube of rose madder and a half-pound lemon yellow, partly used and very dirty.

Wimsey considered this collection for a moment, and then dived confidently into the satchel again. The large compartment, however, yielded nothing further except some dried heather, a few shreds of tobacco and a quantity of crumbs, and he turned his attention to the two smaller compartments.

In the first of these was, first, a small screw of greaseproof paper on which brushes had been wiped; next, a repellent little tin, very sticky about the screw-cap, containing copal medium; and, thirdly, a battered dipper, matching the one attached to the palette.

The third and last compartment of the satchel offered a more varied bag. There was a Swan vesta box, filled with charcoal, a cigarette-tin, also containing charcoal and a number of sticks of red chalk, a small sketchbook, heavily stained with oil, three or four canvas-separators, on which Wimsey promptly pricked his fingers, some wine-corks and a packet of Gold Flakes.

Wimsey's air of idleness had left him. His long and inquisitive nose seemed to twitch like a rabbit's as he turned the satchel upside down and shook it, in the vain hope of extracting something more from its depths. He rose, and searched the easel and the ground about the stool very carefully.

A wide cloak of a disagreeable check pattern lay beside the easel. He picked it up and went deliberately through the pockets. He found a penknife, with one blade broken, half a biscuit, another packet of cigarettes, a box of matches, a handkerchief, two trout-casts in a transparent envelope, and a piece of string.

He shook his head. None of these was what he wanted. He searched the ground again, casting like a hound on the trail, and then, still dissatisfied, began to lower himself gingerly down the smooth face of the rock. There were crannies here into which something might have fallen, clumps of bracken and heather, prickly roots of gorse. He hunted and felt about in every corner, stabbing his fingers again at every move and swearing savagely. Small fragments of gorse worked their way up his trouser-legs and into his shoes. The heat was stifling. Close to the bottom he slipped, and did the last yard or so on his hinderparts, which irritated him. At a shout from the top of the bank he looked up. The Sergeant was grinning down at him.

'Reconstructing the accident, my lord?'

'Not exactly,' said Wimsey. 'Here, wait just a moment, will you?'

He scrambled up again. The corpse was now laid as decently as possible on a stretcher, awaiting removal.

'Have you searched his pockets?' panted Wimsey.

'Not yet, my lord. Time enough for that at the station. It's purely a formality, ye ken.'

'No, it's not,' said Wimsey. He pushed his hat back and wiped the sweat from his forehead. 'There's something funny about this, Dalziel. That is, there may be. Do you mind if I go over his belongings now?'

'Not at all, not at all,' said Dalziel, heartily. 'There's no sic a great hurry. We may as weel dew't first as last.'

Wimsey sat down on the ground beside the stretcher, and the Sergeant stood by with a notebook to chronicle the finds.

The right-hand coat pocket contained another handkerchief, a Hardy catalogue, two crumpled bills and an object which caused the Sergeant to exclaim laughingly, 'What's this, lipstick?'

'Nothing so suggestive,' said Wimsey, sadly, 'it's a holder for lead pencil – made in Germany, to boot. Still, if that's there, there might be something else.'

The left-hand pocket, however, produced nothing more exciting than a corkscrew and some dirt; the breast-pocket, only an Ingersoll watch, a pocket comb and a half-used book of stamps; and Wimsey turned, without much hope, to the trouser-pockets, for the dead man wore no waistcoat.

Here, on the right, they found a quantity of loose cash, the notes and coins jumbled carelessly together, and a bunch of keys on a ring. On the left, an empty matchbox and a pair of folding nail-scissors. In the hip-pocket, a number of dilapidated letters, some newspaper cuttings and a small notebook with nothing in it.

Wimsey sat up and stared at the Sergeant.

'It's not here,' he said, 'and I don't like the look of it at all, Dalziel. Look here, there's just one possibility. It may have rolled down into the water. For God's sake get your people together and hunt for it – now. Don't lose a minute.'

Dalziel gazed at this excitable Southerner in some astonishment, and the constable pushed back his cap and scratched his head.

'What would we be lookin' for?' he demanded, reasonably.

(Here Lord Peter Wimsey told the Sergeant what he was to look for and why, but as the intelligent reader will readily supply these details for himself, they are omitted from this page.)

'It'll be important, then, to your way o' thinking,' said Dalziel, with the air of a man hopefully catching, through a forest of obscurity, the first, far-off glimmer of the obvious.

'Important?' said Wimsey. 'Of course it's important. Incredibly, urgently, desperately important. Do you think I should be sliding all over your infernal granite making a blasted pincushion of myself if it wasn't important?'

This argument seemed to impress the Sergeant. He called his force together and set them to search the path, the bank and the burn for the missing object. Wimsey, meanwhile, strolled over to a shabby old four-seater Morris, which stood drawn well up on the grass at the beginning of the sheep-track.

'Ay,' said Constable Ross, straightening his back and sucking his fingers, preliminary to a further hunt among the prickles, 'yon's his car. Maybe ye'll find what ye're wantin' in it, after all.'

'Don't you believe it, laddie,' said Wimsey. Nevertheless, he subjected the car to a careful scrutiny, concentrated for the most part upon the tonneau. A tarry smear on the back cushions seemed to interest him particularly. He examined it carefully with a lens, whistling gently the while. Then he searched further and discovered another on the edge of the body, close to the angle behind the driver's seat. On the floor of the car lay a rug, folded up. He shook it out and looked it over from corner to corner. Another patch of grit and tar rewarded him.

Wimsey pulled out a pipe and lit it thoughtfully. Then he hunted in the pockets of the car till he found an ordnance map of the district. He climbed into the driver's seat, spread out the map on the wheel, and plunged into meditation.

Presently the Sergeant came back, very hot and red in the face, in his shirtsleeves.

'We've searched high and low,' he said, stooping to wring the water from his trouser-legs, 'but we canna find it. Maybe ye'll be tellin' us now why the thing is so important.'

'Oh?' said Wimsey. 'You look rather warm, Dalziel. I've cooled off nicely, sitting here. It's not there, then?'

'It is not,' said the Sergeant, with emphasis.

'In that case,' said Wimsey, 'you had better go to the coroner – no, of course, you don't keep coroners in these parts. The Procurator Fiscal is the lad. You'd better go to the Fiscal and tell him the man's been murdered.'

'Murdered?' said the Sergeant.

'Yes,' said Wimsey, 'och, ay; likewise hoots! Murrrderrrt is the word.'

'Eh!' said the Sergeant. 'Here, Ross!'

'The constable came up to them at a slow gallop.

'Here's his lordship,' said the Sergeant, 'is of opeenion the man's been murdered.'

'Is he indeed?' said Ross. 'Ay, imph'm. And what should bring his lordship to that conclusion?'

'The rigidity of the corpse,' said Wimsey, 'the fact that you can't find what you're looking for, these smears of tar on the Morris, and the character of the deceased. He was a man anybody might have felt proud to murder.'

'The rigidity of the corpse, now,' said Dalziel. 'That'll be a matter for Dr Cameron.'

'I confess,' said the doctor, who had now joined them, 'that has been puzzling me. If the man had not been seen alive it after ten o'clock this morning, I would have said he had been nearer twelve hours dead.'

'So should I,' said Wimsey. 'On the other hand, you'll notice that that painting, which was put on with a quick-drying copal medium, is still comparatively wet, in spite of the hot sun and the dry air.'

'Ay,' said the doctor. 'So I am forced to the conclusion that the chill of the water produced early rigor.'

'I do not submit to force,' said Wimsey. 'I prefer to believe that the man was killed about midnight. I do not believe in that painting. I do not think it is telling the truth. I know that it is absolutely impossible for Campbell to have been working here on that painting this morning.'

'Why so?' inquired the Sergeant.

'For the reasons I gave you before,' said Wimsey. 'And there's another small point – not very much in itself, but supporting the same conclusion. The whole thing looks – and is meant to look – as though Campbell had got up from his painting, stepped back to get a better view of his canvas, missed his footing and fallen down. But his palette and painting-knife were laid down on his stool. Now it's far more likely that, if he were doing that, he would have kept his palette on his thumb and his knife or brush in his hand, ready to make any little extra touch that was required. I don't say he might not have laid them down. I only say it would have looked more natural if we had found the palette beside the body and the knife halfway down the slope.'

'Ay,' said Ross. 'I've seen 'em dew that. Steppin' back wi' their eyes half-shut and then hoppin' forward wi' the brush as if they was throwin' darts.'

Wimsey nodded.

'It's my theory,' he said, 'that the murderer brought the body here this morning in Campbell's own car. He was wearing Campbell's soft hat and that foul plaid cloak of his so that anybody passing by might mistake him for Campbell. He had the body on the floor of the tonneau and on top of it he had a push-cycle; which has left tarry marks on the cushions. Tucked in over the whole lot he had this rug, which has tar-marks on it too. Then I think he dragged out the corpse, carried it up the sheep-track on his shoulders and tumbled it into the burn. Or possibly he left it lying on the top of the bank, covered with the rug. Then, still wearing Campbell's hat and cloak, he sat down and faked the picture. When he had done enough to create the impression that Campbell had been here painting, he took off the cloak and hat, left the palette and knife on the seat and went away on his push-bike. It's a lonely spot, here. A man might easily commit a dozen murders, if he chose his time well.'

'That's a verra interesting theory,' said Dalziel.

'You can test it,' said Wimsey. 'If anybody saw Campbell this morning to speak to, or close enough to recognise his face, then, of course, it's a wash-out. But if they only saw the hat and cloak, and especially if they noticed anything bulky in the back of the car with a rug over it, then the theory stands. Mind you, I don't say the bicycle is absolutely necessary to the theory, but it's what I should have used in the murderer's place. And if you'll look at this smear of tar under the lens, you'll see traces of the tread of a tyre.'

'I'll no say ye're no richt,' said Dalziel.

'Very well,' said Wimsey. 'Now let's see what our murderer has to do next.' He flapped the map impressively, and the two policemen bent their heads over it with him.

'Here he is,' said Wimsey, 'with only a bicycle to help or hinder him, and he's got to establish some sort of an alibi. He may not have bothered about anything very complicated, but he'd make haste to dissociate himself from this place as quickly as possible. And I don't fancy he'd be anxious to show himself in Newton-Stewart or Creetown. There's nowhere much for him to go northward – it only takes him up into the hills round Larg and the Rhinns of Kells. He could go up to Glen Trool, but there's not much point in that; he'd only have to come back the same way. He might, of course, follow the Cree back on the eastern bank as far as Minniegaff, avoiding Newton Stewart, and strike across country to New Galloway, but it's a long road and keeps him hanging about much too close to the scene of the crime. In my opinion, his best way would be to come back to the road and go north-west by Bargrennan, Cairnderry, Creeside and Drumbain, and strike the railway at Barrhill. That's about nine or ten miles by road. He could do it, going briskly, in an hour, or, as it's a rough road, say an hour and a half. Say he finished the painting at eleven o'clock, that brings him to Barrhill at 12.30. From there he could get a train to Stranraer and Port Patrick, or even to Glasgow, or, of course, if he dumped the bicycle, he might take a motor-bus to somewhere. If I were you, I'd have a hunt in that direction.'

The Sergeant glanced at his colleagues and read approval in their eyes.

'And whae d'ye think, my lord, wad be the likeliest pairson to hae committed the crime?' he inquired.

'Well,' said Wimsey, 'I can think of half a dozen people with perfectly good motives. But the murderer's got to be an artist, and a clever one, for that painting would have to pass muster as Campbell's work. He must know how to drive a car, and he must possess, or have access to, a bicycle. He must be fairly hefty, to have carried the body up here on his back, for I see no signs of dragging. He must have been in contact with Campbell after 9.15 last night, when I saw him leave the McClellan Arms alive and kicking. He must know the country and the people pretty well, for he obviously knew that Campbell lived alone with only a charwoman coming in, so that his early morning departure would surprise nobody. He either lives in the same way himself, or else had a very good excuse for being up and out before breakfast this morning. If you find a man who fulfils all these conditions, he's probably the right one. His railway ticket, if he took one, ought to be traceable. Or it's quite possible I may be able to put my finger on him myself, working on different lines and with rather less exertion.'

'Och, weel,' said the Sergeant, 'if ye find him, ye'll let us know.'

'I will,' said Wimsey, 'though it will be rather unpleasant, because ten to one he'll be some bloke I know and like much better than Campbell. Still, it doesn't do to murder people, however offensive they may be. I'll do my best to bring him in captive to my bow and spear – if he doesn't slay me first.'

'Richard Crookback'

from The Daughter of Time

JOSEPHINE TEY (1897–1952)

'Josephine Tey' was the pseudonym used by Elizabeth Mackintosh for her detective fiction. Mackintosh was born in Inverness and educated at the Royal Academy there and at a college of physical education in England before taking up a career as a school PE teacher. In 1929 she published her first detective story (as 'Gordon Daviot') and continued to write fiction and plays under her two pen names until her death.

The Daughter of Time, first published in 1951, features her Scotland Yard Inspector, Alan Grant, in an unusual example of detective fiction. The detective is confined to a hospital bed (having fallen down an open hatch in hot pursuit of a criminal) and the case is almost 450 years old.

Grant takes up the case of Richard III of England, Richard Crookback, the last king of the House of York, the subject of one of Shakespeare's more memorable pieces of pro-Tudor character assination and the man blamed down through the centuries for the murder of his nephews – the Princes in the Tower. Like other investigators Grant concludes that Richard was not the dark-dyed villain of popular legend.

The novel's title is derived from an old proverb which says that 'Truth is the daughter of time'. The testing of the evidence and the search for bias, malice and motivation interestingly points up the similarities in method between criminal and historical investigation.

Grant lay on his high white cot and stared at the ceiling. Stared at it with loathing. He knew by heart every last minute crack on its nice clean surface. He had made maps of the ceiling and gone exploring on them; rivers, islands, and continents. He had made guessing games of it and discovered hidden objects; faces, birds, and fishes. He had made mathematical calculations of it and rediscovered his childhood; theorems, angles, and triangles. There was practically nothing else he could do but look at it. He hated the sight of it.

He had suggested to The Midget that she might turn his bed round a little so that he could have a new patch of ceiling to explore. But it seemed that that would spoil the symmetry of the room, and in hospitals symmetry ranked just a short head behind cleanliness and a whole length in front of Godliness. Anything out of the parallel was hospital profanity. Why didn't he read? she asked. Why didn't he go on reading some of those expensive brand-new novels that his friends kept on bringing him.

'There are far too many people born into the world, and far too many words written. Millions and millions of them pouring from the presses every minute. It's a horrible thought.'

'You sound constipated,' said The Midget.

The Midget was Nurse Ingham, and she was in sober fact a very nice five-feet two, with everything in just proportion. Grant called her The Midget to compensate himself for being bossed around by a piece of Dresden china which he could pick up in one hand. When he was on his feet, that is to say. It was not only that she told him what he might or might not do, but she dealt with his six-feet-odd with an off-hand ease that Grant found humiliating. Weights meant nothing, apparently, to The Midget. She tossed mattresses around with the absent-minded grace of a plate spinner. When she was off-duty he was attended to by The Amazon, a goddess with arms like the limb of a beech tree. The Amazon was Nurse Darroll, who came from Gloucestershire and was homesick each daffodil season. (The Midget came from Lytham St Anne's, and there was no daffodil nonsense about her.) She had large soft hands and large soft cow's eyes and she always looked very sorry for you, but the slightest physical exertion set her breathing like a suction pump. On the whole Grant found it even more humiliating to be treated as a dead weight than to be treated as if he was no weight at all.

Grant was bed-borne, and a charge on The Midget and The Amazon, because he had fallen through a trap-door. This, of course, was the absolute in humiliation; compared with which the heavings of The Amazon and the light slingings of The Midget were a mere corollary. To fall through a trap-door was the ultimate in absurdity; pantomimic, bathetic, grotesque. At the moment of his disappearance from the normal level of perambulation he had been in hot pursuit of Benny Skoll, and the fact that Benny had careered round the next corner slap into the arms of Sergeant Williams provided the one small crumb of comfort in an intolerable situation.

Benny was now 'away' for three years, which was very satisfactory for the lieges, but Benny would get time off for good behaviour. In hospitals there was no time off for good behaviour.

Grant stopped staring at the ceiling, and slid his eye sideways at the pile of books on his bedside table; the gay expensive pile that The Midget had been urging on his attention. The top one, with the pretty picture of Valetta in unlikely pink, was Lavinia Fitch's annual account of a blameless heroine's tribulations. In view of the representation of the Grand Harbour on the cover, the present Valerie or Angela or Cecile or Denise must be a naval wife. He had opened the book only to read the kind message that Lavinia had written inside.

The Sweat and the Furrow was Silas Weekley being earthy and spade-conscious all over seven hundred pages. The situation, to judge from the first paragraph, had not materially changed since Silas's last book: mother lying-in with her eleventh upstairs, father laid-out after his ninth downstairs, eldest son lying to the Government in the cow-shed, eldest daughter lying with her lover in the hay-loft, everyone else lying low in the barn. The rain dripped from the thatch, and the manure steamed in the midden. Silas never omitted the manure. It was not Silas's fault that its steam provided the only up-rising element in the picture. If Silas could have discovered a brand of steam that steamed downwards, Silas would have introduced it.

Under the harsh shadows and highlights of Silas's jacket was an elegant affair of Edwardian curlicues and Baroque nonsense, entitled *Bells on Her Toes*. Which was Rupert Rouge being arch about vice. Rupert Rouge always seduced you into laughter for the first three pages. About Page Three you noticed that Rupert had learned from that very arch (but of course not vicious) creature George Bernard Shaw that the easiest way to sound witty was to use that cheap and convenient method, the paradox. After that you could see the jokes coming three sentences away.

The thing with a red gun-flash across a night-green cover was Oscar Oakley's latest. Toughs talking out of the corners of their mouths in synthetic American that had neither the wit nor the pungency of the real thing. Blondes, chromium bars, breakneck chases. Very remarkably bunk.

The Case of the Missing Tin-opener, by John James Mark, had three errors of procedure in the first two pages, and had at least provided Grant with a pleasant five minutes while he composed an imaginary letter to its author.

He could not remember what the thin blue book at the bottom of the pile was. Something earnest and statistical, he thought. Tsetse flies, or calories, or sex behaviour, or something.

Even in that, you knew what to expect on the next page. Did no one, any more, no one in all this wide world, change their record now and then? Was everyone nowadays thirled to a formula? Authors today wrote so much to a pattern that their public expected it. The public talked about 'a new Silas Weekley' or 'a new Lavinia Fitch' exactly as they talked about 'a new brick' or 'a new hairbrush'. They never said 'a new book by' whoever it might be. Their interest was not in the book but in its newness. They knew quite well what the book would be like.

It might be a good thing, Grant thought as he turned his nauseated gaze away from the motley pile, if all the presses of the world were stopped for a generation. There ought to be a literary moratorium. Some Superman ought to invent a ray that would stop them all simultaneously. Then people wouldn't send you a lot of fool nonsense when you were flat on your back, and bossy bits of Meissen wouldn't expect you to read them.

He heard the door open, but did not stir himself to look. He had turned his face to the wall, literally and metaphorically.

He heard someone come across to his bed, and closed his eyes against possible conversation. He wanted neither Gloucestershire sympathy nor Lancashire briskness just now. In the succeeding pause a faint enticement, a nostalgic breath of all the fields of Grasse, teased his nostrils and swam about his brain. He savoured it and considered. The Midget smelt of lavender dusting powder, and The Amazon of soap and iodoform. What was floating expensively about his nostrils was *L'Enclos Numéro Cinq*. Only one person of his acquaintance used L'Enclos Number Five. Marta Hallard.

He opened an eye and squinted up at her. She had evidently bent over to see if he was asleep, and was now standing in an irresolute way – if anything Marta did could be said to be irresolute – with her attention on the heap of all too obviously virgin publications on the table. In one arm she was carrying two new books, and in the other a great sheaf of white lilac. He wondered whether she had chosen white lilac because it was her idea of the proper floral offering for winter (it adorned her dressing room at the theatre from December to March), or whether she had taken it because it would not detract from her black-and-white chic. She was wearing a new hat and her usual pearls; the pearls which he had once been the means of recovering for her. She looked very handsome, very Parisian, and blessedly unhospital-like.

'Did I waken you, Alan?'

'No. I wasn't asleep.'

'I seem to be bringing the proverbial coals,' she said, dropping the two books alongside their despised brethren. 'I hope you will find these more interesting than you seem to have found that lot. Didn't you even try a little teensy taste of our Lavinia?'

'I can't read anything.'

'Are you in pain?'

'Agony. But it's neither my leg nor my back.'

'What then?'

'It's what my cousin Laura calls "the prickles of boredom".'

'Poor Alan. And how right your Laura is.' She picked a bunch of narcissi out of a glass that was much too large for them, dropped them with one of her best gestures into the wash-basin, and proceeded to substitute the lilac. 'One would expect boredom to be a great yawning emotion, but it isn't, of course. It's a small niggling thing.'

'Small nothing. Niggling nothing. It's like being beaten with nettles.'

'Why don't you take up something?'

'Improve the shining hour?'

'Improve your mind. To say nothing of your soul and your temper. You might study one of the philosophies. Yoga, or something like that. But I suppose an analytical mind is not the best kind to bring to the consideration of the abstract.'

'I did think of going back to algebra. I have an idea that I never did algebra justice, at school. But I've done so much geometry on that damned ceiling that I'm a little off mathematics.'

'Well, I suppose it is no use suggesting jigsaws to someone in your position. How about crosswords? I could get you a book of them, if you like.'

'God forbid.'

'You could invent them, of course. I have heard that that is more fun than solving them.'

'Perhaps. But a dictionary weighs several pounds. Besides, I always did hate looking up something in a reference book.'

'Do you play chess? I don't remember. How about chess problems? White to play and mate in three moves, or something like that.'

'My only interest in chess is pictorial.'

'Pictorial?'

'Very decorative things, knights and pawns and whatnot. Very elegant.'

'Charming. I *could* bring you along a set to play with. All right, no chess. You could do some academic investigating. That's a sort of mathematics. Finding a solution to an unsolved problem.'

'Crime, you mean? I know all the case histories by heart. And there is nothing more that can be done about any of them. Certainly not by someone who is flat on his back.'

'I didn't mean something out of the files at the Yard. I meant something more – what's the word? – something classic. Something that has puzzled the world for ages.'

'As what, for instance?'

'Say, the casket letters.'

'Oh, *not* Mary Queen of Scots!'

'Why not?' asked Marta, who like all actresses saw Mary Stuart through a haze of white veils.

'I could be interested in a bad woman but never in a silly one.'

'*Silly?*' said Marta in her best lower-register Electra voice.

'*Very* silly.'

'Oh, Alan, how can you!'

'If she had worn another kind of headdress no one would ever have bothered about her. It's that cap that seduces people.'

'You think she would have loved less greatly in a sunbonnet?'

'She never loved greatly at all, in any kind of bonnet.'

Marta looked as scandalised as a lifetime in the theatre and an hour of careful make-up allowed her to.

'Why do you think that?'

'Mary Stuart was six feet tall. Nearly all outsize women are cold. Ask any doctor.'

And as he said it he wondered why, in all the years since Marta had first adopted him as a spare escort when she needed one, it had not occurred to him to wonder whether her notorious level-headedness about men had something to do with her inches. But Marta had not drawn any parallels; her mind was still on her favourite Queen.

'At least she was a martyr. You'll have to allow her that.'

'Martyr to what?'

'Her religion.'

'The only thing she was a martyr to was rheumatism. She married Darnley without the Pope's dispensation, and Bothwell by Protestant rites.'

'In a moment you'll be telling me she wasn't a prisoner!'

'The trouble with you is that you think of her in a little room at the top of a castle, with bars on the window and a faithful old attendant to share her prayers with her. In actual fact she had a personal household of sixty persons. She complained bitterly when it was reduced to a beggarly thirty, and nearly died of chagrin when it was reduced to two male secretaries, several women, an embroiderer, and a cook or two. And Elizabeth had to pay for all that out of her own purse. For twenty years she paid, and for twenty years Mary Stuart hawked the crown of Scotland round Europe to anyone who would start a revolution and put her back on the throne that she had lost; or, alternatively, on the one Elizabeth was sitting on.'

'He looked at Marta and found that she was smiling.

'Are they a little better now?' she asked.

'Are what better?'

'The prickles.'

He laughed.

'Yes. For a whole minute I had forgotten about them. That is at least one good thing to be put down to Mary Stuart's account!'

'How do you know so much about Mary?'

'I did an essay about her in my last year at school.'

'And didn't like her, I take it.'

'Didn't like what I found out about her.'

'You don't think her tragic, then.'

'Oh, yes, very. But not tragic in any of the ways that popular belief makes her tragic. Her tragedy was that she was born a Queen with the outlook of a suburban housewife. Scoring off Mrs Tudor in the next street is harmless and amusing; it may lead you into unwarrantable indulgence in hire-purchase, but it affects only yourself. When you use the same technique on kingdoms the result is disastrous. If you are willing to put a country of ten million people in pawn in order to score off a royal rival, then you end by being a friendless failure.' He lay thinking about it for a little. 'She would have been a wild success as a mistress at a girls' school.'

'Beast!'

'I meant it nicely. The staff would have liked her, and all the little girls would have adored her. That is what I meant about her being tragic.'

'Ah well. No casket letters, it seems. What else is there? The Man In The Iron Mask.'

'I can't remember who that was, but I couldn't be interested in anyone who was being coy behind some tin plate. I couldn't be interested in anyone at all unless I could see his face.'

'Ah, yes. I forgot your passion for faces. The Borgias had wonderful faces. I should think they would provide a little mystery or two for you to dabble in if you looked them up. Or there was Perkin Warbeck, of course. Imposture is always fascinating. Was he or wasn't he. A lovely game. The balance can never come down wholly on one side or the other. You push it over and up it comes again, like one of those weighted toys.'

The door opened and Mrs Tinker's homely face appeared in the aperture surmounted by her still more homely and historic hat. Mrs Tinker had worn the same hat since first she began to 'do' for Grant, and he could not imagine her in any other. That she did possess another one he knew, because it went with something that she referred to as 'me blue'. Her 'blue' was an occasional affair, in both senses, and never appeared at 9 Tenby Court. It was worn with a ritualistic awareness and having been worn it was used in the event as a yardstick by which to judge the proceedings. ('Did you enjoy it, Tink? What was it like?' 'Not worth putting on me blue for.') She had worn it to Princess Elizabeth's wedding, and to various other royal functions, and had indeed figured in it for two flashing seconds in a newsreel shot of the Duchess of Kent cutting a ribbon, but to Grant it was a mere report; a criterion of the social worth of an occasion. A thing was or was not worth putting on 'me blue' for.

'I 'eard you 'ad a visitor,' said Mrs Tinker, 'and I was all set to go away again when I thought the voice sounded familiar like, and I says to meself: "It's only Miss Hallard," I says, so I come in.'

She was carrying various paper bags and a small tight bunch of anemones. She greeted Marta as woman to woman, having been in her time a dresser and having therefore no exaggerated reverence for the goddesses of the theatre world, and looked askance at the beautiful arrangement of lilac sprays that had blossomed under Marta's ministrations. Marta did not see the glance but she saw the little bunch of anemones and took over the situation as if it were something already rehearsed.

'I squander my vagabond's hire on white lilac for you, and then Mrs Tinker puts my nose out of joint by bringing you the Lilies Of The Field.'

'Lilies?' said Mrs Tinker, doubtfully.

'Those are the Solomon in all his glory things. The ones that toiled not neither did they spin.'

Mrs Tinker went to church only for weddings and christenings, but she belonged to a generation that had been sent to Sunday school. She looked with a new interest at the little handful of glory incased by her woollen glove.

'Well, now. I never knew that. Makes more sense that way, don't it. I always pictured them arums. Fields and fields of arums. Awful expensive, you know, but a bit depressing. So they was coloured? Well, why can't they say so? What do they have to call them lilies for!'

And they went on to talk about translation, and how misleading Holy Writ could be ('I always wondered what bread on the waters was,' Mrs Tinker said) and the awkward moment was over.

While they were still busy with the Bible, The Midget came in with extra flower vases. Grant noticed that the vases were designed to hold white lilac and not anemones. They were tribute to Marta; a passport to further communing. But Marta never bothered about women unless she had an immediate use for them; her tact with Mrs Tinker had been mere *savoir faire*: a conditioned reflex. So The Midget was reduced to being functional instead of social. She collected the discarded narcissi from the wash-basin and meekly put them back into a vase. The Midget being meek was the most beautiful sight that had gladdened Grant's eyes for a long time.

'Well,' Marta said, having finished her arrangement of the lilac and placed the result where he could see it, 'I shall leave Mrs Tinker to feed you all the titbits out of those paper bags. It couldn't be, could it, Mrs Tinker darling, that one of those bags contains any of your wonderful bachelor's buttons?'

Mrs Tinker glowed.

'You'd like one or two maybe? Fresh outa me oven?'

'Well, of course I shall have to do penance for it afterwards – those little rich cakes are death on the waist – but just give me a couple to put in my bag for my tea at the theatre.'

She chose two with a flattering deliberation ('I like them a little brown at the edges'), dropped them into her handbag, and said: 'Well, au revoir, Alan. I shall look in, in a day or two, and start you on a sock. There is nothing so soothing, I understand, as knitting. Isn't that so, nurse?'

'Oh, yes. Yes, indeed. A lot of my gentlemen patients take to knitting. They find it whiles away the time very nicely.'

Marta blew him a kiss from the door and was gone, followed by the respectful Midget.

'I'd be surprised if that hussy is any better than she ought to be,' Mrs Tinker said, beginning to open the paper bags. She was not referring to Marta.

But when Marta came back two days later it was not with knitting needles and wool. She breezed in, very dashing in a Cossack hat worn at a casual rake that must have taken her several minutes at her mirror, just after lunch.

'I haven't come to stay, my dear. I'm on my way to the theatre. It's matinée day, God help me. Tea trays and morons. And we've all got to the frightful stage when the lines have ceased to have any meaning at all for us. I don't think this play is ever coming off. It's going to be like those New York ones that run by the decade instead of by the year. It's too frightening. One's mind just won't stay on the thing. Geoffrey dried up in the middle of the second act last night. His eyes nearly popped out of his head. I thought for a moment he was having a stroke. He said afterwards that he had no recollection of anything that happened between his entrance and the point where he came to and found himself half-way through the act.'

'A black-out, you mean?'

'No. Oh, no. Just being an automaton. Saying the lines and doing the business and thinking of something else all the time.'

'If all reports are true that's no unusual matter where actors are concerned.'

'Oh, in moderation, no. Johnny Garson can tell you how much paper there is in the house what time he is sobbing his heart out on someone's lap. But that's different from being "away" for half an act. Do you realise that Geoffrey had turned his son out of the house, quarrelled with his mistress, and accused his wife of having an affaire with his best friend all without being aware of it.'

'What *was* he aware of?'

'He says he had decided to lease his Park Lane flat to Dolly Dacre and buy that Charles the Second house at Richmond that the Latimers are giving up because he has got that Governor's appointment. He had thought about the lack of bathrooms and decided that the little upstairs room with the eighteenth century Chinese paper would make a very good one. They could remove the beautiful paper and use it to decorate that dull little room downstairs at the back. It's full of Victorian panelling, the dull little room. He had also reviewed the drainage, wondered if he had enough money to take the old tiling off and replace it, and speculated as to what kind of cooking range they had in the kitchen. He had just decided to get rid of the shrubbery at the gate when he found himself face to face with me, on a stage, in the presence of nine hundred and eighty-seven people, in the middle of a speech. Do you wonder that his eyes popped. I see that you have managed to read at least one of the books I brought you – if the rumpled jacket is any criterion.'

'Yes. The mountain one. It was a godsend. I lay for hours looking at the pictures. Nothing puts things in perspective as quickly as a mountain.'

'The stars are better, I find.'

'Oh, *no*. The stars merely reduce one to the status of an amoeba. The stars take the last vestige of human pride, the last spark of confidence, from one. But a snow mountain is a nice human-size yard-stick. I lay and looked at Everest and thanked God that I wasn't climbing those slopes. A hospital bed was a haven of warmth and rest and security by comparison, and The Midget and The Amazon two of the highest achievements of civilisation.'

'Ah, well, here are some more pictures for you.'

Marta up-ended the quarto envelope she was carrying, and spilled a collection of paper sheets over his chest.

'What is this?'

'Faces,' said Marta, delightedly. 'Dozens of faces for you. Men, women, and children. All sorts, conditions, and sizes.'

He picked a sheet off his chest and looked at it. It was an engraving of a fifteenth-century portrait. A woman.

'Who is this?'

'Lucrezia Borgia. Isn't she a duck.'

'Perhaps, but are you suggesting that there was any mystery about her?'

'Oh, yes. No one has ever decided whether she was her brother's tool or his accomplice.'

He discarded Lucrezia, and picked up a second sheet. This proved to be the portrait of a small boy in late eighteenth-century clothes, and under it in faint capitals was printed the words: Louis XVII.

'Now there's a *beautiful* mystery for you,' Marta said. 'The Dauphin. Did he escape or did he die in captivity?'

'Where did you get all these?'

'I routed James out of his cubby-hole at the Victoria and Albert, and made him take me to a print shop. I knew he would know about that sort of thing, and I'm sure he has nothing to interest him at the V and A.'

It was so like Marta to take it for granted that a civil servant, because he happened also to be a playwright and an authority on portraits, should be willing to leave his work and delve about in print shops for her pleasure.

He turned up the photograph of an Elizabethan portrait. A man in velvet and pearls. He turned the back to see who this might be and found that it was the Earl of Leicester.

'So that is Elizabeth's Robin,' he said. 'I don't think I ever saw a portrait of him before.'

Marta looked down on the virile fleshy face and said: 'It occurs to me for the first time that one of the major tragedies of history is that the best painters didn't paint you till you were past your best. Robin must have been quite a man. They say Henry the Eighth was dazzling as a young man, but what is he now? Something on a playing card. Nowadays we *know* what Tennyson was like before he grew that frightful beard. I must fly. I'm late as it is. I've been lunching at the Blague, and so many people came up to talk that I couldn't get away as early as I meant to.'

'I hope your host was impressed,' Grant said, with a glance at the hat.

'Oh, yes. She knows about hats. She took one look and said "Jacques Tous, I take it".'

'She!' said Grant surprised.

'Yes. Madeleine March. And it was I who was giving her luncheon. Don't look so astonished: it isn't tactful. I'm hoping, if you must know, that she'll write me that play about Lady Blessington. But there was such a to-ing and fro-ing that I had no chance to make any impression on her. However, I gave her a wonderful meal. Which reminds me that Tony Bittmaker was entertaining a party of seven. Magnums galore. How do you imagine he keeps going?'

'Lack of evidence,' Grant said, and she laughed and went away.

In the silence he went back to considering Elizabeth's Robin. What mystery was there about Robin?

Oh, yes. Amy Robsart, of course.

Well, he wasn't interested in Amy Robsart. He didn't care how she had fallen down stairs, or why.

But he spent a very happy afternoon with the rest of the faces. Long before he had entered the Force he had taken a delight in faces, and in his years at the Yard that interest had proved both a private entertainment and a professional advantage. He had once in his early days dropped in with his Superintendent at an identification parade. It was not his case, and they were both there on other business, but they lingered in the background and watched while a man and a woman, separately, walked down the line of twelve nondescript men, looking for the one they hoped to recognise.

'Which is Chummy, do you know?' the Super had whispered to him.

'I don't know,' Grant had said, 'but I can guess.'

'You can? Which do you make it?'

'The third from the left.'

'What is the charge?'

'I don't know. Don't know anything about it.'

His chief had cast him an amused glance. But when both the man and the woman had failed to identify anyone and had gone away, and the line broke into a chattering group, hitching collars and settling ties preparatory to going back to the street and the world of everyday from which they had been summoned to assist the Law, the one who did not move was the third man from the left. The third man from the left waited submissively for his escort and was led away to his cell again. 'Strewth!' the Superintendent had said. 'One chance out of twelve, and you made it. That was good going. He picked your man out of the bunch,' he said in explanation to the local Inspector.

'Did you know him?' the Inspector said, a little surprised. 'He's never been in trouble before, as far as we know.'

'No, I never saw him before. I don't even know what the charge is.'

'Then what made you pick him?'

Grant had hesitated, analysing for the first time his process of selection. It had not been a matter of reasoning. He had not said: 'That man's face has this characteristic or that characteristic, therefore he is the accused person.' His choice had been almost instinctive; the reason was in his sub-conscious. At last, having delved into his subconscious, he blurted: 'He was the only one of the twelve with no lines on his face.'

They had laughed at that. But Grant, once he had pulled the thing into the light, saw how his instinct had worked and recognised the reasoning behind it. 'It sounds silly, but it isn't,' he had said. 'The only adult entirely without face lines is the idiot.'

'Freeman's no idiot, take it from me,' the Inspector broke in. 'A very wide-awake wide boy he is, believe me.'

'I didn't mean that. I mean that the idiot is irresponsible. The idiot is the standard of irresponsibility. All those twelve men in that parade were thirty-ish, but only one had an irresponsible face. So I picked him at once.'

After that it had become a mild joke at the Yard that Grant could 'pick them at sight'. And the Assistant Commissioner had once said teasingly: 'Don't tell me that you believe that there is such a thing as a criminal face, Inspector.'

But Grant had said no, he wasn't as simple as that. 'If there was only one kind of crime, sir, it might be possible; but crimes being as wide as human nature, if a policeman started to put faces into categories he would be sunk. You can tell what the normal run of disreputable women look like by a walk down Bond Street any day between five and six, and yet the most notorious woman in London looks like a cold saint.'

'Not so saintly of late; she's drinking too much these days,' the AC had said, identifying the lady without difficulty; and the conversation had gone on to other things.

But Grant's interest in faces had remained and enlarged until it became a conscious study. A matter of case records and comparisons. It was, as he had said, not possible to put faces into any kind of category, but it was possible to characterise individual faces. In a reprint of a famous trial, for instance, where photographs of the principal actors in the case were displayed for the public's interest, there was never any doubt as to which was the accused and which the judge. Occasionally, one of the counsel might on looks have changed places with the prisoner in the dock – counsel were after all a mere cross-section of humanity, as liable to passion and greed as the rest of the world, but a judge had a special quality; an integrity and a detachment. So, even without a wig, one did not confuse him with the man in the dock, who had had neither integrity nor detachment.

Marta's James, having been dragged from his 'cubby-hole', had evidently enjoyed himself, and a fine selection of offenders, or their victims, kept Grant entertained until The Midget brought his tea. As he tidied the sheets together to put them away in his locker his hand came in contact with one that had slipped off his chest and had lain all the afternoon unnoticed on the counterpane. He picked it up and looked at it.

It was the portrait of a man. A man dressed in the velvet cap and slashed doublet of the late fifteenth century. A man about thirty-five or thirty-six years old, lean and clean shaven. He wore a rich jewelled collar, and was in the act of putting a ring on the little finger of his right hand. But he was not looking at the ring. He was looking off into space.

Of all the portraits Grant had seen this afternoon this was the most individual. It was as if the artist had striven to put on canvas something that his talent was not sufficient to translate into paint. The expression in the eyes – that most arresting and individual expression – had defeated him. So had the mouth: he had not known how to make lips so thin and so wide look mobile, so the mouth was wooden and a failure. What he had best succeeded in was in the bone structure of the face: the strong cheekbones, the hollows below them, the chin too large for strength.

Grant paused in the act of turning the thing over, to consider the face a moment longer. A judge? A soldier? A prince? Someone used to great responsibility, and responsible in his authority. Someone too-conscientious. A worrier; perhaps a perfectionist. A man at ease in a large design, but anxious over details. A candidate for gastric ulcer. Someone, too, who had suffered ill-health as a child. He had that incommunicable, that indescribable look that childhood suffering leaves behind it; less positive than the look on a cripple's face, but as inescapable. This the artist had both understood and translated into terms of paint. The slight fullness of the lower eyelid, like a child that has slept too heavily; the texture of the skin; the old-man look in a young face.

He turned the portrait over to look for a caption.

On the back was printed: *Richard the Third. From the portrait in the National Portrait Gallery. Artist Unknown.*

Richard the Third.

So that was who it was. Richard the Third. Crouchback. The monster of nursery stories. The destroyer of innocence. A synonym for villainy.

He turned the paper over and looked again. Was that what the artist had tried to convey when he had painted those eyes? Had what he had seen in those eyes been the look of a man haunted?

He lay a long time looking at that face; at those extraordinary eyes. They were long eyes, set close under the brows; the brows slightly drawn in that worried, over-conscientious frown. At first glance they appeared to be peering; but as one looked one found that they were in fact withdrawn, almost absent-minded.

When The Midget came back for his tray he was still staring at the portrait. Nothing like this had come his way for years. It made La

Giaconda look like a poster.

The Midget examined his virgin teacup, put a practised hand against the teapot's tepid cheek, and pouted. She had better things to do, she conveyed, than bring him trays for him to ignore.

He pushed the portrait at her.

What did she think of it? If that man were her patient what would be her verdict?

'Liver,' she said crisply, and bore away the tray in heel-tapping protest, all starch and blonde curls.

But the surgeon, strolling in against her draught, kindly and casual, had other views. He looked at the portrait, as invited, and said after a moment's interested scrutiny:

'Poliomyelitis.'

'Infantile paralysis?' Grant said; and remembered all of a sudden that Richard III had a withered arm.

'Who is it?' the surgeon asked.

'Richard the Third.'

'Really? That's interesting.'

'Did you know that he had a withered arm?'

'Had he? I didn't remember that. I thought he was a hunchback.'

'So he was.'

'What I do remember is that he was born with a full set of teeth and ate live frogs. Well, my diagnosis seems to be abnormally accurate.'

'Uncanny. What made you choose polio?'

'I don't quite know, now that you ask me to be definitive. Just the look of the face, I suppose. It's the look one sees on the face of a cripple child. If he was born hunchbacked that probably accounts for it and not polio. I notice the artist has left out the hump.'

'Yes. Court painters have to have a modicum of tact. It wasn't until Cromwell that sitters asked for "warts and all".'

'If you ask me,' the surgeon said, absent-mindedly considering the splint on Grant's leg, 'Cromwell started that inverted snobbery from which we are all suffering today.' "I'm a plain man, I am; no nonsense about *me*." And no manners, grace, or generosity, either.' He pinched Grant's toe with detached interest. 'It's a raging disease. A horrible perversion. In some parts of the States, I understand, it's as much as a man's political life is worth to go to some constituencies with his tie tied and his coat on. That's being stuffed-shirt. The beau ideal is to be one of the boys. That's looking very healthy,' he added, referring to Grant's big toe, and came back of his own accord to the portrait lying on the counterpane.

'Interesting,' he said, 'that about the polio. Perhaps it really was polio, and that accounts for the shrunken arm.' He went on considering it, making no movement to go. 'Interesting, anyhow. Portrait of a murderer. Does he run to type, would you say?'

'There isn't a murder type. People murder for too many different reasons. But I can't remember any murderer, either in my own experience, or in case histories, who resembled him.'

'Of course he was *hors concours* in his class, wasn't he. He couldn't have known the meaning of scruple.'

'No.'

'I once saw Olivier play him. The most dazzling exhibition of sheer evil, it was. Always on the verge of toppling over into the grotesque, and never doing it.'

'When I showed you the portrait,' Grant said, 'before you knew who it was, did you think of villainy?'

'No,' said the surgeon, 'no, I thought of illness.'

'It's odd, isn't it. I didn't think of villainy either. And now that I know who it is, now that I've read the name on the back, I can't think of it as anything but villainous.'

'I suppose villainy, like beauty, is in the eye of the beholder. Well, I'll look in again towards the end of the week. No pain to speak of now?'

And he went away, kindly and casual as he had come.

It was only after he had given the portrait further puzzled consideration (it piqued him to have mistaken one of the most notorious murderers of all time for a judge; to have transferred a subject from the dock to the bench was a shocking piece of ineptitude) that it occurred to Grant that the portrait had been provided as the illustration to a piece of detection.

What mystery was there about Richard III?

And then he remembered. Richard had murdered his two boy nephews, but no one knew how. They had merely disappeared. They had disappeared, if he remembered rightly, while Richard was away from London. Richard had sent someone to do the deed. But the mystery of the children's actual fate had never been solved. Two skeletons had turned up – under some stairs? – in Charles II's day, and had been buried. It was taken for granted that the skeletons were the remains of the young princes, but nothing had ever been proved.

It was shocking how little history remained with one after a good education. All he knew about Richard III was that he was the younger brother of Edward IV. That Edward was a blond six-footer with remarkable good looks and a still more remarkable way with women; and that Richard was a hunchback who usurped the throne on his brother's death in place of the boy heir, and arranged the death of that heir and his small brother to save himself any further trouble. He also knew that Richard had died at the battle of Bosworth yelling for a horse, and that he was the last of his line. The last Plantagenet.

Every schoolboy turned over the final page of Richard III with relief, because now at last the Wars of the Roses were over and they could get on to the Tudors, who were dull but easy to follow.

When The Midget came to tidy him up for the night Grant said: 'You don't happen to have a history book, by any chance, do you?'

'A history book? No. What would I be doing with a history book.' It was not a question, so Grant did not try to provide an answer. His silence seemed to fret her.

'If you really want a history book,' she said presently, 'you could ask Nurse Darroll when she brings your supper. She has all her school-books on a shelf in her room and it's quite possible she has a history among them.'

How like The Amazon to keep her school books! he thought. She was still homesick for school as she was homesick for Gloucestershire every time the daffodils bloomed. When she lumbered into the room, bearing his cheese pudding and stewed rhubarb, he looked at her with a tolerance that bordered on the benevolent. She ceased to be a large female who breathed like a suction-pump and became a potential dispenser of delight.

Oh yes, she had a history book, she said. Indeed, she rather thought that she had two. She had kept all her school books because she had loved school.

It was on the tip of Grant's tongue to ask her if she had kept her dolls, but he stopped himself in time.

'And of course I loved history,' she said. 'It was my favourite subject. Richard the Lionheart was my hero.'

'An intolerable bounder,' Grant said.

'Oh, no!' she said, looking wounded.

'A hyperthyroid type,' Grant said pitilessly. 'Rocketing to and fro about the earth like a badly made firework. Are you going off duty now?'

'Whenever I've finished my trays.'

'Could you find that book for me tonight?'

'You're supposed to be going to sleep, not staying awake over history books.'

'I might as well read some history as look at the ceiling – which is the alternative. Will you get it for me?'

'I don't think I could go all the way up to the Nurses' Block and back again tonight for someone who is rude about the Lionheart.'

'All right,' he said. 'I'm not the stuff that martyrs are made of. As far as I'm concerned Coeur-de-Lion is the pattern of chivalry, the chevalier sans peur et sans reproche, a faultless commander and a triple DSO. Now will you get the book?

'It seems to me you've sore need to read a little history,' she said, smoothing a mitred sheet-corner with a large admiring hand, 'so I'll bring you the book when I come past. I'm going out to the pictures anyhow.'

It was nearly an hour before she reappeared, immense in a camel-hair coat. The room lights had been put out and she materialised into the light of his reading-lamp like some kindly genie.

'I was hoping you'd be asleep,' she said. 'I don't really think you should start on these tonight.'

'If there is anything that is likely to put me to sleep,' he said, 'it would be an English history book. So you can hold hands with a clear conscience.'

'I'm going with Nurse Burrows.'

'You can still hold hands.'

'I've no patience with you,' she said patiently and faded backwards into the gloom.

She had brought two books.

'One was the kind of history book known as a Historical Reader. It bore the same relation to history as Stories from the Bible bears to Holy Writ. Canute rebuked his courtiers on the shore, Alfred burned the cakes, Raleigh spread his cloak for Elizabeth, Nelson took leave of Hardy in his cabin on the *Victory*, all in nice clear large print and one-sentence paragraphs. To each episode went one full-page illustration.

There was something curiously touching in the fact that The Amazon should treasure this childish literature. He turned to the fly-leaf to see if her name was there. On the fly-leaf was written:

Ella Darroll,
   Form III
     Newbridge High School
      Newbridge
       Gloucestershire.
        England
         Europe
          The World
           The Universe.

This was surrounded by a fine selection of coloured transfers.

Did all children do that, he wondered? Write their names like that, and spend their time in class making transfers. He certainly had. And the sight of those squares of bright primitive colour brought back his childhood as nothing had for many years. He had forgotten the excitement of transfers. That wonderfully satisfying moment when you began the peeling-off and saw that it was coming perfectly. The adult world held few such gratifications. A clean smacking drive at golf, perhaps, was the nearest. Or the moment when your line tightened and you knew that the fish had struck.

The little book pleased him so much that he went through it at his leisure. Solemnly reading each childish story. This, after all, was the history that every adult remembered. This was what remained in their minds when tonnage and poundage, and ship money, and Laud's Liturgy, and the Rye House Plot, and the Triennial Acts, and all the long muddle of schism and shindy, treaty and treason, had faded from their consciousness.

The Richard III story, when he came to it, was called The Princes In The Tower, and it seemed that young Ella had found the Princes a poor substitute for Coeur-de-Lion, since she had filled every small O throughout the tale with neat pencil shading. The two golden-haired boys who played together in the sunbeam from the barred window in the accompanying picture had each been provided with a pair of anachronistic spectacles, and on the blank back of the picture-page someone had been playing Noughts and Crosses. As far as young Ella was concerned the Princes were a dead loss.

And yet it was a sufficiently arresting little story. Macabre enough to delight any child's heart. The innocent children; the wicked uncle. The classic ingredients in a tale of classic simplicity.

It had also a moral. It was the perfect cautionary tale.

> But the King won no profit from this wicked deed. The people of England were shocked by his cold-blooded cruelty and decided that they would no longer have him for King. They sent for a distant cousin of Richard's, Henry Tudor, who was living in France, to come and be crowned King in his stead. Richard died bravely in the battle which resulted, but he had made his name hated throughout the country and many deserted him to fight for his rival.

Well, it was neat but not gaudy. Reporting at its simplest.

He turned to the second book.

The second book was the School History proper. The two thousand years of England's story were neatly parcelled into compartments for ready reference. The compartments, as usual, were reigns. It was no wonder that one pinned a personality to a reign, forgetful that that personality had known and lived under other kings. One put them in pigeon-holes automatically. Pepys: Charles II. Shakespeare: Elizabeth. Marlborough: Queen Anne. It never crossed one's mind that someone who had seen Queen Elizabeth could also have seen George I. One had been conditioned to the reign idea from childhood.

However it did simplify things when you were just a policeman with a game leg and a concussed spine hunting up some information on dead and gone royalties to keep yourself from going crazy.

He was surprised to find the reign of Richard III so short. To have made oneself one of the best-known rulers in all those two thousand years of England's history, and to have had only two years to do it in, surely augured a towering personality. If Richard had not made friends he had certainly influenced people.

The history book, too, thought that he had personality.

Richard was a man of great ability, but quite unscrupulous as to his means. He boldly claimed the crown on the absurd ground that his brother's marriage with Elizabeth Woodville had been illegal and the children of it illegitimate. He was accepted by the people, who dreaded a minority, and began his reign by making a progress through the south, where he was well received. During this progress, however, the two young Princes who were living in the Tower disappeared, and were believed to have been murdered. A serious rebellion followed, which Richard put down with great ferocity. In order to recover some of his lost popularity he held a Parliament, which passed useful statutes against Benevolences, Maintenance, and Livery.

But a second rebellion followed. This took the form of an invasion, with French troops, by the head of the Lancaster branch, Henry Tudor. He encountered Richard at Bosworth, near Leicester, where the treachery of the Stanleys gave the day to Henry. Richard was killed in the battle, fighting courageously, leaving behind him a name hardly less infamous than that of John.

What on earth were Benevolences, Maintenance, and Livery?

And how did the English like having the succession decided for them by French troops?

But, of course, in the days of the Roses, France was still a sort of semi-detached part of England; a country much less foreign to an Englishman than Ireland was. A fifteenth-century Englishman went to France as a matter of course; but to Ireland only under protest.

He lay and thought about that England. The England over which the Wars of the Roses had been fought. A green, green England; with not a chimney-stack from Cumberland to Cornwall. An England still unhedged, with great forests alive with game, and wide marshes thick with wild-fowl. An England with the same small group of dwellings repeated every few miles in endless permutation: castle, church, and cottages; monastery, church, and cottages; manor, church, and cottages. The strips of cultivation round the cluster of dwellings, and beyond that the greenness. The unbroken greenness. The deep-rutted lanes that ran from group to group, mired to bog in the winter and white with dust in the summer; decorated with wild roses or red with hawthorn as the seasons came and went.

For thirty years, over this green uncrowded land, the Wars of the Roses had been fought. But it had been more of a blood feud than a war. A Montague and Capulet affair; of no great concern to the average Englishman. No one pushed in at your door to demand whether you were York or Lancaster and to hale you off to a concentration camp if your answer proved to be the wrong one for the occasion. It was a small concentrated war; almost a private party. They fought a battle in your lower meadow, and turned your kitchen into a dressing-station, and then moved off somewhere or other to fight a battle somewhere else, and a few weeks later you would hear what had happened at that battle, and you would have a family row about the result because your wife was probably Lancaster and you were perhaps York, and it was all rather like following rival football teams. No one persecuted you for being a Lancastrian or a Yorkist, any more than you would be persecuted for being an Arsenal fan or a Chelsea follower.

He was still thinking of that green England when he fell asleep.

And he was not a whit wiser about the two young Princes and their fate.

Concrete Evidence

from A Good Hanging

IAN RANKIN (1960–)

Ian Rankin, born in Fife, educated at Edinburgh University and resident in the city, has written powerfully of the seamier side of Edinburgh, the side largely unseen by the tourist, in his series of detective stories featuring Inspector John Rebus. Rebus, a fully-paid up member of the awkward squad, became a policeman after an earlier army career in the Special Air Service. The level of physical fitness he must have enjoyed in the SAS has now gone, he gets breathless climbing stairs in Edinburgh tenements and is more likely to be seen eating a fish supper than living off the land on snakes and grubs.

Rebus may not be the easiest person to work for. His assistant, Detective Constable Holmes, in another story in this collection, concludes that Rebus was:

> *. . . too clever for Holmes' own good. How was he expected to shine, to be noticed, to push forwards to promotion, when it was always Rebus who, two steps ahead, came up with the answers.*

He is certainly not the easiest subordinate. His much tried Chief Inspector reflects elsewhere: 'He'd said it! Rebus had actually ended a sentence with "sir"!'

But what Rebus does have in large measure is determination. The present story reveals this quality to a high degree, the long-dead body could have been the subject of a perfunctory enquiry but Rebus as usual gets his teeth into the problem and worries out a solution.

The dictionary definition of a 'rebus' is an enigmatic representation of a word, by pictures or other symbols suggesting its parts – in other words a type of puzzle.

✝

'It's amazing what you find in these old buildings,' said the contractor, a middle-aged man in safety helmet and overalls. Beneath the overalls lurked a shirt and tie, the marks of his station. He was the chief, the gaffer. Nothing surprised him any more, not even unearthing a skeleton.

'Do you know,' he went on, 'in my time, I've found everything from ancient coins to a pocket-watch. How old do you reckon he is then?'

'We're not even sure *it* is a he, not yet. Give us a chance, Mr Beesford.'

'Well, when can we start work again?'

'Later on today.'

'Must be gey old though, eh?'

'How do you make that out?'

'Well, it's got no clothes on, has it? They've perished. Takes time for that to happen, plenty of time . . .'

Rebus had to concede, the man had a point. Yet the concrete floor beneath which the bones had been found . . . it didn't look so old, did it? Rebus cast an eye over the cellar again. It was situated a storey or so beneath road-level, in the basement of an old building off the Cowgate. Rebus was often in the Cowgate; the mortuary was just up the road. He knew that the older buildings here were a veritable warren, long narrow tunnels ran here, there and, it seemed, everywhere, semi-cylindrical in shape and just about high enough to stand up in. This present building was being given the full works – gutted, new drainage system, rewiring. They were taking out the floor in the cellar to lay new drains and also because there seemed to be damp – certainly there was a fousty smell to the place – and its cause needed to be found.

They were expecting to find old drains, open drains perhaps. Maybe even a trickle of a stream, something which would lead to damp. Instead, their pneumatic drills found what remained of a corpse, perhaps hundreds of years old. Except, of course, for that concrete floor. It couldn't be more than fifty or sixty years old, could it? Would clothing deteriorate to a visible nothing in so short a time? Perhaps the damp could do that. Rebus found the cellar oppressive. The smell, the shadowy lighting provided by portable lamps, the dust.

But the photographers were finished, and so was the pathologist, Dr Curt. He didn't have too much to report at this stage, except to comment that he preferred it when skeletons were kept in cupboards, not confined to the cellar. They'd take the bones away, along with samples of the earth and rubble around the find, and they'd see what they would see.

'Archaeology's not really my line,' the doctor added. 'It may take me some time to bone up on it.' And he smiled his usual smile.

It took several days for the telephone call to come. Rebus picked up the receiver.

'Hello?'

'Inspector Rebus? Dr Curt here. About our emaciated friend.'

'Yes?'

'Male, five feet ten inches tall, probably been down there between thirty and thirty-five years. His left leg was broken at some time, long before he died. It healed nicely. But the little finger on his left hand had been dislocated and it did *not* heal so well. I'd say it was crooked all his adult life. Perfect for afternoon tea in Morningside.'

'Yes?' Rebus knew damned well Curt was leading up to something. He knew, too, that Curt was not a man to be hurried.

'Tests on the soil and gravel around the skeleton show traces of human tissue, but no fibres or anything which might have been clothing. No shoes, socks, underpants, nothing. Altogether, I'd say he was buried there in the altogether.'

'But did he die there?'

'Can't say.'

'All right, what did he die *of*?'

There was an almost palpable smile in Curt's voice. 'Inspector, I thought you'd never ask. Blow to the skull, a blow of considerable force to the back of the head. Murder, I'd say. Yes, definitely murder.'

There were, of course, ways of tracing the dead, of coming to a near-infallible identification. But the older the crime, the less likely this outcome became. Dental records, for example. They just weren't *kept* in the 50s and 60s the way they are today. A dentist practising then would most probably be playing near-full-time golf by now. And the record of a patient who hadn't been in for his check-up since 1960? Discarded, most probably. Besides, as Dr Curt pointed out, the man's teeth had seen little serious work, a few fillings, a single extraction.

The same went for medical records, which didn't stop Rebus from checking. A broken left leg, a dislocated left pinkie. Maybe some aged doctor would recall? But then again, maybe not. Almost certainly not. The local papers and radio were interested, which was a bonus. They were given what information the police had, but no memories seemed to be jogged as a result.

Curt had said he was no archaeologist, Rebus was no historian either. He knew other cases – contemporary cases – were yammering for his attention. The files stacked up on his desk were evidence enough of that. He'd give this one a few days, a few hours of his time. When the dead ends started to cluster around him, he'd drop it and head back for the here and now.

Who owned the building back in the 1950s? That was easy enough to discover: a wine importer and merchant. Pretty much a one-man operation, Hillbeith Vintners had held the premises from 1948 until 1967. And yes, there was a Mr Hillbeith, retired from the trade and living over in Burntisland, with a house gazing out across silver sands to the grey North Sea.

He still had a cellar, and insisted that Rebus have a 'wee taste' from it. Rebus got the idea that Mr Hillbeith liked visitors – a socially acceptable excuse for a drink. He took his time in the cellar (there must have been over 500 bottles in there) and emerged with cobwebs hanging from his cardigan, holding a dusty bottle of something nice. This he opened and sat on the mantelpiece. It would be half an hour or so yet at the very least before they could usefully have a glass.

Mr Hillbeith was, he told Rebus, seventy-four. He'd been in the wine trade for nearly half a century and had 'never regretted a day, not a day, nor even an hour'. Lucky you, Rebus thought to himself.

'Do you remember having that new floor laid in the cellar, Mr Hillbeith?'

'Oh, yes. That particular cellar was going to be for best claret. It was just the right temperature, you see, and there was no vibration from passing buses and the like. But it was damp, had been ever since I'd moved in. So I got a building firm to take a look. They suggested a new floor and some other alterations. It all seemed fairly straightforward and their charges seemed reasonable, so I told them to go ahead.'

'And when was this, sir?'

'1960. The spring of that year. There you are, I've got a great memory where business matters are concerned.' His small eyes beamed at Rebus through the thick lenses of their glasses. 'I can even tell you how much the work cost me . . . and it was a pretty penny at the time. All for nothing, as it turned out. The cellar was still damp, and there was always that *smell* in it, a very unwholesome smell. I couldn't take a chance with the claret, so it became the general stock-room, empty bottles and glasses, packing-cases, that sort of thing.'

'Do you happen to recall, Mr Hillbeith, was the smell there *before* the new floor was put in?'

'Well, certainly there was *a* smell there before the floor was laid, but the smell afterwards was different somehow.' He rose and fetched two crystal glasses from the china cabinet, inspecting them for dust. 'There's a lot of nonsense talked about wine, Inspector. About decanting, the type of glasses you must use and so on. Decanting can help, of course, but I prefer the feel of the bottle. The bottle, after all, is part of the wine, isn't it?' He handed an empty glass to Rebus. 'We'll wait a few minutes yet.'

Rebus swallowed drily. It had been a long drive. 'Do you recall the name of the firm, sir, the one that did the work?'

Hillbeith laughed. 'How could I forget? Abbot & Ford, they were called. I mean, you just don't forget a name like that, do you? Abbot & Ford. You see, it sounds like Abbotsford, doesn't it? A small firm they were, mind. But you may know one of them, Alexander Abbot.'

'Of Abbot Building?'

'The same. He went on to make quite a name for himself, didn't he? Quite a fortune. Built up quite a company, too, but he started out small like most of us do.'

'How small, would you say?'

'Oh, small, small. Just a few men.' He rose and stretched an arm towards the mantelpiece. 'I think this should be ready to taste, Inspector. If you'll hold out your glass –'

Hillbeith poured slowly, deliberately, checking that no lees escaped into the glass. He poured another slow, generous measure for himself. The wine was reddish-brown. 'Robe and disc not too promising,' he muttered to himself. He gave his glass a shake and studied it. 'Legs not promising either.' He sighed. 'Oh dear.' Finally, Hillbeith suffered the glass anxiously, then took a swig.

'Cheers,' said Rebus, indulging in a mouthful. A mouthful of vinegar. He managed to swallow, then saw Hillbeith spit back into the glass.

'Oxidisation,' the old man said, sounding cruelly tricked. 'It happens. I'd best check a few more bottles to assess the damage. Will you stay, Inspector?' Hillbeith sounded keen.

'Sorry, sir,' said Rebus, ready with his get-out clause. 'I'm still on duty.'

Alexander Abbot, aged fifty-five, still saw himself as the force behind the Abbot Building Company. There might be a dozen executives working furiously beneath him, but the company had grown from *his* energy and from *his* fury. He was Chairman, and a busy man too. He made this plain to Rebus at their meeting in the executive offices of ABC. The office spoke of business confidence, but then in Rebus's experience this meant little in itself. Often, the more dire straits a company was in, the healthier it tried to look. Still, Alexander Abbot seemed happy enough with life.

'In a recession,' he explained, lighting an overlong cigar, 'you trim your workforce pronto. You stick with regular clients, good payers, and don't take on too much work from clients you don't know. They're the ones who're likely to welch on you or go bust, leaving nothing but bills. Young businesses . . . they're always hit hardest in a recession, no back-up you see. Then, when the recession's over for another ten years, you dust yourself off and go touting for business again, re-hiring the men you laid off. That's where we've always had the edge over Jack Kirkwall.'

Kirkwall Construction was ABC's main competitor in the Lowlands, when it came to medium-sized contracts. Doubtless Kirkwall was the larger company. It, too, was run by a 'self-made' man, Jack Kirkwall. A larger-than-life figure. There was, Rebus quickly realised, little love lost between the two rivals.

The very mention of Kirkwall's name seemed to have dampened Alexander Abbot's spirits. He chewed on his cigar like it was a debtor's finger.

'You started small though, didn't you, sir?'

'Oh aye, they don't come much smaller. We were a pimple on the bum of the construction industry at one time.' He gestured to the walls of his office. 'Not that you'd guess it, eh?'

Rebus nodded. 'You were still a small firm back in 1960, weren't you?'

'1960. Let's think. We were just starting out. It wasn't ABC then, of course. Let's see. I think I got a loan from my dad in 1957, went into partnership with a chap called Hugh Ford, another self-employed builder. Yes, that's right. 1960, it was Abbot & Ford. Of course it was.'

'Do you happen to remember working at a wine merchant's in the Cowgate?'

'When?'

'The spring of 1960.'

'A wine merchant's?' Abbot furrowed his brow. 'Should be able to remember that. Long time ago, mind. A wine merchant's?'

'You were laying a new floor in one of his cellars, amongst other work. Hillbeith Vintners.'

'Oh, aye, Hillbeith, it's coming back now. I remember him. Little funny chap with glasses. Gave us a case of wine when the job was finished. Nice of him, but the wine was a bit off as I remember.'

'How many men were working on the job?'

Abbot exhaled noisily. 'Now you're asking. It was over thirty years ago, Inspector.'

'I appreciate that, sir. Would there be any records?'

Abbot shook his head. 'There might have been up to about ten years ago, but when we moved into this place a lot of the older stuff got chucked out. I regret it now. It'd be nice to have a display of stuff from the old days, something we could set up in the reception. But no, all the

Abbot & Ford stuff got dumped.'

'So you don't remember how many men were on that particular job? Is there anyone else I could talk to, someone who might –'

'We were small back then, I can tell you that. Mostly using casual labour and part-timers. A job that size, I wouldn't think we'd be using more than three or four men, if that.'

'You don't recall anyone going missing? Not turning up for work, that sort of thing?'

Abbot bristled. 'I'm a stickler for time-keeping, Inspector. If anyone had done a bunk, I'd remember, I'm pretty sure of that. Besides, we were careful about who we took on. No lazy buggers, nobody who'd do a runner halfway through a job.'

Rebus sighed. Here was one of the dead ends. He rose to his feet. 'Well, thanks anyway, Mr Abbot. It was good of you to find time to see me.' The two men shook hands, Abbot rising to his feet.

'Not at all, Inspector. Wish I could help you with your little mystery. I like a good detective story myself.' They were almost at the door now.

'Oh,' said Rebus, 'just one last thing. Where could I find your old partner Mr Ford?'

Abbot's face lost its animation. His voice was suddenly that of an old man. 'Hugh died, Inspector. A boating accident. He was drowned. Hell of a thing to happen. Hell of a thing.'

Two dead ends.

Mr Hillbeith's telephone call came later that day, while Rebus was ploughing through the transcript of an interview with a rapist. His head felt full of foul-smelling glue, his stomach acid with caffeine.

'Is that Inspector Rebus?'

'Yes, hello, Mr Hillbeith. What can I do for you?' Rebus pinched the bridge of his nose and screwed shut his eyes.

'I was thinking all last night about that skeleton.'

'Yes?' In between bottles of wine, Rebus didn't doubt.

'Well, I was trying to think back to when the work was being done. It might not be much, but I definitely recall that there were four people involved. Mr Abbot and Mr Ford worked on it pretty much full-time, and there were two other men, one of them a teenager, the other in his forties. They worked on a more casual basis.'

'You don't recall their names?'

'No, only that the teenager had a nickname. Everyone called him by that. I don't think I ever knew his real name.'

'Well, thanks anyway, Mr Hillbeith. I'll get back to Mr Abbot and see if what you've told me jogs his memory.'

'Oh, you've spoken to him then?'

'This morning. No progress to report. I didn't realise Mr Ford had died.'

'Ah, well, that's the other thing.'

'What is?'

'Poor Mr Ford. Sailing accident, wasn't it?'

'That's right.'

'Only I remember that, too. You see, that accident happened just after they'd finished the job. They kept talking about how they were going to take a few days off and go fishing. Mr Abbot said it would be their first holiday in years.'

Rebus's eyes were open now. 'How soon was this after they'd finished your floor?'

'Well, directly after, I suppose.'

'Do you remember Mr Ford?'

"Well, he was very quiet. Mr Abbot did all the talking, really. A very quiet man. A hard worker though, I got that impression.'

'Did you notice anything about his hands? A misshapen pinkie?'

'Sorry, Inspector, it *was* a long time ago.'

Rebus appreciated that. 'Of course it was, Mr Hillbeith. You've been a great help. Thank you.'

He put down the receiver. A long time ago, yes, but still murder, still calculated and cold-blooded murder. Well, a path had opened in front of him. Not much of a path perhaps, a bit overgrown and treacherous. Nevertheless . . . Best foot forward, John. Best foot forward.

Of course, he kept telling himself, he was still ruling possibilities out rather than ruling them in, which was why he wanted to know a little more about the boating accident. He didn't want to get the information from Alexander Abbot.

Instead, the morning after Hillbeith's phone call, Rebus went to the National Library of Scotland on George IV Bridge. The doorman let him through the turnstile and he climbed an imposing staircase to the reading room. The woman on the desk filled in a one-day reader's card for him, and showed him how to use the computer. There were two banks of computers, being used by people to find the books they needed. Rebus had to go into the reading room and find an empty chair, note its number and put this on his slip when he'd decided which volume he required. Then he went to his chair and sat, waiting.

There were two floors to the reading room, both enveloped by shelves of reference books. The people working at the long desks downstairs seemed bleary. Just another morning's graft for them; but Rebus found it all fascinating. One person worked with a card index in front of him, to which he referred frequently. Another seemed asleep, head resting on arms. Pens scratched across countless sheets of paper. A few souls, lost for inspiration, merely chewed on their pens and stared at the others around them, as Rebus was doing.

Eventually, his volume was brought to him. It was a bound edition of the *Scotsman*, containing every issue for the months from January to June, 1960. Two thick leather buckles kept the volume closed. Rebus unbuckled these and began to turn the pages.

He knew what he was looking for, and pretty well where to find it, but that didn't stop him browsing through football reports and front page headlines. 1960. He'd been busy trying to lose his virginity and supporting Hearts. Yes, a long time ago.

The story hadn't quite made the front page. Instead, there were two paragraphs on page three. 'Drowning Off Lower Largo.' The victim, Mr Hugh Ford, was described as being twenty-six years of age (a year older than the survivor, Mr Alex Abbot) and a resident of Duddingston, Edinburgh. The men, on a short fishing holiday, had taken a boat out early in the morning, a boat hired from a local man, Mr John Thomson. There was a squall, and the boat capsized. Mr Abbot, a fair swimmer, had made it back to the shore. Mr Ford, a poor swimmer, had not. Mr Ford was further described as a 'bachelor, a quiet man, shy according to Mr Abbot, who was still under observation at the Victoria Hospital, Kirkcaldy'. There was a little more, but not much. Apparently, Ford's parents were dead, but he had a sister, Mrs Isabel Hammond, somewhere out in Australia.

Why hadn't Abbot mentioned any of this? Maybe he wanted to forget. Maybe it still gave him the occasional bad dream. And of course he would have forgotten all about the Hillbeith contract precisely because this tragedy happened so soon afterwards. So soon. Just the one line of print really bothered Rebus; just that one sentence niggled.

'Mr Ford's body has still not been recovered.'

Records might get lost in time, but not by Fife Police. They sent on what they had, much of it written in fading ink on fragile paper, some of it typed – badly. The two friends and colleagues, Abbot and Ford, had set out on Friday evening to the Fishing-Net Hotel in Largo, arriving late. As arranged, they'd set out early next morning on a boat they'd hired from a local man, John Thomson. The accident had taken place only an hour or so after setting out. The boat was recovered. It had been overturned, but of Ford there was no sign. Inquiries were made. Mr Ford's belongings were taken back to Edinburgh by Mr Abbot, after the latter was released from hospital, having sustained a bump to the head when the boat went over. He was also suffering from shock and exhaustion. Mr Ford's sister, Mrs Isabel Hammond, was never traced.

They had investigated a little further. The business run jointly by Messrs Abbot and Ford now became Mr Abbot's. The case notes contained a good amount of information and suspicion – between the lines, as it were. Oh yes, they'd investigated Alexander Abbot, but there had been no evidence. They'd searched for the body, had found none. Without a body, they were left with only their suspicions and their nagging doubts.

'Yes,' Rebus said quietly to himself, 'but what if you were looking for the body in the wrong place?' The wrong place at the wrong time. The work on the cellar had ended on Friday afternoon and by Saturday morning Hugh Ford had ceased to exist.

The path Rebus was on had become less overgrown, but it was still rock-strewn and dangerous, still a potential dead-end.

The Fishing-Net Hotel was still in existence, though apparently much changed from its 1960 incarnation. The present owners told Rebus to arrive in time for lunch if he could and it would be on the house. Largo was north of Burntisland but on the same coastline. Alexander Selkirk, the original of Defoe's Robinson Crusoe, had a connection with the fishing village. There was a small statue of him somewhere which Rebus had been shown as a boy (but only after much hunting, he recalled). Largo was picturesque, but then so were most, if not all, of the coastal villages in Fife's 'East Neuk'. But it was not yet quite the height of the tourist season and the customers taking lunch at the Fishing-Net Hotel were businessmen and locals.

It was a good lunch, as picturesque as its surroundings but with a bit more flavour. And afterwards, the owner, an Englishman for whom life in Largo was a long-held dream come true, offered to show Rebus round, including 'the very room your Mr Ford stayed in the night before he died'.

'How can you be sure?'

'I looked in the register.'

Rebus managed not to look too surprised. The hotel had changed hands so often since 1960, he despaired of finding anyone who would remember the events of that weekend.

'The register?'

'Yes, we were left a lot of old stuff when we bought this place. The store-rooms were choc-a-bloc. Old ledgers and what have you going back to the 1920s and 30s. It was easy enough to find 1960.'

Rebus stopped in his tracks. 'Never mind showing me Mr Ford's room, would you mind letting me see that register?'

He sat at a desk in the manager's office with the register open in front of him, while Mr Summerson's finger stabbed the line. 'There you are, Inspector, H. Ford. Signed in at 11.50 p.m., address given as Duddingston. Room number seven.'

It wasn't so much a signature as a blurred scrawl and above it, on a separate line, was Alexander Abbot's own more flowing signature.

'Bit late to arrive, wasn't it?' commented Rebus.

'Agreed.'

'I don't suppose there's anyone working here nowadays who worked in the hotel back then?'

Summerson laughed quietly. 'People do retire in this country, Inspector.'

'Of course, I just wondered.' He remembered the newspaper story. 'What about John Thomson? Does the name mean anything to you?'

'Old Jock? Jock Thomson? The fisherman?'

'Probably.'

'Oh, yes, he's still about. You'll almost certainly find him down by the dockside or else in the Harbour Tavern.'

'Thanks. I'd like to take this register with me if I may?'

Jock Thomson sucked on his pipe and nodded. He looked the archetype of the 'old salt', from his baggy cord trousers to his chiselled face and silvery beard. The only departure from the norm was, perhaps, the Perrier water in front of him on a table in the Harbour Tavern.

'I like the fizz,' he explained after ordering it, 'and besides, my doctor's told me to keep off the alcohol. Total abstinence, he said, total abstinence. Either the booze goes, Jock, or the pipe does. No contest.'

And he sucked greedily on the pipe. Then complained when his drink arrived without 'the wee slice of lemon'. Rebus returned to the bar to fulfil his mission.

'Oh aye,' said Thomson, 'remember it like it was yesterday. Only there's not much to remember, is there?'

'Why do you say that?'

'Two inexperienced laddies go out in a boat. Boat tips. End of story.'

'Was the weather going to be bad that morning?'

'Not particularly. But there *was* a squall blew up. Blew up and blew out in a matter of minutes. Long enough though.'

'How did the two men seem?'

'How do you mean?'

'Well, were they looking forward to the trip?'

'Don't know, I never saw them. The younger one, Abbot was it? He phoned to book a boat from me, said they'd be going out early, six or thereabouts. I told him he was daft, but he said there was no need for me to be on the dockside, if I'd just have the boat ready and tell him which one it was. And that's what I did. By the time I woke up that morning, he was swimming for the shore and his pal was food for the fish.'

'So you never actually saw Mr Ford?'

'No, and I only saw the lad Abbot afterwards, when the ambulance was taking him away.'

It was fitting into place almost too easily now. And Rebus thought, sometimes these things are only visible with hindsight, from a space of years. 'I don't suppose,' he ventured, 'you know anyone who worked at the hotel back then?'

'Owner's moved on,' said Thomson, 'who knows where to. It might be that Janice Dryman worked there then. Can't recall if she did.'

'Where could I find her?'

Thomson peered at the clock behind the bar. 'Hang around here ten minutes or so, you'll bump into her. She usually comes in of an afternoon. Meantime, I'll have another of these if you're buying.'

Thomson pushed his empty glass over to Rebus. Rebus, most definitely, was buying.

Miss Dryman – 'never married, never really saw the point' – was in her early fifties. She worked in a gift-shop in town and after her stint finished usually nipped into the Tavern for a soft drink and 'a bit of gossip'. Rebus asked what she would like to drink.

Lemonade, please,' she said, 'with a drop of whisky in it.' And she laughed with Jock Thomson, as though this were an old and cherished joke between them. Rebus, not used to playing the part of straight-man, headed yet again for the bar.

'Oh yes,' she said, her lips poised above the glass. 'I was working there at the time all right. Chambermaid and general dogsbody, that was me.'

'You wouldn't see them arrive though?'

Miss Dryman looked as though she had some secret to impart. '*Nobody* saw them arrive, I know that for a fact. Mrs Dennis who ran the place back then, she said she'd be buggered if she'd wait up half the night for a couple of fishermen. They knew what rooms they were in and their keys were left at reception.'

'What about the front door?'

'Left unlocked, I suppose. The world was a safer place back then.'

'Aye, you're right there,' added Jock Thomson, sucking on his sliver of lemon.

'And Mr Abbot and Mr Ford knew this was the arrangement?'

'I suppose so. Otherwise it wouldn't have worked, would it?'

So Abbot knew there'd be nobody around at the hotel, not if he left it late enough before arriving.

'And what about in the morning?'

'Mrs Dennis said they were up and out before she knew anything about it. She was annoyed because she'd already cooked the kippers for their breakfast before she realised.'

So nobody saw them in the morning either. In fact . . .

'In fact,' said Rebus, 'nobody saw Mr Ford at all. Nobody at the hotel, not you, Mr Thomson, nobody.' Both drinkers conceded this.

'I saw his stuff though,' said Miss Dryman.

'What stuff?'

'In his room, his clothes and stuff. That morning. I didn't know anything about the accident and I went in to clean.'

'The bed had been slept in?'

'Looked like it. Sheets all rumpled. And his suitcase was on the floor, only half unpacked. Not that there was much *to* unpack.'

'Oh?'

'A single change of clothes, I'd say. I remember them because they seemed mucky, you know, not fresh. Not the sort of stuff *I'd* take on holiday with me.'

'What? Like he'd been working in them?'

She considered this. 'Maybe.'

'No point wearing clean clothes for fishing,' Thomson added. But Rebus wasn't listening.

Ford's clothes, the clothes he had been working in while laying the floor. It made sense. Abbot bludgeoned him, stripped him and covered his body in fresh cement. He'd taken the clothes away with him and put them in a case, opening it in the hotel room, ruffling the sheets. Simple, but effective. Effective these past thirty years. The motive? A falling out perhaps, or simple greed. It was a small company, but growing, and perhaps Abbot hadn't wanted to share. Rebus placed a five-pound note on the table.

'To cover the next couple of rounds,' he said, getting to his feet. 'I'd better be off. Some of us are still on duty.'

There were things to be done. He had to speak to his superior, Chief Inspector Lauderdale. And that was for starters. Maybe Ford's Australian sister could be traced this time round. There had to be someone out there who could acknowledge that Ford had suffered from a broken leg in youth, and that he had a crooked finger. So far, Rebus could think of only one person – Alexander Abbot.

Somehow, he didn't think Abbot could be relied on to tell the truth, the whole truth.

Then there was the hotel register. The forensics lab could ply their cunning trade on it. Perhaps they'd be able to say for certain that Ford's signature was merely a bad rendition of Abbot's. But again, he needed a sample of Ford's handwriting in order to substantiate that the signature was not genuine. Who did he know who might possess such a document? Only Alexander Abbot. Or Mr Hillbeith, but Mr Hillbeith had not been able to help.

'No, Inspector, as I told you, it was Mr Abbot who handled all the paperwork, all that side of things. If there is an invoice or a receipt, it will be in his hand, not Mr Ford's. I don't recall ever seeing Mr Ford writing anything.'

No through road.

Chief Inspector Lauderdale was not wholly sympathetic. So far all Rebus had to offer were more suppositions to add to those of the Fife Police at the time. There was no proof that Alexander Abbot had killed his partner. No proof that the skeleton was Hugh Ford. Moreover, there wasn't even much in the way of circumstantial evidence. They could bring in Abbot for questioning, but all he had to do was plead innocence. He could afford a good lawyer; and even bad lawyers weren't stupid enough to let the police probe too deeply.

'We need proof, John,' said Lauderdale, 'concrete evidence. The simplest proof would be that hotel signature. If we prove it's not Ford's, then we have Abbot at that hotel, Abbot in the boat and Abbot shouting that his friend has drowned, *all* without Ford having been there. That's what we need. The rest of it, as it stands, is rubbish. You know that.'

Yes, Rebus knew. He didn't doubt that, given an hour alone with Abbot in a darkened alley, he'd have his confession. But it didn't work like that. It worked through the law. Besides, Abbot's heart might not be too healthy. BUSINESSMAN, 55, DIES UNDER QUESTIONING. No, it had to be done some other way.

The problem *was*, there was no other way. Alexander Abbot was getting away with murder. Or was he? Why did his story have to be false? Why did the body have to be Hugh Ford's? The answer was: because the whole thing seemed to fit. Only, the last piece of the jigsaw had been lost under some sofa or chair a long time ago, so long ago now that it might remain missing forever.

He didn't know why he did it. If in doubt, retrace your steps . . . something like that. Maybe he just liked the atmosphere. Whatever, Rebus found himself back in the National Library, waiting at his desk for the servitor to bring him his bound volume of old news. He mouthed the words of 'Yesterday's Papers' to himself as he waited. Then, when the volume appeared, he unbuckled it with ease and pulled open the pages. He read past the April editions, read through into May and June. Football results, headlines – and what was this? A snippet of business news, barely a filler at the bottom right-hand corner of a page. About how the Kirkwall Construction Company was swallowing up a couple of smaller competitors in Fife and Midlothian.

'The 1960s will be a decade of revolution in the building industry,' said Managing Director Mr Jack Kirkwall, 'and Kirkwall Construction aims to meet that challenge through growth and quality. The bigger we are, the better we are. These acquisitions strengthen the company, and they're good news for the workforce, too.'

It was the kind of sentiment which had lasted into the 1980s. Jack Kirkwall, Alexander Abbot's bitter rival. Now there was a man Rebus ought to meet . . .

The meeting, however, had to be postponed until the following week. Kirkwall was in hospital for a minor operation.

'I'm at that age, Inspector,' he told Rebus when they finally met, 'when things go wrong and need treatment or replacing. Just like any bit of well-used machinery.'

And he laughed, though the laughter, to Rebus's ears, had a hollow centre. Kirkwall looked older than his sixty-two years, his skin saggy, complexion wan. They were in his living-room, from where, these days, he did most of his work.

'Since I turned sixty, I've only really wandered into the company headquarters for the occasional meeting. I leave the daily chores to my son, Peter. He seems to be managing.' The laughter this time was self-mocking.

Rebus had suggested a further postponement of the meeting, but when Jack Kirkwall knew that the subject was to be Alexander Abbot, he was adamant that they should go ahead.

'Is he in trouble then?'

He might be,' Rebus admitted. Some of the colour seemed to reappear in Kirkwall's cheeks and he relaxed a little further into his reclining leather chair. Rebus didn't want to give Kirkwall the story. Kirkwall and Abbot were still business rivals, after all. Still, it seemed, enemies. Given the story, Kirkwall might try some underhand tactic, some rumour in the media, and if it got out that the story originally came from a police inspector, well. Hello, being sued and goodbye, pension.

No, Rebus didn't want that. Yet he did want to know whether Kirkwall knew anything, knew of any reason why Abbot might wish, might *need* to kill Ford.

'Go on, Inspector.'

'It goes back quite a way, sir. 1960, to be precise. Your firm was at that time in the process of expansion.'

'Correct.

'What did you know about Abbot & Ford?'

Kirkwall brushed the palm of one hand over the knuckles of the other. 'Just that they were growing, too. Of course, they were younger than us, much smaller than us. ABC still is much smaller than us. But they were cocky, they were winning some contracts ahead of us. I had my eye on them.'

'Did you know Mr Ford at all?'

'Oh yes. Really, he was the cleverer of the two men. I've never had much respect for Abbot. But Hugh Ford was quiet, hardworking. Abbot was the one who did the shouting and got the firm noticed.'

'Did Mr Ford have a crooked finger?'

Kirkwall seemed bemused by the question. 'I've no idea,' he said at last. 'I never actually met the man, I merely knew *about* him. Why? Is it important?'

Rebus felt at last that his meandering, narrowing path had come to the lip of a chasm. Nothing for it but to turn back.

'Well,' he said, 'it would have clarified something.'

'You know, Inspector, my company *was* interested in taking Abbot & Ford under our wing.'

'Oh?'

'But then with the accident, that tragic accident. Well, Abbot took control and he wasn't at all interested in any offer we had to make. Downright rude, in fact. Yes, I've always thought that it was such a *lucky* accident so far as Abbot was concerned.'

'How do you mean, sir?'

'I mean, Inspector, that Hugh Ford was on our side. He wanted to sell up. But Abbot was against it.'

So, Rebus had his motive. Well, what did it matter? He was still lacking that concrete evidence Lauderdale demanded.

'. . . Would it show up from his handwriting?'

Rebus had missed what Kirkwall had been saying. 'I'm sorry, sir, I didn't catch that.'

'I said, Inspector, if Hugh Ford had a crooked finger, would it show from his handwriting?'

'Handwriting?'

'Because I had his agreement to the takeover. He'd written to me personally to tell me. Had gone behind Abbot's back, I suppose. I bet Alex Abbot was mad as hell when he found out about that.' Kirkwall's smile was vibrant now. 'I always thought that accident was a bit too lucky where Abbot was concerned. A bit too neat. No proof though. There was never any proof.'

'Do you still have the letter?'

'What?'

'The letter from Mr Ford, do you still have it?'

Rebus was tingling now, and Kirkwall caught his excitement. 'I never throw anything away, Inspector. Oh yes, I've got it. It'll be upstairs.'

'Can I see it? I mean, can I see it now?'

'If you like,' Kirkwall made to stand up, but paused. '*Is* Alex Abbot in trouble, Inspector?'

'If you've still got that letter from Hugh Ford, then, yes, sir, I'd say Mr Abbot could be in very grave trouble indeed.'

'Inspector, you've made an old man very happy.'

It was the letter against Alex Abbot's word, of course, and he denied everything. But there was enough now for a trial. The entry in the hotel, while it was *possibly* the work of Alexander Abbot was *certainly* not the work of the man who had written the letter to Jack Kirkwall. A search warrant gave the police the powers to look through Abbot's home and the ABC headquarters. A contract, drawn up between Abbot and Ford when the two men had gone into partnership, was discovered to be held in a solicitor's safe. The signature matched that on the letter to Jack Kirkwall. Kirkwall himself appeared in court to give evidence. He seemed to Rebus a different man altogether from the person he'd met previously: sprightly, keening, enjoying life to the full.

From the dock, Alexander Abbot looked on almost reproachfully, as if this were just one more business trick in a life full of them. Life, too, was the sentence of the judge.

7
JUDGEMENT
Introduction

†

At the end of the criminal process comes the lawyer and the judge. At least at the end of the criminal process as mediated through our selection from Scottish literature. After the judge come the jailer and hangman – but they have tended to produce less interesting reading. On the other hand the Scottish Bar and the Scottish Bench have produced a wealth of writing – indeed the practitioners of the law have very often been men of letters themselves. Nor is it entirely surprising that this should be so. For much of the post-Union period the Scottish legal system, a prized symbol of national identity, attracted the country's brightest and best. The law became the favoured career path for the ambitious and a surrogate arena for political activity. The Faculty of Advocates in the eighteenth and early nineteenth centuries played a far larger part in Scottish life than simply being a professional association of lawyers. Many of the nation's leading writers, thinkers and politicians were advocates, the Faculty's Library would become the foundation of the National Library of Scotland, the country's greatest philosopher, David Hume, was the Faculty's Librarian and the keenly fought internal politics of the Faculty mirrored the political tensions and attitudes of the nation.

The list of advocates who were authors is a long and distinguished one – Walter Scott, whose portrayal of the comical legal amateur Bartoline Saddletree from *The Heart of Midlothian* is featured in this chapter, is perhaps the most famous. But he was by no means the only one – in the generation immediately following Scott there were his son-in-law and biographer John Gibson Lockhart and the reviewer and essayist John Wilson 'Christopher North'. Nor should it be forgotten that Robert Louis Stevenson was admitted as an advocate and his legal interests are evident in the extracts we include from *Catriona* and *Weir of Hermiston*.

Many of the eighteenth-century judges, flourishing just before the period Lord Cockburn describes in his lively *Memorials of His Time*, were considerable literary figures. Lord Monboddo was a prolific, if at times eccentric, writer, and Henry Home, Lord Kames, a major intellectual force on the Court of Session for many years, published widely. Cockburn himself has, in addition to *Memorials of His Time*, also left us a vivid diary of his legal travels round Scotland and a major work on the eighteenth-century sedition trials.

James Boswell, the biographer and diarist, was before his wider fame, an advocate, even if he, at times, displayed a somewhat unorthodox approach to the law. In 1774 Boswell was engaged to defend John Reid, charged with the capital offence of sheep-stealing. Reid, eight years earlier, had been Boswell's first criminal client and he had then succeeded in saving his life. Now, however, he was unable to repeat his success and Reid was sentenced to death. Boswell, perhaps more emotionally involved in the case than was wise, worked hard at all the avenues of pardon or commutation of sentence. When the verdict was confirmed Boswell hatched a remarkable plan to recover Reid's body as soon as possible after the execution and attempt to revive the corpse. Boswell thoroughly researched the problems of reviving a hanged man and even consulted Dr Alexander Monro, the Professor of Anatomy at Edinburgh University. Boswell's diary for the 1st September 1774 records the results of this unusual consultation:

> He said that it was more difficult to recover a hanged person than a drowned, because hanging forces the blood up to the brain with more violence, there being a local compression at the neck; but that he thought the thing might be done by heat and rubbing to put the blood in motion, and by blowing air into the lungs; and he said that the best way was to cut a hole in the throat, in the trachea, and introduce a pipe. I laid all this up for service if it should be necessary.

Boswell continued to lay his plans, looking for a property adjacent to the Grassmarket where Reid's body could be taken for the resuscitation attempt. Boswell's unorthodox behaviour was motivated by a strong conviction of John Reid's innocence. Many of the friends he consulted advised against the plan, pointing out, as he noted in his diary:

> A great clamour would be made against me as defying the laws and as doing a ridiculous thing, and that a man in business must pay attention in prudence to the voice of mankind.

He was also affected by the argument that the unfortunate Reid was now resigned to his fate and, as a surgeon friend said:

> He [Reid] will have got over the pain of death. He may curse you for bringing him back. He may tell you that you kept him from heaven.

In the face of the practical and moral obstacles Boswell resolved to give up his plan and Reid was duly executed on 21 September 1774. Boswell's diary notes:

> John died seemingly without much pain. He was effectually hanged, the rope having fixed upon his neck very firmly, and he was allowed to hang near three quarters of an hour; so that any attempt to recover him would have been in vain.

Boswell's proposed conduct, if he had carried it through, was hardly likely to commend him to the legal authorities. He did not, however, hesitate to go outside the law. In 1769, when the verdict in the House of Lords appeal on the long-running Douglas Case – a deeply involved dispute over the succession to the Douglas peerage – became known in Edinburgh, a mob rioted and stoned the houses of those Court of Session judges who had earlier found for the Hamilton claimants. Among this mob who hurled stones at the windows of the Lord President and Lord Hailes was thought to be that rising young advocate, James Boswell, younger of Auchinleck. Boswell's involvement in this criminal behaviour, though widely and probably correctly suspected, was never proved. Lord Hailes seems to have been told that Boswell was part of the mob and wrote to him to give him the chance to deny it:

> I am not at liberty to suppose that you had any hand in such things directly, and I wish that you may have an opportunity of letting me know that you did not countenance the mob when in my neighbourhood and just in the street where I live; I could never ask you any more particular question, for this reason which upon recollection will suggest itself to you, that had you in an unguarded hour forgot yourself and me, and had you acknowledged it, this would [have] been a circumstance for proving one of the greatest insults that has been committed, except those against the President.

Boswell's criminal actions, had they been proved, would doubtless have resulted in his swift expulsion from the Faculty of Advocates.

Such behaviour on the part of a modern-day advocate seems improbable. Boswell was a man of a very different age and our contemporary views of legal and judicial propriety do not necessarily conform too closely to the standards of earlier ages. The habit of judges sitting drinking alcohol while dispensing justice is, for example, one which seems quite alien to our eyes. Lord Cockburn recorded this practice with earnest disapproval:

> Black bottles of strong port were set down beside them on the bench, with glasses, carafes of water, tumblers, and biscuits; and all this without the

slightest attempt at concealment. The refreshment was generally allowed to stand untouched, and as if despised, for a short time. . . . But in a little, some water was poured into the tumbler, and sipped quietly as if merely to sustain nature. Then a few drops of wine were ventured upon, but only with the water: till at last patience could endure no longer, and a full bumper of the pure black element was tossed over, after which the thing went on regularly, and there was a comfortable munching and quaffing, to the great envy of the parched throats in the gallery. The strong-headed stood it tolerably well, but it told, plainly enough, upon the feeble.

It is equally hard to imagine a judge today saying to a condemned man, who he had been in the habit of playing chess with, when sentencing him to death: 'That's checkmate to you, Matthew!' The same chess-playing judge, Henry Home, Lord Kames, on his final appearance at the Court of Session before his death bade farewell to his fellow Senators of the College of Justice in the memorable phrase: 'Fare ye a' weel, ye bitches!'

Boswell, not a man noted for his abstinence from any of the fleshly pleasures of life, recorded in his diary for September 1780 an evening spent at his father's house of Auchinleck in the company of three judges. The elder Boswell was himself a Judge, just recently retired from the Justiciary Bench but still handling civil cases in the Court of Session, and his visitors, in Ayrshire to conduct criminal trials, were Lord Kames and Robert McQueen, Lord Braxfield. Boswell, in a consciously restrained mood writes:

> I drank one glass of Madeira and one of claret. Was somewhat uneasy even by taking so much, and felt the company disturbed the calmness of Auchinleck. Lord Kames raved and Lord Braxfield roared – both bawdy.

'Bartoline Saddletree'

from The Heart of Midlothian

WALTER SCOTT (1771–1832)

As a reminder of that large group of unqualified legal enthusiasts unkindly referred to as 'barrack-room lawyers' we take an extract from Scott's The Heart of Midlothian *(1818). The novel starts with the Porteous Riot in Edinburgh in 1736, when the crowd attempted to free a popular smuggler, Wilson, from the gallows and were fired on by the City Guard under Captain Porteous. (See another extract from* The Heart of Midlothian *in Chapter 5 of this anthology.)*

The events are discussed by a group of Lawnmarket worthies, Peter Plumdamas, Mrs Howden and Grizel Damahoy, who are joined by the saddler and amateur lawyer, Bartoline Saddletree. Saddletree is seduced by the vocabulary of the Scots law, a vocabulary he however fails to pronounce properly and, indeed, a body of law he fails to understand properly. Bartoline is perhaps not to be condemned overmuch. A jurisprudence which can embrace such wonderfully-named crimes as hamesucken, stouthrief, leasing-making and perduellion has its charms.

Scott, himself an advocate, takes evident delight in Saddletree's untutored enthusiasm as he also delighted in the law suit of Peter Peebles in Redgauntlet *(1824).*

✝

'An unco thing this, Mrs Howden,' said old Peter Plumdamas to his neighbour the rouping-wife, or saleswoman, as he offered her his arm to assist her in the toilsome ascent, 'to see the grit folk at Lunnon set their face against law and gospel, and let loose sic a reprobate as Porteous upon a peaceable town!'

'And to think o' the weary walk they hae gien us,' answered Mrs Howden, with a groan; 'and sic a comfortable window as I had gotten, too, just within a penny-stane-cast of the scaffold – I could hae heard every word the minister said – land to pay twalpennies for my stand, and a' for naething!'

'I am judging,' said Mr Plumdamas, 'that this reprieve wadna stand gude in the auld Scots law, when the kingdom *was* a kingdom.'

I dinna ken muckle about the law,' answered Mrs Howden, 'but I ken, when we had a king, and a chancellor, and parliament-men o' our ain, we could aye peeble them wi' stanes when they werena gude bairns – But naebody's nails can reach the length o' Lunnon.'

'Weary on Lunnon, and a' that e'er came out o't!' said Miss Grizel Damahoy, an ancient seamstress. 'They hae taen awa our parliament, and they hae oppressed our trade. Our gentles will hardly allow that a Scots needle can sew ruffles on a sark, or lace on an owerlay.'

'Ye may say that, Miss Damahoy, and I ken o' them that hae gotten raisins frae Lunnon by forpits at ance,' responded Plumdamas, 'and then sic an host of idle English gaugers and excisemen as hae come down to vex and torment us, that an honest man canna fetch sae muckle as a bit anker o' brandy frae Leith to the Lawnmarket, but he's like to be rubbit o' the very gudes he's bought and paid for. Weel, I winna justify Andrew Wilson for pitting hands on what wasna his; but if he took nae mair than his ain, there's an awfu' difference between that and the fact this man stands for.'

'If ye speak about the law,' said Mrs Howden, 'here comes Mr Saddletree, that can settle it as weel as ony on the bench.'

The party she mentioned, a grave elderly person, with a superb periwig, dressed in a decent suit of sad-coloured clothes, came up as she spoke, and courteously gave his arm to Miss Grizel Damahoy.

It may be necessary to mention, that Mr Bartoline Saddletree kept an excellent and highly-esteemed shop for harness, saddles, &c &c at the sign of the Golden Nag, at the head of Bess Wynd. His genius, however (as he himself and most of his neighbours conceived) lay towards the weightier matters of the law, and he failed not to give frequent attendance upon the pleadings and arguments of the lawyers and judges in the neighbouring square, where, to say the truth, he was oftener to be found than would have consisted with his own emolument; but that his wife, an active painstaking person, could, in his absence, make an admirable shift to please the customers and scold the journeymen. This good lady was in the habit of letting her husband take his way, and go on improving his stock of legal knowledge without interruption; but, as if in requital, she insisted upon having her own will in the domestic and commercial departments which he abandoned to her. Now, as Bartoline Saddletree had a considerable gift of words, which he mistook for eloquence, and conferred more liberally upon the society in which he lived than was at all times gracious and acceptable, there went forth a saying, with which wags used sometimes to interrupt his rhetoric, that, as he had a golden nag at his door, so he had a grey mare in his shop. This reproach induced Mr Saddletree, on all occasions, to assume rather a haughty and stately tone towards his good woman, a circumstance by which she seemed very little affected, unless he attempted to exercise any real authority, when she never failed to fly into open rebellion. But such extremes Bartoline seldom provoked; for, like the gentle King Jamie, he was fonder of talking of authority than really exercising it. This turn of mind was, on the whole, lucky for him; since his substance was increased without any trouble on his part, or any interruption of his favourite studies.

This word in explanation has been thrown in to the reader, while Saddletree was laying down, with great precision, the law upon Porteous's case, by which he arrived at this conclusion, that, if Porteous had fired five minutes sooner, before Wilson was cut down, he would have been *versans in licito*; engaged, that is, in a lawful act, and only liable to be punished *propter excessum*, or for lack of discretion, which might have mitigated the punishment to *poena ordinaria*.

'Discretion!' echoed Mrs Howden, on whom, it may well be supposed, the fineness of this distinction was entirely thrown away. 'Whan had Jock Porteous either grace, discretion, or gude manners? I mind when his father –'

'But, Mrs Howden –' said Saddletree.

'And I,' said Miss Damahoy 'mind when his mother –'

'Miss Damahoy –' entreated the interrupted orator –'

'And I,' said Plumdamas, 'mind when his wife –'

'Mr Plumdamas – Mrs Howden – Miss Damahoy,' again implored the orator. 'Mind the distinction, as Counsellor Crossmyloof says – "I," says he, "take a distinction." Now, the body of the criminal being cut down, and the execution ended, Porteous was no longer official; the act which he came to protect and guard, being done and ended, he was no better than *cuivis ex populo*.'

'*Quivis, quivis*, Mr Saddletree, craving your pardon,' said (with a prolonged emphasis on the first syllable) Mr Butler, the deputy schoolmaster of a parish near Edinburgh, who at that moment came up behind them as the false Latin was uttered.

'What signifies interrupting me, Mr Butler? But I am glad to see ye notwithstanding – I speak after Counsellor Crossmyloof, and he said *cuivis*.'

'If Counsellor Crossmyloof used the dative for the nominative, I would have crossed *his* loof with a tight leathern strap, Mr Saddletree; there is not a boy on the booby form but should have been scourged for such a solecism in grammar.'

'I speak Latin like a lawyer, Mr Butler, and not like a schoolmaster,' retorted Saddletree.

'Scarce like a schoolboy, I think,' rejoined Butler.

'It matters little,' said Bartoline 'All I mean to say is, that Porteous has become liable to the *poena extra ordinem*, or capital punishment; which is to say, in plain Scotch, the gallows, simply because he did not fire when he was in office, but waited till the body was cut down, the execution while he had in charge to guard implemented, and he himself exonered of the public trust imposed on him.'

'But, Mr Saddletree,' said Plumdamas, 'do ye really think John Porteous's case wad hae been better if he had begun firing before ony stanes were flung at a'?'

'Indeed do I, neighbour Plumdamas,' replied Bartoline, confidently, 'he being then in point of trust and in point of power, the execution being but inchoat, or, at least, not implemented, or finally ended; but after Wilson was cut down, it was a' ower – he was clean exauctorate, and had nae mair ado but to get awa wi' his guard up this West Bow as fast as if there had been a caption after him. And this is law, for I heard it laid down by Lord Vincovincentem.'

'Vincovincentem? Is he a lord of state, or a lord of seat?' enquired Mrs Howden.

'A lord of seat – a lord of session. I fash mysell little wi' lords o' state; they vex me wi' a wheen idle questions about their saddles, and curpels, and holsters, and horse-furniture, and what they'll cost, and whan they'll be ready – a wheen galloping geese – my wife may serve the like o' them.'

'And so might she, in her day, hae served the best lord in the land, for as little as ye think o' her, Mr Saddletree,' said Mrs Howden, somewhat indignant at the contemptuous way in which her gossip was mentioned; 'when she and I were twa gilpies, we little thought to hae sitten doun wi' the like o' my auld Davie Howden, or you either, Mr Saddletree.'

While Saddletree, who was not bright at a reply, was cudgelling his brains for an answer to this home-thrust, Miss Damahoy broke in on him.

'And as for the lords of state,' said Miss Damahoy, 'ye suld mind the riding o' the parliament, Mr Saddletree, in the gude auld time before the Union – a year's rent o' mony a gude estate gaed for horse-graith and harnessing, forby broidered robes and foot-mantles, that wad hae stude by their lane wi' gold brocade, and that were muckle in my ain line.'

'Ay, and then the lusty banqueting, with sweetmeats and comfits wet and dry, and dried fruits of divers sorts,' said Plumdamas. 'But Scotland was Scotland in these days.'

'I'll tell ye what it is, neighbours,' said Mrs Howden, 'I'll ne'er believe Scotland is Scotland ony mair, if our kindly Scots sit doun with the affront they hae gien us this day. It's not only the blude that is shed, but the blude that might hae been shed, that's required at our hands; there was my daughter's wean, little Eppie Daidle – my oe, ye ken, Miss Grizel had played the truant frae the school, as' bairns will do, ye ken, Mr Butler –'

'And for which,' interjected Mr Butler; 'they should be soundly scourged by their well-wishers.'

'And had just cruppen to the gallows' foot to see the hanging, as was natural for a wean; and what for mightna she hae been shot as weel as the rest o' them, and where wad we a' hae been then? I wonder how Queen Carline (if her name be Carline) wad he liked to hae had ane o' her ain bairns in sic a venture?'

'Report says,' answered Butler, 'that such a circumstance would not have distressed her majesty beyond endurance.'

'Aweel,' said Mrs Howden, 'the sum o' the matter is, that, were I a man, I wad hae amends o' Jock Porteous, be the upshot what like o't, if a' the carles and carlines in England had sworn to the nay-say.'

'I would claw down the tolbooth door wi' my nails,' said Miss Grizel, 'but I wad be at him.'

'Ye may be very right, ladies,' said Butler, 'but I would not advise you to speak so loud.'

'Speak!' exclaimed both the ladies together, 'there will be naething else spoken about frae the Weigh-house to the Water-gate, till this is either ended or mended.'

The females now departed to their respective places of abode. Plumdamas joined the other two gentlemen in drinking their *meridian* (a bumper-dram of brandy) as they passed the well-known low-browed shop in the Lawnmarket, where they were wont to take that refreshment. Mr Plumdamas then departed towards his shop, and Mr Butler, who happened to have some particular occasion for the rein of an old bridle, (the truants of that busy day could have anticipated its application) walked down the Lawnmarket with Mr Saddletree, each talking as he could get a word thrust in, the one on the laws of Scotland, the other on those of Syntax, and neither listening to a word which his companion uttered.

'The Strange Conduct of Lord Grange'

from Traditions of Edinburgh

ROBERT CHAMBERS (1802–1871)

James Erskine of Grange, Lord Justice-Clerk from 1710–34, was hardly a shining example of judicial probity and rectitude. As the presiding officer of the High Court of Justiciary he was at the head of Scotland's criminal justice system, but was involved with various Jacobite conspiracies in the 1720s and 30s. He had married Rachel Chiesley – the Dictionary of National Biography notes: 'Grange had first debauched her and married her under compulsion.' It was an unhappy marriage, Rachel being, again to quote the Dictionary of National Biography: 'proud, violent and jealous . . . drunkard, and at times insane'.

By 1732 her conduct had become dangerous to him as she threatened to expose his Jacobite activities to the authorities. Grange, with the assistance of a number of Highland Jacobites, had Lady Grange kidnapped and held captive in a variety of locations in the Highlands and Islands, including a spell of seven years in the remote archipelago of St Kilda.

Robert Chambers, the Edinburgh printer and publisher, tells this startling story of kidnap and abduction in high society. Erskine of Grange (1679–1754) was the brother of 'Bobbing John' – John Erskine, 11th Earl of Mar who had led the Jacobite forces in the 1715 Rising. Grange resigned from the Court of Session and High Court of Justiciary in 1734, not over any scandal about the abduction of his wife, but in order to become an MP. He later became private secretary to the Prince of Wales. He eventually returned to Scotland and practised unsuccessfully as an advocate before going back to London where he died in 1754, having married his former mistress, a coffee-house keeper.

Lady Grange was rescued by her relatives in 1741 and died in 1745.

Lord and Lady Grange had been married upwards of twenty years, and had had several children, when, in 1730, a separation was determined on between them. It is usually difficult in such cases to say in what degree the parties are respectively blamable; how far there have been positive faults on one side, and want of forbearance on the other, and so forth. If we were to believe the lady in this instance, there had been love and peace for twenty years, when at length Lord Grange took a sudden dislike to his wife, and would no longer live with her. He, on the other hand, speaks of having suffered long from her 'unsubduable rage and madness', and of having failed in all his effort to bring her to a reasonable conduct. There is too much reason to believe that the latter statement is in the main true; although, were it more so, it would still leave Lord Grange unjustifiable in the measures which he took with respect to his wife. It is traditionally stated that, in their unhappy quarrels, the lady did not scruple to remind her husband whose daughter she was – thus hinting at what she was capable of doing if she thought herself deeply aggrieved. However all this might be, in the year 1730 a separation was agreed to (with great reluctance on the part of the lady), his lordship consenting to give her a hundred a year for her maintenance, so long as she should continue to live apart from him.

After spending some months in the country, Lady Grange returned to Edinburgh, and took a lodging near her husband's house, for the purpose, as she tells us, of endeavouring to induce him to take her back, and that she might occasionally see her children. According to Lord Grange, she began to torment him by following him and the children on the street 'in a scandalous and shameful manner', and coming to his house, and calling reproaches to him through the windows, especially when there was company with him. He thus writes: 'In his house, at the bottom of Niddry's Wynd, where there is a court through which one enters the house, one time among others, when it was full of chairs, chairmen, and footmen, who attended the company that were with himself, or his sister Lady Jane Paterson, then keeping house together, she came into this court, and among that mob shamelessly cried up to the windows injurious reproaches, and would not go away, though entreated, till, hearing the late Lord Lovat's voice, who was visiting Mr E—, and seeing two of his servants among the other footmen, "Oh," said she, "is your master here?" and instantly ran off.' He speaks of her having attacked him one day in church; at another time she forced him to take refuge with his son in a tavern for two hours. She even threatened to assault him on the bench, 'which he every day expected, for she professed that she had no shame'.

The traditionary account of Lady Grange represents her fate as having been at last decided by her threatening to expose her husband to the government for certain treasonable practices. It would now appear that this was partially true. In his statement, Lord Grange tells us that he had some time before gone to London, to arrange the private affairs of the Countess of Mar, then become unable to conduct them herself, and he had sent an account of his procedure to his wife, including some reflections on a certain great minister (doubtless Walpole), who had thwarted him much, and been of serious detriment to the interests of his family in this matter. This document she retained, and she now threatened to take it to London, and use it for her husband's disadvantage, being supported in the design by several persons with whom she associated. While denying that he had been concerned in anything treasonable, Lord Grange says, 'he had already too great a load of that great minister's wrath on his back to stand still and see more of it fall upon him by the treachery and madness of such a wife and such worthy confederates'. The lady had taken a seat in a stagecoach for London. Lord Grange caused a friend to go and make interest to get her money returned, and the seat let to another person; in which odd proceeding he was successful. Thus was the journey stayed for the meantime, but the lady declared her resolution to go as soon as possible. 'What,' says Lord Grange, 'could a man do with such a wife? There was great reason to think she would daily go on to do mischief to her family, and to affront and bring a blot on her children, especially her daughters. There were things that could not be redressed in a court of justice, and we had not then a madhouse to lock such unhappy people up in.'

The result of his lordship's deliberations was a plan for what he calls 'sequestrating' his wife. It appears to have been concerted between himself and a number of Highland chiefs, including, above all, the notorious Lord Lovat. We now turn to the lady's narrative, which proceeds to tell that, on the evening of the 22d of January 1732, a party of Highlandmen, wearing the livery of Lord Lovat, made their way into her lodgings, and forcibly seized her, throwing her down and gagging her, then tying a cloth over her head, and carrying her off as if she had been a corpse. At the bottom of the stair was a chair containing a man, who took the hapless lady upon his knees, and held her fast in his arms till they had got to a place in the outskirts of the town. Then they took her from the chair, removed the cloth from her head, and mounted her upon a horse behind a man, to whom she was tied; after which the party rode off 'by the lee light of the moon', to quote the language of the old ballads, whose incidents the present resembles in character.

The treatment of the lady by the way was, if we can believe her own account, by no means gentle. The leader, although a gentleman (Mr Forster of Corsebonny), disregarded her entreaties to be allowed to stop on account of cramp in her side, and only answered by ordering a servant to renew the bandages over her mouth. She observed that they rode along the Long Way (where Princes Street now stands), past the castle, and so to the Linlithgow road. After a ride of nearly twenty miles, they stopped at

Muiravonside, the house of Mr John Macleod, advocate, where servants appeared waiting to receive the lady – and thus shewed that the master of the house had been engaged to aid in her abduction. She was taken up stairs to a comfortable bedroom, but a man being posted in the room as a guard, she could not go to bed, nor take any repose. Thus she spent the ensuing day, and when it was night, she was taken out and remounted in the same fashion as before; and the party then rode along through the Torwood, and so to the place called Wester Polmaise, belonging to a gentleman of the name of Stewart, whose steward or factor was one of the cavalcade. Here was an old tower, having one little room on each floor, as is usually the case in such buildings; and into one of these rooms, the window of which was boarded over, the lady was conducted. She continued here for thirteen or fourteen weeks, supplied with a sufficiency of the comforts of life, but never allowed to go into the open air, till at length her health gave way, and the factor began to fear being concerned in her death. By his intercession with Mr Forster, she was then permitted to go into the court, under a guard; but such was the rigour of her keepers, that the garden was still denied to her.

Thus time passed drearily on until the month of August, during all which time the prisoner had no communication with the external world. At length, by an arrangement made between Lord Lovat and Mr Forster, at the house of the latter, near Stirling, Lady Grange was one night forcibly brought out, and mounted again as formerly, and carried off amidst a guard of horsemen. She recognised several of Lovat's people in this troop, and found Forster once more in command. They passed by Stirling Bridge, and thence onward to the Highlands; but she no longer knew the way they were going. Before daylight they stopped at a house, where she was lodged during the day, and at night the march was resumed. Thus they journeyed for several days into the Highlands, never allowing the unfortunate lady to speak, and taking the most rigid care to prevent any one from becoming aware of her situation. During this time she never had off her clothes: one day she slept in a barn, another in an open enclosure. Regard to delicacy in such a case was impossible. After a fortnight spent at a house on Lord Lovat's ground (probably in Stratherrick, Inverness-shire), the journey was renewed in the same style as before, only Mr Forster had retired from the party, and the lady found herself entirely in the hands of Frasers.

They now crossed a loch into Glengarry's land, where they lodged several nights in cow-houses, or in the open air, making progress all the time to the westward, where the country becomes extremely wild. At Lochour, an arm of the sea on the west coast, the unfortunate lady was transferred to a small vessel which was in waiting for her. Bitterly did she weep, and pitifully implore compassion, but the Highlanders understood not her language, and though they had done so, a departure from the orders which had been given them was not to be expected from men of their character. In the vessel, she found that she was in the custody of Sir Alexander Macdonald, a tenant of one of the Western Islands named Heskir, belonging to Sir Alexander Macdonald of Sleat, and here we have a curious indication of the spirit in which the Highlanders conducted such transactions. 'I told him,' says the lady, 'that I was stolen at Edinburgh, and brought there by force, and that it was contrary to the laws what they were doing. He answered that he would not keep me, or any other, against their will, *except Sir Alexander Macdonald were in the affair.*' While they lay in Lochourn, waiting for a wind, the brother and son of Macdonald of Scothouse came to see, but not to relieve her. Other persons visited the sloop, and among these one William Tolmy, a tenant of the chief of Macleod, and who had once been a merchant at Inverness. This was the first person she had seen who expressed any sympathy with her. He undertook to bear information of her retreat to her friend and 'man of business', Mr Hope of Rankeillor, in Edinburgh, but it does not appear that he fulfilled his promise.

Lady Grange remained in Macdonald's charge at Heskir nearly two years – during the first year without once seeing bread, and with no supply of clothing; obliged, in fact, to live in the same miserable way as the rest of the family. Afterwards some little indulgence was shewn to her. This island was of desolate aspect, and had no inhabitant besides Macdonald and his wife. The wretchedness of such a situation for a lady who had been all her life accustomed to the refined society of a capital, may of course be imagined. Macdonald would never allow her to write to any one, but he went to his landlord, Sir Alexander, to plead for the indulgences she required. On one of these occasions, Sir Alexander expressed his regret at having been concerned in such an affair, and wished he were quit of it. The wonder is, how Erskine should have induced all these men to interest themselves in the 'sequestration' of his wife. One thing is here remarkable: they were all of them friends of the Stuart family, as was Macleod of Macleod, into whose hands the lady subsequently fell. It therefore becomes probable that Erskine had at least convinced them that her seclusion from the world was necessary in some way for the preservation of political secrets important to them.

In June 1734, a sloop came to Heskir to take away the lady; it was commanded by a Macleod, and in it she was conveyed to the remotest spot of ground connected with the British Islands – namely, the isle of St

Kilda, the property of the chief of Macleod, and remarkable for the simple character of the poor peasantry who occupy it. There cannot, of course, be a doubt that those who had an interest in the seclusion of Lady Grange, regarded this as a more eligible place than Heskir, in as far as it was more out of the way, and promised better for her complete and permanent confinement. In some respects it was an advantageous change for the lady: the place was not uninhabited as Heskir very nearly was, and her domestic accommodation was better. In St Kilda, she was placed in a house or cottage of two small apartments, tolerably well furnished, with a girl to wait upon her, and provided with a sufficiency of good food and clothing. Of educated persons the island contained not one, except for a short time a Highland Presbyterian clergyman, named Roderick Maclennan. There was hardly even a person capable of speaking or understanding the English language within reach. No books, no intelligence from the world in which she had once lived. Only once a year did a steward come to collect the rent paid in kind by the poor people, and by him was the lady regularly furnished with a store of such articles, foreign to the place, as she needed – usually a stone of sugar, a pound of tea, six pecks of wheat, and an anker of spirits. Thus she had no lack of the common necessaries of life: she only wanted society and freedom. In this way she spent seven dreary years in St Kilda. How she contrived to pass her time is not known. We learn, however, some particulars of her history during this period from the testimony of those who had a charge over her. If this is to be believed, she made incessant efforts, though without effect, to bribe the islanders to assist in liberating her. Once a stray vessel sent a boat ashore for water: she no sooner heard of it, than she despatched the minister's wife to apprise the sailors of her situation, and entreat them to rescue her, but Mrs Maclennan did not reach the spot till after they had departed. She was kind to the peasantry, giving them from her own stores, and sometimes had the women to come and dance before her; but her temper and habits were not such as to gain their esteem. Often she drank too much, and whenever any one near her committed the slightest mistake, she would fly into a furious passion, and even resort to violence. Once she was detected in an attempt, during the night, to obtain a pistol from above the steward's bed, in the room next to her own: on his awaking and seeing her, she ran off to her own bed. One is disposed, of course, to make all possible allowances for a person in her wretched circumstances, yet there can be little doubt, from the evidence before us, that it was a natural and habitual violence of temper which displayed itself during her residence in St Kilda.

Meanwhile it was known in Edinburgh that Lady Grange had been

forcibly carried away and placed in seclusion by orders of her husband,
but her whereabouts was a mystery to all besides a few who were
concerned to keep it secret. During the years which had elapsed since her
abduction, Mr Erskine had given up his seat on the bench, and entered
into political life as a friend of the Prince of Wales, and opponent of Sir
Robert Walpole. The world had wondered at the events of his domestic
life, and several persons denounced the singular means he had adopted for
obtaining domestic peace. But, in the main, he stood as well with society
as he had ever done. At length, in the winter of 1740–41, a communication
from Lady Grange for the first time reached her friends. It was brought
by the minister Maclennan and his wife, who had left the island in
discontent, after quarrelling with Macleod's steward. The idea of a lady
by birth and education being immured for a series of years in an
outlandish place where only the most illiterate peasantry resided, and this
by the command of a husband who could only complain of her irritable
temper, struck forcibly upon public feeling, and particularly upon the
mind of Lady Grange's legal agent, Mr Hope of Rankeillor, who had all
along felt a keen interest in her fate. Of Mr Hope it may be remarked that
he was also a zealous Jacobite; yet, though all the persons engaged in the
lady's abduction were of that party, he hesitated not to take active
measures on the contrary side. He immediately applied to the Lord
Justice-clerk (supreme criminal judge) for a warrant to search for and
liberate Lady Grange. This application was opposed by the friends of Mr
Erskine, and eventually it was defeated, yet he was not on that account
deterred from hiring a vessel, and sending it with armed men to secure the
freedom of the lady – a step which, as it was illegal and dangerous,
obviously implied no small risk on his own part. This ship proceeded no
farther than the harbour called the Horseshoe, in Lorn (opposite to the
modern town of Oban), where the master quarrelled with and set on
shore Mrs Maclennan, his guide. Apparently the voyage was not
prosecuted, in consequence of intelligence being received that the lady
had been removed to another place, where she was kept in more humane
circumstances. If so, its object might be considered as in part at least,
though indirectly, accomplished.

I have seen a warrant, signed in the holograph of Normand Macleod –
the same insular chief who, a few years after, lost public respect in
consequence of his desertion of the Jacobite cause, and shewing an active
hostility to Prince Charles when in hiding. The document is dated at
Dunvegan, February 17, 1741, and proceeds upon a rumour which has
reached the writer, that a certain gentlewoman, called Lady Grange, was
carried to his isle of St Kilda in 1734, and has ever since been confined

there under cruel circumstances. Regarding this as a scandal which he is bound to inquire into (as if it could have hitherto been a secret to him), he orders his baron-bailie of Harris, Donald Macleod of Bernera (this was a gallant fellow, who went out in the Forty-five), to proceed to that island and make the necessary investigations. I have also seen the original precognition taken by honest Donald, six days thereafter, when the various persons who had been about Lady Grange gave evidence respecting her. The general bearing of this testimony, besides establishing the fact of her confinement as a prisoner, is to the effect that she was treated well in all other respects, having a house forty feet long, with an inner room and a chimney to it, a curtained bed, armchair, table, and other articles; ample store of good provisions, including spirits; and plenty of good clothes; but that she was addicted to liquor, and liable to dreadful outbreaks of anger. Evidence was at the same time taken regarding the character of the Maclennans, upon whose reports Mr Hope had proceeded. It was Mr Erskine's interest to establish that they were worthless persons, and to this effect strong testimony was given by several of the islanders, though it would be difficult to say with what degree of verity. The whole purpose of these precognitions was to meet the clamours raised by Mr Hope as to the barbarities to which Lady Grange had been subjected. They had the effect of stopping for a time the legal proceedings threatened by that gentleman; but he afterwards raised an action in the Court of Session for payment of the arrears of aliment or allowance due to the lady, amounting to £1150, and obtained decreet or judgment in the year 1743 against the defender in absence, though he did not choose to put it in force.

The unfortunate cause of all these proceedings ceased to be a trouble to anyone in May 1745. Erskine, writing from Westminster, June 1, in answer to an intimation of her death, says: 'I most heartily thank you, my dear friend, for the timely notice you gave me of the death of *that person*. It would be a ridiculous untruth to pretend grief for it, but as it brings to my mind a train of various things for many years back, it gives me concern. Her retaining wit and facetiousness to the last surprises me. These qualities none found in her, no more than commonsense or good-nature, before she went to these parts; and of the reverse of all which, if she had not been irrecoverably possest, in an extraordinary and insufferable degree, after many years' fruitless endeavours to reclaim her, she had never seen these parts. I long for the particulars of her death, which, you are pleased to tell me, I am to have by next post.'

Mr Hope's wife and daughters being left as heirs of Lady Grange, an action was raised in their name for the £1150 formerly awarded, and for three years additional of her annuity, and for this compound sum decreet was obtained, which was followed by steps for forcing payment. The Hopes were aware, however, of the dubious character of this claim, seeing that Mr Erskine, from whatever causes, had substituted an actual subsistence since 1732. They accordingly intimated that they aimed at no personal benefit from Lady Grange's bequest, and the affair terminated in Mr Erskine reimbursing Mr Hope for all the expenses he had incurred on behalf of the lady, including that for the sloop which he had hired to proceed to St Kilda for her rescue.

It is humbly thought that this story casts a curious and faithful light upon the age of our grandfathers, shewing things in a kind of transition from the sanguinary violence of an earlier age to the humanity of the present times. Erskine, not to speak of his office of a judge in Scotland, moved in English society of the highest character. He must have been the friend of Lyttelton, Pope, Thomson, and other ornaments of Frederick's court, and, as the brother-in-law of the Countess of Mar, who was sister of Lady Mary Wortley Montagu, he would figure in the brilliant circle which surrounded that star of the age of the second George. Yet he does not appear to have ever felt a moment's compunction at leaving the mother of his children to pine and fret herself to death in a half-savage wilderness –

'Placed far amidst the melancholy main'

for in a paper which expresses his feelings on the subject pretty freely, he justifies the 'sequestration' as a step required by prudence and decency, and, in shewing that the gross necessaries of life were afforded to his wife, seems to have considered that his whole duty towards her was discharged. Such an insensibility could not be peculiar to one man: it indicates the temper of a class and of an age. While congratulating ourselves on the improved humanity of our own times, we may glance with satisfaction to the means which it places in our power for the proper treatment of patients like Mrs Erskine. Such a woman would now be regarded as the unfortunate victim of disease, and instead of being forcibly carried off under cloud of night by a band of Highlanders, and committed to confinement on the outskirts of the world, she would, with proper precautions, be remitted to an asylum, where, by gentle and rational management, it might be hoped that she would be restored to mental health, or, at the worst, enabled to spend the remainder of her days in the utmost comfort which her state admitted of.

Lord Advocate Prestongrange

from Catriona

ROBERT LOUIS STEVENSON (1850–1894)

Stevenson's successful 1886 novel Kidnapped, *which told of the adventures of David Balfour and Alan Breck Stewart and their involvement in the Appin Murder (see extract in Chapter 4 of this anthology) was followed in 1893 by* Catriona. *This novel's action follows on immediately from the end of* Kidnapped *with David Balfour having claimed his rightful inheritance, reached Edinburgh and made contact with a distant cousin, an Edinburgh lawyer, Balfour of Pilrig. David and his Jacobite friend are still wanted by the authorities for their supposed involvement in the Appin Murder – the killing of Colin Campbell of Glenure, the Government factor on the forfeited estate of Stewart of Ardsheal. James Stewart, a kinsman of Alan's, has been arrested for the murder and David, who has evidence that will exculpate James and remove himself and Alan from the wanted list, resolves to call on the Lord Advocate, William Grant of Prestongrange.*

The post of Lord Advocate in the post-Jacobite period was one of unique power. The office of Secretary of State for Scotland had been abolished as part of the Government's response to the Jacobite rising. The Lord Advocate, who was the chief law officer in Scotland and the chief public prosecutor, took on an enhanced political role as London's man in Scotland. This role would grow through the century with the Lord Advocate being the manager of all the Government's Scottish business and, although answerable to a Secretary of State in Westminster, possessed of considerable powers of discretion and freedom of action.

The real-life William Grant (1701–64), was appointed Lord Advocate in February 1746 and held the post until 1754, when he exercised his privilege of appointing himself to the bench of the Court of Session, taking the judicial title of Lord Prestongrange. While Lord Advocate he had also served as Member of Parliament for the Elgin Burghs.

A minor curiosity about both Kidnapped *and* Catriona *is that Stevenson sets them in 1751 although the Appin Murder, as he knew, took place in 1752. Stevenson admitted this inaccuracy in the dedication of* Kidnapped *to his friend Charles Baxter:*

> *... you will likely ask yourself more questions than I should care to answer: as for instance how the Appin murder has come to fall in the year 1751 ... it is more honest to confess at once how little I am touched by the desire of accuracy.*

✝

My kinsman kept me to a meal, 'for the honour of the roof,' he said, and I believe I made the better speed on my return. I had no thought but to be done with the next stage, and have myself fully committed; to a person circumstanced as I was, the appearance of closing a door on hesitation and temptation was itself extremely tempting, and I was the more disappointed when I came to Prestongrange's house, to be informed he was abroad. I believe it was true at the moment, and for some hours after, and then I have no doubt the Advocate came home again, and enjoyed himself in a neighbouring chamber among friends, while perhaps the very fact of my arrival was forgotten. I would have gone away a dozen times, only for this strong drawing to have done with my declaration out of hand and be able to lay me down to sleep with a free conscience. At first I read, for the little cabinet where I was left contained a variety of books. But I fear I read with little profit; and the weather falling cloudy, the dusk coming up earlier than usual, and my cabinet being lighted with but a loophole of a window, I was at last obliged to desist from this diversion (such as it was), and pass the rest of my time of waiting in a very burthensome vacuity. The sound of people talking in a near chamber, the pleasant note of a harpsichord, and once the voice of a lady singing, bore me a kind of company.

I do not know the hour, but the darkness was long come, when the door of the cabinet opened, and I was aware, by the light behind him, of a tall figure of a man upon the threshold. I rose at once.

'Is anybody there?' he asked. 'Who is that?'

'I am bearer of a letter from the laird of Pilrig to the Lord Advocate,' said I.

'Have you been here long?' he asked.

'I would not like to hazard an estimate of how many hours,' said I.

'It is the first I hear of it,' he replied, with a chuckle. 'The lads must have forgotten you. But you are in the bit at last, for I am Prestongrange.'

So saying, he passed before me into the next room, whither (upon his sign) I followed him, and where he lit a candle and took his place before a business-table. It was a long room, of a good proportion, wholly lined with books. That small spark of light in a corner struck out the man's handsome person and strong face. He was flushed, his eye watered and sparkled, and before he sat down I observed him to sway back and forth. No doubt he had been supping liberally, but his mind and tongue were under full control.

'Well, sir, sit ye down,' said he, 'and let us see Pilrig's letter.'

He glanced it through in the beginning carelessly, looking up and bowing when he came to my name, but at the last words I thought I observed his attention to redouble, and I made sure he read them twice. All this while you are to suppose my heart was beating, for I had now crossed my Rubicon and was come fairly on the field of battle.

'I am pleased to make your acquaintance, Mr Balfour,' he said when he had done. 'Let me offer you a glass of claret.'

'Under your favour, my lord, I think it would scarce be fair on me,' said I. 'I have come here, as the letter will have mentioned, on a business of some gravity to myself, and as I am little used with wine, I might be the sooner affected.'

'You shall be the judge,' said he. 'But if you will permit, I believe I will even have the bottle in myself.'

He touched a bell, and a footman came, as at a signal, bringing wine and glasses.

'You are sure you will not join me?' asked the Advocate. 'Well, here is to our better acquaintance! In what way can I serve you?'

'I should perhaps begin by telling you, my lord, that I am here at your own pressing invitation,' said I.

'You have the advantage of me somewhere,' said he, 'for I profess I think I never heard of you before this evening.'

'Right, my lord, the name is indeed new to you,' said I. 'And yet you have been for some time extremely wishful to make my acquaintance, and have declared the same in public.'

'I wish you would afford me a clue,' says he. 'I am no Daniel.'

'It will perhaps serve for such,' said I, 'that if I was in a jesting humour – which is far from the case – I believe I might lay a claim on your lordship for two hundred pounds.'

'In what sense?' he inquired.

'In the sense of rewards offered for my person,' said I.

He thrust away his glass once and for all, and sat straight up in the chair where he had been previously lolling. 'What am I to understand?' said he.

'*A tall strong lad of about eighteen,*' I quoted, '*speaks like a Lowlander, and has no beard.*'

'I recognise those words,' said he, 'which, if you have come here with any ill-judged intention of amusing yourself, are like to prove extremely prejudicial to your safety.'

'My purpose in this,' I replied, 'is just entirely as serious as life and death, and you have understood me perfectly. I am the boy who was speaking with Glenure when he was shot.'

'I can only suppose (seeing you here) that you claim to be innocent,' said he.

'The inference is clear,' I said. 'I am a very loyal subject to King

George, but if I had anything to reproach myself with, I would have had more discretion than to walk into your den.'

'I am glad of that,' said he. 'This horrid crime, Mr Balfour, is of a dye which cannot permit any clemency. Blood has been barbarously shed. It has been shed in direct opposition to his Majesty and our whole frame of laws, by those who are their known and public oppugnants. I take a very high sense of this. I will not deny that, I consider the crime as directly personal to his Majesty.'

'And unfortunately, my lord,' I added, a little drily, 'directly personal to another great personage who may be nameless.'

'If you mean anything by those words, I must tell you I consider them unfit for a good subject; and were they spoke publicly I should make it my business to take note of them,' said he. 'You do not appear to me to recognise the gravity of your situation, or you would be more careful not to pejorate the same by words which glance upon the purity of justice. Justice, in this country, and in my poor hands, is no respecter of persons.'

'You give me too great a share in my own speech, my lord,' said I. 'I did but repeat the common talk of the country, which I have heard everywhere, and from men of all opinions as I came along.'

'When you are come to more discretion you will understand such talk is not to be listened to, how much less repeated,' says the Advocate. 'But I acquit you of an ill intention. That nobleman, whom we all honour, and who has indeed been wounded in a near place by the late barbarity, sits too high to be reached by these aspersions. The Duke of Argyle – you see that I deal plainly with you – takes it to heart as I do, and as we are both bound to do by our judicial functions and the service of his Majesty; and I could wish that all hands, in this ill age, were equally clean of family rancour. But from the accident that this is a Campbell who has fallen martyr to his duty – as who else but the Campbells have ever put themselves foremost on that path? – I may say it, who am no Campbell – and that the chief of that great house happens (for all our advantages) to be the present head of the College of Justice, small minds and disaffected tongues are set agog in every changehouse in the country; and I find a young gentleman like Mr Balfour so ill-advised as to make himself their echo.' So much he spoke with a very oratorical delivery, as if in court, and then declined again upon the manner of a gentleman. 'All this apart,' said he. 'It now remains that I should learn what I am to do with you.'

'I had thought it was rather I that should learn the same from your lordship,' said I.

'Ay, true,' says the Advocate. 'But, you see, you come to me well recommended. There is a good honest Whig name to this letter,' says he, picking it up a moment from the table. 'And – extra-judicially, Mr Balfour

– there is always the possibility of some arrangement. I tell you, and I tell you beforehand that you may be the more upon your guard, your fate lies with me singly. In such a matter (be it said with reverence) I am more powerful than the king's Majesty; and should you please me – and of course satisfy my conscience – in what remains to be held of our interview, I tell you it may remain between ourselves.'

'Meaning how?' I asked.

'Why, I mean it thus, Mr Balfour,' said he, 'that if you give satisfaction, no soul need know so much as that you visited my house, and you may observe that I do not even call my clerk.'

I saw what way he was driving. 'I suppose it is needless anyone should be informed upon my visit,' said I, 'though the precise nature of my gains by that I cannot see. I am not at all ashamed of coming here.'

'And have no cause to be,' says he, encouragingly. 'Nor yet (if you are careful) to fear the consequences.'

'My lord,' said I, 'speaking under your correction I am not very easy to be frightened.'

'And I am sure I do not seek to frighten you,' says he. 'But to the interrogation; and let me warn you to volunteer nothing beyond the questions I shall ask you. It may consist very immediately with your safety. I have a great discretion, it is true, but there are bounds to it.'

'I shall try to follow your lordship's advice,' said I.

He spread a sheet of paper on the table and wrote a heading. 'It appears you were present, by the way, in the wood of Lettermore at the moment of the fatal shot,' he began. 'Was this by accident?'

'By accident,' said I.

'How came you in speech with Colin Campbell?' he asked.

'I was inquiring my way of him to Aucharn,' I replied.

I observed he did not write this answer down.

'H'm, true,' said he, 'I had forgotten that. And do you know, Mr Balfour, I would dwell, if I were you, as little as might be on your relations with these Stewarts? It might be found to complicate our business. I am not yet inclined to regard these matters as essential.'

'I had thought, my lord, that all points of fact were equally material in such a case,' said I.

'You forget we are now trying these Stewarts,' he replied, with great significance. 'If we should ever come to be trying you, it will be very different; and I shall press these very questions that I am now willing to glide upon. But to resume: I have it here in Mr Mungo Campbell's precognition that you ran immediately up the brae. How came that?'

'Not immediately, my lord, and the cause was my seeing of the murderer.'

'You saw him, then?'

'As plain as I see your lordship, though not so near hand.'

'You know him?'

'I should know him again.'

'In your pursuit you were not so fortunate, then, as to overtake him?'

'I was not.'

'Was he alone?'

'He was alone.'

'There was no one else in the neighbourhood?'

'Alan Breck Stewart was not far off, in a piece of a wood.'

The Advocate laid his pen down. 'I think we are playing at cross purposes,' said he, 'which you will find to prove a very ill amusement for yourself.'

'I content myself with following your lordship's advice, and answering what I am asked,' said I.

'Be so wise as to bethink yourself in time,' said he, 'I use you with the most anxious tenderness, which you scarce seem to appreciate, and which (unless you be more careful) may prove to be in vain.'

'I do appreciate your tenderness, but conceive it to be mistaken,' I replied, with something of a falter, for I saw we were come to grips at last. 'I am here to lay before you certain information, by which I shall convince you Alan had no hand whatever in the killing of Glenure.'

The Advocate appeared for a moment at a stick, sitting with pursed lips, and blinking his eyes upon me like an angry cat. 'Mr Balfour,' he said at last, 'I tell you pointedly you go an ill way for your own interests.'

'My lord,' I said, 'I am as free of the charge of considering my own interests in this matter as your lordship. As God judges me, I have but the one design, and that is to see justice executed and the innocent go clear. If in pursuit of that I come to fall under your lordship's displeasure, I must bear it as I may.'

At this he rose from his chair, lit a second candle, and for a while gazed upon me steadily. I was surprised to see a great change of gravity fallen upon his face, and I could have almost thought he was a little pale.

'You are either very simple, or extremely the reverse, and I see that I must deal with you more confidentially,' says he. 'This is a political case – ah, yes, Mr Balfour! Whether we like it or no, the case is political – and I tremble when I think what issues may depend from it. To a political case, I need scarce tell a young man of your education, we approach with very different thoughts from one which is criminal only. *Salus populi suprema lex* is a maxim susceptible of great abuse, but it has that force which we find elsewhere only in the laws of nature: I mean it has the force of necessity. I will open this out to you, if you allow me, at more length. You would have me believe –'

'Under your pardon, my lord, I would have you to believe nothing but that which I can prove,' said I.

'Tut! tut! young gentleman,' says he, 'be not so pragmatical, and suffer a man who might be your father (if it was nothing more) to employ his own imperfect language, and express his own poor thoughts, even when they have the misfortune not to coincide with Mr Balfour's. You would have me to believe Breck innocent. I would think this of little account, the more so as we cannot catch our man. But the matter of Breck's innocence shoots beyond itself. Once admitted, it would destroy the whole presumptions of our case against another and a very different criminal; a man grown old in treason, already twice in arms against his king and already twice forgiven; a fomenter of discontent, and (whoever may have fired the shot) the unmistakable original of the deed in question. I need not tell you that I mean James Stewart.'

'And I can just say plainly that the innocence of Alan and of James is what I am here to declare in private to your lordship, and what I am prepared to establish at the trial by my testimony,' said I.

'To which, I can only answer by an equal plainness, Mr Balfour,' said he, 'that (in that case) your testimony will not be called by me, and I desire you to withhold it altogether.'

'You are at the head of Justice in this country,' I cried, 'and you propose to me a crime!'

'I am a man nursing with both hands the interests of this country,' he replied, 'and I press on you a political necessity. Patriotism is not always moral in the formal sense. You might be glad of it, I think: it is your own protection; the facts are heavy against you; and if I am still trying to except you from a very dangerous place it is in part of course because I am not insensible to your honesty in coming here; in part because of Pilrig's letter, but in part, and in chief part, because I regard in this matter my political duty first and my judicial duty only second. For the same reason – I repeat it to you in the same frank words – I do not want your testimony.'

'I desire not to be thought to make a repartee, when I express only the plain sense of our position,' said I. 'But if your lordship has no need of my testimony, I believe the other side would be extremely blythe to get it.'

Prestongrange arose and began to pace to and fro in the room. 'You are not so young,' he said, 'but what you must remember very clearly the year '45 and the shock that went about the country. I read in Pilrig's letter that you are sound in Kirk and State. Who saved them in that fatal year? I do not refer to His Royal Highness and his ramrods, which were extremely useful in their day; but the country had been saved and the field won before ever Cumberland came upon Drummossie. Who saved it? I repeat, who saved the Protestant religion and the whole frame of our civil institutions? The late Lord President Culloden, for one; he played a man's part, and small thanks he got for it – even as I, whom you see before you, straining every nerve in the same service, look for no reward beyond the conscience of my duties done. After the President, who else? You know the answer as well as I do; 'tis partly a scandal, and you glanced at it yourself, and I reproved you for it, when you first came in. It was the Duke and the great clan of Campbell. Now here is a Campbell foully murdered, and that in the King's service. The Duke and I are Highlanders. But we are Highlanders civilised, and it is not so with the great mass of our clans and families. They have still savage virtues and defects. They are still barbarians, like these Stewarts; only the Campbells were barbarians on the right side, and the Stewarts were barbarians on the wrong. Now be you the judge. The Campbells expect vengeance. If they do not get it – if this man James escape – there will be trouble with the Campbells. That means disturbance in the Highlands, which are uneasy and very far from being disarmed: the disarming is a farce . . .'

'I can bear you out in that,' said I.

'Disturbance in the Highlands makes the hour of our old watchful enemy,' pursued his lordship, holding out a finger as he paced; 'and I give you my word we may have a '45 again with the Campbells on the other side. To protect the life of this man Stewart – which is forfeit already on half a dozen different counts if not on this – do you propose to plunge your country in war, to jeopardise the faith of your fathers, and to expose the lives and fortunes of how many thousand innocent persons? . . . These are considerations that weigh with me, and that I hope will weigh no less with yourself, Mr Balfour, as a lover of your country, good government, and religious truth.'

'You deal with me very frankly, and I thank you for it,' said I. 'I will try on my side to be no less honest. I believe your policy to be sound. I believe these deep duties may lie upon your lordship; I believe you may have laid them on your conscience when you took the oaths of the high office which you hold. But for me, who am just a plain man – or scarce a man yet – the plain duties must suffice. I can think but of two things, of a poor soul in the immediate and unjust danger of a shameful death, and of the cries and tears of his wife that still tingle in my head. I cannot see beyond, my lord. It's the way that I am made. If the country has to fall, it has to fall. And I pray God, if this be wilful blindness, that He may enlighten me before too late.'

He had heard me motionless, and stood so a while longer.

'This is an unexpected obstacle,' says he, aloud, but to himself.

'And how is your lordship to dispose of me?' I asked.

'If I wished,' said he, 'you know that you might sleep in gaol?'

'My lord,' said I, 'I have slept in worse places.'

'Well, my boy,' said he, 'there is one thing appears very plainly upon our interview, that I may rely on your pledged word. Give me your honour that you will be wholly secret, not only on what has passed tonight, but in the matter of the Appin case, and I let you go free.'

'I will give it till tomorrow or any other near day that you may please to set,' said I. 'I would not be thought too wily; but if I gave the promise without qualification your lordship would have attained his end.'

'I had no thought to entrap you,' said he.

'I am sure of that,' said I.

'Let me see,' he continued. 'Tomorrow is the Sabbath. Come to me on Monday by eight in the morning, and give me your promise until then.'

'Freely given, my lord,' said I. 'And with regard to what has fallen from yourself, I will give it for as long as it shall please God to spare your days.'

'You will observe,' he said next, 'that I have made no employment of menaces.'

'It was like your lordship's nobility,' said I. 'Yet I am not altogether so dull but what I can perceive the nature of those you have not uttered.'

'Well,' said he, 'good-night to you. May you sleep well, for I think it is more than I am like to do.'

With that he sighed, took up a candle, and gave me his conveyance as far as the street door.

'Judges and Judgements'

from The Social Life of Scotland in the Eighteenth Century

HENRY GREY GRAHAM (1842–1906)

Henry Grey Graham was a son of the Manse who himself became a minister of the Church of Scotland. Born in North Berwick, he studied at Edinburgh University and was an assistant at Bonhill, Dumbartonshire, before becoming minister of Nenthorn, Berwickshire, in 1868. He was translated to Hyndland parish, Glasgow in 1884 and remained there until his death.

He is best remembered for two books: Scottish Men of Letters of the Eighteenth Century *(1901) and* The Social Life of Scotland in the Eighteenth Century *(1899). These volumes, with their vast store of miscellaneous and fascinating information about daily life in the period are a testament to Graham's wide reading and delight in detail.*

Our extract comes from his chapter on Crime and Punishments *– it concludes with an interesting description of the many local courts, part of the network of private jurisdictions which once formed a significant part of the Scottish criminal justice system. These, as Graham points out, were swept away in the wake of the 1745–46 Jacobite Rising, when the British Government grew concerned about the power of the Highland chiefs and took a variety of measures to reduce their influence. Few tears need be shed for the abolition of heritable jurisdictions whatever one's view about the other measures taken at this time.*

Graham also usefully points out the comparatively mild nature of Scottish criminal justice compared to that in England. Even murderers could escape the ultimate penalty – in 1788 one Isabel Tait, who had been indicted for child-murder, petitioned the High Court and with the concurrence of the Lord Advocate was banished from Scotland for life and given ten weeks to put her affairs in order and be gone. Perhaps the court looked on life in, say, Northumberland, as a fate worse than death.

✝

In the early part of the century the turbulent element was to be found in the swarms of 'randy beggars, thiggers, Egyptian sorners', who haunted outlying districts of the country, and incessantly infested villages, and visited the homes of the people to the terror of their lives and with the plunder of their goods. In former times there were off-hand measures taken for dealing with these vagabonds, statutes still existing which allowed any master of a pit, salt-pans, or mine, to seize them and force them to work as life-long serfs in their service. When Fletcher of Saltoun prescribed slavery as a drastic remedy for beggary, he was propounding no novel or whimsical scheme, but simply urging that existing laws should be enforced on the 200,000 sturdy prowling beggars, who were pests and dangerous to the community. The stalwart republican, however, went further than advocating compulsory slavery; he also urged compulsion on masters to take slaves. At the beginning of the century instances occurred of men, who were scoundrels or escaped hanging for thefts, being consigned as perpetual servants in the silver mines and pits of Scotland, where they were bound as slaves, wearing iron collars riveted round their necks, on which was inscribed their name, their crime, and their owner. Vagabonds who were not condemned to this fate were burnt through the ear with an iron and banished the county, for magistrates were quite satisfied that they had done their duty when they had rid their own district of a nuisance, and had sent him to rob the next, under penalty of being hanged if he returned. More dangerous 'Egyptians' were 'banished furth of Scotland', while those caught in act of theft were regarded as if 'notorious thieves' and straightway hanged.

Harsh as much of the penal code was, it was far from cruel, and was infinitely milder than that of England. Though robbery (theft with violence or terrorism) was liable to penalty of death, even when the article was of trifling value, ordinary thieving called 'pickery' received no capital sentence unless the thief was 'by habit and repute', or after a third offence. Contrast that with the law of England. When Blackstone wrote his *Commentaries* in 1760, there were no fewer than 164 crimes which involved capital punishment, a number which was increased in the course of after years. The same measure was meted out to the man guilty of the foulest murder and the man guilty of the smallest theft, to the starving woman who snatched a loaf from a baker's window and to the boy who took 'privately' from a shop or picked from a pocket a sum valued at 12d.

While lords of session administered justice in the High Courts at Edinburgh, at their stated times they went on circuit to county towns. They proceeded on horseback along the wretched ruts which served as roads, where no coach could pass, to the peril and discomfort of venerable persons, inexpert in horsemanship, whose cloaks fluttered in the wind, and whose wigs got dishevelled at the everlasting jolts and stumbles on the paths. Behind them a cavalcade of clerks and servants followed, carrying papers and books and cloaks for their lordships in their bags. While the judges were trying the criminals in their courts on charges of 'spuilzie' and 'hamesucken', arson and murder, in country towns justices of peace had their arduous labours to preserve order, to punish offenders for 'pickery' with penalties full of quaint barbarity of olden times. Imprisonment was seldom awarded, and only for short periods, partly from frugal dislike to expense, and partly because the jails or 'thieves' holes' were only little hovels, with no jailer to guard them, and uncertain arrangements to feed their lodgers. Other punishments, however, abounded. There were for less offences the jougs or iron collars, attached to the kirk walls (though they were becoming less used), in which the culprits' necks were fastened for 'ye terror to ye others', though they provided more amusement than warning to the community. More excitement filled 'ye others' when they heard that a criminal was to stand bareheaded at the top of the outside stair of the Tolbooth, bound with a chain, and having a label on the breast, stating 'Here I stand for theft and reset of theft', or when two miserable beings were stationed with their placards announcing in local spelling 'Thir are adulterers'. Great public satisfaction was felt when a well-known offender sat upon a cuck-stool, with neck and hand in the pillory having his ears nailed to the same, or, with still further refinement of cruelty, stood with his ear nailed till he summoned resolution to tear away his 'lug with the gristle'. On such occasions the crowd was great and deeply interested. Children played truant from school, the weavers left their looms, the women threw their spindles down, and ran to watch some creature having her 'nose pinched' – a process performed with an iron frame with clips which held secure the cartilage of the victim's nose. A pleasant rural thrill was felt when yet another penalty was inflicted, and they saw the common hangman take his knife and cut off the bleeding ear. The tuck of a drum made everyone run to his doorstep to gaze on the locksman leading a woman, stripped to the waist, through the streets, at certain stations to flog her with his lashes, before taking her to jail, for stealing lawn from a bleaching field. Relapse into immorality might incur as penalty (at recommendation of the Kirk Session) the woman standing at the Market Cross with her head shaved, with the locksman beside her. Such penalties were a town's excitement in an age not too full of fine sensibilities, and wonderfully relieved the monotony of burghal existence.

A very frequent adjunct to such sentences by justices was that of

banishment out of the town or beyond the county, while the judges
sentenced criminals for theft 'furth of Scotland' – a vague destination in
days before they were able to transport them to the colonies. Thus
banished, with threat of being scourged or branded if they returned,
offenders had a fate which in those days was virtual outlawry with the
prospect of a hunted life. For whither could the exile go? By law of
Church and rules of Kirk Sessions no one was allowed to reside in a
parish until he produced a 'testificate' from the Session of his former
place, and this, of course, he could not furnish. The unfortunate creature
banished for stealing a hen or an ell of linen, or for breaking a sapling, was
forced to beg, if not to steal, and yet his doing so insured his at once being
delated by the elders to the justices, by them to be anew scourged, and
either sent to jail or again banished. If in despair he returned to his old
haunts and family he might be incontinently seized, branded,
imprisoned, till an impossible £100 Scots was paid, and yet rebanished
again. This miserable dilemma of being driven from pillar to post existed
up till near the middle of the century, when the Kirk and its elders became
less rigorous, and the people less docile, and towns with growing
populations afforded easier shelter and concealment for fugitives, while
sentences themselves became more mild in a milder age, and prisons more
able to hold offenders.

While the execution of laws in highest crimes lay with the judges of
session, there were other courts over many districts, and especially north
of the Forth, which exercised jurisdiction as full as the Court of Session.
There were over a hundred Courts of Regality, in which the great owners
of land throughout Scotland presided as hereditary barons or sheriffs,
having power to sentence all criminals in their domain. The baron or his
bailie presided over fifteen assessors as jury, and he could wield the right
of punishment of pit and gallows – to hang or imprison. This tremendous
power he held, bound by no legal process, restrained by no fear, guided
by no precedents. However wrongly he might abuse his right, it could
not be withdrawn, for it came by charter, was inherited by birth, and yet
could be sold at his will. Especially high-handed and rigorous were these
barons or chiefs of the Northern and Highland counties, where the voice
of public opinion was never heard, and from which the grievances of
victims were never borne. Whatever verdict the baron desired was
obsequiously given by the servile tenants or humble tacksmen who
formed the jury. If he was a friend the prisoner escaped scot free, however
clear his guilt; if he was a foe, he was pretty certain to be condemned
however clear his innocence.

The records of the courts of these irresponsible hereditary sheriffs in some cases are extant, stating concisely the name of the criminal, the offence, and the verdict, whether 'clenzit' or 'convikt', to the latter being crisply appended the sentence, which is too often 'hangit' or 'drownit'. At other times the sentence was to be scourged, to have his ear nailed to a post, or cut off, and banished the country. By such summary processes Grant of Grant sentenced three persons found guilty of horse-stealing to be carried from the court to the pit or dungeon of Castle Grant, there to remain till Tuesday next, and thence to be carried to the gallowstree at Ballintore, and to be hanged between three and four in the afternoon till they be dead. If a loch was near, as Loch Spynie was to Gordonston, the victim of hereditary jurisdiction was expeditiously drowned. There, for example, an unfortunate woman was put to death for stealing out of a chest thirty rex dollars and two webs of linen, and as she was drowning she was heard (very naturally) 'evacuating curses on her oppressors'. Each gentleman who had the cherished privilege and power had a dempster or hangman who carried out the sentences, which were executed on gallows usually erected on a moor or where two roads met; and in the local names of fields of 'Galloflat' and 'Gallowlaw' there are still reminiscences of the old hanging days of these Courts of Regality. Memories of these oppressive and arbitrary measures were vivid at the end of the century, when stories were still told of the iniquitous doings of the old régime: how one hereditary sheriff acted as both judge and jury, and sentenced at his will; how another hanged a man and afterwards called his faithful jury to convict him; how yet another hanged two brothers on one tree near Abernethy, and burned their bodies on the roadside; and how a chief hanged two notorious thieves, parboiled their heads, and set them on spikes. Tradition lingered of a case where the baron bailie was so odious that the people rose in vengeance and drowned him in the Spey.

The pit and dungeon in the castles or mansion houses were usually noisome holes. Such was the pit at Gordonston in Morayshire, victims of which appealed to the lords of session in 1740, a vault cold, wet, and pitch-dark, secured by an iron grating, without door or window, so wet that the miserable inmates had to stand on stones to raise themselves above the inflowing water that covered the floor. In such a pit untried prisoners were detained for months, and there those convicted even of trifling offences were confined at the risk or cost of life. Although these hereditary barons had no right to transport their convicts, they often made a nefarious and profitable trade of sending them to the Plantations. They offered the prisoners that alternative to death, and many gladly consented to be exported, whereupon the lord of regality in the North sold his victims to those men whose business it was to secure, by means fair or foul, recruits to sell for work in the estates of America or West Indies, where they became serfs of planters, with little hope of ever recovering their freedom.

It was in 1748 that all hereditary jurisdictions were abolished. After the Rebellion of '45 it was felt necessary to break down feudal power and state, especially in the Highlands, to bring under equal law and central authority all officers of justice, and to shear the chieftains of those privileges which had made them dangers to order and menaces to government. Barons and chiefs who had ruled like kings in their districts, and tyrants over their vassals, by the withdrawal of those ancient rights were suddenly reduced to mere subjects – no more superior to law than the meanest of their crofters. Not merely did this abolition involve the loss of prestige, of power, of influence on which they had so long prided themselves; it also implied the loss of gains hardly less coveted. Baron bailies often enriched themselves by the fruits of office, which were called 'duties': a day's labour from every tenant, the goods of all persons sentenced to death, the fines of those who were convicted, the herial cow or horse at the death of each tenant – the best of the cattle being seized from the poor widow and her family. By the abolition of the Courts of Regality and of Barony all these 'duties' and perquisites were lost, as were their personal glory and importance, and the dispossessed lords claimed exorbitant compensation for the loss they had sustained. They, not too modestly, estimated the equivalent at £602,127, but were obliged to be satisfied with £152,000. Whatever might have been the loss to these gentlemen, it was clearly a gain to the country, which under the legal sheriffs who reigned in their stead had a chance of equity and due procedure, of fairer trials, more reasonable verdicts, and less arbitrary sentences. Yet no institutions or men, however bad, ever pass away without mourners when they die – even on the grave of Nero some unknown hand laid flowers – and sentimental lovers of ancient customs and patriarchal ways joined in the lamentation with retainers who had benefited by the partiality of their lairds and lords. Some loyal tenants protested that they 'aye liked gentlemen's law', preferring the possible lenity of their laird to the certain justice of the sheriff. No longer could an Earl of Galloway, as in good old days, hold his court and sentence in a trice criminals caught 'red-hand'. 'Yerl John,' exclaimed one vigorous admirer, 'was the man! He'd hang them up just o' his ain word: nane o' your law!'

'The Scottish Bench'

from Memorials of His Time

HENRY COCKBURN (1779–1854)

Henry Cockburn was one of the most prominent Scottish advocates of the early nineteenth century and was appointed Solicitor General in 1830 and a Court of Session judge in 1834. In his earlier life his enthusiastic support for the Whig party and his advocacy of franchise extension had denied him advancement under successive Tory administrations.

Cockburn is a lively and colourful writer and Memorials of His Time *(published posthumously in 1856) is an important source for Scottish life in Cockburn's period. His journals, published as* Circuit Journeys *in 1888 give a vivid impression of the Scotland Cockburn saw as he travelled around the country on justiciary business between 1837 and May 1854.*

Cockburn is so lively and colourful a writer that his views have often been accepted as entirely reliable and insufficient allowance made for his deep prejudices and, in some cases, lack of first-hand knowledge. This is well demonstrated in this extract in his portrayal of Robert McQueen, Lord Braxfield, the Lord Justice-Clerk. He describes Braxfield's behaviour on the bench in some detail. Until one realises that, during the 1792–93 sedition trials he discusses, Cockburn was a lad of thirteen or fourteen, one assumes that he had been sitting in the Justiciary Court, rather than sitting in a classroom in the High School of Edinburgh. Not only is Cockburn not a first-hand witness to the events he reports, he was temperamentally hostile to Braxfield. As Braxfield's biographer has noted:

> *Between McQueen and Cockburn lies the gulf of fifty-seven years ... But more than a generation gap separates McQueen and Cockburn – they are divided by language, by political ideology, by religious conviction, by social custom, by manners. McQueen was an anachronistic survivor of a fast-vanishing Scotland – a mid eighteenth-century figure, rough, perhaps even gross, in manner. Cockburn as a nineteenth-century Whig was emotionally and intellectually opposed to much that McQueen represented.*

Even in the language Cockburn uses to describe McQueen evident prejudice creeps in – 'a formidable blacksmith', 'accent and dialect were exaggerated Scotch', 'without any taste for refined enjoyment'. McQueen was the grandson of a Lanarkshire gardener, who stubbornly retained a broad Scots tongue and idiom throughout his life – Cockburn was a scion of the Midlothian legal aristocracy.

Braxfield's behaviour on the bench, where cases of sedition were involved, was indeed unacceptable but not, perhaps, surprising. The more general accusation of coarseness and taunting of condemned criminals is not sustained by contemporary accounts or the published accounts of trials he presided over. For example his final words to Deacon Brodie, condemning him to death, were characterised by a sympathetic and genuine feeling; Brodie's accomplice Smith was disposed of with less emotion but without any suggestion of mockery or discourtesy.

Despite these serious reservations about Cockburn's credibility he remains an important chronicler of an age when the Scottish Bench was populated by a colourful group of men.

Of the fifteen judges of those days, some of course were 'heads without name'. Of the others Monboddo, Swinton, and Braxfield had left the scene shortly before I entered the Faculty.

Classical learning, good conversation, excellent suppers, and ingenious though unsound metaphysics were the peculiarities of Monboddo. He was reputed a considerable lawyer in his own time; and his reports shew that the reputation was well founded. Some offence had made him resolve never to sit on the same bench with President Dundas; and he kept this vow so steadily that he always sat at the clerk's table even after Dundas was gone. I never saw him sitting anywhere else. This position enabled him to get easily out and in; and whenever there was a pause he was sure to slip off; gown and all, to have a talk in the Outer House, where I have often seen the shrivelled old man walking about very cheerfully. He went very often to London, almost always on horseback, and was better qualified than most of his countrymen to shine in its literary society. But he was insufficiently appreciated; and he partly justified and indeed provoked this, by taking his love of paradox and metaphysics with him, and dealing them out in a style of academical formality; and this even after he ought to have seen, that all that people cared about his dogmas was to laugh at their author. It is more common to hear anecdotes about his maintaining that men once had tails, and similar follies, than about his agreeable conversation and undoubted learning. All who knew him in Edinburgh concur in describing his house as one of the most pleasant in the place.

I knew Lord Swinton as much as a youth can know an old man, and I have always been intimate with his family. He was a very excellent person; dull, mild, solid, and plodding; and in his person large and heavy. It is only a subsequent age that has discovered his having possessed a degree of sagacity, for which he did not get credit while he lived. So far back as 1765 he published an attack on our system of entails; in 1779 he explained a scheme for a uniform standard of weights and measures; and in 1789 he put forth considerations in favor of dividing the Court of Session into more courts than one, and of introducing juries for the trial of civil causes. All these improvements have since taken place, but they were mere visions in his time; and his anticipation of them, in which, so far as I ever heard, he had no associate, is very honourable to his thoughtfulness and judgment. Notwithstanding the utter dissimilarity of the two men, there was a great friendship between him and Henry Erskine, which it is to the honor of Swinton's ponderous placidity that Erskine's endless jokes upon him never disturbed.

But the giant of the bench was Braxfield. His very name makes people start yet.

Strong built and dark, with rough eyebrows, powerful eyes, threatening lips, and a low growling voice, he was like a formidable blacksmith. His accent and his dialect were exaggerated Scotch; his language, like his thoughts, short, strong, and conclusive.

Our commercial jurisprudence was only rising when he was sinking, and, being no reader, he was too old both in life and in habit to master it familiarly; though even here he was inferior to no Scotch lawyer of his time except Ilay Campbell the Lord President. But within the range of the Feudal and the Civil branches, and in every matter depending on natural ability and practical sense, he was very great; and his power arose more from the force of his reasoning and his vigorous application of principle, than from either the extent or the accuracy of his learning. I have heard good observers describe with admiration how, having worked out a principle, he followed it in its application, fearlessly and triumphantly, dashing all unworthy obstructions aside, and pushed on to his result with the vigour and disdain of a consummate athlete. And he had a colloquial way of arguing, in the form of question and answer, which, done in his clear abrupt style, imparted a dramatic directness and vivacity to the scene.

With this intellectual force, as applied to law, his merits, I fear, cease. Illiterate and without any taste for refined enjoyment, strength of understanding, which gave him power without cultivation, only encouraged him to a more contemptuous disdain of all natures less coarse than his own. Despising the growing improvement of manners, he shocked the feelings even of an age which, with more of the formality, had far less of the substance of decorum than our own. Thousands of his sayings have been preserved, and the staple of them is indecency; which he succeeded in making many people enjoy, or at least endure, by hearty laughter, energy of manner, and rough humour. Almost the only story of him I ever heard that had some fun in it without immodesty, was when a butler gave up his place because his lordship's wife was always scolding him. 'Lord!' he exclaimed, 'ye've little to complain o': ye may be thankfu' ye're no married to her.'

It is impossible to condemn his conduct as a criminal judge too gravely, or too severely. It was a disgrace to the age. A dexterous and practical trier of ordinary cases, he was harsh to prisoners even in his jocularity, and to every counsel whom he chose to dislike. I have heard this attempted to be accounted for and extenuated by the tendency which the old practice of taking all the evidence down in writing, by judicial dictation, had to provoke a wrangle between the court and the bar every moment, and thus to excite mutual impatience and hostility. No doubt there was something in this; but not much. And Braxfield, as might have been expected from his love of domineering, continued the vice after its external cause, whatever it may have been, had ceased. It may be doubted if he was ever so much in his element as when tauntingly repelling the last despairing claim of a wretched culprit, and sending him to Botany Bay or the gallows with an insulting jest; over which he would chuckle the more from observing that correct people were shocked. Yet this was not from cruelty, for which he was too strong and too jovial, but from cherished coarseness.

This union of talent with a passion for rude predomination, exercised in a very discretionary court, tended to form a formidable and dangerous judicial character. This appeared too often in ordinary cases, but all stains on his administration of the common business of his court disappear in the indelible iniquity of the political trials of 1793 and 1794. In these he was the Jeffreys of Scotland. He as the head of the Court, and the only very powerful man it contained, was the real director of its proceedings. The reports make his abuse of the judgment seat bad enough, but his misconduct was not so fully disclosed in formal decisions and charges, as it transpired in casual remarks and general manner. 'Let them bring me prisoners, and I'll find them law' used to be openly stated as his suggestion, when an intended political prosecution was marred by anticipated difficulties. If innocent of this atrocious sentiment, he was scandalously ill-used by his friends, by whom I repeatedly heard it ascribed to him at the time, and who, instead of denying it, spoke of it as a thing understood, and rather admired it as worthy of the man and of the times. Mr Horner (the father of Francis), who was one of the jurors in Muir's case, told me that when he was passing, as was often done then, behind the bench to get into the box, Braxfield, who knew him, whispered 'Come awa, Maister Horner, come awa, and help us to hang ane o' thae daamned scoondrels'. The reporter of Gerald's case could not venture to make the prisoner say more than that 'Christianity was an innovation'. But the full truth is, that in stating this view he added that all great men had been reformers, 'even our Saviour himself'. 'Muckle he made o' that,' chuckled Braxfield in an under voice, 'he was hanget.' Before Hume's Commentaries had made our criminal record intelligible, the forms and precedents were a mystery understood by the initiated alone, and by nobody so much as by Mr Joseph Norris the ancient clerk. Braxfield used to quash anticipated doubts by saying, 'Hoot! Just gie me Josie Norrie and a gude jury, an' I'll doo for the fallow.' He died in 1799, in his seventy-eighth year.

Of the older judges still on the bench in 1800, but who soon left it, there were two who ought not to be allowed to perish. These were the Lord Justice-Clerk Rae, and the Lord President Campbell.

David Rae, Lord Eskgrove, succeeded Braxfield as head of the Criminal Court, and it is his highest honor that he is sometimes mentioned as Braxfield's judicial rival. In so far as law and political partiality went, they were pretty well matched, but in all other respects they were quite different men.

Eskgrove was a very considerable lawyer, in mere knowledge probably Braxfield's superior. But he had nothing of Braxfield's grasp or reasoning, and in everything requiring force or soundness of head, he was a mere child compared with that practical Hercules. Still he was cunning in old Scotch law.

But a more ludicrous personage could not exist. When I first knew him he was in the zenith of his absurdity. People seemed to have nothing to do but to tell stories of this one man. To be able to give an anecdote of Eskgrove, with a proper imitation of his voice and manner, was a sort of fortune in society. Scott in those days was famous for this particularly. Whenever a knot of persons were seen listening in the Outer House to one who was talking slowly, with a low muttering voice and a projected chin, and then the listeners burst asunder in roars of laughter, nobody thought of asking what the joke was. They were sure that it was a successful imitation of Esky, and this was enough. Yet never once did he do or say anything which had the slightest claim to be remembered for any intrinsic merit. The value of all his words and actions consisted in their absurdity.

He seemed, in his old age, to be about the average height, but as he then stooped a good deal, he might have been taller in reality. His face varied, according to circumstances, from a scurfy red to a scurfy blue, the nose was prodigious, the under lip enormous and supported on a huge clumsy chin, which moved like the jaw of an exaggerated Dutch toy. He walked with a slow stealthy step – something between a walk and a hirple, and helped himself on by short movements of his elbows, backwards and forwards, like fins. The voice was low and mumbling, and on the bench was generally inaudible for sometime after the movement of the lips shewed that he had begun speaking, after which the first word that was let fairly out was generally the loudest of the whole discourse. It is unfortunate that, without an idea of his voice and manner, mere narrative cannot describe his sayings and doings graphically.

One of his remarks on the trial of Mr Fysche Palmer for sedition – not given in the report of the trial, but as he made it – is one of the very few things he ever said that had some little merit of its own. Mr John Haggart, one of the prisoner's counsel, in defending his client from the charge of disrespect of the king, quoted Burke's statement that kings are naturally lovers of low company. 'Then, sir, that says very little for you or your client! For if kinggs be lovers of low company, low company ought to be lovers of kinggs!'

Nothing disturbed him so much as the expense of the public dinner for which the judge on the circuit has a fixed allowance, and out of which the less he spends the more he gains. His devices for economy were often very diverting. His servant had strict orders to check the bottles of wine by laying aside the corks. His lordship once went behind a screen at Stirling, while the company was still at table, and seeing an alarming row of corks, got into a warm altercation, which everybody overheard, with John; maintaining it to be 'impossibill' that they could have drunk so much. On being assured that they had, and were still going on – 'Well, then, John, I must just protect myself!' On which he put a handful of the corks into his pocket, and resumed his seat.

Brougham tormented him, and sat on his skirts wherever he went, for above a year. The Justice liked passive counsel who let him dawdle on with culprits and juries in his own way; and consequently he hated the talent, the eloquence, the energy, and all the discomposing qualities of Brougham. At last it seemed as if a court day was to be blessed by his absence, and the poor Justice was delighting himself with the prospect of being allowed to deal with things as he chose; when, lo! his enemy appeared – tall, cool, and resolute. 'I declare,' said the Justice, 'that man Broom, or Broug-ham is the torment of my life!' His revenge, as usual, consisted in sneering at Brougham's eloquence by calling it or him *the Harangue*. 'Well, gentle-men, what did the Harangue say next? Why it said this' (mis-stating it); 'but here, gentle-men, the Harangue was most plainly wrongg, and not intelligibill.'

As usual, then with stronger heads than his, everything was connected by his terror with republican horrors. I heard him, in condemning a tailor to death for murdering a soldier by stabbing him, aggravate the offence thus, 'and not only did you murder him, whereby he was berea-ved of his life, but you did thrust, or push, or pierce, or project, or propell, the le-thall weapon through the belly-band of his regimen-tal breeches, which were his Majes-ty's!'

In the trial of Glengarry for murder in a duel, a lady of great beauty was called as a witness. She came into Court veiled. But before administering the oath Eskgrove gave her this exposition of her duty – 'Youngg woman! You will now consider yourself as in the presence of Almighty God, and of this High Court. Lift up your veil; throw off all modesty, and look me in the face.'

Sir John Henderson of Fordell, a zealous Whig, had long nauseated the civil court by his burgh politics. Their Lordships had once to fix the amount of some discretionary penalty that he had incurred. Eskgrove began to give his opinion in a very low voice, but loud enough to be heard by those next him, to the effect that the fine ought to be fifty pounds, when Sir John, with his usual imprudence, interrupted him, and begged him to raise his voice, adding that if judges did not speak so as to be heard, they might as well not speak at all. Eskgrove, who could never endure any imputation of bodily infirmity, asked his neighbour, 'What does the fellow say?' 'He says that, if you don't speak out, you may as well hold your tongue.' 'Oh, is that what he says? My Lords, what I was sayingg was very simpell. I was only sayingg that in my humbell opinyon, this fine could not be less than two hundred and fifty pounds sterlingg' – this sum being roared out as loudly as his old angry voice could launch it.

His tediousness, both of manner and matter, in charging juries was most dreadful. It was the custom to make juries stand while the judge was addressing them, but no other judge was punctilious about it. Eskgrove however insisted upon it, and if any one of them slipped cunningly down to his seat, or dropped into it from inability to stand any longer, the unfortunate wight was sure to be reminded by his Lordship that 'these were not the times in which there should be any disrespect of this High Court, or even of the law'. Often have I gone back to the court at midnight, and found him, whom I had left mumbling hours before, still going on, with the smoky unsnuffed tallow candles in greasy tin candlesticks, and the poor despairing jurymen, most of the audience having retired or being asleep, the wagging of his Lordship's nose and chin being the chief signs that he was still *char-ging*.

A very common arrangement of his logic to juries was this – 'And so, gentle-men, having shewn you that the pannell's argument is utterly impossibill, I shall now proceed for to shew you that it is extremely improbabill.'

He rarely failed to signalise himself in pronouncing sentences of death. It was almost a matter of style with him to console the prisoner by assuring him that, 'whatever your religi-ous persua-shon may be, or even if, as I suppose, you be of no persua-shon at all, there are plenty of rever-end gentle-men who will be most happy for to shew you the way to yeternal life.'

He had to condemn two or three persons to die who had broken into a house at Luss, and assaulted Sir James Colquhoun and others, and robbed them of a large sum of money. He first, as was his almost constant practice, explained the nature of the various crimes, assault, robbery, and hamesucken – of which last he gave them the etymology; and he then reminded them that they attacked the house and the persons within it, and robbed them – and then came to this climax – 'All this you did – and God preserve us! joost when they were sitten doon to their denner!'

But a whole volume could easily be filled with specimens of his absurdities. Scott, not by invention but by accurate narration, could have done it himself. So could Jeffrey; and William Clerk; and William Erskine; and indeed everybody who had eyes and ears. He was the staple of the public conversation; and so long as his old age lasted (for of his youth I know nothing) he nearly drove Napoleon out of the Edinburgh world. He died in 1804, in his eightieth year; and had therefore been put at the head of the Court when he had reached the age of seventy-six: an incredible appointment, for his peculiarities had been in full flourish long before that. It would have been a pity if the public had lost them; but it was unfortunate that a judicial chair was necessary for their complete exhibition. A story of Eskgrove is still preferred to all other stories. Only, the things that he did and said every day are beginning to be incredible to this correct and flat age.

In the Matter of the Hanging of Duncan Jopp

from Weir of Hermiston

ROBERT LOUIS STEVENSON (1850–1894)

Weir of Hermiston *was Stevenson's last novel – he was at work on it on the day that he died at Vailima in Samoa – and although it is unfinished, there is enough of it to allow it to rank as one of his finest creations. The story of family conflict between the young, idealistic Archie Weir and his hard-bitten father, the Lord Justice-Clerk Adam Weir, Lord Hermiston, has obvious parallels with Stevenson's own frequently-troubled relationship with his father. Thomas Stevenson wanted his son to follow him into the family lighthouse engineering practice (the Stevensons had been from the end of the eighteenth century consulting engineers to the Commissioners for the Northern Lights), but agreed to him training as an advocate instead and then, on qualifying, saw him give up the law to follow an uncertain career in literature and fall in love with a married woman.*

It is hard not to feel when Hermiston tells his student son Archie, 'You're splairging; you're running at lairge in life like a wild nowt', that echoes of conversations between Thomas and Robert are being replayed. Not that Stevenson's portrayal of Hermiston is an unsympathetic one, any more that Stevenson's relationship with his father was an entirely hostile one. The Lord Justice-Clerk, before the central action of the novel starts in the incident described in our extract, loses his wife when his son is aged seven. He perhaps inevitably fails to build any sort of relationship with his sensitive young son Archie. Stevenson writes, in a memorable passage:

> As time went on, the tough and rough old sinner felt himself drawn to the son of his loins and sole continuator of his new family, with softness of sentiment that he could hardly credit and was wholly impotent to express. With a face, voice and manner trained through forty years to terrify and repel, Rhadamanthus may be great but he will scarce be engaging ... If he failed to gain his son's friendship, or even his son's toleration, on he went up the great, bare staircase of his duty, uncheered and undepressed.

The 'tough and rough old sinner' Hermiston, who nonetheless displayed the very Roman (and very Scottish) virtues of gravitas *and* severitas *was, to a very considerable degree based on the equally larger than life figure of Robert McQueen, Lord Braxfield (1722–99). Braxfield was Lord Justice-Clerk, the head of the Scottish criminal judiciary, from 1788–99. Many of the characteristics of Braxfield were borrowed by Stevenson for his fictional, if chronologically slightly later, counterpart: the capacity for drink, the cherished coarseness, the stubborn adherence to a broad Scots accent and idiom, even a house in Edinburgh's George Square.*

Hermiston is, however, not Braxfield, even though the vivid portrayal of the fictional Justice-Clerk has been read back to colour later views of the real Justice-Clerk. Stevenson wrote, good-humouredly, to his friend Sydney Colvin in February 1893:

> *I don't seem to be able to get it into your head that my Lord Hermiston is Lord Hermiston – a person who never existed, which sets me free from any little irksome question of date.*

He had written to Colvin in October 1892 telling him he was starting on a new novel which 'ought to be called, but of course that is impossible – Braxfield'.

The Braxfield figure was one that intrigued Stevenson throughout his life. Braxfield had tried and sentenced the notorious Edinburgh housebreaker Deacon Brodie. Stevenson's nursery at 17 Heriot Row had housed a cabinet made by the Deacon, before his fall from grace as a respectable Edinburgh tradesman and his descent into crime. His awareness of this duality in Brodie's nature is often considered to have informed his portrayal of Dr Jekyll and Mr Hyde in Strange Case of Dr Jekyll and Mr Hyde *(1886), an extract from which appears elsewhere in this anthology. Stevenson also wrote a play on the Brodie case and in his essay* Some Portraits by Raeburn *published in* Virginibus Puerisque *(1881) he included some reflections on Sir Henry Raeburn's portrait of Braxfield:*

> *So sympathetically is the character conceived by the portrait-painter, that it is hardly possible to avoid some movement of sympathy on the part of the spectator. And sympathy is a thing to be encouraged, apart from human considerations, because it supplies us with the materials for wisdom. It is probably more instructive to entertain a sneaking kindness for any unpopular person, and, among the rest, for Lord Braxfield, than to give way to perfect raptures of moral indignation against his abstract vices. He was the last judge on the Scottish bench to employ the pure Scotch idiom. His opinions, thus given in Doric, and conceived in a lively, rugged, conversational style, were full of point and authority. Out of the bar, or off the bench, he was a convivial man, a lover of wine, and one who 'shone peculiarly' at tavern meetings. He left behind him an unrivalled reputation for rough and cruel speech; and to this day his name smacks of the gallows.*

Stevenson sent home for copies of reports of Scottish criminal trials, and details of the justiciary oath, and sought instruction on points of legal procedure, so determined was he to get everything right in what he told his friend Charles Baxter would be his masterpiece.

Possibly Stevenson's judgment of Braxfield owes too much to Lord Cockburn's animus-ridden portrayal (see The Scottish Bench *elsewhere in this section). His portrayal of the Hermiston/Erchie Weir relationship however gives us a nuanced, if tragically incomplete, portrayal of a father/son relationship and an example of Stevenson at his finest.*

IN THE MATTER OF THE HANGING OF DUNCAN JOPP

It chanced in the year 1813 that Archie strayed one day into the Justiciary Court. The macer made room for the son of the presiding judge. In the dock, the centre of men's eyes, there stood a whey-coloured, misbegotten caitiff, Duncan Jopp, on trial for his life. His story, as it was raked out before him in that public scene, was one of disgrace and vice and cowardice, the very nakedness of crime; and the creature heard and it seemed at times as though he understood – as if at times he forgot the horror of the place he stood in, and remembered the shame of what had brought him there. He kept his head bowed and his hands clutched upon the rail; his hair dropped in his eyes and at times he flung it back; and now he glanced about the audience in a sudden fellness of terror, and now looked in the face of his judge and gulped. There was pinned about his throat a piece of dingy flannel, and this it was perhaps that turned the scale in Archie's mind between disgust and pity. The creature stood in a vanishing point, yet a little while, and he was still a man, and had eyes and apprehension; yet a little longer, and with a last sordid piece of pageantry, he would cease to be. And here, in the meantime, with a trait of human nature that caught at the beholder's breath, he was tending a sore throat.

Over against him, my Lord Hermiston occupied the bench in the red robes of criminal jurisdiction, his face framed in the white wig. Honest all through, he did not affect the virtue of impartiality; this was no case for refinement; there was a man to be hanged, he would have said, and he was hanging him. Nor was it possible to see his lordship, and acquit him of gusto in the task. It was plain he gloried in the exercise of his trained faculties, in the clear sight which pierced at once into the joint of fact, in the rude, unvarnished gibes with which he demolished every figment of defence. He took his ease and jested, unbending in that solemn place with some of the freedom of the tavern; and the rag of man with the flannel round his neck was hunted gallowsward with jeers.

Duncan had a mistress, scarce less forlorn and greatly older than himself, who came up, whimpering and curtseying, to add the weight of her betrayal. My lord gave her the oath in his most roaring voice, and added an intolerant warning.

'Mind what ye say now, Janet,' said he. 'I have an e'e upon ye, I'm ill to jest with.'

Presently, after she was tremblingly embarked on her story, 'And what made ye do this, ye auld runt?' the Court interposed. 'Do ye mean to tell me ye was the panel's mistress?'

'If you please, ma loard,' whined the female.

'Godsake! Ye made a bonny couple', observed his lordship; and there was something so formidable and ferocious in his scorn that not even the galleries thought to laugh.

The summing up contained some jewels.

'These two peetiable creatures seem to have made up thegither, it's not for us to explain why.' – 'The panel, who (whatever else he may be) appears to be equally ill set-out in mind and boady.' – 'Neither the panel nor yet the old wife appears to have had so much common sense as even to tell a lie when it was necessary.' And in the course of sentencing, my lord had this *obiter dictum:* 'I have been the means, under God, of haanging a great number, but never just such a disjaskit rascal as yourself.' The words were strong in themselves; the light and heat and detonation of their delivery, and the savage pleasure of the speaker in his task, made them tingle in the ears.

When all was over, Archie came forth again into a changed world. Had there been the least redeeming greatness in the crime, any obscurity, any dubiety, perhaps he might have understood. But the culprit stood, with his sore throat, in the sweat of his mortal agony, without defence or excuse: a thing to cover up with blushes: a being so much sunk beneath the zones of sympathy that pity might seem harmless. And the judge had pursued him with a monstrous, relishing gaiety, horrible to be conceived, a trait for nightmares. It is one thing to spear a tiger, another to crush a toad; there are aesthetics even of the slaughter-house; and the loathsomeness of Duncan Jopp enveloped and infected the image of his judge.

Archie passed by his friends in the High Street with incoherent words and gestures. He saw Holyrood in a dream, remembrance of its romance awoke in him and faded; he had a vision of the old radiant stories, of Queen Mary and Prince Charlie, of the hooded stag, of the splendour and crime, the velvet and bright iron of the past; and dismissed them with a cry of pain. He lay and moaned in the Hunter's Bog, and the heavens were dark above him and the grass of the field an offence. 'This is my father,' he said. 'I draw my life from him; the flesh upon my bones is his, the bread I am fed with is the wages of these horrors.' He recalled his mother, and ground his forehead in the earth. He thought of flight, and where was he to flee to? of other lives, but was there any life worth living in this den of savage and jeering animals?

The interval before the execution was like a violent dream. He met his father; he would not look at him, he could not speak to him. It seemed there was no living creature but must have been swift to recognise that imminent animosity; but the hide of the Justice-Clerk remained impenetrable. Had my lord been talkative, the truce could never have subsisted; but he was by fortune in one of his humours of sour silence; and under the very guns of his broadside, Archie nursed the enthusiasm of rebellion. It seemed to him, from the top of his nineteen years' experience, as if he were marked at birth to be the perpetrator of some signal action, to set back fallen Mercy, to overthrow the usurping devil that sat, horned and hoofed, on her throne. Seductive Jacobin figments, which he had often refuted at the Speculative, swam up in his mind and startled him as with voices: and he seemed to himself to walk accompanied by an almost tangible presence of new beliefs and duties.

On the named morning he was at the place of execution. He saw the fleering rabble, the flinching wretch produced. He looked on for a while at a certain parody of devotion, which seemed to strip the wretch of his last claim to manhood. Then followed the brutal instant of extinction, and the paltry dangling of the remains like a broken jumping-jack. He had been prepared for something terrible, not for this tragic meanness. He stood a moment silent, and then – 'I denounce this God-defying murder,' he shouted; and his father, if he must have disclaimed the sentiment, might have owned the stentorian voice with which it was uttered.

Frank Innes dragged him from the spot. The two handsome lads followed the same course of study and recreation, and felt a certain mutual attraction, founded mainly on good looks. It had never gone deep; Frank was by nature a thin, jeering creature, not truly susceptible whether of feeling or inspiring friendship; and the relation between the pair was altogether on the outside, a thing of common knowledge and the pleasantries that spring from a common acquaintance. The more credit to Frank that he was appalled by Archie's outburst, and at least conceived the design of keeping him in sight, and, if possible, in hand, for the day. But Archie, who had just defied – was it God or Satan? – would not listen to the word of a college companion.

'I will not go with you,' he said. 'I do not desire your company, sir, I would be alone.'

'Here, Weir, man, don't be absurd ' said Innes, keeping a tight hold upon his sleeve. 'I will not let you go until I know what you mean to do with yourself; it's no use brandishing that staff.' For indeed at that moment Archie had made a sudden – perhaps a warlike – movement. 'This has been the most insane affair; you know it has. You know very well that I'm playing the good Samaritan. All I wish is to keep you quiet.'

'If quietness is what you wish, Mr Innes,' said Archie, 'and you will promise to leave me entirely to myself, I will tell you so much, that I am going to walk in the country and admire the beauties of nature.'

'Honour bright?' asked Frank.

'I am not in the habit of lying, Mr Innes,' retorted Archie. 'I have the honour of wishing you good-day.'

'You won't forget the Spec.?' asked Innes.

'The Spec.?' said Archie. 'O no, I won't forget the Spec.'

And the one young man carried his tortured spirit forth of the city and all the day long, by one road and another, in an endless pilgrimage of misery; while the other hastened smilingly to spread the news of Weir's access of insanity, and to drum up for that night a full attendance at the Speculative, where further eccentric developments might certainly be looked for. I doubt if Innes had the least belief in his prediction; I think it flowed rather from a wish to make the story as good and the scandal as great as possible; not from any ill-will to Archie – from the mere pleasure of beholding interested faces. But for all that his words were prophetic. Archie did not forget the Spec.; he put in an appearance there at the due time, and, before the evening was over, had dealt a memorable shock to his companions. It chanced he was the president of the night. He sat in the same room where the Society still meets – only the portraits were not there: the men who afterwards sat for them were then but beginning their career. The same lustre of many tapers shed its light over the meeting; the same chair, perhaps, supported him that so many of us have sat in since. At times he seemed to forget the business of the evening, but even in these periods he sat with a great air of energy and determination. At times he meddled bitterly, and launched with defiance those fines which are the precious and rarely used artillery of the president. He little thought, as he did so, how he resembled his father, but his friends remarked upon it, chuckling. So far, in his high place above his fellow-students, he seemed set beyond the possibility of any scandal; but his mind was made up – he was determined to fulfil the sphere of his offence. He signed to Innes (whom he had just fined, and who just impeached his ruling) to succeed him in the chair, stepped down from the platform, and took his place by the chimney-piece, the shine of many wax tapers from above illuminating his pale face, the glow of the great red fire relieving from behind his slim figure. He had to propose, as an amendment to the next subject in the case-book, 'Whether capital punishment be consistent with God's will or man's policy?'

A breath of embarrassment, of something like alarm, passed round the room, so daring did these words appear upon the lips of Hermiston's only son. But the amendment was not seconded; the previous question was promptly moved and unanimously voted, and the momentary scandal smuggled by. Innes triumphed in the fulfilment of his prophecy. He and Archie were now become the heroes of the night; but whereas every one crowded about Innes, when the meeting broke up, but one of all his companions came to speak to Archie.

'Weir, man! That was an extraordinary raid of yours!' observed this courageous member, taking him confidentially by the arm as they went out.

'I don't think it a raid,' said Archie grimly. 'More like a war. I saw that poor brute hanged this morning, and my gorge rises at it yet.'

'Hut-tut,' returned his companion, and, dropping his arm like something hot, he sought the less tense society of others

Archie found himself alone. The last of the faithful – or was it only the boldest of the curious? – had fled. He watched the black huddle of his fellow-students draw off down and up the street, in whispering or boisterous gangs. And the isolation of the moment weighed upon him like an omen and an emblem of his destiny in life. Bred up in unbroken fear himself, among trembling servants, and in a house which (at the least ruffle in the master's voice) shuddered into silence, he saw himself on the brink of the red valley of war, and measured the danger and length of it with awe. He made a détour in the glimmer and shadow of the streets, came into the back stable lane, and watched for a long while the light burn steady in the Judge's room. The longer he gazed upon that illuminated window-blind, the more blank became the picture of the man who sat behind it, endlessly turning over sheets of process, pausing to sip a glass of port, or rising and passing heavily about his book-lined walls to verify some reference. He could not combine the brutal judge and the industrious, dispassionate student; the connecting link escaped him; from such a dual nature, it was impossible he should predict behaviour; and he asked himself if he had done well to plunge into a business of which the end could not be foreseen? and presently after, with a sickening decline of confidence, if he had done loyally to strike his father? For he had struck him – defied him twice over and before a cloud of witnesses – struck him a public buffet before crowds. Who had called him to judge his father in these precarious and high questions? The office was usurped. It might have become a stranger; in a son – there was no blinking it – in a son, it was disloyal. And now, between these two natures so antipathetic, so hateful to each other, there was depending an unpardonable affront: and the providence of God alone might foresee the manner in which it would be resented by Lord Hermiston.

These misgivings tortured him all night and arose with him in the winter's morning, they followed him from class to class, they made him shrinkingly sensitive to every shade of manner in his companions, they sounded in his ears through the current voice of the professor; and he brought them home with him at night unabated and indeed increased. The cause of this increase lay in a chance encounter with the celebrated Dr Gregory. Archie stood looking vaguely in the lighted window of a book shop, trying to nerve himself for the approaching ordeal. My lord and he had met and parted in the morning as they had now done for long, with scarcely the ordinary civilities of life; and it was plain to the son that nothing had yet reached the father's ears. Indeed, when he recalled the awful countenance of my lord, a timid hope sprang up in him that perhaps there would be found no one bold enough to carry tales. If this were so, he asked himself, would he begin again? and he found no answer. It was at this moment that a hand was laid upon his arm, and a voice said in his ear, 'My dear Mr Archie, you had better come and see me.'

He started, turned round, and found himself face to face with Dr Gregory. 'And why should I come to see you?' he asked, with the defiance of the miserable.

'Because you are looking exceedingly ill,' I said the doctor, 'and you very evidently want looking after, my young friend. Good folk are scarce, you know; and it is not every one that would be quite so much missed as yourself. It is not every one that Hermiston would miss.'

And with a nod and a smile, the doctor passed on.

A moment after, Archie was in pursuit, and had in turn, but more roughly, seized him by the arm.

'What do you mean, what did you mean by saying that? What makes you think that Hermis – my father would have missed me?'

The doctor turned about and looked him all over with a clinical eye. A far more stupid man than Dr Gregory might have guessed the truth; but ninety-nine out of a hundred, even if they had been equally inclined to kindness, would have blundered by some touch of charitable exaggeration. The doctor was better inspired. He knew the father well; in that white face of intelligence and suffering, he divined something of the son; and he told, without apology or adornment, the plain truth.

'When you had the measles, Mr Archibald, you had them gey and ill; and I thought you were going to slip between my fingers,' he said. 'Well, your father was anxious. How did I know it? says you. Simply because I am a trained observer. The sign that I saw him make ten thousand would have missed; and perhaps – *perhaps*, I say, because he's a hard man to judge of – but perhaps he never made another. A strange thing to consider! It was this. One day I came to him: "Hermiston," said I, "there's a change." He never said a word, just glowered at me (if ye'll pardon the phrase) like a wild beast. "A change for the better," said I. And I distinctly heard him take his breath.'

The doctor left no opportunity for anti-climax; nodding his cocked hat (a piece of antiquity to which he clung) and repeating 'Distinctly' with raised eyebrows, he took his departure, and left Archie speechless in the street.

The anecdote might be called infinitely little, and yet its meaning for Archie was immense. 'I did not know the old man had so much blood in him.' He had never dreamed this sire of his, this aboriginal antique, this adamantine Adam, had even so much of a heart as to be moved in the least degree for another – and that other himself, who had insulted him! With the generosity of youth, Archie was instantly under arms upon the other side: had instantly created a new image of Lord Hermiston, that of a man who was all iron without and all sensibility within. The mind of the vile jester, the tongue that had pursued Duncan Jopp with unmanly insults, the unbeloved countenance that he had known and feared for so long, were all forgotten; and he hastened home, impatient to confess his misdeeds, impatient to throw himself on the mercy of this imaginary character.

He was not to be long without a rude awakening. It was in the gloaming when he drew near the doorstep of the lighted house, and was aware of the figure of his father approaching from the opposite side. Little daylight lingered; but on the door being opened, the strong yellow shine of the lamp gushed out upon the landing and shone full on Archie, as he stood, in the old-fashioned observance of respect, to yield precedence. The Judge came without haste, stepping stately and firm; his chin raised, his face (as he entered the lamplight) strongly illumined, his mouth set hard. There was never a wink of change in his expression; without looking to the right or left, he mounted the stair, passed close to Archie, and entered the house. Instinctively, the boy, upon his first coming, had made a movement to meet him; instinctively he recoiled against the railing, as the old man swept by him in a pomp of indignation. Words were needless; he knew all – perhaps more than all – and the hour of judgment was at hand.

It is possible that, in this sudden revulsion of hope, and before these symptoms of impending danger, Archie might have fled. But not even that was left to him. My lord, after hanging up his cloak and hat, turned round in the lighted entry, and made him an imperative and silent gesture with his thumb, and with the strange instinct of obedience, Archie followed him into the house.

All dinner-time there reigned over the Judge's table a palpable silence, and as soon as the solids were despatched he rose to his feet.

'McKillup, tak' the wine into my room,' said he; and then to his son: 'Archie, you and me has to have a talk.'

it was at this sickening moment that Archie's courage, for the first and last time, entirely deserted him. 'I have an appointment,' said he.

'It'll have to be broken, then,' said Hermiston, and led the way into his study.

The lamp was shaded, the fire trimmed to a nicety, the table covered deep with orderly documents, the backs of law books made a frame upon all sides that was only broken by the window and the doors.

For a moment Hermiston warmed his hands at the fire, presenting his back to Archie; then suddenly disclosed on him the terrors of the Hanging Face.

'What's this I hear of ye?' he asked.

There was no answer possible to Archie.

'I'll have to tell ye, then,' pursued Hermiston. 'It seems ye've been skirling against the father that begot ye' and one of his Maijesty's Judges in this land; and that in the public street, and while an order of the Court was being executit. Forbye which, it would appear that ye've been airing your opeenions in a Coallege Debatin' Society'; he paused a moment: and then, with extraordinary bitterness, added: 'Ye damned eediot.'

'I had meant to tell you,' stammered Archie. 'I see you are well informed.'

'Muckle obleeged to ye,' said his lordship, and took his usual seat. 'And so you disapprove of Caapital Punishment?' he added.

'I am sorry, sir, I do,' said Archie.

'I am sorry, too,' said his lordship. 'And now, if you please, we shall approach this business with a little more parteecularity. I hear that at the hanging of Duncan Jopp – and, man! ye had a fine client there – in the middle of all the riff-raff of the ceety, ye thought fit to cry out, "This is a damned murder, and my gorge rises at the man that haangit him?" '

'No, sir, these were not my words,' cried Archie.

'What were yer words, then?' asked the Judge.

'I believe I said, "I denounce it as a murder!" ' said the son. 'I beg your pardon a God-defying murder. I have no wish to conceal the truth,' he added, and looked his father for a moment in the face.

'God, it would only need that of it next!' cried Hermiston. 'There was nothing about your gorge rising, then?'

'That was afterwards, my lord, as I was leaving the Speculative. I said I had been to see the miserable creature hanged, and my gorge rose at it.'

'Did ye, though?' said Hermiston. 'And I suppose ye knew who haangit him?'

'I was present at the trial, I ought to tell you that, I ought to explain. I ask your pardon beforehand for any expression that may seem undutiful. The position in which I stand is wretched,' said the unhappy hero, now fairly face to face with the business he had chosen. 'I have been reading some of your cases. I was present while Jopp was tried. It was a hideous business. Father, it was a hideous thing! Grant he was vile, why should you hunt him with vileness equal to his own? It was done with glee – that is the word – you did it with glee; and I looked on, God help me! with horror.'

'You're a young gentleman that doesna approve of Caapital Punishment,' said Hermiston. 'Weel, I'm an auld man that does. I was glad to get Jopp haangit, and what for would I pretend I wasna? You're all for honesty, it seems; you couldn't even steik your mouth on the public street. What for should I steik mines upon the bench, the King's officer, bearing the sword, a dreid to evil-doers, as I was from the beginning, and as I will be to the end! Mair than enough of it! Heedious! I never gave twa thoughts to heediousness, I have no call to be bonny. I'm a man that gets through with my day's business, and let that suffice.'

The ring of sarcasm had died out of his voice as he went on; the plain words became invested with some of the dignity of the Justice-seat.

'It would be telling you if you could say as much,' the speaker resumed. 'But ye cannot. Ye've been reading some of my cases, ye say. But it was not for the law in them, it was to spy out your faither's nakedness, a fine employment in a son. You're splairging; you're running at lairge in life like a wild nowt. It's impossible you should think any longer of coming to the Bar. You're not fit for it; no splairger is. And another thing: son of mines or no son of mines, you have flung fylement in public on one of the Senators of the Coallege of Justice, and I would make it my business to see that ye were never admitted there yourself. There is a kind of a decency to be observit. Then comes the next of it – what am I to do with ye next? Ye'll have to find some kind of a trade, for I'll never support ye in idleset. What do ye fancy ye'll be fit for? The pulpit? Na, they could never get diveenity into that bloackhead. Him that the law of man whammles is no likely to do muckle better by the law of God. What would ye make of hell? Wouldna your gorge rise at that? Na, there's no room for splairgers under the fower quarters of John Calvin. What else is there? Speak up. Have ye got nothing of your own?'

'Father, let me go the Peninsula,' said Archie. 'That's all I'm fit for – to fight.'

'All? quo' he!' returned the Judge. 'And it would be enough too, if I thought it. But I'll never trust ye so near the French, you that's so Frenchifeed.'

'You do me injustice there, sir,' said Archie. 'I am loyal; I will not boast; but any interest I may have ever felt in the French –'

'Have ye been so loyal to me?' interrupted his father.

There came no reply.

'I think not,' continued Hermiston. 'And I would send no man to be a servant to the King, God bless him! that has proved such a shauchling son to his own faither. You can splairge here on Edinburgh street, and where's the hairm? It doesna play buff on me! And if there were twenty thousand eediots like yourself, sorrow a Duncan Jopp would hang the fewer. But there's no splairging possible in a camp; and if ye were to go to it, you would find out for yourself whether Lord Well'n'ton approves of caapital punishment or not. You a sodger!' he cried, with a sudden burst of scorn. 'Ye auld wife, the sodgers would bray at ye like cuddies!'

As at the drawing of a curtain, Archie was aware of some illogicality in his position, and stood abashed. He had a strong impression, besides, of the essential valour of the old gentleman before him, how conveyed it would be hard to say.

'Well, have ye no other proposeetion?' said my lord again.

'You have taken this so calmly, sir, that I cannot but stand ashamed,' began Archie.

'I'm nearer voamiting, though, than you would fancy,' said my lord.

The blood rose to Archie's brow

'I beg your pardon, I should have said that you had accepted my affront ... I admit it was an affront; I did not think to apologise, but I do, I ask your pardon; it will not be so again, I pass you my word of honour ... I should have said that I admired your magnanimity with – this – offender,' Archie concluded with a gulp.

'I have no other son, ye see,' said Hermiston. 'A bonny one I have gotten! But I must just do the best I can wi' him, and what am I to do? If ye had been younger, I would have wheepit ye for this rideeculous exhibeetion. The way it is, I have just to grin and bear. But one thing is to be clearly understood. As a faither, I must grin and bear it; but if I had been the Lord Advocate instead of the Lord Justice-Clerk, son or no son, Mr Erchibald Weir would have been in a jyle the night.'

Archie was now dominated. Lord Hermiston was coarse and cruel; and yet the son was aware of a bloomless nobility, an ungracious abnegation of the man's self in the man's office. At every word, this sense of the greatness of Lord Hermiston's spirit struck more home; and along with it that of his own impotence, who had struck – and perhaps basely struck – at his own father, and not reached so far as to have even nettled him.

'I place myself in your hands without reserve,' he said.

'That's the first sensible word I've had of ye the night,' said Hermiston. 'I can tell ye, that would have been the end of it, the one way or the other; but it's better ye should come there yourself; than what I would have had to hirstle ye. Weel, by my way of it – and my way is the best – there's just the one thing it's possible that ye might be with decency, and that's a laird. Ye'll be out of hairm's way at the least of it. If ye have to rowt, ye can rowt amang the kye; and the maist feck of the caapital punishment ye're like to come across'll be guddling trouts. Now, I'm for no idle lairdies; every man has to work, if it's only at peddling ballants; to work, or to be wheeped, or to be haangit. If I set ye down at Hermiston I'll have to see you work that place the way it has never been workit yet; ye must ken about the sheep like a herd, ye must be my grieve there and I'll see that I gain by ye. Is that understood?'

'I will do my best,' said Archie.

'Well, then, I'll send Kirstie word the morn, and ye can go yourself the day after,' said Hermiston. 'And just try to be less of an eediot!' he concluded with a freezing smile, and turned immediately to the papers on his desk.

Acknowledgements

'Hook or Me This Time', chapter 15 of *Peter Pan and Wendy*, by J.M. Barrie, reprinted by permission of Great Ormond Street Hospital for Children, London

'Mr Toad', chapter 6 of *The Wind in the Willows*, by Kenneth Grahame © The University Chest, Oxford, reprinted by permission of Curtis Brown Ltd, London

'The Adventure of the Spectacled Roadman', chapter 5 of *The Thirty-Nine Steps*, by John Buchan, reprinted by permission of A.P. Watt on the behalf of The Lord Tweedsmuir and Jean, Lady Tweedsmuir

'The Body Snatchers', pp. 1–5 of *Burke and Hare*, by William Roughead. The publisher acknowledges the Estate of William Roughead

'Ancient Murder', chapter 1 of *The Dark of Summer*, by Eric Linklater, reprinted by permission of Canongate

'Antique Smith', from *The Riddle of the Ruthvens*, by William Roughead. The publisher acknowledges the Estate of William Roughead

'Desperate Characters in Council', chapter 2 of *John Macnab*, by John Buchan, reprinted by permission of A.P. Watt on the behalf of The Lord Tweedsmuir and Jean, Lady Tweedsmuir

'Para Handy – Poacher', from the *Complete Para Handy*, published by Birlinn Limited, reprinted by permission of the Neil Munro Society

'Poaching in Excelsis' by G.K. Menzies, reprinted by permission of the Estate of G.K. Menzies

'The Beachdair', chapters 5 and 6 of *The New Road*, by Neil Munro, reprinted by permission of The Neil Munro Society

'The Adventure of the Greek Interpreter', from *The Memoirs of Sherlock Holmes*, by Arthur Conan Doyle. Copyright © 1996 The Sir Arthur Conan Doyle Copyright Holders. Reprinted by permission of Jonathan Clowes Ltd., London, on behalf of Angela Plunket, Administrator of the Sir Arthur Conan Doyle Copyright

'Three Thief-Catchers', pp. 104–110 of *The Looker-On*, by Neil Munro, reprinted by permission of the Neil Munro Society

'An Artistic Murder', chapters 1 and 2 of *Five Red Herrings*, by Dorothy L. Sayers, published by Hodder & Stoughton

'Richard Crookback', chapters 1 and 2 of *The Daughter of Time*, by Josephine Tey, published by Heineman

'Concrete Evidence' from *A Good Hanging*, © 1992 Ian Rankin, published in Orion paperback

Mungo's City
A Glasgow Anthology

Edited by Brian D. Osborne and Ronald Armstrong

Glasgow – the Dear Green Place, the Second City of the Empire, the Workshop of the World, No Mean City, the City of Culture – her very variety of names suggests a complex history. Glasgow's story has attracted every sort of writer, from medieval chroniclers to nineteenth-century statisticians, from poets and novelists to politicians and journalists.

Mungo's City is a rich and wide-ranging anthology which celebrates the great diversity of human experience – from tobacco lords to slum life – that forms today's Glasgow. To tell this varied story its seven thematic chapters draw on passages of work by some of the great names in Scottish literature, including Scott, Galt and Buchan, and are complemented by a much less familiar but equally rewarding selection of writing dating from the thirteenth to the twentieth century. Emphasising the Glasgow of yesterday, *Mungo's City* places today's flowering of Glasgow writing in context.

ISBN 1 84158 025 2 Price £12.99

Cradle of the Scots
An Argyll Anthology

Edited by Brian D. Osborne, Ronald Armstrong and Ronald Renton

I know corries in Argyle that whisper silken to the wind with juicy grasses, corries where the deer love to prance deep in the cool dew, and the beasts of far-off woods come in bands at their seasons and together rejoice.
– Neil Munro *John Splendid*

Argyll – the enduring heartland, birthplace of the Scottish nation and renowned for its stunning natural beauty. This book is a celebration of the rich literary tradition of an area which has produced many of Scotland's finest writers. From Adomnan in the seventh century to Naomi Mitchison in the twentieth, this anthology also features writers as varied as Neil Munro, Robin Jenkins and, from the Gaelic tradition, Duncan Bàn Macintyre and Iain Crichton Smith.

ISBN 1 84158 041 4 Price £12.99

Echoes of the Sea

Scotland and the Sea – An Anthology

Edited by Brian D. Osborne and Ronald Armstrong

As befits a nation mostly surrounded by water, Scotland has a long and involved relationship with the sea. By the sea invaders have come and bold adventurers departed; on the sea a hard living has been won and lives lost; from the sea have come ageless myths and rattling yarns. Down the centuries come the echoes of the sea: the sailor's cry, a mournful song, the creak of strained rigging, the clang of a shipyard steam-hammer.

Echoes of the Sea is an anthology celebrating Scotland's relationship with the sea as it is found in fiction, ballads, poetry, journal writing and reportage. It includes extracts from the works of the very finest Scottish writers, including Stevenson, Buchan, Linklater and Gunn, but the collection also casts its eye to a wider horizon and dips into the unusual and intriguing with pieces such as Alistair MacLean's first published short story, Gaelic poetry from the eighteenth century to the present day, portraits of Scots seamen by literary giants like Herman Melville and Rudyard Kipling, and selections from those classics of Hebridean humour, *Whisky Galore* and *Para Handy*.

ISBN 0 86241 783 X Price £12.99